MATHEMATICS PLUS

HBJ Harcourt Brace Jovanovich, Inc.

Orlando Austin San Diego Chicago Dallas New York

Printed in the United States of America
ISBN 0-15-300141-0
12   13   14   15   048   97   96

ACKNOWLEDGMENTS

Some computer lessons in this book are based on AppleWorks® by Claris Corporation.
© 1989 by Claris Corporation. All rights reserved. Claris is a registered trademark of Claris Corporation.
AppleWorks is a registered trademark of Apple Computer, Inc. licensed to Claris Corporation.
Apple is a registered trademark of Apple Computer, Inc.

Logo lessons in this book present the Terrapin Logo version. Terrapin
is a registered trademark of Terrapin Software, Inc.

See page H33 for photo and art credits.

AUTHORS

Grace M. Burton
Professor, Department of Curricular Studies
University of North Carolina at Wilmington
Wilmington, North Carolina

Jerome D. Kaplan
Professor of Education
Seton Hall University
South Orange, New Jersey

Martha H. Hopkins
Associate Professor
University of Central Florida
Orlando, Florida

Leonard Kennedy
Professor Emeritus
California State University at Sacramento
Sacramento, California

Howard C. Johnson
Chair, Mathematics Education
Professor of Mathematics and Mathematics Education
Syracuse University
Syracuse, New York

Karen A. Schultz
Professor, Mathematics Education
Georgia State University
Atlanta, Georgia

SENIOR EDITORIAL ADVISOR

Francis (Skip) Fennell
Professor of Education
Western Maryland College
Westminister, Maryland

ADVISORS

Janet S. Abbott
Curriculum Coordinator
Chula Vista Elementary School District
Chula Vista, California

Genevieve M. Knight
Professor of Mathematics
Coppin State College
Baltimore, Maryland

Dorothy S. Strong
Director K–12 Mathematics
Chicago Public Schools
Chicago, Illinois

Don S. Balka
Professor
Saint Mary's College
Notre Dame, Indiana

Charles Lamb
Associate Professor
University of Texas at Austin
Austin, Texas

Steven Tipps
West Foundation Professor
Midwestern State University
Wichita Falls, Texas

Gilbert Cuevas
Professor of Education
University of Miami
Miami, Florida

Marsha W. Lilly
Mathematics Coordinator, K–12
Alief Independent School District
Alief, Texas

David Wells
Retired Assistant Superintendent
for Instruction
Pontiac, Michigan

Michael C. Hynes
Professor
University of Central Florida
Orlando, Florida

Sid Rachlin
Professor
University of Hawaii
Honolulu, Hawaii

Contents

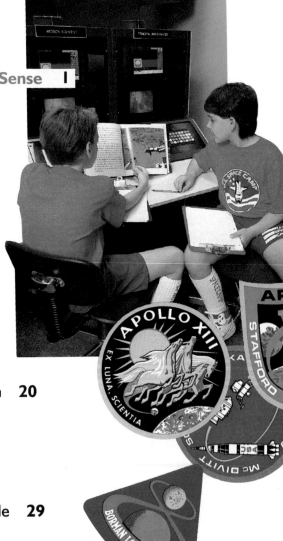

4   Time, Graphing, and Data   108
THEME: *Shopping at the Mall*

Dividing by 1-Digit Numbers   **240**
THEME: *Communication/Media*

9 **Geometry 274**
THEME: *Imagination*

10 **Understanding Fractions and Mixed Numbers** **316**
THEME: *Health and Fitness*

11 **Using Fractions and Exploring Probability** **346**
THEME: *Games*

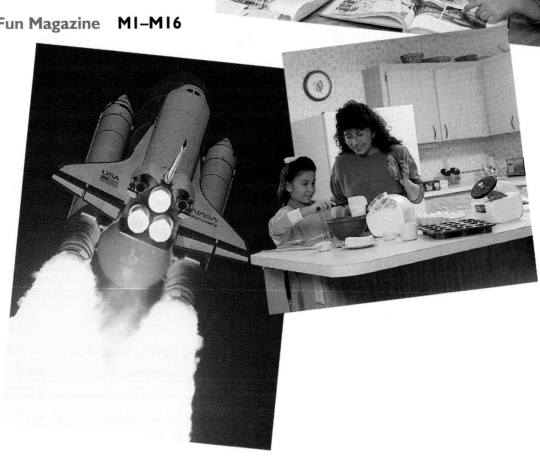

Welcome to MATHEMATICS PLUS

Mathematics is an important part of your daily life. You use it at school, at home, and everywhere you go!

As you learn mathematics this year, look in your book for M.C. Lion. M.C. will give you hints for solving problems and tips for studying math.

This year you are going to use ideas you have already learned in interesting new ways. You will learn more about solving problems. You will use the calculator and the computer as problem-solving tools. You will learn more about numbers—both very large numbers and numbers less than 1. You will discover new and interesting things about plane and solid shapes. You will learn to multiply and divide with large numbers. You will learn to do math in your head and to make estimates—so you can use numbers quickly to solve problems every day!

Math is fun! You will work in groups to share what you are learning. You will have fun solving the puzzles and problems in the **Math Fun Magazine** at the back of this book.

This year
you can make mathematics
a learning adventure!

The Authors

▶ ▶ ▶ ▶ ▶ ▶ ▶ ▶

How Do You Use Math Every Day?

People use math to help them do many things.

shop	weigh
count	measure
share	cook
build	tell time
compare	keep score
estimate	predict

Look at these pictures. Talk about how math is being used. Think of some ways you have used math to solve problems. Share your ideas with a classmate.

Solving Problems

You use math every day to solve problems. In this book you will learn how to solve problems by asking yourself questions. These questions will help you

- UNDERSTAND the problem.
- PLAN a solution.
- SOLVE the problem.
- LOOK BACK and check your solution.

Maria has a problem to solve. Read her problem slowly and carefully.

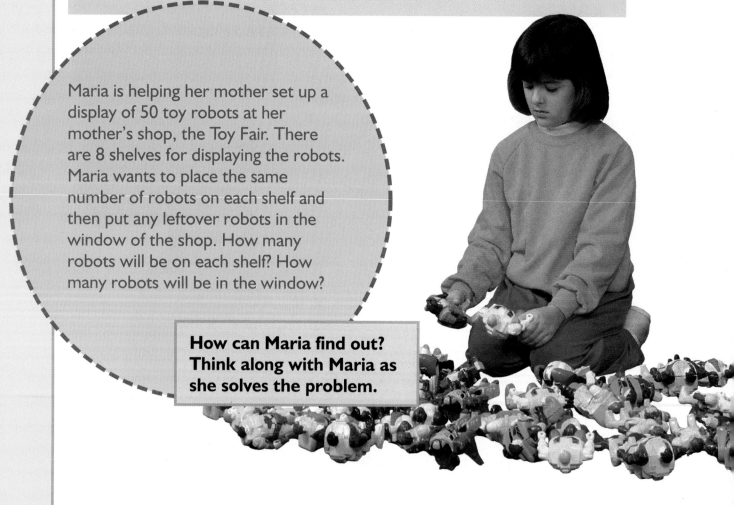

Maria is helping her mother set up a display of 50 toy robots at her mother's shop, the Toy Fair. There are 8 shelves for displaying the robots. Maria wants to place the same number of robots on each shelf and then put any leftover robots in the window of the shop. How many robots will be on each shelf? How many robots will be in the window?

How can Maria find out? Think along with Maria as she solves the problem.

Understand the Problem

First, Maria must UNDERSTAND the problem.

She says the problem to herself. She wants to be sure that she knows what the problem is about. Then she asks herself these questions.

What facts do I have?
There are 50 robots to place on 8 shelves. I need to put the same number of robots on each shelf. I will put the leftover robots in the window.

What must I find?
I must find how many robots will be on each shelf and how many robots will be left over.

How would you say Maria's problem in your own words?

Plan a Solution

Then, Maria must PLAN how to solve her problem.

She thinks about the ways she solves problems. She chooses one of these strategies.

- Guess and check
- Draw a picture
- Make a model
- Act out the problem
- Make a table, chart, or graph
- Write a number sentence

Then she makes a plan by asking herself these questions.

How can I solve the problem?
Since I have the robots and I need to set up the display, I will arrange the robots on the shelves.

How should I act out the problem?
I will divide the robots into 8 equal groups to find how many robots will fit on each shelf and how many will be left over.

What other plan could Maria have made?

▶ ▶ ▶ ▶ ▶ ▶ ▶ ▶

Solve the Problem

Next, Maria must SOLVE the problem.

Maria has decided to act out the problem by using the robots. For some problems Maria may need to decide whether to use a calculator, mental math, or paper and pencil to find the answer.

Maria then thinks about how she will arrange the robots.

I will put 1 robot on each shelf until I have fewer than 8 robots left. When I have fewer than 8 robots left, I know that I cannot add another robot to each shelf and still have equal groups.

I can put 6 robots on each shelf. I will have 2 robots left to put in the window.

Why do you think Maria solved the problem by placing the robots on the shelves? What method would you choose?

▶ ▶ ▶ ▶ ▶ ▶ ▶ ▶

Last, Maria can LOOK BACK and check to see whether her answer is reasonable.

She thinks about a way to check her answer to be sure it is correct. She thinks about whether her solution answers the question.

She asks herself these questions.

How can I check my answer?

I can divide the number of robots by the number of shelves.

$$\begin{array}{r} 6 \ r2 \\ 8{\overline{\smash{\big)}\,50}} \\ -48 \\ \hline 2 \end{array}$$

So, I know there should be 6 robots on each of the 8 shelves. I will have 2 robots left to put in the window.

Does my solution answer the question?

Since I found how many robots will be on each shelf and how many will be left over, my solution answers the question.

How else could Maria check her answer?

Maria solved her problem. She used math to help her set up the robot display.

In Mathematics Plus you will learn to be a problem solver!

How Will You Learn Math?

In Mathematics Plus you will learn math in different ways. All of the ways to learn involve *thinking.*

WORKING TOGETHER

- Listen carefully to other people's ideas.
- Encourage others to share their ideas.
- Discuss ideas in a friendly way.
- Plan how your group is going to share the work.

You will learn math by

- working with a group.
- modeling problems, using objects and drawings.
- listening to your teacher and your classmates.
- talking about math ideas.
- writing about math ideas.
- recording the meanings of new words.
- choosing problem-solving strategies.
- making decisions about how to solve problems.
- using math in school, at home, and everywhere.

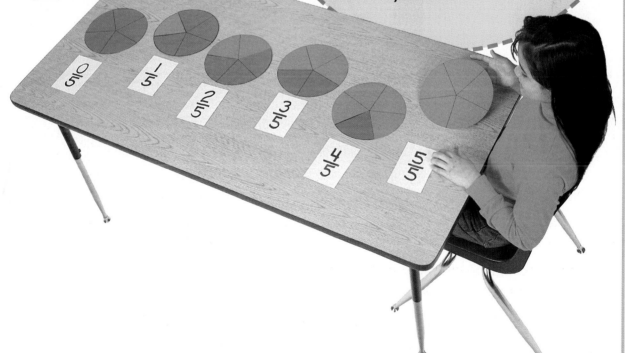

PLACE VALUE
DEVELOPING NUMBER SENSE

Did you know ...

. . . that in space the lunar module traveled at speeds up to 24,300 miles per hour?

Talk About It

On July 21, 1969, Astronaut Neil Armstrong stepped out of the lunar module, *Eagle*, onto the rocky lunar plain. He had traveled 238,857 miles from Earth to the moon. Is the distance from Earth to the moon greater than or less than one million miles?

EXPLORING

Numbers to Thousands

Sometimes it is hard to imagine large numbers. In this lesson you will explore how ones, tens, hundreds, and thousands are related.

Building Understanding

Use graph paper to make place-value models.

Color 1 square, and label it *one*.

Color 10 squares in a row, and label them *ten*.

Color 100 squares in 10 rows of 10, and label them *one hundred*.

Since ▫ = 1, then ▯ = 10, and ▦ = 100.

     one   ten   one hundred

Next, use your graph paper to make models for 40, 90, 200, and 600.

Talk About It

▶ How many hundreds are in each number?

▶ How many tens are in each number? How many ones?

Since ▦ = 100, then ▧ = 1,000.

ten tens   ten hundreds

▶ How many hundreds are in 1,000? How many tens? How many ones?

You can think about numbers in many different ways.

▶ How many pennies are equal to a dime? to 6 dimes?

▶ How many dimes are equal to a dollar? to 5 dollars?

▶ How many pennies are in a dollar? ten dollars?

Making the Connection

1. How many is one thousand? Choose three questions to answer.

What kind of container would hold 1,000 pencils?

Are there a thousand of something in the classroom?

Is there a room in your school that can hold 1,000 students?

What item could you buy with 1,000 pennies?

From the front door of the school, where would you be if you took 1,000 steps?

2. Work in a team. How could you and your team describe 1,000 to someone who has no idea of the size of this number? Decide on an idea, and make a plan to do this. Present your idea to the other teams.

Checking Understanding

Use your graph-paper models to help you answer each question.

3. How many more than 500 is 1,000?

4. What is 100 more than 900?

5. If each of you makes a model for 1,000, how many thousands does your team have in all?

Here are some statements about 1,000. Write *true* or *false*. Think about what seems reasonable.

6. There are more than 1,000 books in the classroom.

7. A line of one thousand squares ☐ would reach from the classroom door to the principal's office door.

8. Ten minutes is greater than 1,000 seconds.

9. You can stay awake for 1,000 minutes.

10. One hundred equals 10 tens.

11. Fifty dollars in dimes is less than 1,000 dimes.

Mr. Cortez, a U.S. SPACE CAMP® instructor, said that the diameter of Mars is about forty-two hundred miles at the equator. Write this number. Use place value to find other names for the same number.

	Thousand	Hundred	Ten	One
Place-Value Blocks	cube	flat	long	unit
Names for Numbers	1 thousand 10 hundreds 100 tens 1,000 ones	1 hundred 10 tens 100 ones	1 ten 10 ones	1 one

Forty-two hundred is another name for four thousand, two hundred.

So, the diameter of Mars at the equator is about 4,200 miles.

More Examples

A. 1,400

1 thousand 4 hundreds
14 hundreds
140 tens
1,400 ones

B. 2,600

2 thousands 6 hundreds
26 hundreds
260 tens
2,600 ones

C. 3,700

3 thousands 7 hundreds
37 hundreds
370 tens
3,700 ones

Check for Understanding

Copy and complete.

1. 20 = ■ ones

2. 100 = ■ tens

3. 500 = ■ hundreds

4. 300 = ■ tens

5. 2,000 = ■ hundreds

6. 2,740 = ■ tens

Write four different names for each.

7. 5,600

8. 1,900

9. 2,200

10. 7,500

11. 8,100

12. 4,300

13. 6,400

14. 9,800

Practice

Copy and complete.

15. $40 = \blacksquare$ tens

16. $800 = \blacksquare$ tens

17. $6,000 = \blacksquare$ hundreds

18. $30 = \blacksquare$ ones

19. $2,390 = \blacksquare$ tens

20. $700 = \blacksquare$ hundreds

Match each number with its value. Write the correct letter.

21. 210

a. 347 tens

22. 3,470

b. 21 tens

23. 8,300

c. 95 hundreds

24. 9,500

d. 83 hundreds

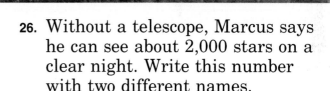

Mixed Applications

25. José read 10 pages of a book about space each day for 30 days. How many pages did he read?

26. Without a telescope, Marcus says he can see about 2,000 stars on a clear night. Write this number with two different names.

27. Mars has two moons. The larger moon, Phobos, is about 5,800 miles from the center of Mars. Write this number with four different names.

28. **Number Sense** The Camp Bookstore gives a prize to every tenth shopper. On Saturday 16 prizes were given away. How many people went to the bookstore on Saturday? (HINT: 16 tens)

VISUAL THINKING

Write the letter of the correct answer.

29.

a. 258
b. 2,058
c. 2,580

30.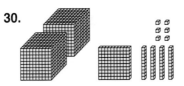

a. 2,056
b. 2,146
c. 3,146

31.

a. 307
b. 2,170
c. 3,007

Why is the number system you use based on 10?

Scott and Julio worked on a report about space travel. Julio told Scott that Saturn's diameter is seventy-four thousand, six hundred miles across. How would Scott write this number? Use a place-value chart.

Thousands			Ones		
Hundreds	Tens	Ones	Hundreds	Tens	Ones
	7	4 ,	6	0	0

Read: seventy-four thousand, six hundred
Write: 74,600

You can express numbers in different ways.

Standard Form	Expanded Form	Words
A. 306	300 + 6	three hundred six
B. 2,110	2,000 + 100 + 10	two thousand, one hundred ten
C. 30,275	30,000 + 200 + 70 + 5	thirty thousand, two hundred seventy-five

Use a calculator. Enter the expanded form of each number above, and read the answer on the display.

Press: 3 0 0 + 6 = | 306.

Talk About It

▶ In the number 306, how would the value of the number change if you removed the zero? Explain.

▶ In the number 74,600, what is the place-value position of the digit 7?

▶ Do all numbers use place value? Think about your telephone number.

Check for Understanding

Express each number in two other ways.

1. four hundred eight

2. eleven thousand, six hundred sixty

3. 73,895   4. 79,245   5. 6,043   6. 11,892   7. 7,102

Practice

Express each number in two other ways. Then enter the expanded form of each number on a calculator. Read and write the answer in the display.

8. two hundred five

9. seven thousand, four hundred sixty

10. ninety-two thousand, six hundred seventy-eight

11. two hundred eighty-three thousand, four hundred ten

12. 80,000 + 2,000 + 20 + 2

13. 700,000 + 50,000 + 2,000 + 100 + 30

14. 6,713   15. 856   16. 4,983   17. 1,200   18. 6,591

Write an example of each.

19. telephone number   20. street address   21. your birth year   22. zip code

Mixed Applications

23. The length of a year on Pluto is about ninety thousand, five hundred twenty Earth days. Write the number in standard form.

24. Mr. Davis wrote a check for $8,253 for the new telescope. Write the number in words.

25. **Number Sense** You want to make a long-distance telephone call. You dial a three-digit area code before the usual seven-digit number. The area code and number are four one five, five five five, two three one five. Write this number as a telephone number.

MIXED REVIEW

Copy and complete.

1. 60 = ▇ ones

2. 7,000 = ▇ hundreds

3. 200 = ▇ tens

4. 9,100 = ▇ hundreds

5. 3,450 = ▇ tens

6. 900 = ▇ tens

7. Write two examples of numbers without place value.

When do you have to write numbers in words?

WRAP
UP...

PROBLEM *Solving*

Carlotta made a tally table of the space patches collected by her team. One tally mark (/) stands for each patch. How many people collected more patches than Carlotta?

A table can sometimes help you organize information and make a plan to solve a problem.

▶ **UNDERSTAND**

What are you asked to find?

What information is given?

▶ **PLAN**

How will you solve the problem?

You can use the table to compare the tally marks.

▶ **SOLVE**

How can you use the table to find the solution?

You know Carlotta has 5 patches.

Find all people with more than 5 patches.

So, 4 people collected more patches than Carlotta.

▶ **LOOK BACK**

What other strategy can you use to solve the problem?

SPACE PATCHES COLLECTED

Juan	
Mike	///
Tony	/
Mickey	////
Bill	///// ///
Nancy	///// /
Carlotta	///
Florence	/////
Lilly	//
Lorenzo	///// ////
	///// //

///// = 5

W H A T
I F... ... Carlotta had 6 patches? How many people earned more patches than Carlotta?

8

Apply

Use the table to solve Exercises 1–4.

Dotty recorded the weather at U.S. SPACE CAMP® every day for three weeks. Use the table she made to answer the questions.

U.S. SPACE CAMP® Weather Table

Week	Weather		
	Cloudy	Rainy	Sunny
1	//	////	/
2	/	/	†††
3	///	//	//

1. Which week had the most rainy days?

2. Which week had the most cloudy days?

3. Which week had the most sunny days?

4. How many rainy days were there in all?

Mixed Applications

Use the table to answer Exercises 5–10.

Lee made a tally table. It shows the number of birthdays per month of the people attending U.S. SPACE CAMP®.

5. How many birthdays are in August?

6. How many birthdays are in September?

7. In which months are there no birthdays?

8. In which month are the most birthdays?

9. In which months are there fewer than five birthdays?

10. How many more birthdays are in November than in April?

U.S. SPACE CAMP® Birthdays

Month	Number of Birthdays
January	////
February	//
March	
April	†††
May	/
June	///
July	
August	////
September	††† ///
October	///
November	††† /
December	††† †††

11. **Write a Question** Use the birthday table or the weather table to write two more questions that can be answered by using a table.

12. **Organize Data** Suppose you want to compare the color of your classmates' eyes. Describe how you would gather and display the information.

PLACE VALUE
to Hundred Thousands

The speaker at the planetarium said that the average distance between the center of the earth and the center of the moon is two hundred thirty-eight thousand, eight hundred fifty-seven miles. How can you write this number in standard form?

Thousands			Ones		
Hundreds	Tens	Ones	Hundreds	Tens	Ones
2	3	8	8	5	7

A **comma** is used to separate periods

Each group of three digits is called a **period**.

Read: two hundred thirty-eight thousand, eight hundred fifty-seven

	Standard Form	**Expanded Form**
Write:	238,857	200,000 + 30,000 + 8,000 + 800 + 50 + 7

Talk About It

In 238,857 the value of the digit 8 in the thousands place is 8,000.

▶ What is the value of the digit 3 in 238,857?

▶ What is the value of the digit 2 in 238,857?

▶ What digits are in the thousands period in 238,857?

Talk About It

Read the numbers in the box.

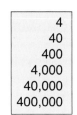

```
4
40
400
4,000
40,000
400,000
```

▶ How does the value of the 4 change as it moves from right to left?

▶ How does changing the number of zeros change the value of the number?

Check for Understanding

Write the value of the blue digit.

1. 6,891
2. 45,034
3. 17,105
4. 367,023
5. 450,924
6. 789,421

7. In 382,017, what three digits are in the thousands period?

Practice

Write the value of the digit 8 in each number.

8. 114,682   **9.** 89,416   **10.** 5,801   **11.** 24,318   **12.** 813,506

Write the value of the blue digit.

13. 3,829   **14.** 116,302   **15.** 465   **16.** 29,497   **17.** 937,227

Express each number in two other ways. Then enter the expanded form on a calculator. Read and write the answer on the display.

18. three thousand, seventy-seven

19. forty-four thousand, twenty-eight

20. seven hundred eleven thousand, forty-five

21. sixty-four thousand, one hundred fifty-two

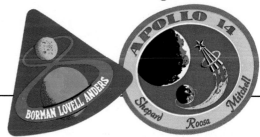

Mixed Applications

22. Adam has a space-sticker collection of thirty-four stickers. Write the number in standard form.

23. How many zeros must you write beside the digit 2 to show a value of two hundred thousand? Write the number.

24. In one month eleven thousand, one hundred sixteen students visited the planetarium. Write the number in standard form and in expanded form.

25. Number Sense Write the largest six-digit number using the digits 6, 7, and 8. Use each digit twice.

| LOGICAL REASONING |

Use place value to solve each riddle.

26. My ones digit is 3. My tens digit is 6. My hundreds digit is 1 more than my tens digit. My thousands digit is the same as my ones digit. What number am I?

27. My ones digit is 3. My hundreds digit is 1 less than my ones digit. My tens digit is 7 more than my hundreds digit. What number am I?

Is the value of the 4 greater in 43,210 or 4,321? How do you know?

WRAP UP...

PLACE VALUE
to Millions

Did you know that Earth's population has increased by about eighty-one million, four hundred sixty thousand people each year over a ten-year period? How would you write this number?

Millions			Thousands			Ones		
Hundreds	Tens	Ones	Hundreds	Tens	Ones	Hundreds	Tens	Ones
	8	1,	4	6	0,	0	0	0

A comma is used to separate periods.

Read: eighty-one million,
four hundred sixty thousand

Write: 81,460,000

> Commas help you read large numbers. Read the number before the comma. Then name the period.

Talk About It

▶ About how many people live in your town or city?

▶ Do you think there are more than or fewer than a million people in your state? Check to see if you are correct.

▶ Give an example of something that can be counted in the millions.

▶ Name the number that is 1,000,000 more than 9,657,021.

Check for Understanding

1. Tell which things are counted in the millions.
   a. the number of students in your school
   b. the number of dollars it cost to build the space shuttle
   c. the number of people in the United States
   d. the number of miles from the earth to the sun

Write the number that is 1,000,000 more.

2. 73,152,633   3. 1,207,631   4. 49,016,657

Practice

Name the period shown by the blue digits.

5. 214,893,487   **6.** 285,306,100   **7.** 447,008,275   **8.** 119,300,378

Express each number in two other ways. Enter the expanded form on a calculator. Read the answer on the display.

9. 200,000 + 30,000 + 7,000 + 100 + 10 + 2   **10.** 8,234,567

11. twenty-one million, five hundred thousand   **12.** 419,809

13. 90,000,000 + 3,000,000 + 700,000 + 30,000 + 9,000

14. four million, two hundred forty thousand, forty-six

15. eighty-nine million, one hundred sixteen thousand, sixty-two

Write the number that is 1,000,000 less.

16. 8,496,283   **17.** 3,389,005   **18.** 86,000,347   **19.** 12,345,678

Mixed Applications

Population of South America	
Argentina	31,965,000
Bolivia	6,918,000
Brazil	144,427,000
Chile	12,668,000
Colombia	30,577,000
Ecuador	10,013,000
Guyana	1,006,000
Paraguay	4,007,000
Peru	21,254,000
Suriname	398,000
Uruguay	3,081,000
Venezuela	20,116,000

Use the table to solve Exercises 20–22.

20. Which country has the largest population?

21. Which country has the smallest population?

22. Which countries have a population between 5,000,000 and 20,000,000?

23. Give an example of something other than population that is counted in millions.

Use a calculator to find how many days it would take to spend $1,000,000 if you could spend $100,000 a day.

More Practice, Lesson 1.6, page H35

1. Mr. Rubin traveled two thousand, one hundred forty-five miles on a business trip. Express this number in two other ways.

2. It is 1,753 miles from Dallas, Texas, to Boston, Massachusetts. It is 1,752 miles from Dallas to San Francisco, California. Which city, Boston or San Francisco, is farther from Dallas?

Use the table for Exercises 3–6.

This table shows the number of students who help in the school library each morning.

3. On which day do the most students help?

4. On which day do 4 students help?

5. On which day do the fewest students help?

6. How many students in all help during the week?

One tally mark (/) can stand for one student.

Library Helpers	
Day	Number of Students
Monday	////
Tuesday	//// /
Wednesday	//
Thursday	//// //
Friday	///

Write the value of the blue digit.

7. 326   8. 497   9. 833   10. 8,621

11. 37,621   12. 84,926   13. 73,483   14. 171,850

Write each number in words.

15. 98   16. 465   17. 3,055   18. 92,721   19. 800,620

Write each number in standard form.

20. eighty-three

21. three hundred twenty-nine

22. six thousand, four

23. forty-two thousand, fifty-one

Copy and complete.

24. 30 = ■ ones

25. 200 = ■ tens

26. 700 = ■ hundreds

27. 7,400 = ■ hundreds

28. 3,980 = ■ tens

29. 65,002 = ■ ones

Spotlight ON PROBLEM SOLVING

Understand
Plan
Solve
Look Back

◆ ◆ Make Predictions ◆ ◆

You can solve a problem by using the facts to make a prediction, or a good guess about what will happen next.

This table shows the price of a cup of juice at the Space Center Restaurant for three years.

Price of a Cup of Juice	
Year	Cost
1	$0.80
2	$1.00
3	$1.20

Talk About It

a How much has the price of a cup of juice changed during the three years?

b Predict how much a cup of juice will cost next year.

c Predict what the price of a cup of juice will be in two years.

A **prediction** is based on information from the past. Many things can keep a prediction from coming true.

d What are some things that could make the cost of a cup of juice become more expensive? become less expensive? remain the same?

◆ ◆ ◆ Apply ◆ ◆ ◆ ◆

Use the table. Which of these predictions will probably be correct? Write **yes** or **no** for Exercises 1–3. Write a sentence to explain your answer.

Juice Cups Used (in dozens)	
Month	Cups Used
January	1,000
February	1,500
March	2,000

1. The restaurant will use more cups in April than in March.

2. The restaurant will sell fewer cups of juice in April.

3. The restaurant may use 2,500 dozen cups in April.

4. If the sale of juice increases, how will this affect the number of cups used?

COMPARING WHOLE NUMBERS

Sarah and Latoya traveled from different cities to U.S. SPACE CAMP® in Titusville, Florida. Sarah traveled 179 miles from Waverly, Georgia. Latoya traveled 174 miles from Ft. Lauderdale, Florida. Who traveled farther to come to U.S. SPACE CAMP®?

A number line can be used to compare numbers.

$$174 \quad 179$$
```
◄┼┼┼┼┼•┼┼┼┼┼•┼┼┼┼┼•┼┼┼↑┼↑┼┼•┼┼┼┼┼•┼┼┼┼┼•┼┼┼┼┼•┼┼┼┼►
   150      160      170      180      190      200
```

Notice that 174 is to the left of 179.	Notice that 179 is to the right of 174.
So, 174 *is less than* 179.	So, 179 *is greater than* 174.
Write: 174 < 179	Write: 179 > 174

So, Sarah traveled farther than Latoya.

> means *is greater than*
< means *is less than*
= means *equals*

You can compare numbers by comparing the digits in the same place-value position.

Compare 2,567 and 2,519.
Line up the digits. Begin at the left.
Check each place-value position until the digits are different.

Step 1	Step 2	Step 3
Compare the thousands.	Compare the hundreds.	Compare the tens.
2,567 Same number of thousands.	2,567 Same number of hundreds.	2,567 Since 6 > 1, 2,567 > 2,519.
↓	↓	↓
2,519	2,519	2,519

So, 2,567 > 2,519 or 2,519 < 2,567.

Check for Understanding

Compare. Write <, >, or = for ●.

1. 319 ● 139
2. 4,228 ● 4,218
3. 1,607 ● 1,607
4. 4,087 ● 987

5. 5,772 ● 5,774
6. 2,117 ● 12,711
7. 6,061 ● 6,091
8. 4,890 ● 4,872

Practice

Compare. Write $<$, $>$, or $=$ for ●.

9. 987 ● 999
10. 2,429 ● 2,567
11. 6,415 ● 6,457

12. 98,104 ● 9,804
13. 62,011 ● 63,110
14. 3,215,861 ● 3,218,427

15. 7,123 ● 7,123
16. 2,345,212 ● 2,345,112
17. 51,959 ● 50,161

Write the numbers using the symbol that means *is less than.*

18. 43; 47
19. 81; 18
20. 121; 211
21. 841; 418

22. 396; 369
23. 239; 236
24. 3,385; 3,358
25. 12,782; 12,278

Write the numbers using the symbol that means *is greater than.*

26. 63; 36
27. 839; 389
28. 2,037; 2,073
29. 3,403; 3,430

Using the number 36,725, write the number that is

30. 1 more.
31. 10 more.
32. 100 more.
33. 100 less.

34. 1 less.
35. 10 less.
36. 1,000 more.
37. 1,000 less.

Mixed Applications

38. Betsy counted 128 stars. Paula counted 218 stars. Compare the numbers by comparing the digits. Write a number sentence using $<$, $>$, or $=$.

39. The land area of Earth is about 57,259,000 square miles. The water area of Earth is about 139,692,000 square miles. Which is greater?

40. On a calculator, how can you change 36,725 to 38,725? Do not use the "clear" button.

41. **Logical Reasoning** Cameron traveled 245 miles to U.S. SPACE CAMP®. Lynn traveled 100 miles farther than Cameron. Jay traveled 100 miles less than Cameron. Find how far each one traveled. Who traveled the greatest distance?

How can you tell that 276,498 $<$ 276,598?

More Practice, Lesson 1.7, page H36

ORDERING WHOLE NUMBERS

The weights of three space probes are listed in this table. Place the weights of the probes in order from greatest to least.

Space Probe	Weight in Tons
Starship	4,636
Probe	4,618
Quest	4,652

You can use a number line.

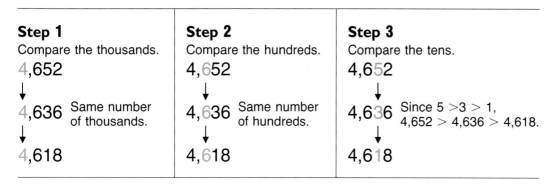

| 4,618 | 4,636 | 4,652 |

4,610   4,620   4,630   4,640   4,650   4,660

Order numbers by comparing them.
Compare the digits in the same place-value positions.

Talk About It

▶ Do you begin at the left or the right?

▶ How do you line up the digits?

▶ When do you stop checking the digits?

Compare 4,636; 4,618; 4,652.

Step 1	**Step 2**	**Step 3**
Compare the thousands.	Compare the hundreds.	Compare the tens.
4,652 ↓	4,652 ↓	4,652 ↓
4,636 ↓ Same number of thousands.	4,636 ↓ Same number of hundreds.	4,636 ↓ Since 5 > 3 > 1, 4,652 > 4,636 > 4,618.
4,618	4,618	4,618

The order of the probes from greatest to least is 4,652; 4,636; 4,618.

Check for Understanding

Write each group of numbers in order from least to greatest.
Draw a number line for Exercises 1 and 4.

1. 346; 341; 314; 431   2. 1,089; 985; 1,917; 1,098   3. 56,032; 2,562; 56,539

4. 7,124; 7,127; 7,129   5. 2,973; 2,193; 2,937   6. 13,709; 13,970; 12,970

Practice

Draw a number line for each set of numbers, and place the numbers in order from least to greatest.

7. $450, 100, 750, 900, 200$ **8.** $90, 60, 110, 100$

Choose the letter that describes how each group of numbers is ordered.

a. from least to greatest   **b.** from greatest to least

9. 19, 26, 46, 62, 91

10. 259, 290, 295, 592

11. 27,449; 27,494; 27,944

12. 1,591; 1,542; 1,519

13. 1,987; 2,062; 2,620

14. 560,908; 560,898; 560,890

Mixed Applications

Use the table to answer Exercises 15–17.

Planet	Distance from Earth in Miles
Mercury	57,000,000
Venus	25,700,000
Mars	48,700,000
Jupiter	390,700,000
Saturn	762,700,000

15. Which planet is closest to Earth?

16. Which of these planets is farthest from Earth?

17. List these planets in the order of their distance from Earth. Begin with the closest planet.

18. Write a Question Last year the Gamez family traveled 2,058 miles on their vacation. This year they traveled 1,508 miles.

SOCIAL STUDIES CONNECTION

19. Large numbers are often used to tell about places and people. For example, the area of Alaska is about 591,000 square miles. The area of California is about 158,700 square miles. Which state is larger?

20. The area of Texas is about 266,800 square miles. Using the information in Exercise 19, write the three states in order from greatest to least according to their areas.

In what situations do you need to order numbers?

WRAP UP...

Look at the pattern on the wallpaper border in Example **A**. In what order can you put the pieces, starting with **A**, to make the pattern of the border?

Finding a pattern can sometimes help you solve a problem.

▶ **UNDERSTAND**

What are you asked to find?

What information are you given?

▶ **PLAN**

How can you place the pieces so that the pattern continues?

Find the pattern of the figures on the wallpaper border.

What is the order of the figures?

The order of the figures is planet, rocket, star.

▶ **SOLVE**

How can you use the pattern to place the pieces of wallpaper border in the correct order?

Since **A** ends with a planet, a rocket must follow.

Since **C** ends with a star, a planet must follow.

So, to make the pattern, the order of the pieces must be **A, C, B**.

▶ **LOOK BACK**

How can you check your answer?

A.

B.

C.

WHAT **IF...** ... the pattern continued? What would be the next figure?

Apply

Complete the pattern.

1

2

3 Create your own pattern. Draw lines so that a classmate can complete the pattern. Exchange patterns and complete.

Jonathan has a puzzle for his classmates. When he says 6, the answer is 16. When he says 9, the answer is 19. When he says 23, the answer is 33.

4 What is the pattern?

5 What is the answer when he says 31?

6 What is the answer when he says 52?

7 If the answer is 37, what does he say?

Copy and find the missing figure.

8

9

Mixed Applications

10 The minimum distance between Earth and its moon is 221,463 miles. From Mars to one of its moons, the distance is about 14,600 miles. Which distance is shorter?

11 On Mondays, Wednesdays, and Fridays, Bert buys planet stickers. On Tuesdays and Thursdays, he trades them. His first buying day was Monday, October 13. Will he trade or buy on October 23?

> **WRITER'S CORNER**

12 Some patterns exist in space. For example, the moon seems to change shape in a regular pattern that takes about a month. Find a picture in a reference book that shows these changes. Write a description of this pattern.

More Practice, Lesson 1.9, page H37

ORDINAL NUMBERS

Marty and his friends are in line at the space shuttle simulator. Marty is at the front of the line. What is Marty's position in line?

Marty is *first* in line. If each person in line were given a number, Marty would have the number one.

Carla is behind Marty. What is her position in line? Carla is *second* in line.

First and *second* are called ordinal numbers.

Cardinal numbers tell how many.		Ordinal numbers tell position or order.	
1	one	1st	first
2	two	2nd	second
11	eleven	11th	eleventh
23	twenty-three	23rd	twenty-third
52	fifty-two	52nd	fifty-second
100	one hundred	100th	one-hundredth

Check for Understanding

Write the next ordinal number.

1. seventeenth
2. thirty-first
3. ninety-ninth
4. 112th

Write the missing number.

5. 2, 6, 10, ▮, 18, 22

6. first, third, ▮, seventh

Write *cardinal* or *ordinal* for each underlined word.

7. Sue was the <u>fifth</u> student to pay the <u>eight</u> dollars for the field trip. She was <u>one</u> out of <u>twenty-four</u> students in the <u>fourth</u> grade.

Practice

Write the next ordinal number in words.

8. thirty-third   **9.** sixty-second   **10.** eightieth   **11.** fortieth

Writing the missing numbers.

12. 25th, ■, ■, 28th, 29th, ■, 31st   **13.** 58, ■, 60, 61, ■

14. 98th, ■, 100th, ■, 102nd   **15.** 219th, ■, 223rd, ■, 227th

Use the calendar to answer each question.

16. What is the date of the first Monday?

17. What is the date of the second Friday?

18. What is the date of the third Tuesday?

19. What is the date of the day before the fourth Sunday?

Mixed Applications

20. What is the name of the fifth chapter in this book?

21. Logical Reasoning Frannie is behind the eighth person in the lunch line. How many people are in front of Frannie?

VISUAL THINKING

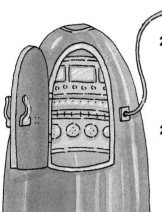

Write the letter of the correct answer.

22. The woman is third in line. How many are in front of her?
     a. 2   **b.** 3   **c.** 4

23. In what place in line is the boy?
     a. 2nd   **b.** 3rd   **c.** 4th

24. Which person is second in line?
     a. girl   **b.** boy   **c.** man

How are ordinal numbers and cardinal numbers different?

WRAP UP...

The radio announcer said that the satellite orbited the earth at about 300 miles. The satellite's orbit was actually at an altitude of 283 miles. Would the announcer have been more accurate if he had estimated the altitude at 200 miles?

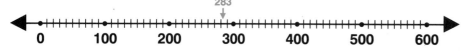

283

```
◄─•┼┼┼┼┼┼┼┼┼•┼┼┼┼┼┼┼┼┼•┼┼┼┼┼┼┼┼┼•┼┼┼┼┼┼┼┼┼•┼┼┼┼┼┼┼┼┼•┼┼┼┼┼┼┼┼┼•─►
   0        100       200       300       400       500       600
```

The radio announcer's estimate of 300 miles was closer to 283 miles than the estimate of 200 miles.

The place value you round a number to depends on how exact your estimate needs to be.

You can estimate by rounding numbers to different places. Use these rules.

- Find the digit in the place to be rounded.
- Now look at the digit to its right.
- If the digit to the right is less than 5, the digit being rounded remains the same.
- If the digit to the right is 5 or more, the digit being rounded is increased by 1.

Examples

A.

Round 4,385 to the nearest thousand.

Digit to be rounded is 4. 4,385   3 < 5

So, do not change the thousands digit. 4,000

B.

Round 4,385 to the nearest hundred.

Digit to be rounded is 3. 4,385   8 > 5

So, increase the digit in the hundreds place by 1. 4,400

C.

Round 4,385 to the nearest ten.

Digit to be rounded is 8. 4,385   5 = 5

So, increase the digit in the tens place by 1. 4,390

Talk About It

▶ If a number rounded to the nearest ten is 40, what are all of the possible exact numbers?

Use the same rules to estimate money amounts.

Round to the nearest ten cents.	Round to the nearest dollar.	Round to the nearest ten dollars.
$0.87 → $0.90	$7.25 → $7.00	$27.95 → $30.00

Check for Understanding

Estimate by rounding to the nearest dollar.

1. $2.50
2. $32.70
3. $37.17
4. $6.49
5. $7.58

6. Round 563,297 to the nearest

    a. ten.
    b. hundred.
    c. thousand.
    d. ten thousand.

Practice

Estimate by rounding to the nearest ten cents and to the nearest dollar.

7. $0.62
8. $5.43
9. $7.91
10. $79.19
11. $7.45
12. $83.12

Estimate by rounding to the nearest thousand or to the nearest ten dollars.

13. 3,500
14. $13.96
15. 38,466
16. $466.85
17. $717.84

Mixed Applications

18. Becky's model rocket traveled to an altitude of 379 feet. Estimate the altitude to the nearest hundred feet.

19. Earth's diameter at the equator is 7,926 miles. Estimate the diameter to the nearest thousand.

20. **Number Sense** A scientist gave a talk about space travel. About 80 students attended. What is the least number and the greatest number of students that could have attended?

21. **Logical Reasoning** Jim says the number of his space stickers rounds to 320 and also to 300. Does he have more than 324 stickers or fewer than 324 stickers? Explain your answer.

MIXED REVIEW

Express each number in two other ways.

1. 410
2. 3,898
3. 90,000 + 3,000 + 400 + 20 + 5
4. six hundred seven

Write each missing ordinal number.

5. forty-fifth, ▓, forty-seventh, ▓, ▓

6. 16th, 18th, 20th, ▓, 24th

Name some situations in which you might use rounding.

Vocabulary Check

Choose a word or words from the box to complete each sentence.

| cardinal |
| expanded |
| hundreds |
| ordinal |
| period |
| round |
| standard |
| ten thousands |

Remember to use commas to separate periods in a number.

1. A number written as 2,000 + 400 + 60 + 7 is written in _?_ form. *(page 6)*

2. Forty-fifth is an _?_ number. *(page 22)*

3. Another name for 3,600 is 36 _?_. *(page 4)*

4. An ordinal number tells position, while a _?_ number tells how many. *(page 22)*

5. When you change the number 78 to 80, you _?_ the number 78 to the nearest ten. *(page 24)*

6. Each group of three digits in a number is a _?_. *(page 10)*

7. The number 6,823 is written in _?_ form. *(page 6)*

8. In the number 137,406 the 3 is in the _?_ place. *(page 10)*

Concept Check

Write in expanded form. *(page 6)*

9. 4,813   10. 891,704   11. 72,591   12. 479,000

Use a calculator. Enter the expanded form and read the answer on the display. Then write it in standard form. *(page 6)*

13. 400 + 30 + 6   14. 70,000 + 5,000 + 200 + 9

15. 1,000,000 + 700,000   16. 300,000 + 20,000 + 600 + 70 + 3

17. two million, fifty-six thousand, nine hundred seven

Write the value of the digit 4 in each number. *(pages 10–13)*

18. 1,429   19. 437,261   20. 64,093   21. 4,258,107

Write another name for each number. *(page 4)*

22. 2 tens   23. 4,500 ones   24. 51 hundreds   25. 3 thousands   26. 600 tens

Skill Check

Copy and complete. *(page 4)*

27. 4,000 = ▧ hundreds   **28.** 600 = ▧ tens   **29.** 23,000 = ▧ thousands

Compare. Write < or > for ●. *(page 16)*

30. 34,803 ● 41,985   **31.** 503,944 ● 650,093   **32.** 947,653 ● 947,563

33. 2,761,999 ● 2,761,987   **34.** 693,704,441 ● 640,769,013

Round to the nearest ten and hundred. *(page 24)*

35. 59   **36.** 55   **37.** 176   **38.** 6,408   **39.** 945

Round to the nearest thousand. *(page 24)*

40. 2,871   **41.** 45,883   **42.** 671,500   **43.** 7,499   **44.** 107,933

Write four different names for each number. *(page 4)*

45. 5,600   **46.** 1,200

Problem-Solving Check

Mrs. Ramos kept track of the miles she drove for her job selling television satellite equipment. Use the table to answer Exercises 47–51. *(page 8)*

Day	Miles
Monday	51
Tuesday	92
Wednesday	13
Thursday	25
Friday	36

47. On what day did she drive the least?

48. How many miles did Mrs. Ramos drive from Monday through Friday?

49. On what day did Mrs. Ramos drive the most?

50. What day had the greatest increase over the day before?

51. Write the miles for each day in order from greatest to least.

Complete the pattern. *(page 20)*

52. ⌐ ⌐ ⌐ ⌐ ⌐ ⌐ ⌐ **?**   **53.** ∫∽?∽∫∽?∽∫∽ **?**

CHAPTER TEST

Write in expanded form.

1. 536

2. 4,267

3. 13,080

Write in standard form.

4. six thousand, two hundred eighty-one

5. $70,000 + 2,000 + 500 + 40$

6. four million, sixty-two thousand, nine

Compare. Write < or > for ●.

7. 452 ● 459

8. 86,304 ● 8,604

9. 43,127 ● 45,216

10. 4,907 ● 4,097

Write the value of the digit 5 in each number.

11. 41,253

12. 126,521,460

13. 135,962,340

> means *greater* than
< means *less* than
= means *equals*

14. Write four different names for 1,700.

Write *cardinal* or *ordinal* for each underlined word.

15. Tom was <u>sixth</u> out of <u>twelve</u> players on the <u>fifth</u>-grade soccer team.

Estimate by rounding to the nearest hundred or dollar.

16. 295

17. 317

18. 56

19. $0.73

20. $4.13

21. $29.69

Jo kept a record of the number of books she read. Use the table for Exercises 22–23.

22. In which month did she read the most books?

23. In which month did she read four books?

Month	Number of Books Read
January	///
February	/
March	//////
April	////

24. Tom plays a number game. When he says 1, the answer is 10. When he says 2, the answer is 20. When he says 3, the answer is 30. What is the answer when he says 4?

25. Write the missing part of the pattern.

 ?

Teamwork P-R-O-J-E-C-T

Create a Time Capsule

A time capsule is a container for facts and objects that represent what the world is like at a given time. Work with your teammates to make a time capsule that will be opened in 25 years. Make it no larger than a shoebox. Include objects and a list of facts that you think are important.

Decide

▶ Discuss what objects should be in the time capsule. Choose 20 objects.

▶ Discuss which important facts should be included. Your team may want to include facts about the population of the earth, the United States, and your state.

Do

▶ Make a list of 20 interesting facts. Check to make sure that your facts are correct.

▶ Collect or make the 20 objects. Pack the list and the objects into your time capsule.

▶ Decorate your time capsule.

Share

▶ Compare your group's capsule with those of other groups.

▶ Tell why you chose each object or fact.

Talk About It

★ What interesting facts did you learn?

★ What large numbers are included in your facts?

★ What other number facts might be interesting to people in the future?

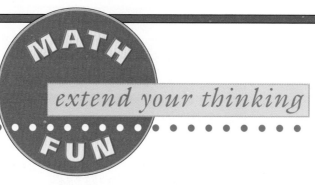

MATH FUN

extend your thinking

Activity

Spin a Number

Play this game with one, two, or three partners. You will need a spinner like the one in the picture. Each player will need a place-value chart.

The first player calls "greatest" or "least" to tell the other players whether to try to write the greatest number possible or the least number possible. The first player then spins the spinner six times. After each spin, each player decides in which place to put that number on his or her place-value chart. The player who writes the greatest (or least) six-digit number scores one point.

The second player then calls "greatest" or "least" and spins the spinner six times for the six digits in the second number. The first player to score ten points wins the game.

Hundred Thousands	Ten Thousands	Thousands	, Hundreds	Tens	Ones

Logical Reasoning

Challenge

Number Sense

◇ Write two numbers that round to 100 when rounded to the nearest ten.
Use all of these digits, but use each digit only once.

$$4 \bullet 8 \bullet 1 \bullet 0 \bullet 9$$

◇ Write two numbers that round to 10,000 when rounded to the nearest ten thousand, thousand, hundred, and ten.
Use all of these digits, but use each digit only once.

$$0 \bullet 2 \bullet 9 \bullet 9 \bullet 1 \bullet 9 \bullet 0 \bullet 0 \bullet 9$$

Suppose that you are given $100,000 to spend any way you wish.

◇ If you spend $100 a day, how many days will it take to spend the whole amount? About how many years is that?

◇ Suppose you save $100 a day. How many days will it take to save $1,000,000? About how many years is that?

CUMULATIVE REVIEW

CHAPTER 1

Write the letter of the correct answer.

1. Which number is another name for 350 tens?

   A. 350   B. 3,500
   C. 35,000   D. 350,000

2. Which number is an ordinal number?

   A. eleventh   B. twenty-three
   C. forty-seven   D. not here

3. Which number has the digit 4 in the ten thousands place?

   A. 24,671   B. 340,795
   C. 1,034,792   D. 2,136,402

4. Round 238 to the nearest ten.

   A. 200   B. 230
   C. 240   D. 300

5. Give the standard form for 20,000 + 7,000 + 400 + 10.

   A. 24,710   B. 27,410
   C. 274,010   D. 20,740,010

6. Round 452 to the nearest hundred.

   A. 400   B. 450
   C. 500   D. 600

7. Order 692; 296; and 629 from greatest to least.

   A. 692; 629; 296   B. 629; 296; 692
   C. 296; 629; 692   D. not here

8. Which number is 10,000,000 more than 38,396,103?

   A. 38,406,103   B. 39,396,103
   C. 48,396,130   D. not here

9. Which item could you buy for about $100?

   A. a car   B. a bicycle
   C. a house   D. soccer ball

10. Which number is 100 greater than 95?

    A. 85   B. 195
    C. 295   D. 1,095

11. Jon kept this record of the number of chores he did each day.

Mon.	Tues.	Wed.	Thurs.
///	////	/	////／

    On which day did he do the most chores?

    A. Monday   B. Tuesday
    C. Wednesday   D. Thursday

12. Look at the pattern. Choose the missing shape.

     ?

    A.   B.

    C.   D.

2

ADDING AND SUBTRACTING WHOLE NUMBERS

Did you know . . .

. . . the Magnum, a roller coaster in Sandusky, Ohio, has a drop of 201 feet, and when it reaches the bottom of the drop, it is going 70 miles per hour?

Talk About It

Stephanie is waiting to ride the roller coaster at the fair. When it reaches the bottom of the 68-foot drop, it is going 29 miles per hour. How could Stephanie compare the speeds of the two roller coasters?

ADDITION
Reviewing Fact Strategies

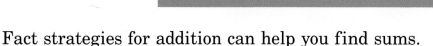

Fact strategies for addition can help you find sums.

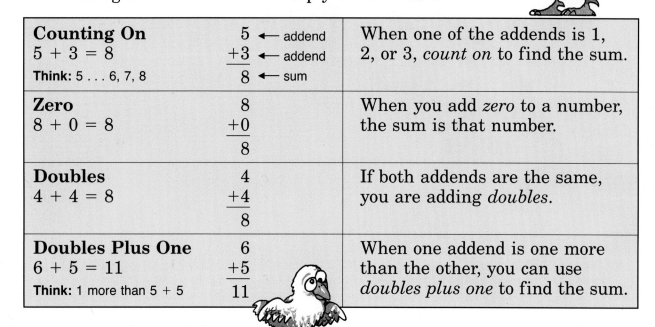

Counting On 5 + 3 = 8 **Think:** 5 . . . 6, 7, 8	5 ← addend +3 ← addend 8 ← sum	When one of the addends is 1, 2, or 3, *count on* to find the sum.
Zero 8 + 0 = 8	8 +0 8	When you add *zero* to a number, the sum is that number.
Doubles 4 + 4 = 8	4 +4 8	If both addends are the same, you are adding *doubles*.
Doubles Plus One 6 + 5 = 11 **Think:** 1 more than 5 + 5	6 +5 11	When one addend is one more than the other, you can use *doubles plus one* to find the sum.

Talk About It

Use the fact strategies for addition to find patterns in the addition table.

▶ Use the *zero* strategy to find sums in the addition table. What pattern do you notice?

▶ Use the *doubles* strategy to find sums in the addition table. What pattern do you notice?

▶ Use the *doubles plus one* strategy to find sums in the addition table. What pattern do you notice?

Addition Table

+	0	1	2	3	4	5	6	7	8	9
0	0	1	2	3	4	5	6	7	8	9
1	1	2	3	4	5	6	7	8	9	10
2	2	3	4	5	6	7	8	9	10	11
3	3	4	5	6	7	8	9	10	11	12
4	4	5	6	7	8	9	10	11	12	13
5	5	6	7	8	9	10	11	12	13	14
6	6	7	8	9	10	11	12	13	14	15
7	7	8	9	10	11	12	13	14	15	16
8	8	9	10	11	12	13	14	15	16	17
9	9	10	11	12	13	14	15	16	17	18

Check for Understanding

Find the sum. Name the fact strategy for addition.

1. 3
   +6

2. 9
   +9

3. 7
   +3

4. 9
   +0

5. 1
   +3

6. 6
   +6

7. 8
   +9

Practice

Find the sum. Name the fact strategy for addition.

8. $8 + 7 = $ ▨   **9.** $4 + 0 = $ ▨   **10.** $2 + 3 = $ ▨   **11.** $4 + 3 = $ ▨

12. $6 + 3 = $ ▨   **13.** $11 + 3 = $ ▨   **14.** $0 + 12 = $ ▨   **15.** $9 + 2 = $ ▨

Find the sum.

16. $6 + 2 = $ ▨   **17.** $4 + 4 = $ ▨   **18.** $1 + 4 = $ ▨   **19.** $7 + 7 = $ ▨

20. $6 + 6 = $ ▨   **21.** $5 + 3 = $ ▨   **22.** $8 + 0 = $ ▨   **23.** $5 + 6 = $ ▨

24. $\begin{array}{r} 7 \\ +6 \\ \hline \end{array}$ **25.** $\begin{array}{r} 3 \\ +5 \\ \hline \end{array}$ **26.** $\begin{array}{r} 4 \\ +9 \\ \hline \end{array}$ **27.** $\begin{array}{r} 6 \\ +0 \\ \hline \end{array}$ **28.** $\begin{array}{r} 8 \\ +9 \\ \hline \end{array}$ **29.** $\begin{array}{r} 2 \\ +3 \\ \hline \end{array}$

30. $\begin{array}{r} 4 \\ +6 \\ \hline \end{array}$ **31.** $\begin{array}{r} 1 \\ +8 \\ \hline \end{array}$ **32.** $\begin{array}{r} 8 \\ +6 \\ \hline \end{array}$ **33.** $\begin{array}{r} 5 \\ +5 \\ \hline \end{array}$ **34.** $\begin{array}{r} 9 \\ +4 \\ \hline \end{array}$ **35.** $\begin{array}{r} 0 \\ +6 \\ \hline \end{array}$

Mixed Applications

36. Claire waited 6 minutes for Mark at the exhibit of farm animals. Then she waited 5 more minutes for Cherie. How long did Claire wait for Mark and Cherie?

37. Robbie won 4 stuffed bears and 5 stuffed rabbits. How many stuffed animals did Robbie win?

38. Make Up a Problem Nadia won 6 prizes and Hans won 7 prizes. Write an addition problem about their prizes. Exchange with a partner and solve. Name the strategy you used.

39. Logical Reasoning Erica's 2 sisters each bought 2 jars of homemade jam at the fair. Then Erica and her brother each bought a jar. How many jars of jam were bought in all?

NUMBER SENSE

If ▨ $+$ ▨ $= 13$, what are the addends when their

40. difference is 1?   **41.** difference is 3?   **42.** difference is 5?

Explain how the *doubles plus one* strategy uses the *doubles* strategy.

WRAP UP...

ADDITION
Grouping Addends

Janell bought balloons at a booth on the midway. She bought 6 red balloons, 3 blue balloons, and 5 yellow balloons. How many balloons did she buy?

Add. $6 + 3 + 5 = $ ■

You can use the **Grouping Property of Addition** to find the sum. Do the work in parentheses first.

$(6 + 3) + 5 = $ ■   or $6 + (3 + 5) = $ ■

$\quad 9 \quad + 5 = 14 \qquad 6 + \quad 8 \quad = 14$

> **Grouping Property**   Addends may be grouped differently. The sum does not change.

So, Janell bought 14 balloons.

You can sometimes group addends to make a ten. This can help you add quickly.

Examples

A.
$$\begin{array}{r} 2 \\ 8 \\ + \ 4 \\ \hline 14 \end{array}$$
$2, 8 \rangle 10$

B.
$$\begin{array}{r} 7 \\ 6 \\ + \ 3 \\ \hline 16 \end{array}$$
$7, 6 \rangle 10$

C.
$$\begin{array}{r} 2 \\ 8 \\ 1 \\ + \ 9 \\ \hline 20 \end{array}$$
$2, 8 \rangle 10$
$1, 9 \rangle 10$

Check for Understanding

Use parentheses to show another way to group the addends. Find the sum.

1. $8 + (7 + 4) = $ ■   **2.** $(2 + 8) + 5 = $ ■   **3.** $7 + (6 + 3) = $ ■   **4.** $(5 + 5) + (4 + 6) = $ ■

Look for tens. Find the sum. Check by grouping the addends differently.

5.	**6.**	**7.**	**8.**	**9.**	**10.**	**11.**
8	7	6	5	4	7	9
2	4	4	1	8	3	2
6	5	3	3	9	4	9
+3	+5	+1	+7	+3	+6	+1

Practice

Use parentheses to show another way to group the addends. Find the sum.

12. $2 + (5 + 8) = \blacksquare$ 13. $(8 + 3) + 7 + 1 = \blacksquare$ 14. $9 + 4 + (8 + 6) = \blacksquare$

15. $5 + (7 + 1) = \blacksquare$ 16. $(7 + 7) + (7 + 7) = \blacksquare$ 17. $6 + 1 + (3 + 7) = \blacksquare$

18. $(6 + 8) + 5 = \blacksquare$ 19. $(8 + 3) + (1 + 4) = \blacksquare$ 20. $2 + (4 + 6) + 9 = \blacksquare$

Look for tens. Find the sum. Check by grouping the addends differently.

21. 9	22. 8	23. 7	24. 6	25. 5	26. 4	27. 3
2	4	6	8	3	5	7
+1	+2	+3	+4	+5	+6	+7

28. 1	29. 2	30. 7	31. 8	32. 2	33. 8	34. 5
9	8	4	6	8	9	4
+7	+4	+3	+7	+6	+9	+8

Write an addition word problem that uses each set of numbers. Then solve.

35. $5, 7, 6, 1$ 36. $3, 9, 1, 4$ 37. $9, 7, 3, 4$ 38. $10, 9, 13$

Mixed Applications

39. Ted read 7 books in September. He read 4 books in October and 9 in November. How many books did he read in the three months?

40. Phyllis has 9 pinwheels. Her classmates Lori and Jane each have 7 pinwheels. How many pinwheels do the girls have altogether?

41. Mrs. King baked 3 apple pies, 2 pecan pies, and 4 peach pies for the pie-baking contest. Her family ate 1 pie. How many pies were left to enter in the contest?

42. **Number Sense** Use the digits 4, 0, 8, and 5. Write the greatest four-digit number possible. Then write the least four-digit number possible.

How can grouping addends help you add quickly?

ESTIMATING SUMS

Alicia wants to ride the roller coaster, the Ferris wheel, and the Whip. She has $4.00. Look at the price list and estimate whether she has enough money for all three rides.

You can estimate in two different ways.

Cost of Rides	
Roller Coaster	$1.55
Ferris Wheel	$1.10
Whip	$1.25

Front-end Digits
Add the front-end digits only.

$1.55 → $1.00
$1.10 →   1.00
$1.25 → + 1.00
            $3.00

Rounding
Round to the nearest dollar.

$1.55 → $2.00
$1.10 →   1.00
$1.25 → + 1.00
            $4.00

> Remember: Write your answer in dollars and cents.

Since both estimates are $4.00 or less, Alicia should have enough money for all three rides.

Now, use a calculator to find the exact answer. **Press:**

1 . 5 5 + 1 . 1 0 + 1 . 2 5 =   3.9

$3.90

Talk About It

▶ Which estimate is closer to the exact answer?

▶ If you are rounding to estimate whether you have enough money to buy several items, should you round each price higher or lower than it actually is? Explain your choice.

▶ Why did the front-end example give an underestimate?

Check for Understanding

Estimate the sum by using both methods. Then use a calculator to find which estimate is closer to the exact answer.

1. $3.45 + 7.94	2. 203 +418	3. $5.37 + 1.08	4. 125 +888	5. $4.50 + 5.05	6. 994 +744

Practice

Estimate the sum.

7. $4.53
   +$3.07

8. $5.68
   +$2.37

9. $8.74
   +$8.17

10. $7.65
    +$8.17

11. $4.48
    +$3.11

12. 897
    +278

13. 573
    +486

14. 440
    +919

15. 913
    +598

16. 147
    +403

17. $8.23 + $0.94 = ■

18. 564 + 207 + 911 = ■

19. $6.83 + $8.76 = ■

Estimate the sum by using both methods. Then use a calculator to find which estimate is closer to the exact answer.

20. $6.11 + $2.81 = ■

21. 529 + 410 = ■

22. $5.03 + $2.68 = ■

Mixed Applications

23. The county fair cafe served 185 hot lunches and 442 sandwich plates. About how many meals were served?

24. Mr. Hill travels 22 miles each morning to the fair. In the afternoon he travels the same distance home. About how many miles does he travel in two days?

25. **Making Choices** At the snack booth, Joy wants popcorn for $1.75 and a drink for $0.95. The *Special* is popcorn and a drink for $2.50. Which is the better buy?

26. **Logical Reasoning** No one was riding the carousel. Then 18 riders got on. At the next stop, 4 more riders got on and 6 riders got off. How many riders were left?

MIXED REVIEW

Find the sum or difference.

1. 4
   +7

2. 11
   − 3

3. 9
   +8

4. 16
   − 8

5. 6
   +5

6. 13
   − 7

7. 7
   +5

8. 4 + 5 + 7 = ■

9. 2 + 8 + 9 = ■

10. (2 + 9) − (2 + 3) = ■

Will you ever get the same estimate by using both front-end digits and rounding? Why?

PROBLEM Solving

Lake County has a soccer competition at the county fair. This year the Blue team won more games than the Yellow team. The Green team won more games than the Red team. The Green team won 2 fewer games than the Yellow team. Which team won the most games?

Sometimes, *drawing a picture* can help you understand a problem and plan a solution.

▶ **UNDERSTAND**

What are you asked to find?

What information are you given?

▶ **PLAN**

How can you solve the problem?

You can use the facts in the problem to draw a picture.

▶ **SOLVE**

How can you draw a picture to find the solution?

Draw and label a line.

Show the Blue team ahead of the Yellow team.

Show the Green team ahead of the Red team but behind the Yellow team.

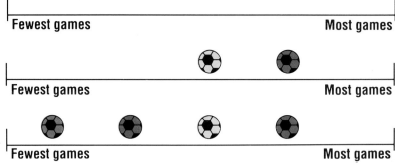

So, the Blue team won the most games.

▶ **LOOK BACK**

What other strategy can you use to solve the problem?

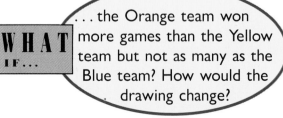

WHAT IF... ...the Orange team won more games than the Yellow team but not as many as the Blue team? How would the drawing change?

40

Apply

Solve by drawing a picture.

(1) Six players lined up in order from the tallest to the shortest for a team photo. Tim is taller than Jon. Don is shorter than Jon but taller than Roberto. Roberto is taller than Ann. Losa is the tallest on the team. In what order should the players line up?

(2) Cindy started from her home. She walked 1 block south to the cleaners and then 3 blocks east to the library. From there she went 5 blocks west to the market. How many blocks must she walk to get home if she takes the shortest route?

Mixed Applications ➤	**STRATEGIES**	• Draw a Picture • Use Estimation • Find a Pattern • Work Backward

Choose a strategy and solve.

(3) Keisha has some raisins for a snack. She gave 14 raisins to her brother. She gave 12 raisins to each of 3 friends. She has 18 raisins left. How many raisins did she start with?

(4) Before the game, four soccer players ran around the field. Sue finished after Jeremy. Ehida finished before Jeremy but after Gwen. Who finished first?

(5) Complete the pattern.

(6) Mr. Faye worked 39 hours one week, 41 hours the next, and 37 hours the week after that. Estimate the total number of hours he worked during the three weeks.

WRITER'S CORNER

(7) Draw a picture of your school playground. Show where the equipment is located. Also show baseball, soccer, and football fields. Then write a paragraph describing the playground. Tell the exact location of each object or field. Use words like *right, left,* and *next to.* Exchange papers with a partner. Draw a picture from your partner's description.

ADDING
Two-Digit Numbers

Molly earned 27 points in the pie-baking contest at the county fair. She earned 35 points in the cow-milking contest. How many points did Molly earn in both contests?

You can add to find how many points she earned.

Add. 27 + 35 = ▨

Step 1	Step 2	Step 3
Add the ones. 7 + 5 = 12 ones	Regroup. 12 ones = 1 ten 2 ones	Add the tens.
27 +35	1 27 +35 2	1 27 +35 62

Molly earned 62 points in all.

More Examples

A. 47
   +32
   ────
    79

B.   1
    35
   +59
   ────
    94

C.   83
   + 65
   ────
   148

D.   1
    58
   + 74
   ────
   132

Talk About It

▸ In which example was it *not* necessary to regroup?

▸ Which columns were regrouped in Examples B, C, and D?

▸ How do you know when you have to regroup?

Check for Understanding

Find the sum. Circle the columns in which you needed to regroup.

1. 26
   +17

2. 45
   +28

3. 74
   +39

4. 43
   +85

5. 91
   +49

6. 63
   +12

Practice

Find the sum. In Exercises 7–18, circle the columns in which you needed to regroup.

7. 52
    + 9

8. 15
    + 6

9. 14
    + 9

10. 63
    +12

11. 21
    +19

12. 54
    +18

13. 13
    +47

14. 18
    +17

15. 65
    +39

16. 24
    +16

17. 44
    +28

18. 38
    +69

19. 72 + 19 =

20. 29 + 32 = ■

21. 66 + 28 =

22. 48 + 65 = ■

23. 69 + 37 = ■

24. 98 + 89 = ■

Mixed Applications

25. The Oak Street School band traveled 38 miles to the fair. On the return trip, they went a different way and traveled 29 miles. How many miles did they travel?

26. On opening day of the county fair, 68 children were given pony rides. The next day 73 children were given pony rides. How many pony rides were given on the first two days of the fair?

27. **Mental Math** Celia buys lemonade for $0.85. She gives the clerk $1.00. There are no dimes or pennies in the cash register. How can the clerk give Celia her change?

28. **Logical Reasoning** In a magic square, the sum of the numbers in any row, column, or diagonal is the same. Find the addends.

12	7	14
13	■	9
8	■	10

MIXED REVIEW

Write the value of the blue digit.

1. 4,395,028

2. 3,492

3. 63,992,004

4. 428,783

Write the number that is 100,000 more.

5. 345,829

6. 1,893,400

7. 23,400,000

8. 200,438

Why do you have to regroup twice to add 43 + 57 but only once for 90 + 70?

WRAP
UP...

The county fair sponsored hayrides to raise money for the Farmers' Association. On Friday 154 tickets were sold. On Saturday 167 tickets were sold. How many hayride tickets were sold on both days?

You can add to find how many hayride tickets were sold on both days.

Add. 154 + 167 = ■

Step 1

Add the ones. 4 + 7 = 11 ones. Regroup.
11 ones = 1 ten 1 one

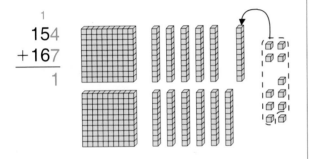

$$\begin{array}{r} \overset{1}{1}54 \\ +167 \\ \hline 1 \end{array}$$

Step 2

Add the tens. 1 + 5 + 6 = 12 tens. Regroup.
12 tens = 1 hundred 2 tens
Add the hundreds.

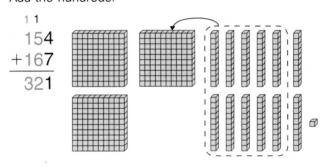

$$\begin{array}{r} \overset{1\;1}{1}54 \\ +167 \\ \hline 321 \end{array}$$

There were 321 hayride tickets sold.

Talk About It

▶ Why is it important to line up the digits in each column?

▶ Why is it helpful to write the regrouped digit above the column?

▶ When you add $2.31 and $0.67, what do you do differently?

Check for Understanding

Find the sum. Circle the columns in which you needed to regroup.

1. 152	2. 279	3. 523	4. 976	5. $2.78	6. $7.65
+175	+808	+748	+815	+ 9.89	+ 9.17

Practice

Find the sum. In Exercises 7–18, circle the columns in which you needed to regroup.

7. 169
    + 26

8. 213
    + 94

9. 462
    +318

10. 670
    +297

11. 337
    +145

12. $6.55
    + 9.57

13. 318
    +198

14. 422
    +278

15. 197
    +413

16. 276
    +935

17. 479
    +460

18. $3.89
    + 7.35

19. $3.99 + $2.11 = ■

20. $2.55 + $5.46 = ■

21. $4.83 + $1.18 = ■

22. $8.55 + $2.95 = ■

23. $4.69 + $5.45 = ■

24. $6.33 + $7.49 = ■

Mixed Applications

25. On Thursday 293 people registered for the grand prize. On Friday 428 people registered. How many people registered in all?

26. Dave bought 3 balloons for $2.25, popcorn for $0.75, and a wallet for $7.98. How much did Dave spend for all three items?

27. **Mental Math** Several door prizes were awarded at the fair. Marcia won $100, Joanne won $50, and Chuck won $25. How much money was awarded at the fair?

28. **Number Sense** I am a number that is 19 ones and 9 tens greater than 389. What number am I?

LOGICAL REASONING

Find the missing digits.

29.   6 7 ■
    +   9 7 6
    ─────────────
      1 , ■ 5 4

30.   7 5 ■
    +   8 ■ 9
    ─────────────
      1 , 6 3 3

31.   9 5 ■
    +   ■ 4 8
    ─────────────
      1 , 0 ■ 5

32.   6 4 2
    +   ■ 7 8
    ─────────────
      ■ , 5 2 0

What is the greatest possible sum when you add two 3-digit numbers?

WRAP
UP...

REVIEW AND MAINTENANCE

1. Barbara has a puzzle for her classmates. When she says 6, the answer is 21. When she says 9, the answer is 24. When she says 12, the answer is 27. What is the answer when Barbara says 20?

2. Four students are growing plants for a science project. Miranda's plant is shorter than Tina's. Karl's plant is taller than Tina's and shorter than Anthony's. Whose plant is the shortest?

Use the table to solve Exercises 3–4.

3. How many more calories are in the sandwich than are in the soup?

4. Find the total number of calories for a lunch of all five items.

Counting Calories	
Food	Calories
Sandwich	285
Salad	68
Soup	156
Apple	75
Lemonade	130

> I read problems several times until I understand them.

Estimate the sum.

5. $\begin{array}{r} 67 \\ +42 \\ \hline \end{array}$

6. $\begin{array}{r} 93 \\ +56 \\ \hline \end{array}$

7. $\begin{array}{r} 100 \\ +\ 57 \\ \hline \end{array}$

Find the sum.

8. $\begin{array}{r} 17 \\ +\ 8 \\ \hline \end{array}$

9. $\begin{array}{r} 96 \\ +38 \\ \hline \end{array}$

10. $\begin{array}{r} 894 \\ +699 \\ \hline \end{array}$

11. $\begin{array}{r} 903 \\ +885 \\ \hline \end{array}$

12. $\begin{array}{r} 287 \\ +\ 96 \\ \hline \end{array}$

13. $3 + 7 = \blacksquare$

14. $(2 + 9) + 8 = \blacksquare$

15. $13 + 8 = \blacksquare$

Compare. Write <, >, or = for ●.

16. 416 ● 461

17. 3,724 ● 986

18. 12,364 ● 12,364

Express each number in two other ways.

19. three hundred fourteen

20. 26,948

21. 926

22. 5,000 + 300 + 50 + 4

23. one million, four hundred thousand

24. 278,211

25. one thousand, four hundred sixty-three

26. 783,213

27. three million, four hundred thirty-eight thousand, six hundred fifty-nine

Spotlight ON

PROBLEM SOLVING

Analyze Relationships

Tables allow you to analyze and compare data to solve problems.

Ms. Cole is the owner of Cole's Chicken Farm. Her chickens always win blue ribbons at the state fair. She wanted to know how the number of chickens she raised each year had changed during the past six years. She made a table to show the number of chickens raised on the farm each year.

Number of Chickens						
Year	1987	1988	1989	1990	1991	1992
Number	51	68	93	124	139	148

Talk About It

Make a plan to solve the problems. Discuss your plan with a partner, and then solve the problems.

- How many more chickens were raised on the farm in 1990 than in 1987?

- In which of the years displayed in the table were the most chickens raised? the fewest?

- Were there more or fewer chickens raised each year on the farm?

- In which year did the number of chickens raised increase the most?

- Make up a problem using the table. Exchange problems and solve.

Apply

Stacey, Heather, and Brett each raise rabbits. They kept a record of how long they worked with their rabbits over the weekend.

Rabbit Work			
	Brett	Heather	Stacey
Time	2 hr 15 min	1 hr 30 min	45 min

Analyze the data and answer the questions:

1. Who spent the most time with the rabbits? the least?

2. How much more time did Brett spend with the rabbits than Stacey spent? than Heather?

ADDING
Three or More Addends

Todd, Mark, and Susan played games on the midway to try to win a stuffed animal. Todd scored 277 points. Mark scored 185 points, and Susan scored 456 points. How many points did they score in all?

Add. 277 + 185 + 456 = ▧

Step 1 Add the ones. Regroup. 18 ones = 1 ten 8 ones	**Step 2** Add the tens. Regroup. 21 tens = 2 hundreds 1 ten	**Step 3** Add the hundreds.
$\overset{1}{2}77$ 185 +456 ——— 8 7 + 5 + 6 = 18 ones	$\overset{2\,1}{2}77$ 185 +456 ——— 18 1 + 7 + 8 + 5 = 21 tens	$\overset{2\,1}{2}77$ 185 +456 ——— 918 2 + 2 + 1 + 4 = 9 hundreds

Todd, Mark, and Susan scored 918 points in all.

Another Method

You can also use a calculator to add several numbers. Estimate the sum to decide whether your answer is reasonable.

$$
\begin{array}{rcl}
324 & \rightarrow & 300 \\
98 & \rightarrow & 100 \\
+987 & \rightarrow & 1{,}000 \\
\hline
 & & 1{,}400
\end{array}
$$

Then, use a calculator to find the exact sum.

Press: ⟨3⟩ ⟨2⟩ ⟨4⟩ ⟨+⟩ ⟨9⟩ ⟨8⟩ ⟨+⟩ ⟨9⟩ ⟨8⟩ ⟨7⟩ ⟨=⟩ | 1409. |

Since 1,409 is close to 1,400, the answer is reasonable.

Check for Understanding

Find the sum.

1.	2.	3.	4.	5.	6.
246 43 +435	$726.35 51.62 + 141.28	$ 0.76 92.90 + 1.90	7,471 195 + 86	3,790 1,013 + 862	846 107 +4,082

Practice

Estimate the sum. Then use a calculator to find the exact answer.

	7.	8.	9.	10.	11.
	65	93	123	281	119
	38	33	936	924	375
	+18	+86	+318	+ 98	+267

Find the sum.

	12.	13.	14.	15.	16.
	3,892	1,204	3,007	8,112	3,980
	115	629	2,195	3,068	8,435
	+ 341	+2,031	+ 14	+ 432	+2,104

	17.	18.	19.	20.	21.
	23	94	$5.39	$12.98	$ 9.98
	9	234	2.11	3.50	7.85
	18	483	4.05	1.59	0.99
	+76	+ 15	+ 9.87	+ 40.15	+ 25.50

22. $251 + 49 + 810 =$ ■   **23.** $3,027 + 185 + 94 =$ ■   **24.** $34 + 29 + 91 + 77 =$ ■

Mixed Applications

25. Emilio spent $1.75 for a taco, $1.25 for potato salad, and $1.59 for lemonade. How much money did he spend in all?

26. Mrs. Bertz sold 378 burritos on Thursday, 419 on Friday, and 572 on Saturday. How many burritos did she sell in three days?

Use the table to complete Exercises 27–29.

27. Find the total number of points earned by each person.

28. Who earned the most points? the fewest points?

29. Write the players' names in order, from the one with the most points to the one with the fewest points.

Fair Competition			
Event	Points Earned		
	Bill	Jill	Will
Pie-eating contest	30	20	10
Balloon throw	45	35	55
Horseshoes	40	45	35
Ringtoss	10	28	19

Why is it important to estimate the answer first when you use a calculator?

WRAP UP...

ESTIMATING DIFFERENCES

The county fair sponsored the twenty-third annual Corn Festival. On Friday night 389 ears of corn were cooked. On Saturday night 513 ears were cooked. About how many more ears of corn were cooked on Saturday than on Friday?

Estimate the difference by rounding.

Round each number to its greatest place value. Then subtract.

$$513 \rightarrow 500$$
$$-389 \rightarrow -400$$
$$100$$

So, about 100 more ears of corn were cooked on Saturday night than on Friday night.

More Examples

A.
$$\$6.02 \rightarrow \$6.00$$
$$- 3.77 \rightarrow - 4.00$$
$$ \$2.00$$

B.
$$756 \rightarrow 800$$
$$-445 \rightarrow -400$$
$$ 400$$

C.
$$6,098 \rightarrow 6,000$$
$$- 2,785 \rightarrow - 3,000$$
$$ 3,000$$

Talk About It

▶ If you estimate Example C by using front-end digits, how will your answer be different than your rounded answer?

▶ In Example B will the exact answer be greater than or less than 500? How do you know?

Check for Understanding

Estimate the difference by rounding.

1.
$$219$$
$$- 98$$

2.
$$8,278$$
$$-1,877$$

3.
$$\$8.90$$
$$- 5.67$$

4.
$$355$$
$$-223$$

5.
$$\$5,398$$
$$- 1,745$$

6.
$$\$10.89$$
$$- 7.33$$

7.
$$558$$
$$-217$$

8.
$$8,488$$
$$-5,821$$

9.
$$\$9.05$$
$$- 5.79$$

10.
$$412$$
$$-111$$

Practice

Estimate the difference by rounding.

11. 816 -289	**12.** 298 $-\ 91$	**13.** 467 -318	**14.** 503 -196	**15.** 981 -438

16. 4,119 $-2,863$	**17.** 9,792 $-6,369$	**18.** \$3.19 $-\ 1.77$	**19.** \$8.88 $-\ 3.75$	**20.** \$18.94 $-\ 9.16$

21. 27,895 − 8,174 = ■   **22.** 11,205 − 4,029 = ■   **23.** \$999.99 − \$329.65 = ■

Mixed Applications

24. Lisa had \$19.05 when she arrived at the Corn Festival. She spent \$7.99 on food and souvenirs. About how much money did she have left?

25. Lex has \$4.65 to buy lunch. He spends \$3.36 on a sandwich and juice. He needs \$1.09 to buy a dessert. Does he have enough money?

Use the table for Exercises 26–27.

26. What was the total attendance at the Corn Festival in 1990?

27. What was the total attendance at the festival in 1990 and 1991?

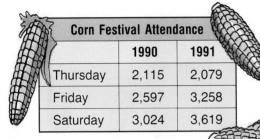

Corn Festival Attendance		
	1990	**1991**
Thursday	2,115	2,079
Friday	2,597	3,258
Saturday	3,024	3,619

NUMBER SENSE • ESTIMATION

Choose the best estimate. Check your estimate by using a calculator.

28. 489,211 $-\ 16,176$
- **a.** greater than 500,000
- **b.** greater than 400,000
- **c.** less than 400,000
- **d.** less than 300,000

29. \$8,244.84 $-\ 6,879.48$
- **a.** greater than \$3,000
- **b.** greater than \$2,000
- **c.** less than \$2,000
- **d.** less than \$1,000

How does estimating help you use mental math to find sums and differences?

WRAP UP...

SUBTRACTING
Two-Digit Numbers

Tony and his 4-H Club raised 43 sheep for their club project. This year they entered 19 sheep in competition at the county fair. How many of their sheep were not entered in the fair this year?

To find how many sheep were not entered this year, subtract. $43 - 19 = $ ■

Step 1	Step 2	Step 3
Decide whether to regroup. $9 > 3$ So, regroup 4 tens 3 ones as 3 tens 13 ones.	Subtract the ones.	Subtract the tens.

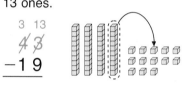
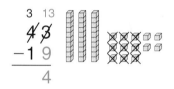

So, 24 sheep were not entered in the fair this year.

Talk About It

▶ In which columns did you need to regroup?

▶ How do you know when you need to regroup?

▶ How would you have estimated the difference?

▶ How can you check your subtraction?

Check for Understanding

Find the difference. Circle the columns in which you needed to regroup.

1. 67 −34	2. 85 −12	3. 86 −47	4. 91 −48	5. 44 −27	6. 61 −34
7. 32 −14	8. 97 −36	9. 60 −45	10. 52 −22	11. 71 −19	12. 83 −15

Practice

Find the difference. Circle the columns in which you needed to regroup.

13. $\begin{array}{r} 99 \\ -23 \\ \hline \end{array}$

14. $\begin{array}{r} 36 \\ -12 \\ \hline \end{array}$

15. $\begin{array}{r} 43 \\ -34 \\ \hline \end{array}$

16. $\begin{array}{r} 67 \\ -27 \\ \hline \end{array}$

17. $\begin{array}{r} 80 \\ -49 \\ \hline \end{array}$

18. $\begin{array}{r} 82 \\ -76 \\ \hline \end{array}$

Find the difference.

19. $\begin{array}{r} 78 \\ -19 \\ \hline \end{array}$

20. $\begin{array}{r} 56 \\ -27 \\ \hline \end{array}$

21. $\begin{array}{r} 22 \\ -13 \\ \hline \end{array}$

22. $\begin{array}{r} 75 \\ -57 \\ \hline \end{array}$

23. $\begin{array}{r} 41 \\ -29 \\ \hline \end{array}$

24. $\begin{array}{r} 37 \\ -18 \\ \hline \end{array}$

25. $\begin{array}{r} 58 \\ -28 \\ \hline \end{array}$

26. $\begin{array}{r} 83 \\ -37 \\ \hline \end{array}$

27. $\begin{array}{r} 74 \\ -45 \\ \hline \end{array}$

28. $\begin{array}{r} 68 \\ -19 \\ \hline \end{array}$

29. $\begin{array}{r} 92 \\ -73 \\ \hline \end{array}$

30. $\begin{array}{r} 85 \\ -37 \\ \hline \end{array}$

31. $56 - 28 = $ ■

32. $31 - 18 = $ ■

33. $47 - 18 = $ ■

34. $95 - 76 = $ ■

35. $80 - 35 = $ ■

36. $42 - 26 = $ ■

37. $66 - 29 = $ ■

38. $77 - 53 = $ ■

Mixed Applications

39. Last year the Hilldale 4-H Club won 17 blue ribbons in the livestock exhibits. This year the club won 25 blue ribbons. How many more blue ribbons did the club win this year than last year?

40. On Thursday morning there were 72 cakes at the bake sale. At the end of the day, 14 cakes had not been sold. How many cakes were sold during the day?

41. **Number Sense**   Joyce used a calculator to find $50.00 - $46.80. The calculator displayed 3.2. How much money is this?

VISUAL THINKING

42. Choose the correct number sentence. Write **a, b,** or **c.**

    a. $20 + 26 = 46$
    b. $46 - 24 = 22$
    c. $46 - 26 = 20$

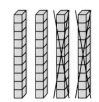

Explain why subtraction and addition are called opposite operations.

WRAP UP...

More Practice, Lesson 2.9, page H40

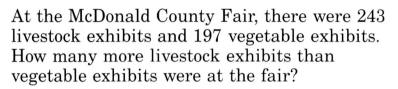

SUBTRACTING
Three-Digit Numbers

At the McDonald County Fair, there were 243 livestock exhibits and 197 vegetable exhibits. How many more livestock exhibits than vegetable exhibits were at the fair?

Subtract. 243 − 197 =

Step 1	**Step 2**	**Step 3**
Decide whether to regroup. 7 > 3 So, regroup 4 tens 3 ones as 3 tens 13 ones. Then subtract the ones.	9 > 3 So, regroup 2 hundreds 3 tens as 1 hundred 13 tens. Then subtract the tens.	Subtract the hundreds.
$\begin{array}{r} 3\ 13 \\ 2\ \cancel{4}\ \cancel{3} \\ -1\ 9\ 7 \\ \hline 6 \end{array}$	$\begin{array}{r} 13 \\ 1\ \cancel{3}\ 13 \\ \cancel{2}\ \cancel{4}\ \cancel{3} \\ -1\ 9\ 7 \\ \hline 4\ 6 \end{array}$	$\begin{array}{r} 13 \\ 1\ \cancel{3}\ 13 \\ \cancel{2}\ \cancel{4}\ \cancel{3} \\ -1\ 9\ 7 \\ \hline 4\ 6 \end{array}$

There were 46 more livestock exhibits than vegetable exhibits.

Subtract amounts of money the same way you subtract whole numbers.

Subtract. $4.87 − $2.69 =

$$\begin{array}{r} \$4.87 \\ -\ 2.69 \end{array} \rightarrow \begin{array}{r} {}^{7\ 17} \\ 4\ \cancel{8}\cancel{7} \\ -\ 2\ 69 \\ \hline \$2.18 \end{array}$$

> Remember: Place the dollar sign and decimal point in the answer.

Check for Understanding

Find the difference.

1. 613	2. 842	3. 684	4. 926	5. $4.25	6. $5.16
−243	−191	−295	−568	− 1.06	− 0.49

Practice

Find the difference.

7. 465
    −124

8. 688
    −317

9. 975
    −461

10. 738
    −527

11. 437
    −218

12. $2.13
    − 0.98

13. $4.35
    − 1.46

14. $5.82
    − 3.94

15. $7.32
    − 5.45

16. $8.48
    − 4.59

17. 822
    −419

18. 492
    −189

19. 785
    −289

20. $8.49 − = $6.58

21. 315 − 149 =

22. Write a word problem in which you must subtract to solve. Write the solution.

Mixed Applications

23. At the vegetable exhibit, there were 112 tomatoes entered in competition. The air conditioning broke down, and 65 tomatoes spoiled. How many tomatoes were left to be judged?

24. **Number Sense** On Thursday 378 people attended the grandstand show. On Saturday 523 people attended the show. Estimate how many more people attended the show on Saturday.

NUMBER SENSE

25. Write three subtraction problems whose answers are between 200 and 300. Use the calculator to help you.

Example Press: 5 2 8 − 2 7 2 = | 256.

26. Write three addition problems whose answers are between 3,000 and 5,000. Use the calculator to help you.

To subtract 400 − 34, how many times do you regroup? Explain.

PROBLEM *Solving*

The table shows the items that Mrs. Patterson is interested in buying at the arts-and-crafts show. She has $200 to spend. She can buy more than one of each item. What combinations of items can she buy?

Arts-and-Crafts Show	
Item	Price
Clay Vase	$48
Pair of earrings	$27
Wooden box	$35

You can *make a table* to analyze data.

▶ **UNDERSTAND**

What are you asked to find?

What facts are given?

▶ **PLAN**

What strategy can you use to solve this problem?

Make a table that shows the cost of different numbers of each item.

▶ **SOLVE**

How can you solve this problem?

Use the table to find all the combinations of things Mrs. Patterson can buy for $200. This is one possible combination.

3 clay vases $144
2 pairs of earrings   54
TOTAL $198

What is another combination of items she can buy at the show?

▶ **LOOK BACK**

What other strategy can you use to solve the problem?

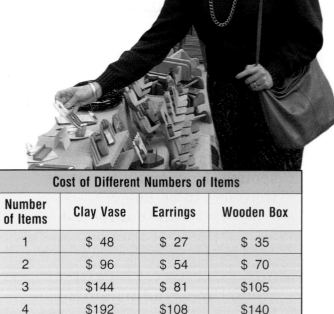

Cost of Different Numbers of Items			
Number of Items	Clay Vase	Earrings	Wooden Box
1	$ 48	$ 27	$ 35
2	$ 96	$ 54	$ 70
3	$144	$ 81	$105
4	$192	$108	$140
5		$135	$175
6		$162	
7		$189	

WHAT IF... ... Mrs. Patterson had $100 to spend? What is one combination of items she could buy at the show?

Apply

The table shows some of the arts-and-crafts exhibits at the fair.
Use the table to answer Exercises 1–3.

Arts-and-Crafts Exhibits		
Exhibit	**Hours**	**Location**
Basket Weaving	Mon., 2 P.M.–4 P.M.	Booth 45
Ceramics	Sat., 1 P.M.–6 P.M.	Booth 116
Flower Arranging	Sat., 1 P.M.–6 P.M.	Booth 73
Glassblowing	Daily 3 P.M.–6 P.M.	Booth 44
Jewelry Artistry	Daily 2 P.M.–4 P.M.	Booth 69
Photography	Thurs., All day	Booth 90
Quilt Making	Daily 2 P.M.–4 P.M.	Booth 2
Woodworking	Wed., 3 P.M.–6 P.M.	Booth 100

(1) What three things can you learn from reading the table?

(2) Make a table to show when and where you will visit four exhibits.

(3) If you are going to the fair on Saturday, how many exhibits can you visit?

Mixed Applications ▶ **STRATEGIES**
- Draw a Picture • Write a Number Sentence
- Find a Pattern • Make a Table

Choose a strategy and solve.

(4) Mrs. Ross owns a party-supply store. One morning she sold 50 balloons and 32 prizes. That afternoon she sold 46 favors and 25 decorations. Of which item did she sell the most?

(5) On Friday Mrs. Chang took 323 orders for her hand-painted T-shirts. On Saturday she took 199 orders. How many orders did she take in all?

(6) Six friends ran in a race. Jose finished the race behind Tammy. Gabby finished last. Sam finished ahead of Nick and right behind Tammy. Linda finished right after Jose. Who won the race?

(7) Delta County holds its county fair every 2 years. The first fair was in 1898. The twenty-sixth fair was in 1948. In what year will the Delta County Fair be held for the one hundredth time?

WRITER'S CORNER

(8) Make a table to show a menu for a restaurant at the fair. Include food items, prices, and the hours the restaurant is open. Write three questions that can be answered by using the table.

(9) Workers at the fishing booth attach rings, jacks, whistles, and balls to the fishhooks as prizes. Write a problem that could be solved by using a table. Then make the table.

EXPLORING

Subtraction and Money

I can use money to model subtraction across zeros.

Knowing how to subtract across zeros will help you figure the correct change when you buy something.

Nicole spent $2.75 on a souvenir at the fair. She had $4.00. How much money will she have left?

WORK TOGETHER

Building Understanding

Use dollars, dimes, and pennies to model the problem. Then show the difference on a place-value mat.

Start.   Regroup and subtract.

Talk About It

▶ How many dollar bills did you start with?

▶ How can you regroup 1 dollar bill and 1 dime so that you can subtract?

▶ How can you show the difference using money?

▶ How many dollar bills, dimes, and pennies are left after you take away $2.75?

▶ Write a number sentence to show what you did.

Use play money to find each difference.
Show the difference on a place-value mat.

a. $3.10 − $1.90 = ■   **b.** $2.00 − $0.35 = ■   **c.** $10.00 − $6.51 = ■

Making the Connection

Write each problem in expanded notation. Then regroup and subtract.
Use play money to help you.

Example

Add. → Start.

$5.25
− 3.85

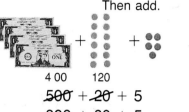

Expanded
notation

500 + 20 + 5
−300 + 80 + 5

Regroup and subtract.
Then add.

```
      4 00   120
     5̶0̶0̶ + 2̶0̶ + 5
    −300 + 80 + 5
    ─────────────────
     100 + 40 + 0 = 140 = $1.40
```

1. $2.00
 − 1.69

2. $6.11
 − 4.71

3. $9.03
 − 7.29

4. $3.37
 − 2.99

5. $90.00
 − 71.64

Checking Understanding

Write each in expanded notation. Then find the difference.

6. $5.13
 − 2.64

7. $8.90
 − 0.45

8. 3,000
 − 647

9. $51.06
 − 12.35

10. 1,411
 − 882

Find the difference.

11. $239.45
 − 128.67

12. $11.45
 − 9.56

13. $14.95
 − 9.99

14. $365.96
 − 197.44

15. $112.43
 − 87.54

16. Varick spent $24.45 on a wallet
and a T-shirt at the fair. The
wallet cost $9.95. How much did
the T-shirt cost?

17. **Logical Reasoning** Dustin spent
$2.07 on a hamburger at the fair.
The amount he paid included
$0.12 tax. How much did the
hamburger cost before tax?

NUMBER SENSE • ESTIMATION

18. Draw triangles as shown. Write the digits 3, 4, 5, 6,
7, and 8 in them to make the least difference, the
greatest difference, and the difference closest to 100.

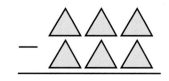

More Practice, Lesson 2.12, page H41

ADD AND SUBTRACT
with Greater Numbers

Weekends are the busiest days at the fair. On Saturday 3,878 people attended the fair. On Sunday 5,395 people attended. How many more people attended on Sunday?

$$\begin{array}{r} {\scriptstyle 4\quad 13\ 8\ 15} \\ \cancel{5},\cancel{3}\cancel{9}\cancel{5} \\ -3,878 \\ \hline 1,517 \end{array}$$

Subtract. 5,395 − 3,878 = ■

On Sunday 1,517 more people attended the fair.

- How many people attended the fair on Saturday and Sunday?

You can use a calculator to add or subtract large numbers. Add 3,878 and 5,395.

First, estimate. 4,000 + 5,000 = 9,000
Then, use a calculator to find the exact sum.

Press:

So, 9,273 people attended the fair on Saturday and Sunday.

- How can you use your estimate to decide whether your answer is reasonable?

Check for Understanding

First, estimate the sum or difference. Then, use a calculator or pencil and paper to find the exact answer.

1. 3,769
   +1,043

2. 5,925
   −2,378

3. 8,306
   +4,455

4. 88,407
   −27,672

5. 35,973
   +78,119

6. 23,447
   +84,260

7. 56,831
   −27,906

8. $34,698.27
   − 11,683.12

9. $4,769.26
   + 8,694.45

10. $8,497.65
   − 7,259.98

11. 34,904 − 10,556 = ■   12. 85,901 + 24,558 = ■   13. 71,223 − 19,959 = ■

Practice

First, estimate the sum or difference.
Then find the exact answer.

14. 6,841
   +7,982

15. 8,109
   −4,361

16. 7,448
   −1,737

17. 6,901
   −2,405

18. 4,187
   +4,219

19. 43,625
   −24,219

20. 58,105
   +92,736

21. 77,129
   −48,506

22. 98,406
   +21,597

23. 26,976
   + 7,377

24. $7,740 - 6,946 = $ ▩

25. $26,840 + 67,204 = $ ▩

26. $99,995 - 48,786 = $ ▩

Mixed Applications

27. On Tuesday 4,576 pizzas were sold at the fair. On Wednesday 4,656 pizzas were sold. How many pizzas were sold in all?

28. Mr. Sykes had 1,500 leather belts in his crafts booth. He sold 264 of them. How many belts does he have left?

Use the table for Exercises 29–30.

29. On which day did Sara have the most visitors? the fewest visitors?

30. Write the days in order from the one with the most visitors to the one with the fewest visitors.

Visitors to Sara's Booth	
Tuesday	1,463
Wednesday	1,334
Thursday	2,063
Friday	3,245
Saturday	3,791

NUMBER SENSE

Without adding, use what you know about place value to enter each sum on a calculator. Do not use the ⊞ key. Write the number that appears on the calculator display.

31. $4,000,000 + 200,000 + 70,000 + 5,000 + 300 + 60 + 8$

32. $80,000,000 + 50,000 + 1,000 + 20 + 6$

33. How many keys do you have to press to enter 90,608,005 in expanded notation?

Add a five-digit number and a four-digit number. What is the greatest sum possible?

Vocabulary Check

Choose a word or words from the box to complete each sentence.

addends
doubles
front-end
group
Grouping
hundred
regroup
round
ten

Fact strategies can help you remember addition facts.

1. The _?_ Property states that when the addends are grouped differently, the sum does not change. *(page 36)*

2. Numbers that are added are called _?_. *(page 34)*

3. When you change 67 to 70, you _?_ the number to the nearest _?_. *(page 38)*

4. When you add only the first digits to estimate, you are using _?_ estimation. *(page 38)*

5. A strategy used to help you remember addition facts such as 6 + 6 = 12 and 9 + 9 = 18 is called _?_. *(page 34)*

6. When you add 64 and 28, you must _?_ the ones. *(page 42)*

7. When you add 7 + 3 + 9, you _?_ two _?_ first. *(page 36)*

8. When you change 350 to 400, you _?_ the number to the nearest _?_. *(page 38)*

Concept Check

Find the sum. Name the fact strategy for addition. *(page 34)*

| 9. $\begin{array}{r}5\\+6\\\hline\end{array}$ | 10. $\begin{array}{r}8\\+8\\\hline\end{array}$ | 11. $\begin{array}{r}9\\+0\\\hline\end{array}$ | 12. $\begin{array}{r}11\\+\ 2\\\hline\end{array}$ | 13. $\begin{array}{r}8\\+9\\\hline\end{array}$ | 14. $\begin{array}{r}13\\+\ 2\\\hline\end{array}$ | 15. $\begin{array}{r}0\\+6\\\hline\end{array}$ |

Complete the number sentence. Write + or − for ●. *(pages 42, 52)*

16. 16 ● 25 = 41   17. 13 ● 26 = 39   18. 13 ● 9 = 4   19. 47 ● 18 = 29

20. 39 ● 15 = 24   21. 12 ● 28 = 40   22. 26 ● 13 = 13   23. 39 ● 27 = 12

Find the sum or difference. Circle the problems where you needed to regroup. *(pages 42, 44, 52, 54)*

| 24. $\begin{array}{r}13\\+22\\\hline\end{array}$ | 25. $\begin{array}{r}57\\-35\\\hline\end{array}$ | 26. $\begin{array}{r}87\\+39\\\hline\end{array}$ | 27. $\begin{array}{r}178\\-152\\\hline\end{array}$ | 28. $\begin{array}{r}507\\-298\\\hline\end{array}$ | 29. $\begin{array}{r}967\\+858\\\hline\end{array}$ |

Skill Check

Find the sum or difference. *(pages 36–60)*

30. 294
       +475

31. 6
        8
        3
       +8

32. 802
       −158

33. 18
        29
         6
       +17

34. 83
        49
        16
       +30

35. 254
       − 85

36. 3,582
       −1,803

37. 24,801
       −17,394

38. 491
       +359

39. 4,982
       +2,078

40. 377
       +2,042

Estimate the sum or difference. *(pages 38, 50)*

41. 431
       +289

42. 705
       −180

43. 3,019
       −1,735

44. 5,682
       +1,087

45. 2,902
       −1,358

46. 4,395
       +2,748

47. 4,021
       −1,175

48. 9,138
       +8,180

49. 489
       +122

50. 978
       −224

Problem-Solving Check *(pages 40, 56)*

51. June, Pam, Ed, and Greg ordered pizzas from Gino's Pizzeria. June ordered a small pepperoni pizza. Pam ordered a large sausage pizza. Ed ordered a medium mushroom pizza, and Greg ordered a small cheese pizza. Gino needs a table to record the orders. Make the table.

52. Sadie and three of her classmates live in a four-story apartment building. Sadie lives in the apartment below Jack. Bob lives in an apartment below Sadie. Gail lives in the apartment above Bob. Each person lives on a different floor. Who lives on the highest floor?

53. From Della's house it is 3 miles to school and 2 miles to the library. It is 4 miles from school to the library. If Della rode her bicycle from home to school, back home, and then to the library, how far did she ride on her bicycle?

54. Lance wants to make a table to show his earnings for mowing lawns. In June he earned $96. In July he earned $168. In August he earned $144, and in September he earned $121. Make the table.

CHAPTER TEST

Find the sum. Name the fact strategy for addition.

Counting On	Zero	Doubles	Doubles Plus One

1. $3 + 4 = $ ▨

2. $7 + 7 = $ ▨

3. $2 + 0 = $ ▨

4. $8 + 3 = $ ▨

Find the sum. Look for a ten.

5.
$$\begin{array}{r} 7 \\ 3 \\ +4 \\ \hline \end{array}$$

6.
$$\begin{array}{r} 2 \\ 3 \\ +8 \\ \hline \end{array}$$

7.
$$\begin{array}{r} 5 \\ 4 \\ +6 \\ \hline \end{array}$$

8.
$$\begin{array}{r} 3 \\ 5 \\ +5 \\ \hline \end{array}$$

9.
$$\begin{array}{r} 2 \\ 8 \\ +7 \\ \hline \end{array}$$

Always read the directions carefully.

Estimate the sum or difference.

10.
$$\begin{array}{r} 294 \\ -128 \\ \hline \end{array}$$

11.
$$\begin{array}{r} 412 \\ +461 \\ \hline \end{array}$$

12.
$$\begin{array}{r} 918 \\ +333 \\ \hline \end{array}$$

Find the sum or difference.

13. $(9 + 3) + 5 = $ ▨

14. $(2 + 3) + (8 + 10) = $ ▨

15. $\$0.19 + \$0.35 = $ ▨

16.
$$\begin{array}{r} \$4.00 \\ -\ 2.63 \\ \hline \end{array}$$

17.
$$\begin{array}{r} 158 \\ +884 \\ \hline \end{array}$$

18.
$$\begin{array}{r} \$23.90 \\ +\ 99.99 \\ \hline \end{array}$$

19.
$$\begin{array}{r} 401 \\ -346 \\ \hline \end{array}$$

20.
$$\begin{array}{r} 3,920 \\ 1,082 \\ +6,957 \\ \hline \end{array}$$

21.
$$\begin{array}{r} 14,060 \\ 953 \\ +\ 2,154 \\ \hline \end{array}$$

Solve.

22. Four players lined up in order from the tallest to the shortest. Earl was taller than Rob. Dan was shorter than Rob but taller than Korosh. In what order did the players line up?

23. Randall has a total of 401 football, baseball, and basketball cards. He has 70 football cards, 296 baseball cards, and 35 basketball cards. Make a table to show this information.

24. Louisa got on the elevator on the fourth floor. She went down 2 floors and then up 6 floors where she got off the elevator. On which floor did Louisa get off the elevator?

25. Bettina counted the coins in her collection. She has 3 coins from England, 4 from Germany, 6 from Canada, 25 from Mexico, 8 from Japan, and 2 from France. Make a table to show this information.

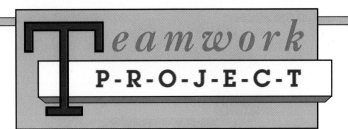
A Day at the Fair

Visitors to the fair spend money on amusements and food. With your teammates, act out a day at the fair.

Decide

Talk about how you can use play money and index cards to make models for buying and spending at the fair.

Do

Work with your teammates. Cut out and label $0.50 tickets for rides and $0.75 tickets for food.

Buy 5 tickets in all. Pay a banker with $5.00 in play money. Count the change you have left.

Draw pictures to show how the money was spent and how much was left.

Share

Show your tickets, money, and pictures to the other teams. Describe how buying and spending at the fair compare with buying and spending for other entertainment and food.

Talk About It

- How can you use your models to plan your family's entertainment and food expenses at a fair?

- Why is it important to know how to estimate when planning an activity such as going to the fair?

- In what everyday activities do you add and subtract money?

Palindromes

A *palindrome* is a word or a number that reads the same from left to right and from right to left.

These are word palindromes.   **DAD • TOOT • MADAM, I'M ADAM.**

These are number palindromes.   **5,885 • 49,094 • 1,234,321**

A number palindrome can be made by using addition. Follow these steps.

1. Write a number.   349
2. Reverse the digits.   +943
3. Add.   1,292
4. Reverse these digits.   +2,921
5. Add.   4,213
6. Continue until you get   +3,124
   a **palindrome.**   →   7,337

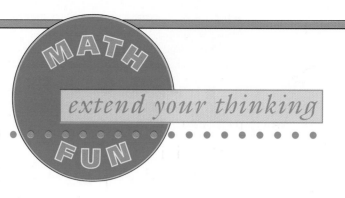

Use these numbers to make palindromes.

1. 29
2. 685
3. 1,864
4. 3,259

Choose other three-digit and four-digit numbers. Use them to make palindromes. If you choose a number that requires many steps, you may want to use a calculator.

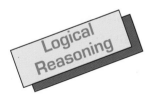
Logical Reasoning

Challenge

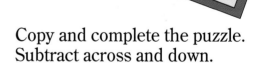
Number Puzzle

1. Julie bought a cassette tape for $6. She sold it to Matt for $7. She bought it back from Matt for $8 and sold it to Mandy for $9. How much money did Julie make or lose in buying and selling the tape?

2. Phil bought a used bike for $40. He sold it to John for $45. John sold it back to Phil for $50. Now Beth is buying the bike from Phil. For how much should Phil sell the bike to "break even"?

Copy and complete the puzzle. Subtract across and down.

9,489	−	■	=	2,771
−		−		−
2,997	−	1,308	=	■
=		=		=
■	−	5,410	=	1,082

Write the letter of the correct answer.

1. What is the value of the digit 7 in 876?

A. 7 ones; 7   B. 7 tens; 70
C. 8 tens; 80   D. 7 hundreds; 700

2. Order from least to greatest.
5,493   4,935   4,539

A. 4,539; 4,935; 5,493
B. 4,539; 5,493; 4,935
C. 5,493; 4,935; 4,539
D. not here

3. Which digit is in the millions place in 12,345,678?

A. 1   B. 3
C. 6   D. not here

4. Which circle is shaded?

A. first   B. fourth
C. sixth   D. seventh

5. Round each number to the nearest hundred. Estimate the sum.
488 + 215 = ▨

A. 600   B. 680
C. 700   D. 800

6. What is another name for 5,700?

A. 570 ones   B. 57 hundreds
C. 5 thousands   D. not here

7. 8 + 4 + 2 + 6 = ▨

A. 18   B. 20
C. 21   D. 22

8.
$$83 \\ -15$$

A. 62   B. 68
C. 72   D. 78

9.
$$608 \\ -\ 49$$

A. 559   B. 569
C. 641   D. 669

10.
$$42{,}825 \\ +\ 6{,}765$$

A. 48,580   B. 48,590
C. 49,590   D. not here

11. Tom has 12 markers that are either blue or red. He has 2 more blue markers than red markers. How many markers of each color does he have?

A. 2 blue and 4 red
B. 4 blue and 2 red
C. 6 blue and 6 red
D. 7 blue and 5 red

12. Four students have birthdays in October. Melissa's birthday comes before Robyn's. Heather's birthday comes between Robyn's and Melissa's. Jason's birthday comes after Robyn's. Whose birthday comes first?

A. Melissa's   B. Heather's
C. Robyn's   D. Jason's

3

MULTIPLICATION AND DIVISION
USING FACTS

Did you know ...

... that the skateboarding record for a "high air" jump is $9\frac{1}{2}$ feet? In competition or just for fun, skateboarding has become a popular sport.

Talk About It

Hoa and 7 of her friends are building a skateboard ramp so they can learn to do jumps. The materials for the ramp cost $72. How can Hoa find the amount of each person's share?

EXPLORING
Multiplication and Division

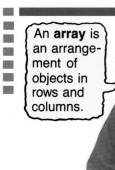

An **array** is an arrangement of objects in rows and columns.

Use counters to explore how multiplication and division are related.

WORK TOGETHER

Building Understanding

Arrange counters in an array to show 4 rows with 2 counters in each row.

Column 1   Column 2
Row 1
Row 2
Row 3
Row 4

Arrange 8 counters into 4 equal groups.

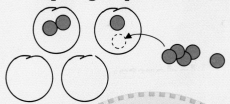

Talk About It

▶ How can you count to find the total number of counters?

▶ How can you add to find the total number of counters?

▶ How are addition and multiplication alike?

▶ How can you multiply to find the total number of counters? Write a number sentence to show this.

▶ How many different arrays can you make with 8 counters?

Talk About It

▶ How can you count to find the number of counters in each group?

▶ How can you subtract to find the number of groups?

▶ How are subtraction and division alike?

▶ How can you divide to find the number of groups? Write a number sentence to show this.

▶ How many different ways can 8 counters be separated into equal groups?

• How are multiplication and division related?

• What are the four number sentences you can write using 4, 2, and 8?

Making the Connection

A set of related multiplication and division sentences using the same numbers is called a **fact family**. You can use 6 counters to model the fact family for 2, 3, and 6.

$$2 \times 3 = 6 \qquad 3 \times 2 = 6 \qquad 6 \div 2 = 3 \qquad 6 \div 3 = 2$$

Use counters to model the fact family for each set of numbers.

1. $3, 6, 18$
2. $2, 7, 14$
3. $3, 4, 12$
4. $5, 3, 15$

Checking Understanding

Draw an array for each and find the product.

5. 2 rows
   4 columns

6. 5 rows
   6 columns

7. 8 rows
   2 columns

8. 4 rows
   5 columns

Write a multiplication number sentence for each picture.

9.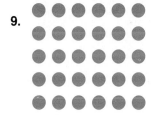

10.

11.

Write a division number sentence for each picture.

12.

13.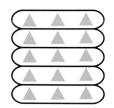

14.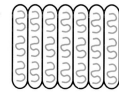

Write the three other facts for each fact family.

15. $6 \times 5 = 30$
16. $28 \div 7 = 4$
17. $3 \times 9 = 27$
18. $8 \times 4 = 32$

MULTIPLICATION
2 and 3 as Factors

Donna and 4 friends rode their bicycles to the park. The word *bicycle* has the prefix *bi*, which means 2. The prefix *bi* refers to the number of wheels. How many wheels do the 5 bicycles have?

Think about ways to find the total number of wheels.

5 bicycles
2 wheels on *each* bicycle
So, you can multiply 5 × 2.

$$5 \times 2 = 10$$

number of   number of   total number
bicycles   wheels on   of wheels
            each bicycle

$$\begin{array}{r} 2 \leftarrow \text{factor} \\ \times\ 5 \leftarrow \text{factor} \\ \hline 10 \leftarrow \text{product} \end{array}$$

The 5 bicycles have 10 wheels.

The first tricycle was developed about 1870. The prefix *tri*, which means 3, refers to the number of wheels. How many wheels do 4 tricycles have?

4 tricycles
3 wheels on *each* tricycle
So, you can multiply 4 × 3.

$$4 \times 3 = \blacksquare \qquad \begin{array}{r} 3 \\ \times 4 \\ \hline \end{array}$$

You can use a number line to find the product.

1 tricycle   2 tricycles   3 tricycles   4 tricycles

```
 0      3        6        9       12
      wheels   wheels   wheels   wheels
```

The 4 tricycles have 12 wheels.

Check for Understanding

Write a multiplication sentence for each picture.

1.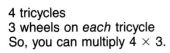

2.

Copy and complete each multiplication table.

3.

X	0	1	2	3	4	5	6	7	8	9
2	■	■	■	■	■	■	■	■	■	■

4.

X	0	1	2	3	4	5	6	7	8	9
3	■	■	■	■	■	■	■	■	■	■

5. What pattern do you see in each table?

Practice

Write a multiplication sentence for each picture.

6.

7.

8.

Draw an array to solve.

9. $3 \times 6 = \blacksquare$ **10.** $2 \times 6 = \blacksquare$ **11.** $5 \times 2 = \blacksquare$ **12.** $3 \times 8 = \blacksquare$

Find the product.

13. $\begin{array}{r} 8 \\ \times 3 \\ \hline \end{array}$	**14.** $\begin{array}{r} 3 \\ \times 4 \\ \hline \end{array}$	**15.** $\begin{array}{r} 2 \\ \times 6 \\ \hline \end{array}$	**16.** $\begin{array}{r} 4 \\ \times 3 \\ \hline \end{array}$	**17.** $\begin{array}{r} 8 \\ \times 2 \\ \hline \end{array}$	**18.** $\begin{array}{r} 6 \\ \times 3 \\ \hline \end{array}$	**19.** $\begin{array}{r} 5 \\ \times 2 \\ \hline \end{array}$
20. $\begin{array}{r} 2 \\ \times 2 \\ \hline \end{array}$	**21.** $\begin{array}{r} 3 \\ \times 2 \\ \hline \end{array}$	**22.** $\begin{array}{r} 2 \\ \times 4 \\ \hline \end{array}$	**23.** $\begin{array}{r} 3 \\ \times 7 \\ \hline \end{array}$	**24.** $\begin{array}{r} 2 \\ \times 9 \\ \hline \end{array}$	**25.** $\begin{array}{r} 3 \\ \times 3 \\ \hline \end{array}$	**26.** $\begin{array}{r} 2 \\ \times 7 \\ \hline \end{array}$

27. $2 \times 6 = \blacksquare$ **28.** $3 \times 5 = \blacksquare$ **29.** $3 \times 9 = \blacksquare$ **30.** $7 \times 3 = \blacksquare$ **31.** $4 \times 3 = \blacksquare$

Mixed Applications

32. The 2 sides of Meadow Lane are lined with maple trees. There are 5 trees on each side. How many trees are on Meadow Lane?

33. Each of the 4 corner houses on Meadow Lane has 2 sidewalks. How many sidewalks do the corner houses have in all?

34. There are bicycles and tricycles in the bicycle rack. There are 12 wheels in all. How many bicycles are there?

35. **Make Up a Problem** Suppose there are 8 bicycles in a bicycle rack. Write a problem about the bicycles that uses addition, subtraction, or multiplication. Exchange with a partner and solve.

How is counting by threes related to multiplying by three?

MULTIPLICATION
4 and 5 as Factors

Each school has 4 runners on the relay team. Last Friday 6 relay teams ran in the state tournament. How many runners were in the race?

6 teams
4 runners on *each* team
So, multiply to find how many in all.

$6 \times 4 = \blacksquare$

$$\begin{array}{r} 4 \\ \times 6 \\ \hline \end{array}$$

Think:
You can count by fours.
4, 8, 12, 16, 20, 24

You can add.
$4 + 4 + 4 + 4 + 4 + 4 = 24$

There were 24 runners in the race.

There are 7 teams competing in the girls' track meet. Each team has 5 girls. How many girls are competing in the meet?

7 teams
5 girls on each team
So, you can multiply 7×5.

$7 \times 5 = \blacksquare$

$$\begin{array}{r} 5 \\ \times 7 \\ \hline \end{array}$$

Think:
You can count by fives.
5, 10, 15, $\blacksquare$, $\blacksquare$, $\blacksquare$, $\blacksquare$

Talk About It

▶ How can you add to find the total number of girls competing in the meet? So, how many girls are competing?

▶ Why can you use both addition and multiplication to solve?

Check for Understanding

Write a multiplication sentence for each picture.

1.

2.

3.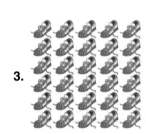

Copy and complete each multiplication table.

4.

X	0	1	2	3	4	5	6	7	8	9
4	■	■	■	■	■	■	■	■	■	■

5.

X	0	1	2	3	4	5	6	7	8	9
5	■	■	■	■	■	■	■	■	■	■

6. What pattern do you see in each table?

Practice

Write a multiplication sentence for each picture.

7.

8. X X X X X X X
   X X X X X X X
   X X X X X X X
   X X X X X X X
   X X X X X X X

9.

Draw an array for each multiplication sentence.

10. $4 \times 7 = 28$

11. $5 \times 6 = 30$

12. $9 \times 5 = 45$

13. $3 \times 4 = 12$

Find the product.

14. $\begin{array}{r} 6 \\ \times 4 \\ \hline \end{array}$

15. $\begin{array}{r} 9 \\ \times 5 \\ \hline \end{array}$

16. $\begin{array}{r} 3 \\ \times 4 \\ \hline \end{array}$

17. $\begin{array}{r} 2 \\ \times 5 \\ \hline \end{array}$

18. $\begin{array}{r} 2 \\ \times 4 \\ \hline \end{array}$

19. $\begin{array}{r} 4 \\ \times 5 \\ \hline \end{array}$

20. $\begin{array}{r} 3 \\ \times 5 \\ \hline \end{array}$

21. $\begin{array}{r} 7 \\ \times 4 \\ \hline \end{array}$

22. $\begin{array}{r} 5 \\ \times 5 \\ \hline \end{array}$

23. $\begin{array}{r} 4 \\ \times 8 \\ \hline \end{array}$

24. $\begin{array}{r} 5 \\ \times 6 \\ \hline \end{array}$

25. $\begin{array}{r} 4 \\ \times 4 \\ \hline \end{array}$

26. $\begin{array}{r} 5 \\ \times 7 \\ \hline \end{array}$

27. $\begin{array}{r} 4 \\ \times 9 \\ \hline \end{array}$

28. $\begin{array}{r} 5 \\ \times 9 \\ \hline \end{array}$

29. $\begin{array}{r} 5 \\ \times 8 \\ \hline \end{array}$

Mixed Applications

Write a number sentence. Solve.

30. This year 2,078 students participated in the Fun Run. Last year only 1,859 students ran in this event. How many more students participated this year?

31. Janet ran the hurdles race 4 times. There are 8 hurdles in the race. She knocked over only 1 hurdle in all 4 races. How many hurdles did she clear?

SOCIAL STUDIES CONNECTION

32. The Olympic Games are scheduled to take place every 4 years. In each Olympiad year, Summer Games and Winter Games are held. How many Summer and Winter games should take place beginning with the 1960 Olympic Games through the games played in 1992?

What facts in the fours and fives have the same products?

WRAP
UP...

Maska and Nina keep their baseball cards in an album. Maska puts 3 rows of 2 cards each on his page. Nina puts 2 rows of 3 cards each on her page. Who has more cards?

Order Property
Two numbers can be multiplied in any order. The product is always the same.

So, Maska and Nina have the same number of cards.

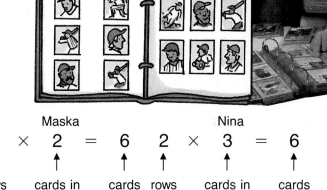

Maska

$$3 \times 2 = 6$$

↑ rows
↑ cards in each row
↑ cards in all

Nina

$$2 \times 3 = 6$$

↑ rows
↑ cards in each row
↑ cards in all

More Properties

Property of One
When one of two factors is 1, the product is the other number.

$$3 \times 1 = 3$$

$$\begin{array}{r} 1 \\ \times 3 \\ \hline 3 \end{array}$$

Zero Property
When one of the factors is zero, the product is zero.

$$2 \times 0 = 0$$

$$\begin{array}{r} 0 \\ \times 2 \\ \hline 0 \end{array}$$

Grouping Property
When the grouping of factors is changed, the product remains the same.

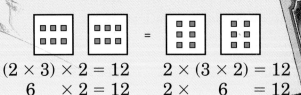

$$(2 \times 3) \times 2 = 12 \qquad 2 \times (3 \times 2) = 12$$
$$6 \times 2 = 12 \qquad 2 \times 6 = 12$$

Check for Understanding

1. Which property shows that $5 \times 7 = 7 \times 5$?

2. Is the product of $(3 \times 4) \times 2$ the same as the product of $3 \times (4 \times 2)$? Why or why not?

3. How can you use the multiplication properties to solve this problem? $(2 \times 5) \times 7 \times (8 \times 3) \times 5 \times 0 = $ ▪

Practice

Draw a picture to show each property. Use the models on page 76 to help you.

4. $7 \times 1 = 7$

5. $3 \times 4 = 4 \times 3$

6. $4 \times (3 \times 2) = (4 \times 3) \times 2$

Write **a, b, c,** or **d** to tell which property is shown.

a. Order Property   **b.** Property of One   **c.** Zero Property   **d.** Grouping Property

7. $9 \times 0 = 0$

8. $1 \times 6 = 6$

9. $6 \times (3 \times 2) = (6 \times 3) \times 2$

10. $2 \times 1 = 1 \times 2$

11. $3 \times 2 = 2 \times 3$

12. $(1 \times 4) \times 2 = 1 \times (4 \times 2)$

Use the multiplication properties to solve.

13. $4 \times 9 = 36$
$9 \times 4 = \blacksquare$

14. $3 \times 7 = 21$
$7 \times 3 = \blacksquare$

15. $3 \times 4 = 12$
$4 \times 3 = \blacksquare$

16. $8 \times 3 = 24$
$3 \times 8 = \blacksquare$

17. $\begin{array}{r} 6 \\ \times 0 \\ \hline \end{array}$

18. $\begin{array}{r} 0 \\ \times 4 \\ \hline \end{array}$

19. $\begin{array}{r} 5 \\ \times 1 \\ \hline \end{array}$

20. $\begin{array}{r} 8 \\ \times 0 \\ \hline \end{array}$

21. $\begin{array}{r} 1 \\ \times 7 \\ \hline \end{array}$

22. $\begin{array}{r} 10 \\ \times 1 \\ \hline \end{array}$

23. $\begin{array}{r} 0 \\ \times 9 \\ \hline \end{array}$

24. $6 \times (3 \times 2) = \blacksquare$

25. $(3 \times 3) \times 3 = \blacksquare$

26. $1 \times (537 \times 0) = \blacksquare$

Mixed Applications

27. Willie has 25 pages in his new scrapbook. He has not put his pictures in the book yet. Write a number sentence to show how many pictures Willie has in his scrapbook.

28. Make Up a Problem Write a word problem for each number sentence.

$1 \times 6 = 6$ $9 \times 0 = 0$

NUMBER SENSE

Use mental math and the properties to find the missing number.

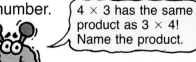
4 × 3 has the same product as 3 × 4! Name the product.

29. $4{,}739 \times 0 = \blacksquare$

30. $1{,}280{,}456 \times 1 = \blacksquare$

31. $4{,}002 \times \blacksquare = 4{,}002$

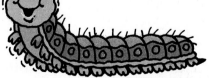

Which multiplication properties can you use to explain $1 \times 0 = 0$?

W R A P
U P . . .

PROBLEM Solving

Too Much or Too Little Information

Mr. Clark is taking his class on a field trip to the Baseball Museum. They will need 7 vans to make the trip. Mr. Clark says each van will hold the same number of students. How many students are going to the museum?

Sometimes, a problem has too much information or too little information.

▶ **UNDERSTAND**

What are you asked to find?

What facts are given?

▶ **PLAN**

Is there too much information or too little information to solve the problem?

There is too little information.

$$7 \qquad \times \qquad \blacksquare \qquad = \qquad \blacksquare$$

number of vans | number of students in each van | total number of students

What fact is missing?

Mr. Clark does not say how many students will ride in each van.

▶ **SOLVE**

Mr. Clark says 5 students will ride in each van. You now have enough information to find the solution.

How do you solve this problem?

Multiply. $7 \times 5 = \blacksquare$

There are 35 students going to the Baseball Museum.

▶ **LOOK BACK**

How can you check your answer?

WHAT IF... ... it had been stated in the problem that 8 students would ride in each van? Which piece of information would not be necessary?

Apply

If the problem has too little information, write what fact is missing. If the problem has too much information, tell which fact is not needed. Solve the problem if you can.

(1) Marco watches 5 baseball games every week. He has been watching games for 2 years. How many games does he watch in 5 weeks?

(2) Patricia buys 6 baseball cards for $2.43, 1 program for $5.00, and a pin for $1.29. How much change does she receive?

Mixed Applications	**STRATEGIES**	• Find a Pattern • Make a Table • Make a Table to Analyze Data • Draw a Picture

Choose a strategy and solve.

(3) Brett took a taxi ride to the airport. The cost was $2 for the first 5 miles. For each mile after that, the cost was $1. The distance to the airport was 11 miles. How much did Brett's taxi ride cost?

(4) Four students from Oak Street School live on the same street. Jojo's house is farther from school than Tiffany's house. Lon's house is between Jojo's and Tiffany's. Tiffany's house is farther from school than Ty's. Whose house is farthest from the school?

Use the table for Exercises 5–6.

(5) What was the total points scored?

(6) How many players scored more than 5 points? fewer than 5 points?

(7) Mr. Ashley's tennis shop had a sale on Friday and Saturday. On Friday he sold 32 cans of balls, 21 rackets, 65 shirts, and 35 pairs of shoes. On Saturday he sold a total of 67 cans of balls, 54 rackets, 102 shirts, and 60 pairs of shoes. Make a table to compare the numbers of items sold during the two days of the sale.

Player	Points Scored
Joe	///
Paul	//
Sam	𝗧𝗛𝗟 ///
Rod	/
Art	𝗧𝗛𝗟 /
Bert	////

MULTIPLICATION
6 and 7 as Factors

In many communities, Americans of Scottish descent celebrate their heritage with games, food, and music at the Scottish Highland Games. There are 6 teams competing at the games. Each team has 5 members. How many team members are at the games? Use counters.

6 teams
5 members on *each* team
So, multiply 6 × 5 = ■.

$$\begin{array}{r} 5 \\ \times 6 \\ \hline \end{array}$$

Think: Since you know that 5 × 6 = 30, you know that 6 × 5 = 30.

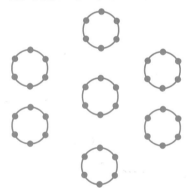

You can use the Order Property to find the product.

There are 30 team members at the Scottish Highland Games.

Mary MacBride and her dance class are taking part in the Highland Games. They form 7 circles with 6 dancers in each circle. How many dancers are taking part?

7 circles
6 dancers in *each* circle
So, multiply 7 × 6.
7 × 6 = ■

$$\begin{array}{r} 6 \\ \times 7 \\ \hline \end{array}$$

Think: Since you know that 6 × 7 = 42, you know that 7 × 6 = 42.

There are 42 dancers.

Check for Understanding

Write a number sentence for each picture.

1.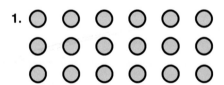

2.

Copy and complete the multiplication table.

3.

X	0	1	2	3	4	5	6	7	8	9
6	■	■	■	■	■	■	■	■	■	■

4. What pattern do you notice in the products of this multiplication table?

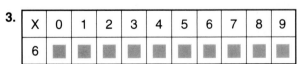
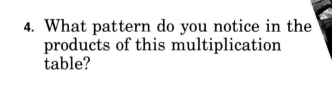

Practice

Write a number sentence for each picture.

5.

6. ☆ ☆ ☆ ☆ ☆ ☆ ☆
   ☆ ☆ ☆ ☆ ☆ ☆

7. ⬤⬤⬤⬤⬤⬤⬤
   ⬤⬤⬤⬤⬤⬤⬤
   ⬤⬤⬤⬤⬤⬤⬤
   ⬤⬤⬤⬤⬤⬤⬤
   ⬤⬤⬤⬤⬤⬤⬤

Complete.

8. Since $6 \times 5 = 30$,
   $5 \times 6 = $ ■.

9. Since $7 \times 6 = 42$,
   $6 \times 7 = $ ■.

10. Since $6 \times 4 = 24$,
    $4 \times 6 = $ ■.

Find the product.

11. $\begin{array}{r} 6 \\ \times 7 \\ \hline \end{array}$

12. $\begin{array}{r} 7 \\ \times 8 \\ \hline \end{array}$

13. $\begin{array}{r} 9 \\ \times 6 \\ \hline \end{array}$

14. $\begin{array}{r} 6 \\ \times 8 \\ \hline \end{array}$

15. $\begin{array}{r} 7 \\ \times 7 \\ \hline \end{array}$

16. $\begin{array}{r} 6 \\ \times 5 \\ \hline \end{array}$

17. $\begin{array}{r} 7 \\ \times 9 \\ \hline \end{array}$

18. $\begin{array}{r} 2 \\ \times 6 \\ \hline \end{array}$

19. $\begin{array}{r} 4 \\ \times 7 \\ \hline \end{array}$

20. $\begin{array}{r} 6 \\ \times 4 \\ \hline \end{array}$

21. $\begin{array}{r} 6 \\ \times 3 \\ \hline \end{array}$

22. $\begin{array}{r} 3 \\ \times 7 \\ \hline \end{array}$

23. $\begin{array}{r} 5 \\ \times 7 \\ \hline \end{array}$

24. $\begin{array}{r} 8 \\ \times 7 \\ \hline \end{array}$

Mixed Applications

25. A costume maker needs ribbons for 6 costumes. He will put 7 ribbons on each costume. How many ribbons will he need?

26. Trish bought 4 cassette tapes for her dance team and 3 cassette tapes for herself. Each tape cost $9. How much did Trish spend?

27. The product is 63. The sum of the factors is 16. Their difference is 2. What are the factors?

28. **Number Sense** The product of 2 numbers is 16. Name all the possible factor pairs for 16.

MIXED REVIEW

Write the fact family for each set of numbers.

1. $4, 5, 20$

2. $2, 6, 12$

3. $3, 4, 12$

4. $21, 3, 7$

5. How are addition and multiplication alike?

6. How are multiplication and division alike?

How can you show that 6×7 and 7×6 have the same product?

WRAP UP...

MULTIPLICATION
8 and 9 as Factors

Mario brought the pickles to the football team's annual picnic. If each pickle jar contains 8 pickles, how many pickles are in 3 jars?

3 jars
8 pickles in *each* jar
So, multiply 3 × 8.

$$\begin{array}{r} 8 \\ \times 3 \\ \hline \end{array}$$

There are 24 pickles in 3 jars.

Patterns of numbers can help you check that the product is correct. Find each product.

1 × 9 = 9	4 × 9 = ■	7 × 9 = ■
2 × 9 = ■	5 × 9 = ■	8 × 9 = ■
3 × 9 = ■	6 × 9 = ■	9 × 9 = ■

Add the digits in each product.   **Example**

$$2 \times 9 = 18$$
$$(1 + 8 = 9)$$

Talk About It

▶ What do you notice about the sums of the digits in the products?

▶ What pattern do you see in the products?

▶ What other patterns do you see?

Check for Understanding

Write a number sentence for each picture.

1.

2.

Copy and complete each multiplication table.

3.
X	0	1	2	3	4	5	6	7	8	9
8	■	■	■	■	■	■	■	■	■	■

4.
X	0	1	2	3	4	5	6	7	8	9
9	■	■	■	■	■	■	■	■	■	■

Practice

Write a number sentence for each picture.

5.

6.

7.

Draw an array to solve.

8. $8 \times 8 = \blacksquare$
9. $9 \times 8 = \blacksquare$
10. $7 \times 8 = \blacksquare$
11. $9 \times 9 = \blacksquare$

Find the product.

12.	13.	14.	15.	16.	17.	18.
8	9	8	9	8	9	8
$\times 3$	$\times 5$	$\times 7$	$\times 9$	$\times 2$	$\times 4$	$\times 6$

19.	20.	21.	22.	23.	24.	25.
9	8	9	4	9	8	3
$\times 7$	$\times 8$	$\times 6$	$\times 8$	$\times 8$	$\times 5$	$\times 9$

Mixed Applications

26. Each picnic table seats 8 people. There are 9 picnic tables. How many people can be seated at the tables?

27. The football team has 8 cheerleaders. Every other cheerleader wears a blue skirt, starting with the first one in line. The rest wear orange skirts. What color skirt is the eighth cheerleader wearing?

28. **Mental Math** Which is the better buy, 8 forks for $0.40 or 9 forks for $0.36?

29. **Logical Reasoning** At the picnic there are 9 packages of hot-dog buns, with 8 buns in a package. There are 8 packages of hot dogs, with 8 hot dogs in a package. How many buns will be left over?

How can you find the product of 9×9 if you know that $8 \times 9 = 72$?

More Practice, Lesson 3.7, page H43

83

MULTIPLICATION
Practicing Facts

Use the multiplication table to solve the riddle.

Copy the blanks and complete the riddle.

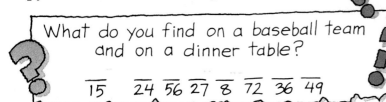

What do you find on a baseball team and on a dinner table?

$\overline{15}$ $\overline{24}$ $\overline{56}$ $\overline{27}$ $\overline{8}$ $\overline{72}$ $\overline{36}$ $\overline{49}$

Find the products. Fill in each blank of the riddle with the letter that matches each product.

Find 5

×	0	1	2	3	4	5	6	7	8	9
0	0	0	0	0	0	0	0	0	0	0
1	0	1	2	3	4	5	6	7	8	9
2	0	2	4	6	8	10	12	14	16	18
3	0	3	6	9	12	15	18	21	24	27
4	0	4	8	12	16	20	24	28	32	36
5	0	5	10	15	20	25	30	35	40	45
6	0	6	12	18	24	30	36	42	48	54
7	0	7	14	21	28	35	42	49	56	63
8	0	8	16	24	32	40	48	56	64	72
9	0	9	18	27	36	45	54	63	72	81

Find 3 →

Find the point at which the row and column meet.

Example $3 \times 5 = \blacksquare$ →

$$\begin{array}{c} 5 \\ \times 3 \\ \hline \end{array}$$ A = $\blacksquare$
$$\begin{array}{c} 4 \\ \times 3 \\ \hline \end{array}$$ B = $\blacksquare$
$$\begin{array}{c} 2 \\ \times 4 \\ \hline \end{array}$$ C = $\blacksquare$
$$\begin{array}{c} 8 \\ \times 5 \\ \hline \end{array}$$ D = $\blacksquare$
$$\begin{array}{c} 9 \\ \times 4 \\ \hline \end{array}$$ E = $\blacksquare$
$$\begin{array}{c} 5 \\ \times 4 \\ \hline \end{array}$$ F = $\blacksquare$
$$\begin{array}{c} 3 \\ \times 6 \\ \hline \end{array}$$ G = $\blacksquare$
$$\begin{array}{c} 9 \\ \times 8 \\ \hline \end{array}$$ H = $\blacksquare$
$$\begin{array}{c} 8 \\ \times 7 \\ \hline \end{array}$$ I = $\blacksquare$

$$\begin{array}{c} 7 \\ \times 4 \\ \hline \end{array}$$ J = $\blacksquare$
$$\begin{array}{c} 6 \\ \times 1 \\ \hline \end{array}$$ K = $\blacksquare$
$$\begin{array}{c} 3 \\ \times 7 \\ \hline \end{array}$$ L = $\blacksquare$
$$\begin{array}{c} 7 \\ \times 2 \\ \hline \end{array}$$ M = $\blacksquare$
$$\begin{array}{c} 8 \\ \times 4 \\ \hline \end{array}$$ N = $\blacksquare$
$$\begin{array}{c} 1 \\ \times 9 \\ \hline \end{array}$$ O = $\blacksquare$
$$\begin{array}{c} 8 \\ \times 3 \\ \hline \end{array}$$ P = $\blacksquare$
$$\begin{array}{c} 8 \\ \times 8 \\ \hline \end{array}$$ Q = $\blacksquare$
$$\begin{array}{c} 7 \\ \times 7 \\ \hline \end{array}$$ R = $\blacksquare$

$$\begin{array}{c} 4 \\ \times 4 \\ \hline \end{array}$$ S = $\blacksquare$
$$\begin{array}{c} 9 \\ \times 3 \\ \hline \end{array}$$ T = $\blacksquare$
$$\begin{array}{c} 7 \\ \times 3 \\ \hline \end{array}$$ U = $\blacksquare$
$$\begin{array}{c} 5 \\ \times 6 \\ \hline \end{array}$$ V = $\blacksquare$
$$\begin{array}{c} 9 \\ \times 5 \\ \hline \end{array}$$ W = $\blacksquare$
$$\begin{array}{c} 6 \\ \times 9 \\ \hline \end{array}$$ X = $\blacksquare$
$$\begin{array}{c} 8 \\ \times 6 \\ \hline \end{array}$$ Y = $\blacksquare$
$$\begin{array}{c} 9 \\ \times 9 \\ \hline \end{array}$$ Z = $\blacksquare$

▶ What pattern do you see in the multiplication table that is made by the products of the doubles facts?

▶ What pattern is formed when you find the products using the Zero Property?

Check for Understanding

Use the multiplication table to find the product.

1. $\begin{array}{c} 8 \\ \times 2 \\ \hline \end{array}$
2. $\begin{array}{c} 4 \\ \times 5 \\ \hline \end{array}$
3. $\begin{array}{c} 7 \\ \times 3 \\ \hline \end{array}$
4. $\begin{array}{c} 6 \\ \times 4 \\ \hline \end{array}$
5. $\begin{array}{c} 9 \\ \times 8 \\ \hline \end{array}$
6. $\begin{array}{c} 1 \\ \times 6 \\ \hline \end{array}$

7. $6 \times 2 = \blacksquare$
8. $3 \times 4 = \blacksquare$
9. $8 \times 2 = \blacksquare$
10. $5 \times 5 = \blacksquare$

Connection, pages 446–447

Practice

Name the two factors and the product for each array.

11.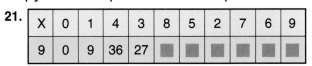

12.

13.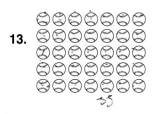

Find the product.

14. 2
    ×1

15. 4
    ×2

16. 6
    ×3

17. 8
    ×4

18. 3
    ×5

19. 5
    ×6

20. 7
    ×7

Copy and complete each multiplication table.

21.

X	0	1	4	3	8	5	2	7	6	9
9	0	9	36	27	■	■	■	■	■	■

22.

X	0	1	2	7	4	9	6	5	8	3
6	0	6	12	42	■	■	■	■	■	■

23.

X	0	1	2	9	4	5	3	7	8	6
3	0	3	6	■	12	■	■	21	■	■

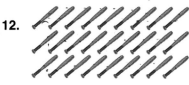

Mixed Applications

24. The school marching band will form an array of 7 rows of 8 students each. Draw an array to find how many students are in the school marching band.

25. The cheerleaders each collect 8 donations for new uniforms, except the squad captain, who collects 10. There are 9 cheerleaders. How many donations do the cheerleaders collect altogether?

NUMBER SENSE

When you multiply two equal factors, the product is called a *square number*. The array of a square number makes a square.

Use graph paper to make and color a model of each square number.

Example

   4 ← factor
 × 4 ← factor
  16 ← square number

26. 49   27. 100   28. 36   29. 64   30. 25

How can you tell that there are 100 multiplication facts on a multiplication table?

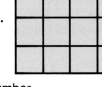

W R A P
U P...

Use the inverse operation to check your answer.

1. Ellis memorized 46 songs. He memorized 18 more songs than Hannah. How many songs did Hannah memorize?

2. On one day the pet store sold $423.95 worth of pet supplies, and 3 kittens for $22.50 each. What was the store's sales total for the day?

3. The Bay County Farmers' Co-op recorded 6 inches of rain in May, 6 inches in June, 4 inches in August, 4 inches in September, and 9 inches in October. Make a table to display this information.

Express each number in two other ways.

4. six thousand nineteen

5. 500 + 70 + 8

6. 2,000 + 100 + 90 + 2

7. three hundred forty-five

Find the sum or difference.

8. 4,625
   +2,177

9. 3,099
   +7,611

10. 5,001
    −1,421

11. 8,254
    +4,357

12. 9,815
    −5,286

Compare. Use <, >, or = for ⬤.

13. 34,809 ⬤ 34,890

14. 704,125 ⬤ 800,902

15. 5 × 8 ⬤ 8 × 5

Each team played a total of 31 games. Use the table to answer Exercises 16–20.

16. How many games did the Stingrays win?

17. How many games did each team lose?

18. How many more games did the Sharks win than the Dolphins?

19. Which teams won more games than they lost?

20. How many games did the teams win in all?

Softball Games		
Teams	Games Won	Games Lost
Sharks	23	8
Stingrays	19	⬛
Dolphins	15	⬛
Scorpions	14	⬛

Spotlight ON PROBLEM SOLVING

? ? ? **W**rite **Q**uestions ? ? ?

The information given in a problem determines which questions can be answered.

Ellie is selling snacks at her brother's football game. She opens a large box of raisins. There are 8 packs of raisins in a box.

Talk About It

Decide which questions can be answered using the information given. Be prepared to discuss your solution.

a. How much does each pack of raisins weigh?
b. How many calories are in a box of raisins?
c. How many boxes of raisins would Ellie need to open to sell 50 packs?
d. How many packs of raisins are in 4 boxes?

What number sentences can be used to solve the problem?

What is another question that can be answered using the information given?

Apply

Choose the question that can be answered using the information given. Solve.

1. Lee had 25 cassette tapes. He gave 5 to Mark.
   a. How many tapes are vocals?
   b. How many tapes does Lee have now?

2. Nita buys 40 computer disks. The disks come in 4 packages.
   a. How many disks are in each package?
   b. What size are the disks?

Write a question and then solve.

3. Carl works at the post office. He sold 2,567 stamps on Monday and 1,869 on Tuesday.

4. Julio is 6 years old. His cousin Anita is 3 times his age.

87

Yoshi and Shameka will learn 20 techniques in self-defense class. They will learn the same number of techniques during each of the 5 weeks of class. How many techniques will they learn each week?

Multiplication and division are opposite, or **inverse,** operations.

So, you can use multiplication or division to solve the problem.

Think:

5	×	4	=	20
↑		↑		↑
weeks in class (factor)		techniques each week (factor)		techniques in all (product)

20	÷	5	=	4
↑		↑		↑
techniques in all (dividend)		weeks in class (divisor)		techniques each week (quotient)

They will learn 4 techniques each week.

You can use multiplication facts to find quotients. Find the quotient of 12 ÷ 4.

Think: 4 × ■ = 12
     4 × 3 = 12
     So, 12 ÷ 4 = 3.

You can use division facts to find **missing factors.**
Find the missing factor.
5 × ■ = 10

Think: 10 ÷ 5 = 2
     So, the missing factor is 2.

Check for Understanding

Complete. Write another number sentence to show the inverse operation.

1. ■ × 8 = 16   2. 24 ÷ 6 = ■   3. ■ × 9 = 63

4. 32 ÷ 8 = ■   5. 9 × ■ = 54   6. 21 ÷ 7 = ■

Complete the multiplication number sentence and the division number sentence for each picture.

7.

   _?_ × _?_ = ■   _?_ ÷ _?_ = ■

8. × ×
   × ×
   × ×
   × ×

   _?_ × _?_ = ■   _?_ ÷ _?_ = ■

Practice

Complete the multiplication number sentence and the division number sentence for each picture.

9.

10.

11.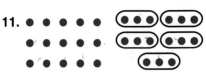

$\underline{?} \times \underline{?} = $ ▨ $\underline{?} \div \underline{?} = $ ▨ $\underline{?} \times \underline{?} = $ ▨ $\underline{?} \div \underline{?} = $ ▨ $\underline{?} \times \underline{?} = $ ▨ $\underline{?} \div \underline{?} = $ ▨

Complete. Write another number sentence to show the inverse operation.

12. $20 \div 4 = $ ▨

13. $3 \times $ ▨ $= 18$

14. $36 \div 4 = $ ▨

15. ▨ $\times 9 = 63$

Find the missing factor.

16. $9 \times $ ▨ $= 72$

17. ▨ $\times 3 = 27$

18. $7 \times $ ▨ $= 42$

19. ▨ $\times 4 = 28$

20. $7 \times $ ▨ $= 35$

21. ▨ $\times 8 = 40$

22. $6 \times $ ▨ $= 30$

23. ▨ $\times 3 = 24$

Mixed Applications

Choose the correct number sentence for each problem. Solve.

24. Mrs. Krenn had 14 T-shirts. She gave each of her students 2 shirts. How many students received T-shirts?
    a. $14 \times 2 = $ ▨
    b. $14 \div 2 = $ ▨

25. Leah sold 3 tickets to each of 5 classmates. How many tickets did she sell in all?
    a. $3 \times 5 = $ ▨
    b. ▨ $\div 5 = 3$

Write a word problem for each number sentence.

26. $9 \times 1 = 9$

27. $36 \div 4 = 9$

28. $48 \div 8 = 6$

29. $2 \times 8 = 16$

CHALLENGE

The missing addends in each number sentence are all the same. Divide to find the missing addends.

30. ▨ $+ $ ▨ $+ $ ▨ $= 12$

31. ▨ $+ $ ▨ $+ $ ▨ $+ $ ▨ $= 32$

32. ▨ $+ $ ▨ $+ $ ▨ $+ $ ▨ $= 20$

33. ▨ $+ $ ▨ $+ $ ▨ $+ $ ▨ $+ $ ▨ $= 45$

How are all four operations related to each other?

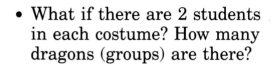

The Chinese New Year is celebrated every February in San Francisco. In one parade 6 students dress as dragons.

• What if there are 2 students in each costume? How many dragons (groups) are there?

| Divide to find how many groups. |

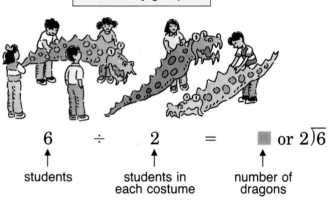

$$6 \div 2 = \blacksquare \text{ or } 2\overline{)6}$$

students   students in each costume   number of dragons

So, there are 3 dragons.

• What if there are 3 dragons? How many students are in each dragon costume?

| Divide to find how many in each group. |

$$6 \div 3 = \blacksquare \text{ or } 3\overline{)6}$$

students   number of dragons   students in each costume

So, there are 2 students in each dragon costume.

Talk About It

▶ What are two ways to use division?

Check for Understanding

Complete each number sentence. Write whether you divided to find *how many groups* or *how many in each group*.

1. $10 \div 2 = \blacksquare$

2. $12 \div 4 = \blacksquare$

Find the quotient.

3. $8 \div 2 = \blacksquare$

4. $9 \div 3 = \blacksquare$

5. $12 \div 2 = \blacksquare$

6. $6 \div 3 = \blacksquare$

7. $3\overline{)18}$

8. $2\overline{)12}$

9. $3\overline{)9}$

10. $2\overline{)8}$

11. $3\overline{)15}$

Practice

Complete each number sentence. Choose **a** or **b** to explain your division.
a. how many groups   **b.** how many in each group

12.    **13.** 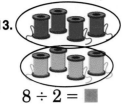   **14.** 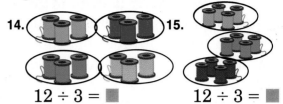 **15.**

$10 \div 2 = $ ▥ $8 \div 2 = $ ▥ $12 \div 3 = $ ▥ $12 \div 3 = $ ▥

Draw a picture to solve.

16. $18 \div 3 = $ ▥   **17.** $15 \div 3 = $ ▥   **18.** $16 \div 2 = $ ▥   **19.** $12 \div 2 = $ ▥

Complete the number sentence.

20. $2 \times $ ▥ $ = 18$ **21.** ▥ $\times 3 = 21$ **22.** $2 \times $ ▥ $ = 10$ **23.** ▥ $\times 3 = 27$

Find the quotient.

24. $3\overline{)15}$ **25.** $2\overline{)18}$ **26.** $3\overline{)27}$

Mixed Applications

27. Name the numbers from 0 through 18 that can be divided evenly by 2. What do you notice about the ones place in the numbers?

28. **Logical Reasoning** Explain why this fact family is made up of only two number sentences.
$3 \times 3 = 9$ $9 \div 3 = 3$

29. It takes about 9 yards of fabric to make one dragon costume. About how many yards of fabric will it take to make 3 dragon costumes?

30. On one float, teams of rowers show how it can move in water. Suppose there are 8 rowers on each side of the float. Two people handle each oar. How many oars are on the float?

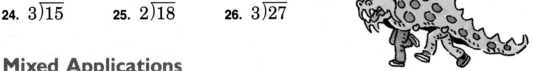

MIXED REVIEW

Estimate the sum or difference by rounding to the nearest hundred or dollar.

1. 478 **2.** $\$6.17$ **3.** $\$12.42$ **4.** $1,411$ **5.** $68,096$
$+717$ $-\ 3.39$ $+\ 16.95$ $-\ 864$ $+17,498$

How can you demonstrate the two ways to use division?

WRAP UP...

DIVIDING
by 4 and 5

Ms. Pace's class of 24 students is going to a basketball game. Each of 4 adults will supervise an equal number of students. How many students will each adult supervise?

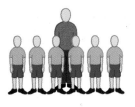

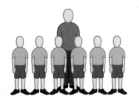

You can divide to find how many students are in *each* group.

Finding the missing factor can help you find a quotient.

Think: $4 \times \blacksquare = 24$

↑
missing factor

Now, divide. $24 \div 4 = 6$ or $4\overline{)24}$ with 6 above

↑
quotient

So, each adult will supervise 6 students.

Talk About It

▶ How can you use a multiplication fact to help you divide?

▶ Is the missing factor the divisor, the dividend, or the quotient of a division problem?

Check for Understanding

Find the missing factor.

1. $4 \times \blacksquare = 16$ **2.** $5 \times \blacksquare = 20$ **3.** $4 \times \blacksquare = 28$ **4.** $5 \times \blacksquare = 45$

Find the quotient.

5. $4\overline{)8}$ **6.** $5\overline{)20}$ **7.** $4\overline{)24}$ **8.** $5\overline{)15}$

9. $16 \div 4 = \blacksquare$ **10.** $30 \div 5 = \blacksquare$ **11.** $36 \div \blacksquare = 6$ **12.** $32 \div 4 = \blacksquare$

Practice

Find the missing factor.

13. $4 \times \blacksquare = 32$ **14.** $5 \times \blacksquare = 35$ **15.** $9 \times \blacksquare = 36$ **16.** $7 \times \blacksquare = 28$

Find the quotient.

17. $45 \div 5 = \blacksquare$ **18.** $25 \div 5 = \blacksquare$ **19.** $40 \div 5 = \blacksquare$ **20.** $12 \div 4 = \blacksquare$

Complete the table.

21.

Divide by 4	
4	1
8	$\blacksquare$
36	$\blacksquare$
20	$\blacksquare$
28	$\blacksquare$

22.

Divide by 5	
10	2
20	$\blacksquare$
40	$\blacksquare$
25	$\blacksquare$
35	$\blacksquare$

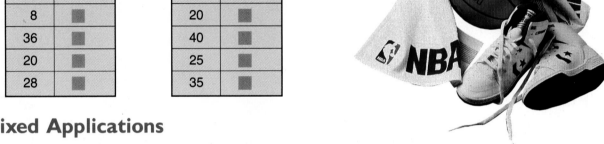

Mixed Applications

23. How many basketball teams of 5 players each can be formed from 40 players?

24. The basketball team runs 5 laps in the gym each day. How many laps does each player run in 5 days of practice?

25. The coach has 47 new uniforms for the basketball league. There are 5 teams in the league, with 9 players on each team. How many extra uniforms will there be?

26. **Logical Reasoning**   There are 16 cars and bicycles in the school parking lot. There are 50 wheels in all. How many vehicles of each kind are there?

VISUAL THINKING

Use toothpicks to make calculator display digits.

Example   It takes five toothpicks to make a 2.

27. Which digit takes the most toothpicks?

28. Which digit takes the fewest toothpicks?

Why is it true that numbers that can be divided by 4 can also be divided by 2?

WRAP UP...

There are 9 players on the City High School football team who qualify for the All Star team. They have been given 81 tickets to the All Star game. Each player received the same number of tickets. How many tickets did each player receive?

Writing a number sentence is an important part of planning the solution to a problem.

▶ **UNDERSTAND**

What are you asked to find?

What facts are given?

▶ **PLAN**

What number sentences can you write to find how many tickets each player received?

You can write a multiplication number sentence or a division number sentence.

▶ **SOLVE**

How can you solve this problem?

Find the missing factor.

$$9 \quad \times \quad \blacksquare \quad = \quad 81 \qquad \textbf{Think: } 9 \times 9 = 81.$$

players   tickets to each player   total tickets
(missing factor)

Find the quotient.

So, each player received 9 tickets.

$$81 \quad \div \quad 9 \quad = \quad \blacksquare$$

total tickets   players   tickets to each player
(quotient)

▶ **LOOK BACK**

What operation can you use to check your answer?

WHAT IF... . . . the players had been given 63 tickets? How many tickets would each player receive?

Apply

Write a number sentence and solve.

1. Don practiced for 21 hours last week. He practiced for the same number of hours each day for 7 days. For how many hours did he practice each day?

2. Alana scored 402 points during the last two basketball seasons. Irene scored 548 points. How many points did they score in all?

3. A field goal is worth 3 points. Vernon scored 27 points by making field goals. How many field goals did he make?

4. Hugh shot 38 baskets during practice, and Sonia shot 53 baskets. How many more baskets did Sonia shoot?

Mixed Applications → **STRATEGIES** • Make a Table to Analyze Data • Draw a Picture • Find a Pattern • Use a Table

Choose a strategy and solve.

5. Garrett did 10 sit-ups the first day of practice. The second day he did 12 sit-ups. The third day he did 14, and so on. At this rate of increase, how many sit-ups did he do on the seventh day?

6. Connie, Dot, Ned, and Frank stood in line at the ticket booth. Connie stood behind Frank. Frank stood behind Dot. Ned was last in line. Who was second in line?

7. Use the table that Walt made. How many more cards did he buy at the discount store than at the Mall Sports Store?

Location	Number of Cards Bought
Discount store	189
Trade show	67
Mall Sports Store	98
Flea market	12

WRITER'S CORNER

8. Write two number sentences using the numbers 4, 7, and 28. Write one sentence with a missing factor. Write the other sentence with a missing quotient. Then write two word problems using these numbers. Exchange with a partner and solve.

DIVISION
with Zero and One

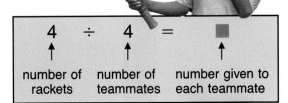

Jared has 4 tennis rackets. He gives the same number to each of 4 teammates. How many tennis rackets does Jared give to each teammate?

You can divide to find how many tennis rackets Jared gives to each teammate.

4	$\div$	4	$=$	■
↑		↑		↑
number of rackets		number of teammates		number given to each teammate

A. When a number is divided by itself, the quotient is always 1. $4 \div 4 = 1$

So, Jared gave 1 tennis racket to each teammate.

More Examples

B. When a number is divided by 1, the quotient is always that number. $3 \div 1 = 3$

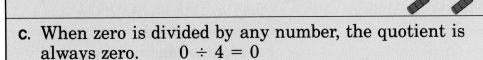

C. When zero is divided by any number, the quotient is always zero. $0 \div 4 = 0$

D. You cannot divide by zero.

$2 \div 0$ does not equal 0 because 0×0 does not equal 2.
$2 \div 0$ does not equal 2 because 2×0 does not equal 2.

There is no number that when multiplied by zero will equal 2.

Talk About It

▶ Which rule shows that $0 \div 6$ is zero?

▶ If the dividend and divisor are the same, what is the quotient?

Check for Understanding

Find the quotient. Write the letter of the rule that you used.

1. $3 \div 3 = $ ■

2. $0 \div 2 = $ ■

3. $5 \div 1 = $ ■

4. $7 \div 7 = $ ■

5. $15\overline{)0}$

6. $20\overline{)20}$

7. $6\overline{)0}$

8. $1\overline{)27}$

Practice

Find the quotient. Write the letter of the rule that you used.

9. $6 \div 6 = $

10. $0 \div 5 = $

11. $3 \div 1 = $

12. $8 \div 8 = $

13. $15\overline{)0}$

14. $19\overline{)19}$

15. $5\overline{)5}$

16. $1\overline{)5}$

Find the quotient.

17. $0 \div 6 = $

18. $1 \div 1 = $

19. $6 \div 6 = $

20. $0 \div 1 = $

21. $67 \div 1 = $

22. $4 \div 4 = $

23. $81 \div 1 = $

24. $9 \div 1 = $

25. $7\overline{)7}$

26. $5\overline{)0}$

27. $9\overline{)9}$

28. $1\overline{)8}$

29. $1\overline{)1}$

30. $8\overline{)8}$

31. $3\overline{)0}$

32. $3\overline{)3}$

33. $1\overline{)7}$

34. $1\overline{)8}$

Mixed Applications

35. Shawn has $5. How many plastic visors can he buy if each visor costs $1?

36. Tracy takes 6 tennis lessons in 6 days. She takes the same number of lessons each day. How many lessons does she take each day?

37. **Logical Reasoning** Vince needs to practice 40 hours for a tennis tournament. If he practices for 5 hours each day, how many days will it take Vince to practice for 2 tournaments?

38. Carol wants to share her peanuts with 3 other tennis players. The package is empty. How many peanuts can she give to each person? Show your answer in a number sentence.

LOGICAL REASONING

39. I am a one-digit number. I am inside the circle and the square. I am not in the rectangle. What is the quotient when I am divided by 1?

9 4 6
7 3
5

How can you use what you know about division with 0 and 1 to help you divide mentally?

WRAP
UP...

DIVIDING
by 6 and 7

Kathy and Eric compete in a gymnastics league. There are 48 gymnasts in the league. Each team has 6 gymnasts. How many teams are in the league?

You can divide to find how many teams are in the league.

$$48 \div 6 = \blacksquare \quad \text{or} \quad 6\overline{)48}$$

total number of gymnasts   number on each team   number of teams

Use a multiplication fact to help you.

Think: $\blacksquare \times 6 = 48$

$$8 \times 6 = 48 \quad \text{or} \quad 6\overline{)48}^{\,8}$$

So, there are 8 teams in the league.

Another Example

Find the quotient of $42 \div 7$.

First, find the missing factor.

Think: $\blacksquare \times 7 = 42$

$6 \times 7 = 42 \qquad$ So, $42 \div 7 = 6$.

Check for Understanding

Complete the number sentence.

1. $\blacksquare \times 8 = 48$
2. $\blacksquare \times 7 = 49$
3. $8 \times \blacksquare = 56$
4. $4 \times \blacksquare = 28$

Find the quotient.

5. $6\overline{)18}$
6. $7\overline{)63}$
7. $8\overline{)24}$
8. $7\overline{)56}$

9. $18 \div 6 = \blacksquare$
10. $21 \div 7 = \blacksquare$
11. $24 \div 6 = \blacksquare$
12. $35 \div 7 = \blacksquare$

Practice

Draw a picture to solve.

13. $18 \div 6 = \blacksquare$ **14.** $21 \div 7 = \blacksquare$ **15.** $30 \div 6 = \blacksquare$ **16.** $28 \div 7 = \blacksquare$

Complete the number sentence.

17. $6 \times \blacksquare = 36$ **18.** $7 \times \blacksquare = 56$ **19.** $\blacksquare \times 6 = 54$ **20.** $\blacksquare \times 7 = 63$

Find the quotient.

21. $40 \div 5 = \blacksquare$ **22.** $49 \div 7 = \blacksquare$ **23.** $42 \div 7 = \blacksquare$ **24.** $35 \div 7 = \blacksquare$

25. $30 \div 5 = \blacksquare$ **26.** $28 \div 4 = \blacksquare$ **27.** $63 \div 7 = \blacksquare$ **28.** $54 \div 6 = \blacksquare$

29. $6\overline{)36}$ **30.** $7\overline{)42}$ **31.** $7\overline{)21}$ **32.** $6\overline{)6}$ **33.** $7\overline{)0}$

34. $5\overline{)35}$ **35.** $6\overline{)54}$ **36.** $5\overline{)45}$ **37.** $4\overline{)36}$ **38.** $7\overline{)56}$

Mixed Applications

39. In one year Sue, Lynn, and Iris won 27 medals. They each won the same number of medals. How many medals did each girl win?

40. The gymnastics season lasts 49 days. For how many weeks does the gymnastics season last?

41. Logical Reasoning The product of two numbers is 36. Their quotient is 1. What are the two numbers?

MIXED REVIEW

Find the sum or difference.

1. $\begin{array}{r} 1,000 \\ -596 \\ \hline \end{array}$ **2.** $\begin{array}{r} 4,697 \\ +8,954 \\ \hline \end{array}$ **3.** $\begin{array}{r} 6,052 \\ -3,493 \\ \hline \end{array}$ **4.** $\begin{array}{r} 26,761 \\ +89,549 \\ \hline \end{array}$ **5.** $\begin{array}{r} 2,113 \\ -845 \\ \hline \end{array}$

Write the inverse number sentence.

6. $21 \div 3 = 7$ **7.** $4 \times 3 = 12$ **8.** $35 \div 5 = 7$ **9.** $7 \times 4 = 28$

How does knowing that $7 \times 8 = 56$ help you to find $56 \div 7$?

There are 56 skaters on Bobby's ice hockey team. During practice they are organized into 8 squads, with the same number of skaters on each squad. How many skaters are on each squad?

Divide to find how many skaters are on each squad.

$$56 \div 8 = \blacksquare \quad \text{or} \quad 8\overline{)56}$$

total number of skaters   number of squads   number of skaters on each squad

Or, you can find the missing factor.

Think: $8 \times \blacksquare = 56$

$8 \times 7 = 56 \qquad 8\overline{)56}^{\,7}$

So, there are 7 skaters on each squad.

Talk About It

▶ Did you divide to find how many groups or how many in each group?

▶ How can you use multiplication to find quotients?

Another Example

Find the quotient of $45 \div 9$.

Think: $\blacksquare \times 9 = 45$

$5 \times 9 = 45 \qquad$ So, $45 \div 9 = 5$.

Check for Understanding

Complete the number sentence.

1. $5 \times \blacksquare = 45$ 2. $32 \div 8 = \blacksquare$ 3. $\blacksquare \times 7 = 56$ 4. $64 \div 8 = \blacksquare$

Find the quotient.

5. $16 \div 8 = \blacksquare$ 6. $24 \div 8 = \blacksquare$ 7. $36 \div 9 = \blacksquare$ 8. $45 \div 9 = \blacksquare$

9. $8\overline{)8}$ 10. $9\overline{)27}$ 11. $8\overline{)64}$ 12. $9\overline{)72}$ 13. $9\overline{)81}$

Practice

Draw a picture to solve.

14. $18 \div 9 = $

15. $36 \div 9 = $

16. $32 \div 8 = $

17. $24 \div 8 = $

Complete the number sentence.

18. $8 \times \blacksquare = 72$

19. $\blacksquare \times 9 = 45$

20. $\blacksquare \times 8 = 40$

21. $9 \times \blacksquare = 81$

Find the quotient.

22. $64 \div 8 = $

23. $63 \div 9 = $

24. $56 \div 8 = $

25. $54 \div 9 = $

26. $18 \div 18 = $

27. $48 \div 8 = $

28. $45 \div 5 = $

29. $72 \div 8 = $

30. $4\overline{)24}$

31. $6\overline{)42}$

32. $7\overline{)49}$

33. $8\overline{)24}$

34. $9\overline{)27}$

35. $7\overline{)21}$

36. $5\overline{)40}$

37. $7\overline{)35}$

38. $1\overline{)9}$

39. $2\overline{)14}$

Mixed Applications

40. The Green County Hockey League has 63 games scheduled. If 9 games are played each week, for how many weeks will the league's season last?

41. **Logical Reasoning** Manuel wants to invite some friends to see a hockey game with him. He has $48. Each ticket costs $8. How many friends can Manuel invite?

42. Teri and her dad packed hockey uniforms into boxes. On Friday they packed 142 uniforms. On Saturday they packed 230 uniforms. How many more uniforms did they pack on Saturday?

LOGICAL REASONING

Find the missing factors to complete each table.

	Multiply by 8	
	Input	Output
43.	$\blacksquare$	48
44.	$\blacksquare$	64
45.	$\blacksquare$	72

46.

	Multiply by $\blacksquare$	
	Input	Output
	6	54
	8	72
	9	81

Write a fact family for 72, 8, and 9. How are the products and dividends related?

WRAP UP...

Vocabulary Check

Choose a word or words from the box to complete each sentence.

array
fact family
factors
Grouping
inverse
One
Order
product
quotient
zero

If you do not understand a problem, look back in the chapter on the page listed.

1. The number sentence $4 \times 1 = 4$ is an example of the Property of _?_ for Multiplication. *(page 76)*

2. The answer to a multiplication problem is the _?_. *(page 72)*

3. The answer to a division problem is the _?_. *(page 88)*

4. The numbers we multiply to find a product are called _?_. *(page 72)*

5. The number sentences $5 \times 4 = 20$ and $20 \div 4 = 5$ belong to the same _?_. *(page 70)*

6. The number sentence $(3 \times 2) \times 4 = 3 \times (2 \times 4)$ is an example of the _?_ Property of Multiplication. *(page 76)*

7. The number sentence $6 \times 7 = 7 \times 6$ is an example of the _?_ Property of Multiplication. *(page 76)*

8. When 0 is divided by any nonzero number, the quotient is always _?_. *(page 96)*

9. A model of objects in rows and columns is called an _?_. *(page 70)*

10. Multiplication and division are opposite, or _?_, operations. *(page 88)*

Concept Check

Write a multiplication and a division number sentence for each picture. *(pages 71, 88)*

11.

12.

13.

Which property is shown by each number sentence? *(page 76)*

14. $6 \times 1 = 6$

15. $(2 \times 3) \times 4 = 2 \times (3 \times 4)$

16. $3 \times 0 = 0$

17. $5 \times 7 = 7 \times 5$

Write the other facts for each fact family. *(pages 70, 88)*

18. $3 \times 4 = 12$

19. $7 \times 7 = 49$

20. $72 \div 9 = 8$

21. $54 \div 6 = 9$

22. $4 \times 1 = 4$

23. $12 \div 2 = 6$

Complete. Write another number sentence to show the inverse operation. *(page 88)*

24. $14 \div 2 = \blacksquare$

25. $6 \times \blacksquare = 30$

26. $16 \div 4 = \blacksquare$

27. $42 \div 6 = \blacksquare$

28. $32 \div 4 = \blacksquare$

29. $5 \times \blacksquare = 40$

30. $\blacksquare \times 7 = 56$

31. $18 \div 3 = \blacksquare$

Skill Check

Find the product or quotient. *(pages 72–101)*

32. $3 \times 9 = \blacksquare$

33. $4 \times 6 = \blacksquare$

34. $12 \div 2 = \blacksquare$

35. $15 \div 3 = \blacksquare$

36. $32 \div 8 = \blacksquare$

37. $5 \times 7 = \blacksquare$

38. $8 \times 6 = \blacksquare$

39. $72 \div 9 = \blacksquare$

40. $\begin{array}{r} 3 \\ \times 5 \\ \hline \end{array}$

41. $\begin{array}{r} 7 \\ \times 9 \\ \hline \end{array}$

42. $\begin{array}{r} 9 \\ \times 3 \\ \hline \end{array}$

43. $\begin{array}{r} 8 \\ \times 6 \\ \hline \end{array}$

44. $\begin{array}{r} 5 \\ \times 8 \\ \hline \end{array}$

45. $\begin{array}{r} 5 \\ \times 5 \\ \hline \end{array}$

46. $9\overline{)54}$

47. $7\overline{)49}$

48. $8\overline{)40}$

49. $6\overline{)48}$

50. $8\overline{)48}$

51. $6\overline{)36}$

Problem-Solving Check

Write a number sentence and solve. *(page 94)*

52. Alberto makes 8 calls a day on his job. He works 5 days a week. How many calls does he make in 2 weeks?

53. Vanessa has to wait 56 days until her birthday. How many weeks are there until her birthday?

Write whether there is *too much* or *too little* information to solve the problem. Solve the problem if you can. *(page 78)*

54. Donya collected 28 recipes for salads. She divided them equally into 4 categories. Fruit salad is her favorite category. How many recipes are in each category?

55. Tad has 42 seashells. He places an equal number of seashells in each of 6 different boxes. How many conch shells are there in each box?

CHAPTER TEST

Write a multiplication sentence and a division sentence for each picture.

1.  2.  3.

Complete. Write another number sentence to show the inverse operation.

4. $\blacksquare \times 4 = 36$ 5. $2 \times \blacksquare = 16$ 6. $28 \div 4 = \blacksquare$

Which property is shown by each number sentence?

7. $6 \times 8 = 8 \times 6$ 8. $(3 \times 4) \times 2 = 3 \times (4 \times 2)$

Find the product or quotient.

Check your answers.

9. $\begin{array}{r} 2 \\ \times 7 \\ \hline \end{array}$
10. $\begin{array}{r} 5 \\ \times 6 \\ \hline \end{array}$
11. $\begin{array}{r} 8 \\ \times 7 \\ \hline \end{array}$
12. $\begin{array}{r} 9 \\ \times 5 \\ \hline \end{array}$
13. $\begin{array}{r} 8 \\ \times 4 \\ \hline \end{array}$

14. $3\overline{)24}$ 15. $6\overline{)18}$ 16. $8\overline{)64}$ 17. $9\overline{)54}$ 18. $3\overline{)21}$

19. $6 \times 3 = \blacksquare$ 20. $7 \times 6 = \blacksquare$ 21. $20 \div 5 = \blacksquare$

Problem Solving

Write whether there is *too much* or *too little* information to solve the problem.
Solve the problem if you can.

22. Lorna bought a belt for $2.00 and a scarf for $3.50. How much change did she receive?

23. Wally bought 6 books and 3 markers. The books cost $2 each. How much did Wally spend on the books?

Write a number sentence and solve.

24. Lloyd has taken 4 math tests this year. Last year he took 3 times as many math tests. How many math tests did Lloyd take last year?

25. Allie practiced the piano for 14 hours last week. She practiced for the same number of hours each day. For how many hours did she practice each day?

Teamwork PROJECT

Cost Analysis

In every community people enjoy a variety of sports and other recreational activities. Some activities require special equipment and clothing for protection and comfort or because of tradition and style. With your teammates, select an activity and determine how much the equipment and clothing would cost.

Decide
Brainstorm the kinds of sports and other recreational activities in which you have participated or would like to participate. Make a list.

Choose one activity.

Make a list of sources for prices of equipment and clothing.

Do
Research the prices.

Design and prepare a table, naming the activity and identifying the price of each item of equipment and clothing.

Share
With other teams, compare the cost of different activities.

Talk About It

- How much would your activity cost for one person? for all your teammates? for a whole sports team? for your whole class?

- Which activity requires the most equipment and clothing? the least?

- Which activity is the most expensive in terms of equipment? clothing? fees?

- To participate in an activity, what other costs might you have to pay?

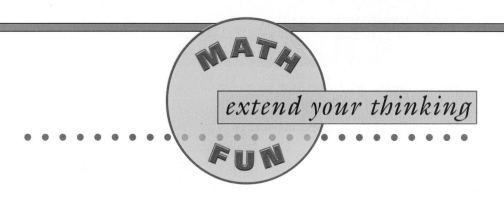
Prime Factors

A prime number has exactly two factors, itself and 1.

So, 2 is a prime number.
Its factors are 1 and 2.
$1 \times 2 = 2$

However, 4 is not a prime number.
Its factors are 1, 2, and 4.
$1 \times 4 = 4$
$2 \times 2 = 4$

> 1 is not a prime number.

Prime Numbers

1	②	③	4	⑤	6	⑦	8	9	10
⑪	12	⑬	14	15	16	⑰	18	⑲	20
21	22	㉓	24	25	26	27	28	㉙	30
㉛	32	33	34	35	36	㊲	38	39	40
㊶	42	㊸	44	45	46	㊼	48	49	50

A prime factor is a factor that is a prime number.

This factor tree shows the prime factors of 24.

Find two factors whose product is 24. These are the first two branches of the tree. Find factors whose products are 4 and 6. These are the next four branches of the tree. These last factors are prime factors.

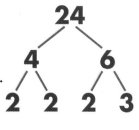

The prime factorization of 24 is $2 \times 2 \times 2 \times 3$.

Find the prime factors of each. Draw a factor tree.

1. 36 **2.** 28 **3.** 54 **4.** 56 **5.** 100

Challenge

Number Puzzles

Copy. Write +, −, ×, or ÷ for each ●. Do the operations in parentheses first.

1. 4 ● 3 ● 5 = 2 ● 6
2. (8 ● 3) ● 6 = 4 ● 1
3. (9 ● 0) ● 9 = 36 ● (3 ● 1)
4. (4 ● 2) ● (3 ● 2) = 5 ● 7
5. 56 ● 8 = 4 ● 4 ● 1

Logical Reasoning

Write *true* or *false* for each statement.

1. All of the factors of 4 are factors of 8.
2. All of the factors of 8 are factors of 4.
3. None of the factors of 5 are factors of 7.
4. Some of the factors of 24 are factors of 8.

Write the letter of the correct answer.

1. What is the value of the digit 5 in 254,021?

   A. 50 B. 500
   C. 50,000 D. 500,000

2. Which number is 100 more than 8,642?

   A. 8,643 B. 8,742
   C. 9,642 D. 9,652

3. Estimate by rounding 2,345 to the nearest hundred.

   A. 2,200 B. 2,300
   C. 2,400 D. 2,500

4. $8 + 5 + 2 + 1 = \blacksquare$

   A. 14 B. 15
   C. 16 D. 17

5.
   $$\begin{array}{r} 500 \\ -123 \\ \hline \end{array}$$

   A. 323 B. 377
   C. 423 D. not here

6.
   $$\begin{array}{r} 2,529 \\ +3,544 \\ \hline \end{array}$$

   A. 5,073 B. 6,063
   C. 6,073 D. 6,173

7. Estimate by rounding 12,567 to the nearest ten.

   A. 12,068 B. 12,560
   C. 12,570 D. 12,600

8. 8×0 is an example of which property of multiplication?

   A. Zero B. One
   C. Grouping D. not here

9. Choose the missing factor.
   $9 \times \blacksquare = 72$

   A. 7 B. 8
   C. 9 D. 10

10.
    $$\begin{array}{r} 5 \\ \times 7 \\ \hline \end{array}$$

    A. 25 B. 32
    C. 45 D. not here

11. $8 \times \blacksquare = 48$

    A. 4 B. 6
    C. 7 D. 9

12. $28 \div 7 = \blacksquare$

    A. 4 B. 6
    C. 8 D. 9

13. Mindy has 8 cats and dogs. She has 2 more dogs than cats. How many dogs does Mindy have?

    A. 3 dogs B. 4 dogs
    C. 5 dogs D. 6 dogs

14. Tanya jogs 6 miles each week. Paulo jogs 5 miles each week. How many miles will Tanya jog in 8 weeks?

    A. 11 miles B. 19 miles
    C. 40 miles D. 48 miles

4

TIME, GRAPHING, AND DATA

Did you know ...

... that the highest price ever paid for a teddy bear was $15,840? The teddy bear was purchased in London, England.

Ever since Mr. Barker opened his teddy bear store at the mall, his profits have increased. Records for the past five months show sales of 250, 350, 500, 650, and 800 teddy bears. How can Mr. Barker display this data on a graph?

Sam rides the bus to the Oakdale Shopping Center. It leaves at 2:00. What is the time on the clock at the bus station? Has Sam missed the bus?

The time on the clock is 1:45, or 15 minutes *before* 2:00. So, Sam is in time to ride the bus.

Write: 1:45
Read: one forty-five, or fifteen minutes before two, or a quarter to two

analog clock

digital clock

This is an analog clock. Write the time in numbers.

Talk About It

▶ What are three ways to say the time in words?

▶ How can you tell the hour when the hour hand is not pointing directly to a number?

▶ How does the hour hand move differently from the minute hand?

▶ How is a digital clock different from an analog clock?

More Examples

A.

6:42

six forty-two, forty-two minutes past six, or eighteen minutes to seven

B.

3:30

three-thirty, thirty minutes past three, or half past three

Check for Understanding

Write the time in two different ways.

1.

2.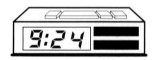

3.

Draw an analog clock and a digital clock for each time.

4. two twenty-two   **5.** eight-thirty   **6.** a quarter to three

Practice

Write the time in two different ways.

7.

8.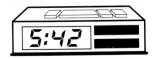

9.

10. nine thirty-five

11. a quarter past two

12. six fifty

Draw an analog clock and a digital clock for each time.

13. four eighteen

14. half past eleven

15. five minutes to one

Match the time with the clock. Write the letter.

a. one minute to seven	b. half past nine
c. fourteen minutes to one	d. twenty-two minutes to twelve
e. a quarter to two	f. six minutes past four

16.

17.

18.

19.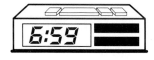

20.

21.

Mixed Applications

22. It took 25 minutes for Barb and her mother to buy two dresses and 18 minutes to buy a new pair of shoes. How many minutes did it take to make both purchases?

23. The boat show at the mall started at 2:00. Sara arrived at 1:54. Roxie arrived at a quarter to two. Who arrived at the boat show first?

24. Shawn came to the bus stop at 4:52. The bus arrived at a quarter past five. How long did Shawn wait for the bus?

What is a good way to compute the time between 2:42 and 3:17?

WRAP **UP...**

TIME
A.M. and P.M.

Jill and her mother plan to go to a fashion show that starts at 7:30 P.M. How do they know whether it starts at 7:30 in the morning or 7:30 in the evening?

A.M. and P.M. tell what part of the day it is. Each day has 24 hours. Since the clockface shows 12 hours, the hour hand goes around once for the A.M. hours and once for the P.M. hours.

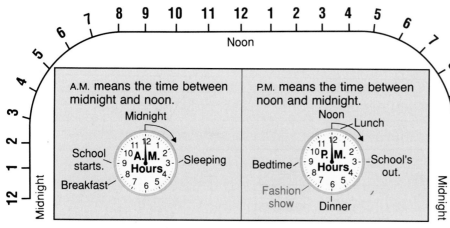

So, the fashion show takes place in the evening.

Talk About It

▶ Name three other things you do in the A.M. hours.

▶ Name three other things you do in the P.M. hours.

Check for Understanding

Write the time by using numbers and A.M. or P.M.

1. Doug eats dinner.

2. Ann sees the sunset.

3. Ty dresses for school.

Write A.M. or P.M. to complete each sentence.

4. Rick has lunch at 12:30 _?_ .

5. It is 2:00 _?_ in the middle of the night.

6. I sleep during more _?_ hours than _?_ hours.

Practice

Write the time by using numbers and A.M. or P.M.

7. The mall closes.

8. The Card Shop opens for business.

9. Mrs. May takes an afternoon break.

10. your bedtime

11. the time you arrive home from school

12. the time you eat breakfast

13. the time your favorite television show begins

14. the time a bakery sells the most pastries

15. the time you would get up to watch the sunrise

Mixed Applications

16. On Saturdays Aaron and Danny work at a video store in the mall. Aaron reports to work at 10:00 A.M. Danny reports to work at 4:30 P.M. Who reports to work at a later time?

17. Mrs. Romano and her daughter Julie ate lunch at the mall at 11:55 A.M. They spent 30 minutes eating lunch. Write the time that they finished eating lunch. Use A.M. or P.M.

LOGICAL REASONING

On Saturday morning Lois bought a birthday gift at the mall. At 12:15 P.M. she bought a bouquet of flowers at the mall flower shop. Lois left the gift at Mona's house at 2:00 P.M. The mall opened at 10:00 A.M.

18. Did Lois buy the gift before going to the flower shop?

19. Did Lois buy the flowers before going to Mona's house?

20. Did Lois reach Mona's house before or after 12:15 P.M.?

Is midnight A.M. or P.M.?

"Jason, try on these shoes."
"I'll do it in a second, Dad."

- Can Jason try on the shoes in a second?

No, a second will not be enough time.

Talk About It

▶ How can you measure a second? a minute?

▶ What unit of time is more appropriate to use in this example?

▶ Give another example of when you might estimate time.

_____

Here is a table showing different units of time.

Talk About It

▶ What can be done in about 1 minute? in about 1 hour? in about 1 week? in about 1 month? in about 1 year?

Units of Time

60 seconds (sec)	= 1 minute (min)
60 minutes	= 1 hour (hr)
24 hours	= 1 day (d)
7 days	= 1 week (wk)
12 months (mo)	= 1 year (yr)
about 52 weeks	= 1 year
365 days	= 1 year
366 days	= 1 leap year

Check for Understanding

Choose the most reasonable unit of time for each (*sec, min, hr, d, wk, mo, yr*).

1. It takes about 20 _?_ to take a bath.

2. Most school years last about 10 _?_ .

3. Summer camp lasts about 2 _?_ .

4. One complete day at school takes 7 _?_ .

5. One birthday to the next is 1 _?_ .

6. A blink of your eye takes 1 _?_ .

Practice

Choose the most reasonable unit of time for each (*sec, min, hr, d, wk, mo, yr*).

7. Winter lasts about 3 _?_ .

8. A movie lasts about 2 _?_ .

9. To brush and floss your teeth takes about 5 _?_ .

10. It may take 6 _?_ to get an item from a mail-order catalog.

Choose the best estimate for each.

11. the time it takes to walk 5 miles
   a. 20 minutes
   b. 20 hours
   c. 2 hours

12. the time it takes to jog 1 mile
   a. 10 minutes
   b. 2 minutes
   c. 1 hour

13. the time it takes to drive 500 miles
   a. 1 hour
   b. 10 hours
   c. 10 weeks

The minute hand has fallen off these clocks. Estimate the time.

14.

15.

16.

Mixed Applications

17. Number Sense Brian jogged for 37 minutes. Then he walked 26 minutes to cool off. Did his jogging and walking take more or less than 1 hour?

18. Mike called his aunt to tell her he would be home in about an hour. It was 4:50 when he called. Estimate the time Mike's aunt should expect him home.

ANALYZE DATA

Paul and his sister earn their allowances by doing household chores. Use the table to answer Exercises 19–20.

19. Which of Paul's chores take about $\frac{1}{2}$ of an hour to complete?

20. Which of Paul's chores takes him the longest to complete?

Time for Paul's Chores (In min)					
	Mon.	Tues.	Wed.	Thurs.	Fri.
Walk dog	25		25		25
Mow lawn			90		
Feed cats		15		15	
Clean room	35				35

About how much time do you spend in school each day?

EXPLORING

Elapsed Time

Elapsed time is the time that passes from the start of an activity to the end of that activity.

About how much time has elapsed since you arrived at school?

WORK TOGETHER

Building Understanding

Use a clock to explore elapsed time.

Buck works in his aunt's bath shop. He started to rearrange the towels at 3:10 P.M. He finished at 3:45 P.M. How long did it take Buck to complete this activity?

Buck and Maria went out to lunch at 11:35 A.M. They returned to the bath shop at 1:10 P.M. How long were they gone?

Starting Time　　　Ending Time

Talk About It
► How many hours pass each time the minute hand makes one trip around the clock?

► How can you find the elapsed time between when they went to lunch and when they returned?

► Tell the method that you used to find the elapsed time.

Talk About It
► When did the activity start? Mark this time on your clockface.

► When did the activity end? Mark this time on your clockface.

► How can you find the elapsed time?

► What is the elapsed time?

Making the Connection

In your everyday activities, you can use elapsed time to find the starting time and ending time. Complete this table. Remember to use A.M. and P.M. correctly.

	Activity	Starting Time	Ending Time	Elapsed Time
	Example: football game	2:00 P.M.	4:45 P.M.	2 hr 45 min
1.	cleaning garage	10:40 A.M.	1:10 P.M.	▪
2.	shopping at mall	11:20 A.M.	▪	4 hr 30 min
3.	riding bike	5:12 P.M.	6:18 P.M.	▪
4.	dentist appointment	3:50 P.M.	▪	45 min
5.	recess	▪	12:23 P.M.	28 min

Use the clocks to help you answer Exercises 6–7.

6. How many minutes pass from 1:15 A.M. to 1:55 A.M.?

7. How many hours pass from 10:00 P.M. to 5:00 A.M.?

8. If you know the starting time and elapsed time, what can you find? How do you find it?

9. If you know the starting time and ending time, what can you find? How do you find it?

10. If you know the ending time and elapsed time, what can you find? How can you find it?

Checking Understanding

Tell how much time has elapsed.

11.

Begin A.M.   End A.M.   Begin A.M.   End P.M.

Write the time for each.

13. Start: 4:25 P.M.
    35 min elapsed
    End: __?__

14. Start: __?__ P.M.
    2 hr 25 min elapsed
    End: 7:00 P.M.

15. Start: 7:00 A.M.
    Elapsed time: __?__
    End: 4:20 P.M.

THE CALENDAR

ATTENTION ALL ANTIQUE LOVERS

Use this August calendar to answer the questions.

Talk About It

▶ How many days are there in August?

▶ About how many weeks are there in August?

▶ How many Thursdays are there? Which days occur four times?

▶ What is the date of the fifth Wednesday?

▶ What day of the week is the last day of the month?

▶ On what dates will the Craft Fair be held?

AUGUST

Sun.	Mon.	Tues.	Wed.	Thurs.	Fri.	Sat.
			1	2	3	4
5	6	7	8	9	10	11
12	13	14	15	16	17	18
19	20	21	22	23	24	25
26	27	28	29	30	31	

THE TIMES

Weekend Events   Thursday Aug 2.

The 14th Annual Craft Fair will be held from 10 A.M. to 7 P.M. this Friday through August 5th at the Alamo Plaza.

Check for Understanding

Use a one-year calendar to answer the questions.

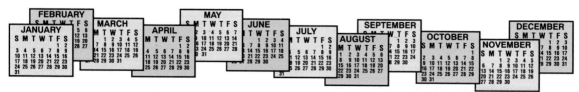

1. Which month is the fifth month of the year?

2. Which month comes after the tenth month?

3. Flag Day is the fourteenth day of the sixth month. Name the month.

4. Julie's birthday will be 3 months from August 5. When is Julie's birthday?

5. What is the 100th day of the year?

Practice

Use the calendars to answer Exercises 6–11.

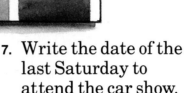

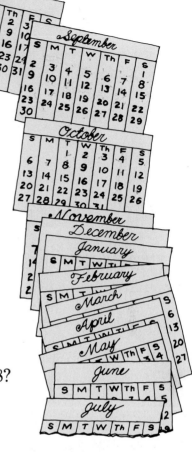

6. About how many weeks will the car show last?

7. Write the date of the last Saturday to attend the car show.

8. Write the date that is 6 weeks before the car show ends.

9. Write the date that is exactly 3 months before your birthday.

10. How many days are between September 3 and October 16?

11. How many months are there from August 8 to January 8?

Mixed Applications

Write the day and date. Use the August, September, and October calendars.

12. 3 days after August 12

13. 5 days before August 17

14. 2 months before Tuesday, October 22

15. 3 months after Wednesday, August 1

16. the second Wednesday of August

17. the third Friday of the tenth month

18. 2 weeks and 3 days before September 21

19. 1 week and 6 days after August 26

Solve.

20. Abby's family left on Saturday for a trip to the Mountain Crafts Festival. They returned 12 days later. On what day of the week did they return?

21. Postcards at the craft fair cost $0.35 each. Leigh bought 5 postcards and gave the clerk $2.00. How much did Leigh spend for the postcards?

About how much time has elapsed from the first day in second grade to the first day in fourth grade?

PROBLEM *Solving*

Use a Table or a Schedule

The Cinema 6 at the mall is having a cartoon movie festival. Sherry and Kathy want to see *The Little Mermaid, The Jungle Book,* or *Bambi,* but they must be home by 3:00. It is 12:30 now. It takes 15 minutes to get home. Which movie can they see?

Sometimes you can use a table or schedule to solve a problem.

▶ **UNDERSTAND**

What are you asked to find?

What facts are given?

▶ **PLAN**

How can you make a plan to solve the problem?

You can use the schedule to find the time that each movie starts. Then find the ending time by computing the elapsed time for each.

▶ **SOLVE**

How can you solve the problem?

You can find the ending time for each movie by adding 1 hour 30 minutes to each starting time.

Cinema 6 Movie Schedule

Cinema	Movie	Time
1	Cinderella	12:45
2	The Little Mermaid	1:00
3	Lady & the Tramp	1:20
4	Bambi	1:30
5	The Jungle Book	1:45
6	101 Dalmatians	2:00

Each movie lasts about 1 hour 30 minutes.

Movie	Starts		Ends
The Little Mermaid	1:00	+ 1 hr 30 min	= 2:30
Bambi	1:30	+ 1 hr 30 min	= 3:00
The Jungle Book	1:45	+ 1 hr 30 min	= 3:15

If Sherry and Kathy see *Bambi* or *The Jungle Book,* they will not be home on time.

They can see *The Little Mermaid* and still be home on time.

▶ **LOOK BACK**

What other strategy can you use to solve the problem?

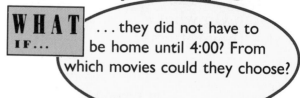

WHAT IF... ...they did not have to be home until 4:00? From which movies could they choose?

 Connection, pages 452–453

Apply

Use the train schedule to answer Exercises 1–6.

Train Schedule					
Train Number	Leaves Argus	Arrives Landview	Arrives Elk City	Arrives El Mirado	Arrives Burlington
14	5:00 A.M.	6:10 A.M.	7:26 A.M.	8:18 A.M.	9:36 A.M.
76	10:15 A.M.	11:25 A.M.	12:41 P.M.	1:33 P.M.	2:51 P.M.
588	2:30 P.M.	3:40 P.M.	4:56 P.M.	5:48 P.M.	7:02 P.M.
1142	7:00 P.M.	8:10 P.M.	9:26 P.M.	10:18 P.M.	11:36 P.M.

(1) Which train arrives in Elk City at 4:56 P.M.?

(2) Which train arrives in Landview closest to noon?

(3) Which train makes the earliest arrival in El Mirado?

(4) Which train arrives in Burlington closest to midnight?

(5) How long is the train ride from Argus to El Mirado?

(6) Which train leaves Argus before noon and arrives in Burlington just before 3:00 P.M.?

Mixed Applications ➤ **STRATEGIES**   • Find a Pattern   • Draw a Picture   • Write a Number Sentence

Choose a strategy and solve.

(7) A train ticket from Ada to Etta costs $67.95. A ticket from Ada to Homa costs $75.00. Find the difference between the costs of the two tickets.

(8) Train M arrived before Train P. Train G arrived between the arrival times of Train P and Train M. Which train had the earliest arrival?

(9) This freight train has ten cars.

Write the next car in the pattern.

(10) Linda and Jerry flew to visit their aunt and uncle. Linda left on Monday, August 6. Jerry left 6 days earlier. On what day and date did Jerry leave?

VISUAL THINKING

(11) Which two designs are exactly the same?

a.

b.

c.

d.

COLLECTING DATA

Angela and Eric took a survey at their school for a social studies project. They asked the students to name their favorite restaurant at the Maple Mall. They used tally marks (/) to record the data and then made a frequency table. How can they find the total number of people who participated in the survey?

Restaurant	Tallies
Burger World	ꞮꞮꞮꞮ ꞮꞮꞮꞮ
Taco-Ria	ꞮꞮꞮꞮ ꞮꞮꞮꞮ ꞮꞮꞮ
Hot Dog Haven	ꞮꞮꞮꞮ
Julie's Pizza	ꞮꞮꞮꞮ ꞮꞮꞮꞮ ꞮꞮꞮꞮ
Sizzling Subs	ꞮꞮꞮꞮ
Pasta Factory	ꞮꞮꞮ

Tally Table

Choice	Frequency
Burger World	9
Taco-Ria	13
Hot Dog Haven	5
Julie's Pizza	15
Sizzling Subs	5
Pasta Factory	3

Frequency Table

A **frequency table** is a table that shows how often an item occurs.

Use a calculator to find the total number of people surveyed.

$$9 + 13 + 5 + 15 + 5 + 3 = \boxed{50.}$$

So, 50 people were surveyed in all.

Talk About It

▶ What do you need to think about when you plan a survey?

▶ How many votes does each tally mark (/) represent?

▶ How was the data displayed for this project?

Check for Understanding

Answer these questions about the restaurant survey.

1. How do you know what numbers to put in the frequency table?

2. How many more people chose Taco-Ria than Sizzling Subs?

3. Which restaurant is the most popular according to the survey?

4. List the restaurants in order from most popular to least popular.

Idea Bank, page 454, Exercise 5

Practice

Use this tally table to answer Exercises 5–8.

Favorite Fruit Juices	
Juice	Tally
Orange	卌 卌 I
Grape	III
Apple	卌 卌 卌
Pineapple	卌 II

5. Which juice is the most popular?

6. Which juice is the least popular?

7. How many people like apple juice or orange juice?

8. Change the tally table into a frequency table.

Use the frequency table to answer Exercises 9–11.
You may wish to use a calculator.

Stan's Juice Stand	
Day	Bottles Sold
Monday	120
Tuesday	194
Wednesday	239
Thursday	248

9. On which day did Stan sell the most bottles of juice?

10. How many more bottles of juice were sold on Thursday than on Wednesday?

11. How many bottles of juice did Stan sell in all?

Mixed Applications

12. **Organize Data** Take a survey of at least ten people to find their favorite sandwich. Make a frequency table from your tallies.

13. List the sandwiches in order from the most popular to the least popular.

14. How many more people chose the most popular sandwich than the least popular sandwich?

15. **Logical Reasoning** In the checkout line at the fruit stand, Casey was behind Sheila. Lex was in front of Sheila and behind Addie. Casey was between Sheila and Brent. Who was last in line?

16. The mall cafeteria served 918 people on Thursday, 1,293 people on Friday, and 1,412 people on Saturday. How many people did the cafeteria serve during those three days?

How are a tally table and a frequency table alike? How are they different?

WRAP UP...

PICTOGRAPHS

Ricardo is writing a report about video games. He wants to make a pictograph to show the favorite video games at his school. How can he make the pictograph?

First, he can record each vote on a tally table. Then, he can make a frequency table.

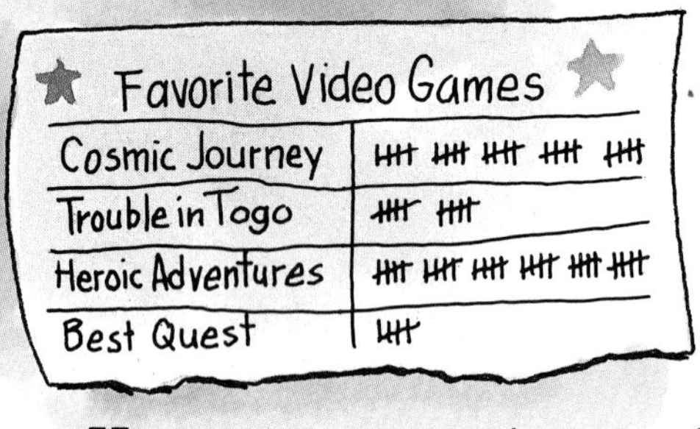

Choice	Frequency
Cosmic Journey	25
Trouble in Togo	10
Heroic Adventures	30
Best Quest	5

A **pictograph** is a graph that uses pictures to show and compare information.

He can create a picture of a video-game character. Each character stands for 5 votes.

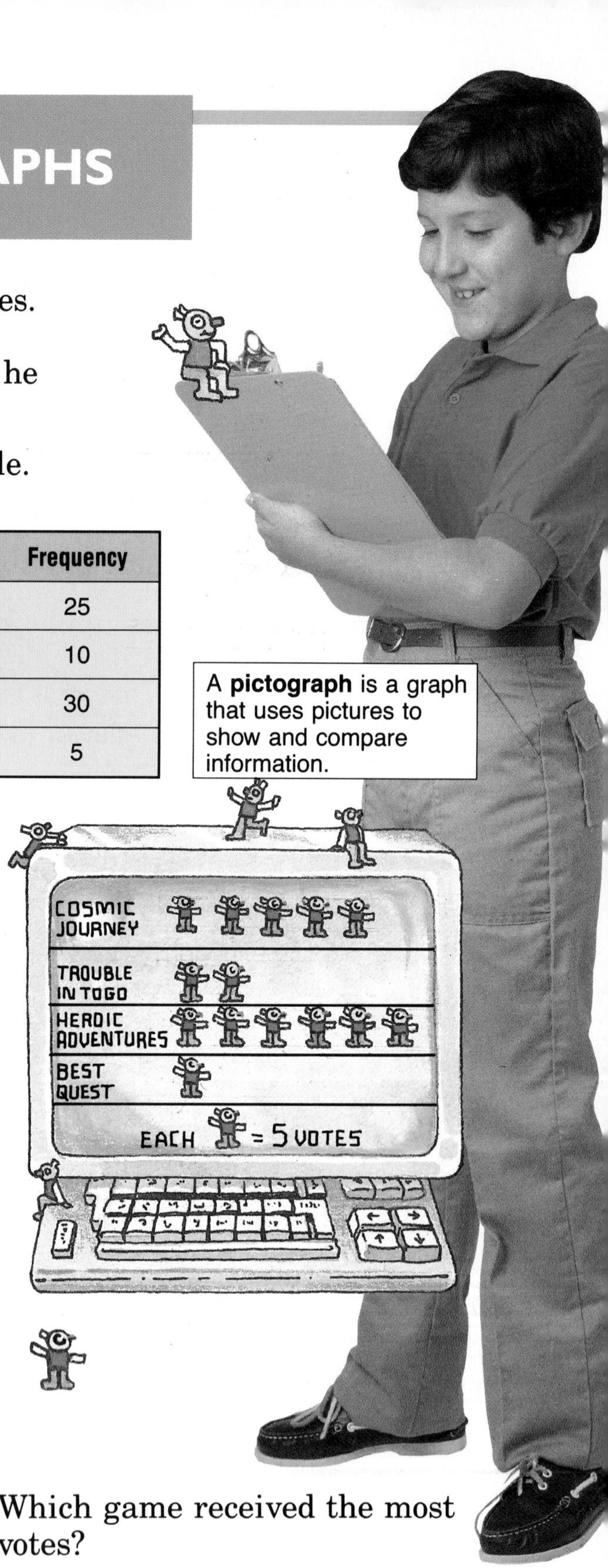

Next, he can draw the correct number of characters to represent the votes.

Talk About It

- ▶ Why is Trouble in Togo represented by two characters?
- ▶ What is a good title for the pictograph?
- ▶ Why is a pictograph a good way to display data?

Check for Understanding

Use the pictograph to answer each question.

1. What is the total number of people represented on the graph?
2. Which game received the most votes?
3. How many more people liked Heroic Adventures than Best Quest?
4. Make a pictograph to show how many boys and how many girls are in your class. Let  stand for two people.

Practice

Use the pictograph to answer Exercises 5–10. You may use a calculator to help you.

Videos Rented in Last Five Months	
July	📹📹📹📹📹📹📹
August	📹📹📹📹📹📹📹📹
September	📹📹📹📹
October	📹📹📹
November	📹📹📹📹📹📹
Key: Each 📹 stands for 50 videos.	

5. In which month were the most videos rented?

6. In which month were the fewest videos rented?

7. In which two months were the same number of videos rented?

8. How many videos were rented in August? September? November?

9. How many more videos were rented in July than in October?

10. Suppose each 📹 stands for 75 videos. How many videos were rented in July? October? November?

Mixed Applications

Use the pictograph to answer Exercises 11–12.

11. How many more compact discs were sold in the first two weeks than in the last two weeks?

12. How many compact discs were sold during the entire month?

Number of CD's Sold in February	
Week 1	♪ ♪ ♪ ♪ ♪ ♪
Week 2	♪ ♪ ♪ ♪
Week 3	♪ ♪ ♪ ♪ ♪
Week 4	♪ ♪
Key: Each ♪ stands for 100 CD's.	

Solve the problem if possible. If you cannot solve, explain why.

13. Beau spent $10.99 on a cassette tape and $16.99 on a compact disc. How much change did he get back?

14. Liz bought a shirt for $18.99, a skirt for $26.99, and a belt for $12.00. She received $2.42 in change. How much did Liz spend?

MIXED REVIEW

Draw an analog clock and a digital clock for each time. Then write the time for each exercise in two other ways.

1. eight twelve

2. one forty-two

3. half past four

4. a quarter to six

What is a disadvantage of a graph compared to a table of data?

WRAP UP...

I can use the data in the table.

Abe's Grill	
Sales for October 8–13	
Sandwich	Number Sold
Chicken	749
Hamburger	936
Hot dog	948
BLT	677

Use the table to answer Exercises 1–3.

1. What was the least popular food sold at Abe's Grill?

2. How many more hamburgers than BLT's did Abe sell?

3. How many hamburgers and hot dogs did Abe sell?

4. On Friday 118 people ate at Abe's Grill. Abe cooked over 75 hamburgers that day. On Saturday 165 people ate at Abe's. How many people ate at Abe's Grill on Friday and Saturday?

5. Harry, Eli, Macy, and Sandy are standing in line at Abe's Grill. Harry is just behind Eli. Macy is between Harry and Sandy. Who is first in line?

Round to the nearest thousand.

6. 3,819   7. 5,211   8. 1,072   9. 6,723   10. 4,338

Compare. Write <, >, or = for ●.

11. 2,076 ● 2,067   12. 42,739 ● 42,397   13. 419,385 ● 418,385

Find the sum or difference.

14. 396
   −187

15. 899
   +475

16. 3,926
   +9,876

17. 4,003
   −1,564

18. 23,994
   − 4,887

19. 45,682
   +68,598

20. 34,896
   −15,924

21. 3,000
   − 543

22. 4,123
   +9,667

23. 17,211
   +85,899

Find the product or quotient.

24. $2 \times 8 =$ ■   25. $6 \times 7 =$ ■   26. $7 \times 8 =$ ■   27. $36 \div 4 =$ ■   28. $63 \div 7 =$ ■

Write the time in two different ways.

29. three forty-five   30. six ten   31. five twenty-two

Analyze and Compare Data

When you solve problems, it is useful to analyze and compare information before you draw conclusions.

Reid's mother sent him to the store to buy 6 bottles of mixed fruit juices. She gave him $5.00 and said he could keep the change from the purchase. Reid noticed that Super Fresh Market sold juice for $0.45 per bottle or $1.99 per carton of 6. At school Reid can buy juice from a machine for $0.50 per bottle.

 **TALK ABOUT IT** Work with a partner and answer the questions below. Use a calculator. Be prepared to discuss your solutions with the class.

a. If Reid bought 6 bottles of juice at school, how much would they cost? How much money could he keep? (**HINT:** Use addition and then subtraction.)

b. Which is cheaper at Super Fresh Market, 6 bottles of juice bought separately or a carton of 6?

c. Which would be Reid's best buy? How much money could Reid keep?

 **APPLY**

Solve. Use a calculator.

1. Which is the better buy, 3 tomatoes for $1.17 or 4 tomatoes for $1.44?

2. Cans of corn are priced at 6 for $2.50 or $0.40 a can. Which is the better buy?

3. You have to travel to work at the mall 5 days a week. You can take the bus to the mall for $1.50 one way or buy a weekly round-trip ticket for $14.00. Which is the better buy?

4. Marie has three choices for her trip. She can fly round-trip for $230. She can travel by train for $116 each way, or she can spend $19 a day to travel 10 days by car. Which trip is least expensive, not including food or lodging?

BAR GRAPHS

Margaret keeps a record of the books she sells in her store. Each month she adds information to her computer files, and then she prints a bar graph to show her employees.

A **bar graph** uses bars of different heights or lengths to show and compare information.

Talk About It

▶ How can you find how many of each kind of book were sold this month?

▶ Which type of book sold the most this month?

▶ How do you read a bar that is halfway between two numbers on the scale?

▶ If the graph's scale is marked off by tens and the data is given in ones (like 57), how can you estimate to draw a bar?

▶ What is a good title for the graph?

▶ How are the vertical and horizontal bar graphs alike? How are they different?

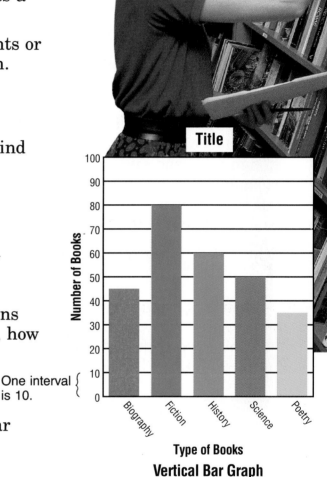

One interval is 10.

Type of Books
Vertical Bar Graph

Check for Understanding

Use the bar graphs to answer each question.

1. How are the bars labeled?

2. How is the scale labeled?

3. How many books in all were sold?

4. How many more fiction than poetry books were sold?

5. Write an example of when to use a bar graph.

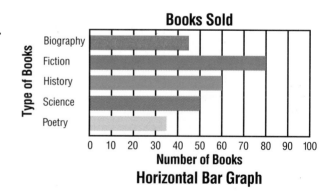

Horizontal Bar Graph

Practice

Use this graph to answer Exercises 6–10.

6. Is this a vertical bar graph or a horizontal bar graph?

7. What do the numbers on the left side of the graph tell?

8. What does each interval of the scale represent?

9. Which clerk had the highest sales?

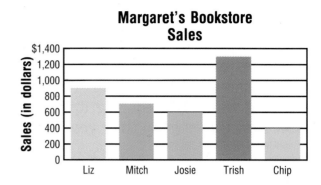

Margaret's Bookstore Sales

10. Which clerks had sales of more than $700?

Mixed Applications

Use the graph above to answer Exercises 11–14.

11. How much more did Liz sell than Chip?

12. Which two clerks together had sales of $1,000?

13. Margaret gave a bonus to the clerks who sold more than $800 worth of books on a Saturday. Who received a bonus?

14. Margaret herself had sales of $1,200 on Saturday. What were the total sales for Saturday?

READING CONNECTION

Sometimes a graph in a magazine or a newspaper is drawn like a picture.

15. What did the artist use instead of bars in this graph?

16. Which two kinds of graphs are similar to this graph?

17. In which city do the residents spend the most on books?

18. In which city is more spent on books than in Boston but less than in Madison, Wisconsin?

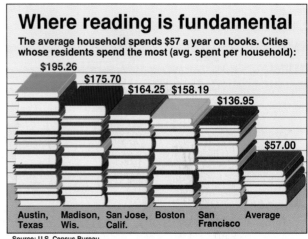

Where reading is fundamental

The average household spends $57 a year on books. Cities whose residents spend the most (avg. spent per household):

$195.26 $175.70 $164.25 $158.19 $136.95 $57.00

Austin, Texas   Madison, Wis.   San Jose, Calif.   Boston   San Francisco   Average

Source: U.S. Census Bureau

When might you use a pictograph instead of a bar graph?

WRAP UP...

EXPLORING

Making a Bar Graph

Mr. Moore's class wrapped gifts at the mall to raise money for a class trip. The number of gifts wrapped was recorded. A graph will be made to show how many gifts they wrapped each day.

Gifts Wrapped	
Day	Number
Monday	20
Tuesday	35
Wednesday	65
Thursday	60
Friday	70
Saturday	75

WORK TOGETHER

Building Understanding

Use graph paper and the information from the table to make a bar graph.

Talk About It

▶ How do you know how many spaces high and how many spaces wide the graph needs to be?

▶ How will you label the bottom of the graph?

▶ How can you label the number scale? Always begin the scale with zero.

▶ What can you use to be sure that the top of each bar is drawn correctly?

▶ What is a good title for your graph?

▶ How can you find the day when the most gifts were wrapped?

Lily kept track of the number of gifts each student wrapped on Wednesday. Make a bar graph using the information from the table.

Talk About It

Should you make a vertical or a horizontal bar graph? Explain.

Gifts Wrapped on Wednesday	
Students	Number Wrapped
Sara	10
T. J.	20
Roland	15
Karen	5
Liane	15

Idea Bank, page 455, Exercises 15–16

Making the Connection

Work in a group to make a bar graph to compare the heights of the group members.

1. Draw a scale marked in inches and feet. The scale will go up from the floor to 6 feet.

2. Place the top of the scale on the chalkboard, and draw a line across the chalkboard at 3 ft, 4 ft, and 5 ft.

3. Write three questions that you can ask about your graph.

4. Each group should take a turn as bars on a graph while other students record the heights and answer the questions.

Checking Understanding

The table shows where Mr. Moore's students wanted to go for their class trip. Use the frequency table for Exercises 5–8.

Possible Trips	Votes
Planetarium	12
Railroad museum	5
Children's theater	8
Newspaper plant	4

5. Analyze the results and make a bar graph.

6. Where did most of the students want to go?

7. How many students did not choose the planetarium as their first choice?

8. Suppose three students who wanted to go to the children's theater decided on the planetarium later. How would this change the graph?

9. **Find Data** Take a survey to find where your classmates would like to go on a "dream vacation." Make a bar graph of the information.

MIXED REVIEW

Find the missing number.

1. $7 \times 8 = $ ■

2. $8 \times $ ■ $ = 64$

3. ■ $\times 6 = 36$

4. $7 \times 6 = $ ■

5. $45 \div 9 = $ ■

6. $63 \div $ ■ $ = 7$

7. ■ $\div 7 = 8$

8. $48 \div $ ■ $ = 8$

GRAPHING
Points on a Grid

A sign at the mall is like a map. It shows the locations of the stores.

You can use a pair of numbers, or an **ordered pair,** to find a point on a grid.

Find the Movie Theater at the point represented by the ordered pair (1,3).

a. Always start at 0.
b. First, move 1 space to the *right*.
c. Then, move 3 spaces *up*.

Find the Neat Jeans store on the map.

Talk About It

▶ Where do you start?

▶ How many spaces do you move to the right?

▶ How many spaces do you move up?

▶ What is the ordered pair for the Neat Jeans store?

▶ Find (1,7) on the grid. Why is it a different location than (7,1)?

Check for Understanding

Mall Directory

Use the map of the mall to write the name of the location for each ordered pair.

1. (2,5)   2. (7,3)   3. (5,2)   4. (1,9)

Use the map of the mall to write the ordered pair for each store.

5. Pet Shop   6. Clothes Horse   7. Shoe Shop   8. Snack Shop

Practice

Use the map of Flower Valley Mall to write the ordered pair for each store.

9. Valley Pharmacy

10. Mall Card Shop

11. Henri's Deli

12. Nature's Supply

13. Flowers by Jill

Name the store that is found at each point.

14. (3,8)   15. (15,1)   16. (5,2)   17. (4,4)   18. (3,0)

Mixed Applications

19. Make a grid like the one above. Assign each letter of the alphabet a point on the grid. Then write the ordered pair for each letter of your first and last name. Connect the points.

20. **Make Up a Problem**   Write a question whose answer is one word. Then write the ordered pairs from Exercise 19 for the letters in the word. Exchange with a partner and solve.

Henri's Deli Work Schedule		
	Friday	Saturday
9:30–1:30	Lynn	Henri
12:30–6:30	Katy	Dee
9:30–4:30	Dee	Katy
4:30–9:30	Henri	Lynn

Use the table for Exercises 21–23.

21. How many hours did Katy work in all?

22. Which two people worked the most hours?

23. If employees are paid $5.00 per hour, how much will each one earn on both days?

ART CONNECTION

Graph these points and letters for each ordered pair. Start at *A* and connect the points in alphabetical order. Name the figure.

24. $C(7,7)$ 25. $H(5,3)$ 26. $K(4,7)$ 27. $B(8,7)$ 28. $G(5,1)$ 29. $J(5,7)$

30. $A(6,10)$ 31. $I(2,3)$ 32. $F(7,1)$ 33. $E(7,3)$ 34. $D(10,3)$

What is the difference in the location of the points (2,5) and (5,2)?

WRAP
UP...

LINE GRAPHS

Mr. Diaz keeps track of the monthly income at his pet store so he can see at a glance how it changes each year. Have the pet store's earnings increased or decreased from January, 1991 to December, 1991?

Find the income for January. Follow the line from month to month, checking to see where each point lines up on the earnings scale.

The pet store's income increased from January, 1991 to December, 1991.

Pet Store Income for 1991

A **line graph** shows changes over a period of time.

Talk About It

▶ How much was the pet store's income in January?

▶ How much was the pet store's income in December?

▶ During which two months was the pet store's income $4,000?

▶ Estimate the income for the month of February.

▶ How is a line graph different from a bar graph?

Check for Understanding

Use this line graph to answer Exercises 1–4.

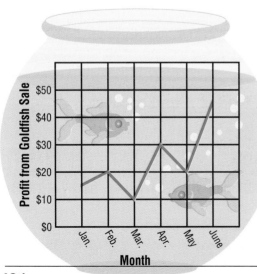

1. In which month was the profit from the sale of goldfish the least? the greatest?

2. About how much was the profit from the sale of goldfish in January?

3. Between which two months was the greatest increase in profit?

4. What is a good title for this graph?

Practice

Use the graph to answer Exercises 5–6.

Pet Kitchen Sales

5. During which two months were the sales about the same?

6. Between which two months was the greatest increase in sales? the greatest decrease?

Mixed Applications

Use the graph above to answer Exercises 7–10.

7. In which three months were the sales less than $5,000?

8. Find the total sales for all six months shown on the graph.

9. In December Pet Kitchen set a goal to increase sales by $2,000 each month. Predict what sales will be for next July.

10. Order the months according to sales, starting with the month that had the greatest sales.

11. Last year Mr. Diaz sold 454 dog collars. This year he sold 600 collars. How many more collars did he sell this year?

12. Mr. Diaz walks to work. He walks 1 block south, 3 blocks west, and then 2 blocks south. How many blocks does he walk to work?

ANALYZE DATA

Sometimes data about two different items is displayed on a double-line graph.

13. How much more dog food than cat food was sold in 1987?

14. How much more dog food than cat food was projected to sell in 1992?

15. In what year do you predict that cat food will catch up with dog food?

16. When should a double-line graph be used instead of a single-line graph?

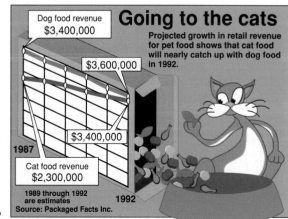

Dog food revenue $3,400,000

Going to the cats

Projected growth in retail revenue for pet food shows that cat food will nearly catch up with dog food in 1992.

$3,600,000

$3,400,000

1987

Cat food revenue $2,300,000

1989 through 1992 are estimates
Source: Packaged Facts Inc.

1992

How does knowing how to find points on a grid help you make a line graph?

WRAP UP...

Day	Temperature
Sunday	24°
Monday	27°
Tuesday	30°
Wednesday	41°
Thursday	42°
Friday	32°
Saturday	36°

The outside temperature at the mall skating rink must stay below 40°F for the rink to be open. The highest daily temperatures for one week in December are recorded in this table. Make a line graph to show how the temperature changed.

WORK TOGETHER

Building Understanding

Talk About It

▶ How do you know how many spaces high and how many spaces wide the graph needs to be?

▶ How will you label the bottom of the graph?

▶ Why does a scale sometimes increase by twos, fives, or tens?

▶ What do the broken lines mean?

▶ How can you connect the points on the graph?

▶ What is a good title for the graph?

▶ On which days was the rink closed?

Use graph paper and the information from the table to make a line graph.

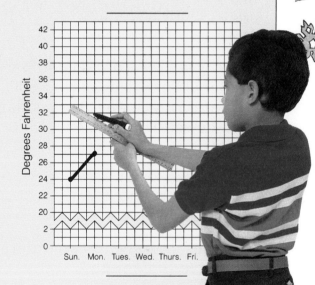

Michelle kept track of the average temperature each week at the rink during the months of December and January. Work in a group to make a line graph using the information from the table. Write three questions about your graph that you can ask classmates to answer.

Week	Temperature
1	43°
2	40°
3	38°
4	32°
5	40°
6	30°
7	28°
8	27°

Making the Connection

1. Kit's mother has kept a record of Kit's height each school year, beginning with kindergarten. Copy and complete the line graph. Use the table to help you. Why was a line graph a good choice?

Kit's Height

Grade in School	Height
Kindergarten	46
First	48
Second	51
Third	54
Fourth	59

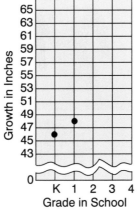

Growth in Inches

65 63 61 59 57 55 53 51 49 47 45 43 0

K 1 2 3 4
Grade in School

Checking Understanding

You can use a line graph to display data about your health. This table shows a record of pulse rates after exercising.

Use the data to make a line graph.

2.

Rest time in minutes	0	1	2	3	4	5	6	7	8	9	10
Pulse rate per minute	130	110	100	90	85	80	75	72	70	70	70

Solve.

3. **Analyze Data** Jess recorded temperatures as she hiked at camp. Write two sentences to describe what this graph tells about her hike.

Temperature Changes On My Hike

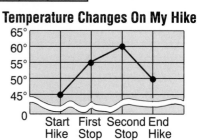

65° 60° 55° 50° 45° 0

Start First Second End
Hike Stop Stop Hike

VISUAL THINKING

4. Complete the pattern. Draw the design that goes in the last box.

PROBLEM *Solving*

Analyze Data to Make Decisions

Rick's father owns a toy store in the mall. He wants to compare the profits from sales of action figures over the last six months. Rick wants to make a graph to help his father. What kind of graph should he make?

Sometimes analyzing data can help you make a decision.

▶ **UNDERSTAND**

What are you asked to find?

What facts are given?

▶ **PLAN**

What decision has to be made?

You must decide which type of graph will best display the data. Think about the advantages and disadvantages of each type of graph.

Action Figures Sold

MONTH	PROFIT
May	$150
June	$225
July	$250
August	$375
September	$450
October	$500

Type of Graph	Description	Advantages and Disadvantages
Pictograph	Uses pictures to show and compare data	Makes an attractive display; cannot show exact data clearly
Bar graph	Uses bars to show and compare data	Bars can show closer estimates of data than pictographs.
Line graph	Shows changes over time	Shows data as it changes over time

▶ **SOLVE**

How can you solve the problem?

Now you can analyze the data to make your decision. A pictograph or bar graph would show and compare the data but a line graph is best for showing a change over time. Rick should make a line graph because he needs to show a change over time.

Action Figure Profits

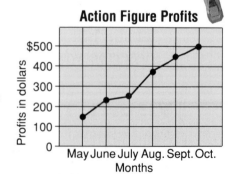

▶ **LOOK BACK**

How can you check whether you made the right decision?

WHAT IF... ... Rick had drawn a pictograph and each symbol stood for $50 profit from action figures? How many symbols would he draw for the month of October?

138

Apply

Make a different type of graph for each situation.

(1) Beth, Alex, and Arnold have saved money to buy kite-building kits. Beth has saved the most money. Create the data and graph their savings.

(2) Paul earned $40 during the first week. His earnings increased by $15 each week over the next six weeks. Make a graph of his earnings.

Mixed Applications → **STRATEGIES** • Find a Pattern • Use a Table • Analyze Data to Make Decisions • Use a Graph

Use the graph to answer Exercises 3–6.

(3) Which kind of graph is shown?

(4) How many hours did Glen work?

(5) How many hours did Mr. and Mrs. Sims work altogether?

(6) How many more hours did Mr. Sims work than Quinn?

Sims's Toy Store	
	Hours Worked
Quinn	★ ★ ★
Mr. Sims	★ ★ ★ ★ ★ ★ ★ ★ ★
Shirley	★ ★
Mrs. Sims	★ ★ ★ ★ ★ ★
Glen	★ ★ ★ ★ ★ ★ ★
Key: Each ★ stands for 20 hours.	

Use the table to answer Exercises 7–8.

(7) Ava buys a birthday card for $0.89. How much tax does she pay?

(8) If Ava buys a yo-yo for $0.76 and a mini-puzzle for $0.33, how much will she pay including tax?

Tax Table	
Amount of Purchase	**Tax**
$0.01–0.10	$0.01
0.11–0.27	0.02
0.28–0.47	0.03
0.48–0.68	0.04
0.69–0.89	0.05
0.90–1.09	0.06

(9) Jasmine wants to buy a set of paints that costs $14.79. She saves $0.25 the first week. She plans to double the amount she saves each week until she has saved enough. When will she have enough money?

WRITER'S CORNER

(10) Write three problems, one for each type of graph you have studied. Exchange problems with another group. Make the appropriate graph for each problem. Discuss which graph is easiest to understand and which was easiest to make.

Vocabulary Check

Choose a word or words from the box to complete each sentence.

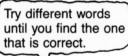

A.M.
bar graph
digital
frequency table
line graph
ordered pair
pictograph
P.M.

Try different words until you find the one that is correct.

1. The two kinds of clocks are analog and __?__. *(page 110)*

2. __?__ means the time between noon and midnight. *(page 112)*

3. A __?__ uses pictures to show and compare information. *(page 124)*

4. You can use an __?__ to find a point on a grid. *(page 132)*

5. A __?__ shows how something changes over a period of time. *(page 134)*

6. A __?__ uses bars of different heights or lengths to show and compare information. *(page 128)*

7. A __?__ shows how often items occur. *(page 122)*

8. __?__ means the time between midnight and noon. *(page 112)*

Concept Check

Write the time by using numbers and A.M. or P.M. *(page 112)*

9. Mrs. Holt went on her morning walk at seven twenty-five.

10. Brad finished lunch at twelve eighteen.

11. The last train of the day left at five minutes after ten.

Make a frequency table from the tally table below. *(page 122)*

12.

Favorite Color	Number of Votes
Blue	ⅢⅢ /
Green	///
Orange	//
Purple	ⅢⅢ /
Red	ⅢⅢ

Use the grid to write the ordered pair for each letter. *(page 132)*

13. *A*   14. *B*   15. *C*   16. *W*   17. *Y*

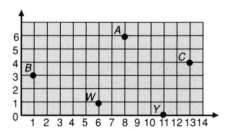

Skill Check

Write the time in two different ways. *(page 110)*

18.

19.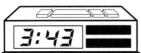

20.

Tell how much time has elapsed. *(page 116)*

21.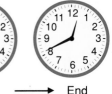

Begin ⟶ End

22.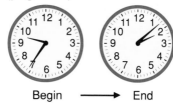

Begin ⟶ End

23.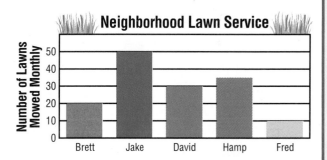

Begin ⟶ End

Use the graph to answer Exercises 24–27. *(page 128)*

24. How many people work with the neighborhood lawn service?

25. How many lawns does Fred mow?

26. Who mows 35 lawns?

27. Who mows the most lawns?

Problem-Solving Check

Use the schedule to answer Exercises 28–29. *(page 120)*

28. On which days are no classes scheduled to go to the library?

29. How many times does each class go to the library each week?

Library Schedule				
	Mon.	**Tues.**	**Wed.**	**Thurs.**
9–10 A.M.	4 A	3 A	4 A	3 A
10–11 A.M.	4 B	3 B	4 B	3 B
1–2 P.M.	4 C	3 C	4 C	3 C
2–3 P.M.	4 D	3 D	4 D	3 D

Analyze each situation. Make an appropriate graph for each.
(page 138)

30. Mel, Faye, and Harvey collect stamps. Mel has 200 stamps, Faye has 150 stamps, and Harvey has 75 stamps. Graph the number of stamps in their collections.

31. The monthly rainfall in Harbor City was 12 inches in April, 8 inches in May, and 15 inches in June. Graph the amount of rainfall for each month to show any increase or decrease.

Write the time by using numbers and A.M. or P.M.

1. Mason eats dinner at seven ten.

2. Shelby arrives at school at eight fifteen.

3. Al goes to bed at nine forty-five.

Choose the best estimate for each.

4. the time it takes to brush your teeth
  a. 3 seconds
  b. 3 minutes
  c. 3 hours

5. the time it usually takes to watch a movie
  a. 2 hours
  b. 20 days
  c. 20 minutes

6. the time it takes to write your name
  a. 3 seconds
  b. 3 minutes
  c. 3 hours

Tell how much time has elapsed.

7.

Starting Time   Ending Time

8.

Starting Time   Ending Time

Count the hours, and then the minutes.

9. Use this information to make a tally table and a frequency table. Lou surveyed the number of student absences each month for three months: September, 15; October, 35; November, 20.

10. Make a bar graph using the information in Exercise 9.

11. Make a line graph using the information in the table.

Use the grid to write the ordered pair for each letter.

12. *K* **13.** *J* **14.** *M* **15.** *R*

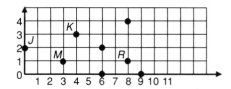

Day of the Week	M	Tu	W	Th	F
High Temperature	86° F	84° F	90° F	88° F	85° F

Use the table for Exercises 16–18.

16. How many hours does Wilson work on Saturday?

17. How many hours does Lynn work on Friday and Saturday?

18. On Friday, how many more hours does Saundra work than Lynn?

Weekend Work Schedule for Super Salads		
Employee	**Hours Worked**	
	Friday	**Saturday**
Lynn	2 P.M.–9 P.M.	9 A.M.–6 P.M.
Saundra	9 A.M.–6 P.M.	4 P.M.–9 P.M.
Mr. Phipps	9 A.M.–9 P.M.	9 A.M.–2 P.M.
Wilson	12 Noon–9 P.M.	2 P.M.–9 P.M.

Where Do You Shop?

Shoppers flock to malls to make purchases of all types. With your teammates, find out in which kinds of stores fourth graders are most likely to shop.

Decide

Work with your teammates. Talk about how you can use a graph to organize and display your data.

- Who will you survey?

- Where will you conduct the survey?

- How many students will you survey?

Do

- List five categories of stores, such as sporting goods, toy, department, clothing, and food. Make a tally table for the five categories.

- Survey as many people as you can. Ask them to choose the kind of store in which they are most likely to shop. Record responses with tally marks.

- Show the results in a bar graph.

Share

Present your graph to the other teams. Ask three questions about your graph, and have volunteers answer them.

Talk About It

- How can you use your graph to predict which kind of store will sell the most items? the fewest items?

- In your everyday activities, what other data have you seen presented in bar graphs?

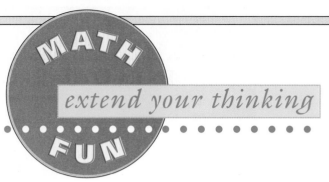

Activity

Pictures from Ordered Pairs

A. You can draw a picture by graphing these ordered pairs.

A (1,6)	G (9,9)	M (6,0)
B (4,7)	H (8,7)	N (5,4)
C (3,9)	I (11,6)	O (3,3)
D (5,8)	J (8,5)	P (4,5)
E (6,12)	K (9,3)	
F (7,8)	L (7,4)	

B. Follow these steps to draw the picture on a grid.

Step 1 Number a grid 12 by 12.

Step 2 Locate a point for each ordered pair. Place the point on the grid, and label it with its letter.

Step 3 Connect the dots in alphabetical order returning to A.

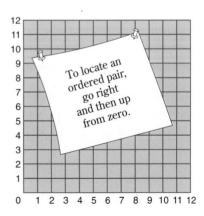

To locate an ordered pair, go right and then up from zero.

What did you draw?

Challenge

Logical Reasoning

Beth went to the pet store to buy a puppy. Guess which puppy she chose. Use the clues to help you.

1. The white puppy is in the first place.
2. The black puppy is next to the brown puppy.
3. The brown puppy is in the middle.
4. The gray puppy is next to the white one.
5. The spotted puppy is at the end.
6. Beth's puppy is in the fourth place.

Everyday Math

Enlarge this picture of a house. Multiply each number in the ordered pairs by 2. Then graph and connect the new points. You will need a 12-by-12 grid.

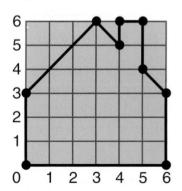

CUMULATIVE REVIEW

CHAPTERS 1–4

Write the letter of the correct answer.

1. Which number is another name for 25 hundreds?

   A. 250 B. 2,500
   C. 25,000 D. 250,000

2. Which number is 100,000 greater than 1,653,296?

   A. 1,653,396 B. 1,753,296
   C. 2,653,296 D. 2,753,296

3. 5,000 − 823 = ■

   A. 4,177 B. 4,187
   C. 4,287 D. 4,298

4. 22 + 19 + 48 + 96 = ■

   A. 185 B. 187
   C. 190 D. 195

5. 6 × ■ = 30

   A. 5 B. 6
   C. 7 D. 8

6. ■ × 5 = 45

   A. 7 B. 8
   C. 9 D. 10

7. 5 × 7 = 7 × 5 is an example of which property of multiplication?

   A. Grouping B. Zero
   C. Order D. not here

8. Tell how much time has elapsed.

   A. 13 minutes B. 18 minutes
   C. 25 minutes D. 28 minutes

9. Which person received the most votes?

Name	Number of Votes
Angie	ⵊⵊⵊ ⵊⵊⵊ ////
Beth	ⵊⵊⵊ ⵊⵊⵊ ⵊⵊⵊ
Carl	ⵊⵊⵊ ⵊⵊⵊ //

   A. Angie B. Beth
   C. Carl D. Ann

10. For which day is the highest temperature recorded?

    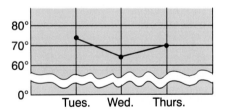

    A. Tuesday B. Wednesday
    C. Thursday D. not here

11. Evie read 3 books each week for 8 weeks. How many books did she read in all?

    A. 5 books B. 11 books
    C. 24 books D. 26 books

12. James bought 4 boxes of pencils with 8 pencils in each box. He also bought 3 boxes of markers with 10 markers in each box. How many pencils did he buy?

    A. 24 pencils B. 25 pencils
    C. 30 pencils D. 32 pencils

5

MULTIPLYING
BY 1-DIGIT NUMBERS

Did you know . . .

. . . that an animated film is made up of thousands of still pictures? One movement is really 24 pictures flashing across the screen in one second.

Ana is making her own cartoon. How can Ana find out how many still pictures she needs to draw for her cartoon to last 5 seconds?

EXPLORING
Patterns in Multiplication

Counting by tens to 100 names **multiples** of 10.
Name some multiples of 100 and 1,000.
In this lesson you will be looking for patterns with
multiples of 10, 100, and 1,000.

WORK TOGETHER

Building Understanding

Use place-value blocks to model
each problem. Then find the
product.

a. $3 \times 2 = \blacksquare$ **b.** $3 \times 20 = \blacksquare$

c. $3 \times 200 = \blacksquare$ **d.** $3 \times 2,000 = \blacksquare$

Look for a pattern in each group
of problems. Use mental math to
find the products.

a. $4 \times 6 = \blacksquare$ **b.** $5 \times 8 = \blacksquare$
$4 \times 60 = \blacksquare$ $5 \times 80 = \blacksquare$
$4 \times 600 = \blacksquare$ $5 \times 800 = \blacksquare$
$4 \times 6,000 = \blacksquare$ $5 \times 8,000 = \blacksquare$

Talk About It

▶ Which place-value
blocks did you use to
model these problems?

▶ How are these problems alike?
How are they different?

▶ What pattern do you see in the
factors?

▶ Tell how you can use a basic fact to
find the product of $7 \times 9,000$.

Talk About It

▶ What pattern
do you see in the
products?

▶ What difference do you see
between the patterns in **a**
and **b**?

▶ Why are there more zeros
in the products in
pattern **b**?

148

Making the Connection

Look for patterns in multiplication.

Example

	Place Value	
2×4	$= 2 \times 4$ ones	$\rightarrow$
2×40	$= 2 \times 4$ tens	$\rightarrow$
2×400	$= 2 \times 4$ hundreds	$\rightarrow$
$2 \times 4,000$	$= 2 \times 4$ thousands	$\rightarrow$

Place-Value Chart			
Thousands	**Hundreds**	**Tens**	**Ones**
			8
		8	0
	8	0	0
8	0	0	0

The same basic fact helps me find the products.

Rewrite the problem like the example. Then record the product on a place-value chart like the one above.

1. 3×6
   3×60
   3×600
   $3 \times 6,000$

2. 6×5
   6×50
   6×500
   $6 \times 5,000$

3. 7×4
   7×40
   7×400
   $7 \times 4,000$

4. 8×8
   8×80
   8×800
   $8 \times 8,000$

5. Why are the zeros needed on the chart? What is the least number of zeros in a multiple of thousands? of hundreds? of tens?

6. How is the pattern of zeros in the products of Exercise 1 different from the pattern in the products of Exercise 2?

Checking Understanding

Complete each pattern.

7. $3 \times 5 = \blacksquare$
   $3 \times \blacksquare = 150$
   $\blacksquare \times 500 = 1,500$
   $3 \times \blacksquare = 15,000$

8. $3 \times 7 = \blacksquare$
   $\blacksquare \times 70 = 210$
   $3 \times \blacksquare = 2,100$
   $3 \times 7,000 = \blacksquare$

9. $5 \times 2 = \blacksquare$
   $5 \times \blacksquare = 100$
   $5 \times 200 = \blacksquare$
   $\blacksquare \times 2,000 = 10,000$

Find the product. Then, continue each pattern multiplying the multiples of 10, 100, and 1,000.

10. $7 \times 8 = \blacksquare$

11. $5 \times 4 = \blacksquare$

12. $4 \times 3 = \blacksquare$

13. $8 \times 5 = \blacksquare$

The All-Star softball team practices 3 hours a week. The season lasts 16 weeks. About how many hours does the team practice during the entire season?

Three different team members estimated the product.

Rachel estimated $3 \times 10 = 30$ hours.

Ashley estimated $3 \times 20 = 60$ hours.

Merita estimated $3 \times 15 = 45$ hours.

Talk About It

▶ How did Rachel calculate her estimate?

▶ How did Ashley calculate her estimate?

▶ How did Merita calculate her estimate?

▶ Compare the three estimation strategies. Which strategy would you choose? Explain your choice.

More Examples

A.
$$\begin{array}{r} 162 \rightarrow \\ \times\ \ 4 \\ \hline \end{array} \qquad \begin{array}{r} 200 \\ \times\ \ 4 \\ \hline 800 \end{array}$$

B.
$$\begin{array}{r} 374 \rightarrow \\ \times\ \ 6 \\ \hline \end{array} \qquad \begin{array}{r} 300 \\ \times\ \ 6 \\ \hline 1{,}800 \end{array}$$

C.
$$\begin{array}{r} 2{,}738 \rightarrow \\ \times\ \ 8 \\ \hline \end{array} \qquad \begin{array}{r} 3000 \\ \times\ \ 8 \\ \hline 24{,}000 \end{array}$$

• Which strategies were used in Examples A, B, and C?

Check for Understanding

1. What is the greatest place-value position of 45, 607, and 4,598?

2. How can you estimate $7 \times 2{,}965$? Name the strategy that you used.

Estimate the product. Name the strategy that you used.

3. $8 \times 49 = $ ■
4. $6 \times 125 = $ ■
5. $4 \times 319 = $ ■
6. $5 \times 2{,}734 = $ ■

Practice

Estimate the product. Name the strategy that you used.

7. $7 \times 613 = \blacksquare$ **8.** $6 \times 2{,}174 = \blacksquare$ **9.** $4 \times 68 = \blacksquare$ **10.** $5 \times 485 = \blacksquare$

11. $3 \times 5{,}752 = \blacksquare$ **12.** $9 \times 32 = \blacksquare$ **13.** $8 \times 409 = \blacksquare$ **14.** $9 \times 187 = \blacksquare$

Estimate the product.

15. 32
    $\times\ 4$

16. 248
    $\times\ \ \ 3$

17. 79
    $\times\ 5$

18. 361
    $\times\ \ \ 6$

19. 1,935
    $\times\ \ \ \ \ 5$

20. 549
    $\times\ \ \ 4$

21. 2,805
    $\times\ \ \ \ \ 7$

22. 659
    $\times\ \ \ 9$

23. 82
    $\times\ 7$

24. 8,652
    $\times\ \ \ \ \ 3$

25. 3,148
    $\times\ \ \ \ \ 2$

26. 53
    $\times\ 9$

27. 4,018
    $\times\ \ \ \ \ 8$

28. 935
    $\times\ \ \ 4$

29. 172
    $\times\ \ \ 5$

Mixed Applications

30. There are 7 teams in the play-offs. If each team has 18 players, about how many players are there?

31. The softball teams need $2,000 to buy new uniforms. In one month they raised $732. If they continue earning money at the same rate, about how many more months will it be before they have enough money?

32. Logical Reasoning   There were 1,000 tickets for the play-offs. Team A used 312 of them, Team B used 298, and Team C used 304. How can you use multiplication to estimate the total number of tickets used?

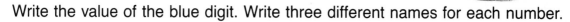

MIXED REVIEW

Write the value of the blue digit. Write three different names for each number.

1. 600   **2.** 1,800   **3.** 2,040   **4.** 5,700   **5.** 490,000

6. 370   **7.** 4,250   **8.** 9,000   **9.** 73,000   **10.** 6,200,000

How do you estimate products?

WRAP UP...

EXPLORING

Multiplication

I can use money or place-value blocks to model a multiplication problem.

Dwight is learning to play a trumpet.
His family pays $12 a month to rent the trumpet.
How much will they pay for the first 6 months' rent?

WORK TOGETHER

Building Understanding

Use ten-dollar and one-dollar bills to model the problem. Then show the product on a place-value mat.

$$6 \times 12 = \blacksquare$$

months   dollars a month

Talk About It

▶ How is the product found using the dollar bills?

▶ How many one-dollar bills were combined?

▶ How can you regroup the one-dollar bills?

▶ How many ten-dollar bills were combined?

▶ What is done with the regrouped ten?

▶ How much will Dwight's family pay to rent the trumpet?

▶ How is using place-value blocks like using money?

Use place-value blocks to find each product. Show the product on a place-value mat. Have a member of your group record how each product is found.

a. $3 \times 312 = \blacksquare$ **b.** $4 \times 26 = \blacksquare$ **c.** $2 \times 263 = \blacksquare$

Making the Connection

Compare these two methods.

Find the product of 3 × 146 using place-value blocks on a place-value mat.

Hundreds	Tens	Ones

Talk About It

▶ How is the place-value mat helpful?

▶ How many ones are there? What regrouping must be done?

▶ How many tens are there? What regrouping must be done?

You can compute 3 × 146 by finding **partial products.** The product is the sum of the partial products.

Think: 146 = 100 + 40 + 6

	Hundreds	Tens	Ones
	1	4	6
×			3
3 × 6 ⟶		1	8
partial products 3 × 40 ⟶	1	2	0
3 × 100 ⟶	3	0	0

1. What is the product of 3 × 146?

2. What are partial products?

3. How are these two methods alike? How are they different?

Checking Understanding

Find each product using place-value blocks on a mat and the partial product method.

4.
H	T	O
2	6	5
×		3

5.
T	O
2	7
×	3

6.
H	T	O
3	8	2
×		2

7.
T	O
2	9
×	3

8.
H	T	O
1	3	2
×		6

MULTIPLYING
Two-Digit Numbers

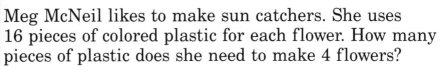

Meg McNeil likes to make sun catchers. She uses 16 pieces of colored plastic for each flower. How many pieces of plastic does she need to make 4 flowers?

Estimate. Front-end: $4 \times 10 = 40$

Rounding: $4 \times 20 = 80$

Use place-value blocks to model 4×16. Then compare what you did with this method.

Step 1	**Step 2**	**Step 3**
Multiply the ones. 4×6 ones $= 24$ ones	Regroup 24 ones as 2 tens 4 ones. Record the 2 tens above the 1 ten.	Multiply the tens. Then add the regrouped tens. 4 tens $+ 2$ tens $= 6$ tens
$\begin{array}{r} 16 \\ \times\ 4 \\ \hline \end{array}$	$\begin{array}{r} 2 \\ 16 \\ \times\ 4 \\ \hline 4 \end{array}$	$\begin{array}{r} 2 \\ 16 \\ \times\ 4 \\ \hline 64 \end{array}$

So, Meg needs 64 pieces of plastic. Since 64 is between 40 and 80, the answer is reasonable.

Talk About It

▶ Compare the method at the right with the shorter method shown above. Explain how the methods differ.

▶ Explain why the 40 is not shown in the problem above.

T	O
1	6
×	4
2	4
4	0
6	4

Check for Understanding

Estimate the product.

1. $2 \times 34 = $ **2.** $3 \times 26 = $ **3.** $2 \times 37 = $ **4.** $4 \times 59 = $

Find the product. Write *yes* if there was regrouping in the exercise.

5. $3 \times 12 = $ **6.** $6 \times 23 = $ **7.** $3 \times 28 = $ **8.** $5 \times 34 = $

9. $\begin{array}{r} 18 \\ \times\ 4 \\ \hline \end{array}$ **10.** $\begin{array}{r} 23 \\ \times\ 3 \\ \hline \end{array}$ **11.** $\begin{array}{r} 34 \\ \times\ 6 \\ \hline \end{array}$ **12.** $\begin{array}{r} 32 \\ \times\ 4 \\ \hline \end{array}$ **13.** $\begin{array}{r} 43 \\ \times\ 7 \\ \hline \end{array}$ **14.** $\begin{array}{r} 52 \\ \times\ 8 \\ \hline \end{array}$

Practice

Estimate the product.

15. 27 × 5	**16.** 45 × 2	**17.** 54 × 4	**18.** 28 × 3	**19.** 29 × 5

Find the product.

20. 79 × 4	**21.** 39 × 8	**22.** 92 × 7	**23.** 56 × 9	**24.** 33 × 7

25. 28 × 5	**26.** 62 × 7	**27.** 37 × 4	**28.** 52 × 6	**29.** 43 × 8

30. $3 \times 72 =$ ■   **31.** $6 \times 35 =$ ■   **32.** $4 \times 59 =$ ■   **33.** $7 \times 64 =$ ■

34. $5 \times 48 =$ ■   **35.** $3 \times 86 =$ ■   **36.** $6 \times 17 =$ ■   **37.** $9 \times 56 =$ ■

Mixed Applications

38. Maria uses a silk screen to print T-shirts. There are 12 T-shirts in each box. How many T-shirts will she print to make 9 boxes?

39. Leon sold 27 pieces of pottery. Pete sold twice as many as Leon. How many pieces of pottery did Pete sell?

Use the pictograph for Exercises 40–42.

40. How many more sun catchers than pieces of pottery were sold?

41. What is the total number of puppets and T-shirts sold?

42. **Making Decisions** If you owned the crafts store, which kind of craft would you order in the largest quantity?

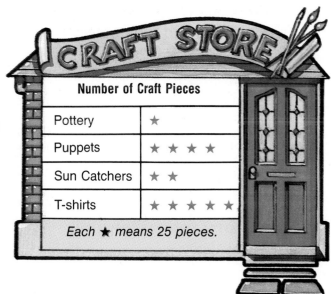

Number of Craft Pieces	
Pottery	★
Puppets	★ ★ ★ ★
Sun Catchers	★ ★
T-shirts	★ ★ ★ ★ ★
Each ★ means 25 pieces.	

After you multiply 7 × 4 in 34 × 7, what do you do with the regrouped tens?

WRAP UP...

MULTIPLYING
Three-Digit Numbers

The hobby club had an art show. Each of the 214 members entered 3 pieces. How many pieces were entered in the art show?

Estimate. $3 \times 200 = 600$
Multiply. $3 \times 214 = $ ■

Step 1	**Step 2**	**Step 3**
Multiply the ones.	Multiply the tens.	Multiply the hundreds.
3×4 ones $= 12$ ones	3×1 ten $= 3$ tens	3×2 hundreds $= 6$ hundreds
Regroup 12 ones as 1 ten 2 ones.	3 tens + 1 ten = 4 tens	
$\begin{array}{r} 1 \\ 214 \\ \times\ \ 3 \\ \hline 2 \end{array}$ 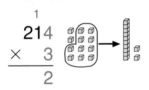	$\begin{array}{r} 1 \\ 214 \\ \times\ \ 3 \\ \hline 42 \end{array}$ and	$\begin{array}{r} 1 \\ 214 \\ \times\ \ 3 \\ \hline 642 \end{array}$ 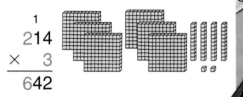

So, 642 pieces were entered in the art show.

Talk About It

▶ Is your answer reasonable? How do you know?

▶ In what order do you multiply the digits?

▶ Why is the regrouped ten added after you multiply the digit in the tens place?

More Examples

A. $\begin{array}{r} 1 \\ 264 \\ \times\ \ 2 \\ \hline 528 \end{array}$ Regroup 12 tens as 1 hundred 2 tens.

B. $\begin{array}{r} 1 \\ 240 \\ \times\ \ 4 \\ \hline 960 \end{array}$ Regroup 16 tens as 1 hundred 6 tens.

C. $\begin{array}{r} 2\ 1 \\ 143 \\ \times\ \ 5 \\ \hline 715 \end{array}$ Regroup 15 ones as 1 ten 5 ones.
Regroup 21 tens as 2 hundreds 1 ten.

Check for Understanding

Find the product.

1. $\begin{array}{r} 230 \\ \times\ \ 3 \end{array}$

2. $\begin{array}{r} 123 \\ \times\ \ 4 \end{array}$

3. $\begin{array}{r} 106 \\ \times\ \ 2 \end{array}$

4. $\begin{array}{r} 231 \\ \times\ \ 4 \end{array}$

5. $\begin{array}{r} 123 \\ \times\ \ 5 \end{array}$

Practice

Find the product.

6. 314
   × 3

7. 213
   × 3

8. 105
   × 5

9. 112
   × 4

10. 313
    × 3

11. 110
    × 7

12. 332
    × 2

13. 427
    × 2

14. 310
    × 3

15. 212
    × 4

16. 325
    × 3

17. 171
    × 4

18. 136
    × 4

19. 347
    × 2

20. 294
    × 3

21. 219
    × 4

22. 321
    × 3

23. 482
    × 2

24. 235
    × 3

25. 364
    × 2

26. $2 \times 325 = $ ▨

27. $3 \times 312 = $ ▨

28. $8 \times 111 = $ ▨

29. $4 \times 216 = $ ▨

30. $(2 \times 2) \times 102 = $ ▨

31. $4 \times (111 \times 2) = $ ▨

32. $(3 \times 1) \times 245 = $ ▨

Mixed Applications

33. Sherry sees some quilts at the show. She counts 122 blocks on 1 quilt. If 4 quilts are made exactly the same way, how many blocks are quilted?

34. There were 5 boxes of pottery shipped to the show. Each box had 36 pieces. If all the pieces in 3 of the boxes were damaged, how many pieces could be sold?

35. **Write a Question** Roberto sold wooden puzzles he had made. He sold 57 puzzles with 250 pieces each. He sold 84 puzzles with 100 pieces each.

36. **Logical Reasoning** Ginny makes a floral wreath in about 30 minutes. How many wreaths can she make in 8 hours?

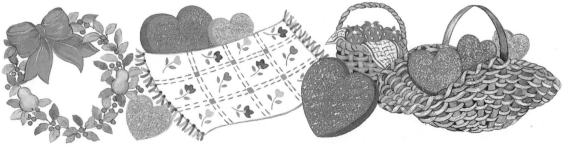

How do you use what you know about place value to help you multiply?

WRAP UP...

PROBLEM Solving

Ed bought a basketball for $22 and wristbands for $3. Later, his father gave him $5. Then Ed had $7. How much money did he have before he bought the basketball and wristbands?

Sometimes you can solve a problem by using the *work backward* strategy. To work backward, use opposite operations.

► UNDERSTAND

What are you asked to find?

What facts are given?

► PLAN

What strategy can you use?

A good strategy is to start with the amount Ed had left and work backward.

Draw a picture, or flowchart, to show the steps as they happened. To work backward, draw a second flowchart that reverses the steps and uses the opposite operations.

► SOLVE

How can you solve the problem?

Draw a flowchart to show the operations. Then reverse the flowchart using opposite operations.

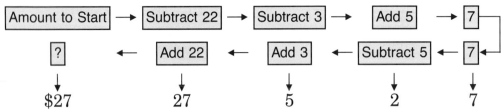

So, Ed had $27 before he bought the basketball and wristbands.

► LOOK BACK

What other strategy can you use to solve the problem?

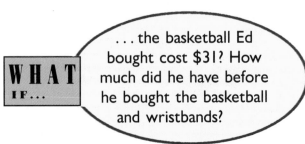

WHAT IF... ...the basketball Ed bought cost $31? How much did he have before he bought the basketball and wristbands?

 Idea Bank, page 454, Exercise 8

Apply

Solve. Make a flowchart and work backward.

1 Andy and his dad went to a basketball game. Andy spent $12 for a T-shirt and $4 for snacks. Later, his dad gave him $5. He then had $9. How much did Andy have when he arrived at the game?

2 Lisa and 5 of her friends divided a box of colored pencils. Lisa brought 2 extra pencils. Then she gave her total of 9 pencils to her sister. No pencils were left. How many pencils were in the box?

Mixed Applications ➔ **STRATEGIES** • Guess and Check • Work Backward • Write a Number Sentence • Draw a Picture

Choose a strategy and solve.

3 Lydia made 7 doll dresses. Each dress took 6 days to make. How many days did it take her to make all of the dresses?

4 Felix built 3 wooden toy cars. He used 17 screws for one car, 20 screws for another, and 19 screws for a third. How many screws did he use?

5 Tammy and Helen were playing a number game. First, Helen picked a number and added 4. Then, she multiplied by 6. Last, she subtracted 3. The result was 51. What number did Helen pick?

6 Thomas bought tacks for $3, colored paper for $2, and stick-on letters for $3. Later, his brother gave him $1 to help pay for the paper. Then Thomas had $4. How much did he have before he bought all the items?

WRITER'S CORNER

7 Look at the picture. Then write a word problem that uses addition.

8 Look at the picture. Then write a word problem that uses multiplication.

5 Swordtail —— $1.50
3 Neon Tetra —— $1.50
2 Black Mollie —— $1.25
1 Platys —— $1.25

1. The school library has two thousand, one hundred eight books. Write the number in standard form.

I have to first find how many tapes Julie bought.

2. There were 6 softball teams. Each team had 9 players. How many players were there?

3. Julie buys 4 rock-and-roll tapes and 3 jazz tapes. Each tape costs $7.00. How much does Julie spend?

4. The team ran one lap. Joey finished after Juan. Kim finished before Juan but after Sal. Who finished first?

5. Mr. Chang left his home at 7:30 A.M. He drove for 5 hours and 40 minutes. At what time did he reach Lakeland?

Round to the nearest hundred.

6. 236
7. 708
8. 450
9. 980
10. 95
11. 502

Write in standard form.

12. four million, seven hundred thirty-five thousand, eight hundred fifty-three

13. two hundred ninety thousand, nine hundred seventy-eight

Find the sum or difference.

14. 2,768
    +1,873

15. 8,058
    −2,473

16. 34,094
    −12,806

17. 45,927
    + 7,227

18. 697
    −509

For each picture, write the four number sentences that make up a fact family.

19.

20.

Write the multiplication fact shown on the number line.

21.

22.

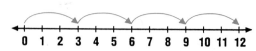

Spotlight ON
PROBLEM SOLVING

Understand
Plan
Solve
Look Back

? ? ? ? ? Write Questions ? ? ? ? ?

Many problems you must solve in everyday life do not state the question. Before you can solve a problem, you must know the question.

Work Together

Read the information given and talk about the questions that can be asked and answered.

Josh makes wooden figures to put on key chains. He paid $4 for wood, $6 for paint, $3 for varnish, and $2 for key chains. He has enough supplies to make 30 key chains.

TALK ABOUT IT

Which of the following questions can be answered using the data in the problem?

a. How much money did Josh spend on supplies?

b. How much should Josh charge for each key chain?

c. How many hours will it take Josh to make all the key chains?

d. How many key chains must Josh sell to pay for the cost of the supplies?

Answer the question you chose. Tell why each of the remaining questions cannot be answered.

APPLY

Write a question that can be answered for each situation.

1. Josh finished making 25 key chains. He sold 15 for $1 each.

2. Josh can make one key chain in 2 hours. If he works on 10 key chains at once, he can finish them all in 6 hours.

3. Josh made all 30 key chains. He sold 15 for $1.00 each, 10 for $0.75 each, and 5 for $0.50 each.

4. Josh paid $15 for supplies and sold the key chains for a total of $30.

161

MULTIPLYING
More Practice

This year Dan put 189 vacation photos in albums. If his family takes the same number of photos each year, how many photos will he put in albums during the next 4 years?

Estimate. Front-end: 4 × 100 = 400   Rounding: 4 × 200 = 800
Multiply. 4 × 189 =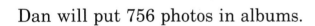

Step 1	**Step 2**	**Step 3**
Multiply the ones. 4 × 9 ones = 36 ones Regroup.	Multiply the tens. 4 × 8 tens = 32 tens Add 3 tens. Regroup.	Multiply the hundreds. 4 × 1 hundred = 4 hundreds Add 3 hundreds.
$\begin{array}{r} 3 \\ 189 \\ \times 4 \\ \hline 6 \end{array}$ 36 ones = 3 tens 6 ones	$\begin{array}{r} 3\,3 \\ 189 \\ \times 4 \\ \hline 56 \end{array}$ 32 tens + 3 tens = 35 tens, or 3 hundreds 5 tens	$\begin{array}{r} 3\,3 \\ 189 \\ \times 4 \\ \hline 756 \end{array}$ 4 hundreds + 3 hundreds = 7 hundreds

Dan will put 756 photos in albums.

• Is your answer reasonable? How do you know?

More Examples

A. $\begin{array}{r} 1\,1 \\ 236 \\ \times 3 \\ \hline 708 \end{array}$ Regroup the ones and the tens.

B. $\begin{array}{r} 2 \\ 74 \\ \times 5 \\ \hline 370 \end{array}$ Regroup 20 ones as 2 tens 0 ones.

C. $\begin{array}{r} 3 \\ 408 \\ \times 4 \\ \hline 1,632 \end{array}$ Regroup 32 ones as 3 tens 2 ones. 0 tens + 3 tens = 3 tens

Check for Understanding

Estimate the product.

1. $\begin{array}{r} 37 \\ \times 4 \\ \hline \end{array}$
2. $\begin{array}{r} 225 \\ \times 5 \\ \hline \end{array}$
3. $\begin{array}{r} 52 \\ \times 7 \\ \hline \end{array}$
4. $\begin{array}{r} 304 \\ \times 8 \\ \hline \end{array}$

Find the product.

5. $\begin{array}{r} 49 \\ \times 2 \\ \hline \end{array}$
6. $\begin{array}{r} 402 \\ \times 3 \\ \hline \end{array}$
7. $\begin{array}{r} 393 \\ \times 4 \\ \hline \end{array}$
8. $\begin{array}{r} 95 \\ \times 8 \\ \hline \end{array}$

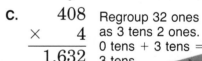

Practice

Estimate the product.

9. $8 \times 895 = $ ▩ **10.** $3 \times 215 = $ ▩ **11.** $7 \times 58 = $ ▩ **12.** $5 \times 659 = $ ▩

Find the product.

13. 623×7 **14.** 58×3 **15.** 107×9 **16.** 720×8 **17.** 46×5

18. 348×4 **19.** 87×7 **20.** 409×5 **21.** 327×8 **22.** 670×9

23. 705×6 **24.** 549×4 **25.** 830×7 **26.** 678×3 **27.** 98×9

28. 49×8 **29.** 470×3 **30.** 295×6 **31.** 903×2 **32.** 77×7

Mixed Applications

33. The Giovannis drove 275 miles each day on Saturday and Sunday. For the next 5 days they drove about 165 miles each day. How many miles did they drive in that week?

34. Write a Question Last year the Giovannis traveled 1,067 miles. This year they traveled 2,750 miles.

MIXED REVIEW

Complete each pattern.

1. $4 \times 8 = $ ▩
$4 \times 80 = $ ▩
$4 \times 800 = $ ▩
$4 \times 8{,}000 = $ ▩

2. $2 \times 5 = $ ▩
$2 \times $ ▩ $ = 100$
▩ $\times 500 = 1{,}000$
$2 \times 5{,}000 = $ ▩

3. $9 \times 6 = $ ▩
▩ $\times 60 = 540$
$9 \times $ ▩ $ = 5{,}400$
$9 \times 6{,}000 = $ ▩

How does knowing $4 \times 8 = 32$ help you find 40×80?

WRAP UP...

Tanya rides her bicycle around the pond 3 times each day. The path around the pond is 2,840 feet. How far does she ride her bicycle around the pond each day?

Estimate. 3 × 3,000 = 9,000
Multiply. 3 × 2,840 =

Step 1	Step 2	Step 3	Step 4
Multiply the ones. 3 × 0 ones = 0 ones	Multiply the tens. 3 × 4 tens = 12 tens Regroup 12 tens as 1 hundred 2 tens.	Multiply the hundreds. 3 × 8 hundreds = 24 hundreds Add. Regroup 25 hundreds as 2 thousands 5 hundreds.	Multiply the thousands. 3 × 2 thousands = 6 thousands Add.
2,840 × 3 = 0	1 2,840 × 3 = 20	2 1 2,840 × 3 = 520	2 1 2,840 × 3 = 8,520

So, Tanya rides her bicycle 8,520 feet around the pond each day.

Another Method

Use a calculator to find the product of two numbers.

7 × 8,346 =   First, estimate the product. → 7 × 8,000 = 56,000

Then use a calculator to find the exact product.

Press: 58422.

- Is your estimate close to the calculated answer?

- Why is it wise to estimate first?

Check for Understanding

Estimate. Then use a calculator to find the product.

1. 5 × 9,601 =   2. 3 × 2,604 =   3. 8 × 5,217 =   4. 8 × 3,671 =

5. 2 × 6,725 =   6. 4 × 8,037 =   7. 5 × 1,285 =   8. 6 × 2,316 =

Practice

Estimate. Then use a calculator to find the product.

9.	10.	11.	12.	13.
2,346 × 6	1,902 × 3	2,124 × 3	6,701 × 5	3,132 × 3

14.	15.	16.	17.	18.
3,724 × 8	8,250 × 2	4,918 × 6	5,294 × 7	6,531 × 4

19. $6 \times 7,027 = $ ▦

20. $4 \times 6,723 = $ ▦

21. $5 \times 2,468 = $ ▦

22. $3 \times 2,736 = $ ▦

23. $7 \times 1,234 = $ ▦

24. $5 \times 7,210 = $ ▦

25. $(3 \times 3) \times 1,752 = $ ▦

26. $(15 - 10) \times 4,639 = $ ▦

27. $(11 - 9) \times 8,472 = $ ▦

Mixed Applications

28. Uncle Roscoe's Balloon Antics sold tickets for 1,247 rides in six months. In the next six months, twice as many tickets were sold. How many tickets were sold in the whole year?

29. Finding Data   A hot-air balloon company kept a record to find which of its balloons were ridden most often. It found that 2,463 people rode Hefty Rider. The company found that 4 times as many rode Breeze Away, and 3 times as many rode Light and Fluffy. Use this information to complete the table.

Name of Balloon	Number of Riders
Hefty Rider	2,463
Breeze Away	▦
Light and Fluffy	▦
TOTAL	▦

PATTERNS AND RELATIONSHIPS

The Blue Sky Balloon Company uses this table to compute the money collected for rides each day.

Number of Rides	1	2	3	4	5	6
Money Collected	$125	$250	▦	$500	$625	▦

30. How much money is collected for 3 rides?

31. How much money is collected for 6 rides?

Why is estimation important when you use a calculator?

Nancy wants to go to summer camp for 3 weeks. Each week costs $76. She has saved $232. Does she have enough money to go for 3 weeks?

You can solve a problem by using different methods of computation.

▶ **UNDERSTAND**

What do you need to find?

What facts are given?

▶ **PLAN**

What strategy can you use?

You can write and solve a number sentence. Then compare the solution with the amount of money Nancy has saved.

▶ **SOLVE**

How can you solve this problem?

Choose a method of computation.

Method	Example
Calculator	Use with large numbers or when you need an answer quickly.
Mental Math	Use with small numbers and multiples of tens, hundreds, thousands, and so on.
Objects	Use objects to model the situation.
Paper and Pencil	Use when a calculator is not available and the problem is too difficult to solve mentally.

You can use paper and pencil to solve the number sentence.

$$3 \times 76 = \blacksquare$$

$$\begin{array}{r} {}^{1} \\ 76 \\ \times 3 \\ \hline 228 \end{array} \rightarrow \$228$$

So, Nancy needs $228. Since she has saved $232, she has enough money.

▶ **LOOK BACK**

How can you check your answer?

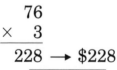 **WHAT IF...**

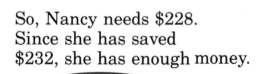 ... each week of summer camp costs $100? What method of computation would you use?

Apply

Tell which method of computation you would use to solve the problem. Solve.

① There are 10 rowboats on the lake. Each rowboat holds 6 campers. How many campers can be in the rowboats at the same time?

② The camp has 18 horses for riding classes. If 5 different groups ride each day, how many campers can sign up for riding classes?

| Mixed Applications | STRATEGIES | • Write a Number Sentence • Work Backward • Guess and Check • Draw a Picture |

Choose a strategy and solve.

③ Emma and Doug went shopping. Emma spent $4.50 and $2.50. Later, Doug gave her $3.00. Then she had $6.00. How much money did Emma have before she went shopping?

④ During June, July, and August, Lois and her mother went to 12 plays. They saw the same number of plays each month. How many plays did they see each month?

⑤ Jennifer played in 24 softball games last season. In each game she was at bat 4 times. How many times did she go to bat last season?

⑥ The script for the play is 47 pages long. Olga makes 7 copies of the script. How many copied pages does Olga have?

⑦ Tim placed 36 photos in his new photo album. The album has 20 pages. Each page holds 4 photos. How many pages did he fill? How many pages were not filled?

⑧ Ashley pitched her tent between the woods and the stream. Betty's tent was on the other side of the stream. Sarah's tent was between Ashley's and Betty's tent. Whose tent was closest to the woods?

Brian practices his golf swing at the driving range once a week after school. One bucket of balls costs $3.49. How much do three buckets of balls cost?

Estimate. 3 × $3.00 = $9.00
Multiply. 3 × $3.49 =

Multiply amounts of money as if you were multiplying whole numbers. Write the product in dollars and cents.

$3.49 →
$$\begin{array}{r} 349 \\ \times\ \ \ \ 3 \\ \hline 1{,}047 \end{array} \to \$10.47$$
or
$$\begin{array}{r} \$3.49 \\ \times\ \ \ \ 3 \\ \hline \$10.47 \end{array}$$

So, 3 buckets of balls cost $10.47.

Talk About It

▶ Is the estimate greater than or less than the product?

▶ If you estimate by rounding $3.49 to $3.00, does the estimate give you a good idea of how much money Brian needs? Why or why not?

You can estimate to make sure you have enough money by rounding to the next higher dime, dollar, or ten dollars, whichever will give you an estimate greater than the product.

More Examples

A.
$$\begin{array}{r} \overset{1}{\ }\$0.48 \\ \times\ \ \ \ 2 \\ \hline \$0.96 \end{array} \to \begin{array}{r} \$0.50 \\ \times\ \ \ \ 2 \\ \hline \$1.00 \end{array}$$
To the next higher dime, $0.48 rounds to $0.50.

B.
$$\begin{array}{r} \overset{1}{\ }\$5.26 \\ \times\ \ \ \ 3 \\ \hline \$15.78 \end{array} \to \begin{array}{r} \$6.00 \\ \times\ \ \ \ 3 \\ \hline \$18.00 \end{array}$$
To the next higher dollar, $5.26 rounds to $6.00.

Check for Understanding

Estimate by rounding to the next higher dime, dollar, or ten dollars. Then find the product.

1. $0.26
   × 3

2. $1.39
   × 4

3. $4.16
   × 2

4. $12.76
   × 5

5. $18.04
   × 6

Practice

Estimate by rounding to the next higher dime, dollar, or ten dollars. Then find the product.

6. $3 \times \$2.15 = $ ■

7. $8 \times \$1.72 = $ ■

8. $3 \times \$0.27 = $ ■

9. $6 \times \$5.14 = $ ■

10. $4 \times \$3.24 = $ ■

11. $7 \times \$4.68 = $ ■

12. $5 \times \$0.84 = $ ■

13. $9 \times \$18.86 = $ ■

14. $6 \times \$2.75 = $ ■

Find the product.

15. $\$1.36$ $\times\ 2$	16. $\$2.16$ $\times\ 4$	17. $\$3.01$ $\times\ 9$	18. $\$0.27$ $\times\ 5$	19. $\$0.95$ $\times\ 2$
20. $\$5.12$ $\times\ 6$	21. $\$4.05$ $\times\ 5$	22. $\$16.23$ $\times\ 4$	23. $\$13.12$ $\times\ 3$	24. $\$10.24$ $\times\ 5$
25. $\$0.87$ $\times\ 9$	26. $\$6.75$ $\times\ 4$	27. $\$10.57$ $\times\ 7$	28. $\$7.68$ $\times\ 6$	29. $\$15.25$ $\times\ 3$

Mixed Applications

30. **Making Choices** Ashley has $10 to buy 3 boxes of golf balls. She wants to be sure she has enough money before she takes 3 boxes of either brand to the checkout. Which brand should she choose?

31. There are 35 balls in each bucket. How many balls could Brian hit if he pays for 3 buckets of balls?

Use the price list for Exercise 32.

32. **Making Choices** Joseph wants enough film to take 48 pictures. Which combination of film is the best buy?

Price List	
Color film for 12 photos	$1.99
Color film for 24 photos	$2.59
Color film for 36 photos	$3.49

When you want to be sure you have enough money, how do you estimate?

WRAP UP...

Vocabulary Check

Choose a word or words from the box to complete each sentence.

| basic facts |
| calculator |
| estimate |
| factors |
| multiples |
| product |

1. The answer to a multiplication problem is the _?_.
   (page 148)

2. The numbers you name when counting by tens are _?_ of ten. *(page 148)*

3. The two numbers you multiply are _?_. *(page 148)*

4. By using place value and _?_, you can multiply any whole number. *(page 148)*

Use mental math to multiply multiples of 10.

5. To _?_ products, you can round numbers to multiples of 10, 100, or 1,000 and then multiply. *(page 150)*

6. The fast way to multiply a very large number is to use a _?_. *(page 164)*

Concept Check

Find the product. Then continue each pattern by multiplying the multiples of 10, 100, and 1,000. *(page 148)*

7. $7 \times 4 = $ ■

8. $9 \times 3 = $ ■

9. $5 \times 4 = $ ■

10. $6 \times 8 = $ ■

Estimate the product. Name the strategy that you used. *(page 150)*

11. 529	12. 39	13. 6,183	14. 736	15. 5,729
$\times\ \ 4$	$\times\ 7$	$\times\ \ \ \ 5$	$\times\ \ 8$	$\times\ \ \ \ 4$

Find each product using place-value blocks on a mat and the partial product method. *(page 152)*

16.

T	O
1	9
×	4

17.

T	O
3	4
×	2

18.

H	T	O
2	4	5
×		3

19.

H	T	O
3	2	6
×		3

20.

H	T	O
4	1	7
×		2

Idea Bank, page 455, Exercise 13

Skill Check

Find the product. *(pages 154–157, 162–165, 168–169)*

21. 41— $\times$ 3	22. 22 $\times$ 4	23. 14 $\times$ 3	24. 25 $\times$ 2	25. 29 $\times$ 3	26. 19 $\times$ 8
27. 263 $\times$ 4	28. 364 $\times$ 7	29. 288 $\times$ 3	30. 271 $\times$ 9	31. 472 $\times$ 8	32. 526 $\times$ 6
33. 5,026 $\times$ 3	34. 7,217 $\times$ 5	35. 3,947 $\times$ 2	36. 4,456 $\times$ 4		37. 6,254 $\times$ 8

Estimate by rounding to the next higher dime, dollar, or ten dollars. Then find the product. *(pages 166, 168)*

38. $3 \times \$6.70 = $ ▨

39. $6 \times \$7.22 = $ ▨

40. $9 \times \$4.59 = $ ▨

41. $4 \times \$11.20 = $ ▨

42. $7 \times \$25.71 = $ ▨

43. $8 \times \$44.89 = $ ▨

Problem-Solving Check *(pages 158, 166)*

44. Each of 8 students made 8 mugs. Each student kept 1 mug, and some mugs broke in the kiln. These students donated 46 mugs to the crafts fair. How many mugs broke?

45. At the museum Jesse bought 6 greeting cards. He also bought a poster for $15.00. He had $1.30 left from $28.00. How much did the cards cost?

Solve. Write **a**, **b**, **c**, or **d** to show the method of computation you used.

a. calculator	b. paper and pencil	c. mental math	d. objects

46. The art museum owns 1,700 paintings. There are 9 paintings hanging on each wall. There are 164 walls. How many paintings are in storage?

47. There are 6 libraries that share books. Each library has about 4,500 books. About how many books are in the entire library system?

CHAPTER TEST

Find the product. Then continue each pattern by multiplying the multiples of 10, 100, and 1,000.

1. $4 \times 7 = $

2. $6 \times 5 = $

3. $8 \times 7 = $

Estimate the product.

4. $\begin{array}{r} 37 \\ \times\ 4 \\ \hline \end{array}$

5. $\begin{array}{r} 346 \\ \times\ \ 2 \\ \hline \end{array}$

6. $\begin{array}{r} 836 \\ \times\ \ 5 \\ \hline \end{array}$

7. $\begin{array}{r} 25 \\ \times\ 7 \\ \hline \end{array}$

8. $\begin{array}{r} 580 \\ \times\ \ 6 \\ \hline \end{array}$

9. $\begin{array}{r} 1,262 \\ \times\ \ \ \ 4 \\ \hline \end{array}$

Find the product.

10. $\begin{array}{r} 16 \\ \times\ 8 \\ \hline \end{array}$

11. $\begin{array}{r} 312 \\ \times\ \ 3 \\ \hline \end{array}$

12. $\begin{array}{r} 45 \\ \times\ 3 \\ \hline \end{array}$

13. $\begin{array}{r} 125 \\ \times\ \ 4 \\ \hline \end{array}$

14. $\begin{array}{r} 3,471 \\ \times\ \ \ \ 8 \\ \hline \end{array}$

15. $\begin{array}{r} 2,150 \\ \times\ \ \ \ 6 \\ \hline \end{array}$

16. $7 \times 25 = $

17. $2 \times 218 = $

18. $4 \times 3,206 = $

Estimate by rounding to the next higher dime, dollar, or ten dollars. Then find the product.

19. $7 \times \$2.63 = $

20. $9 \times \$0.38 = $

21. $4 \times \$15.30 = $

Solve.

22. Pedro bought a book for $3.00. He also bought 2 markers. He gave the clerk $5.00 and received $1.50 in change. How much did the 2 markers cost?

23. Robyn told Jane to follow these steps. First, choose a number from 1 to 5. Multiply by 4. Then add 6. Last, divide by 2. Jane's answer was 7. With what number did Jane begin?

You might use a calculator when computing large numbers.

Solve. Write the method of computation you used.

24. There are 4 schools that share computer programs. Each school has 210 programs. How many programs do the schools have altogether?

25. Anna bought a poster for $12.98, wrapping paper for $2.79, and a bow for $0.59. How much did she spend in all?

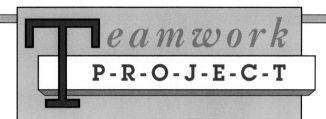

Create Animated Cartoons

Filmmakers create animated cartoon characters by photographing pictures of the same character many times. The action of the character is made by the gradual change in the cartoon figure. It takes 24 pictures for the eye to see 1 second of movement. With your teammates, create an animated cartoon character.

Decide

Work with your teammates. Talk about how you can use index cards, markers, and string to make a flip-book for a 3-second cartoon.

Choose one of the still pictures shown at the right, or create your own character.

Decide how you want the character to move. Then determine which pictures each of you will draw and how many.

Do

Draw all the pictures you will need. Put them in the right order to create the action sequence. Then tie them together with the string.

Share

Let the other teams use your flip-book, and have them tell how your character moves.

Talk About It

- How many pictures are in your flip-book?

- How can you use this number to calculate the number of pictures needed for a 30-second cartoon?

- How many pictures would be needed for a 1-minute cartoon?

- Why is multiplication the best way to calculate the number of pictures?

Multiplication Spin-Off

The game can be played with 1, 2, or 3 players. The players need a spinner and a calculator. Each player also needs a worksheet of blank grids like the ones shown.

■ Each player tries to form a problem with the greatest product. The first player spins the spinner. Each player writes the digit shown on the spinner in any box of the first grid. The first player continues to spin until all boxes in the first grid are full.

■ Each person then solves his or her problem and checks the answer with the calculator. The player with the greatest correct score wins the round and gets one point.

■ The second player then spins numbers for the next round. The game continues until all the grids are filled.

■ The winner is the player with the most points at the end of the game.

◆◆◆◆◆ Challenge ◆◆◆◆◆

Visual Thinking

How many stars are missing from the center of the picture?

Number Puzzles

Fill in the missing digits. You may use a calculator.

1.   56
   × ■
  448

2.   3■2
   × ■
  1,610

3.   ■31
   × 7
  6,■17

4.   6,3■9
    × 9
  ■6,781

Write the letter of the correct answer.

1. Order from least to greatest.
389,618   389,681   389,600

A. 389,600; 389,618; 389,681
B. 389,618; 389,681; 389,600
C. 389,681; 389,600; 389,618
D. not here

2. Which number is an odd number?

A. 34   B. 78
C. 89   D. 98

3. 38
      +49

A. 78   B. 87
C. 144   D. 788

4. 402
      −269

A. 133   B. 233
C. 243   D. 671

5. 38,592
      +43,375

A. 71,777   B. 71,867
C. 71,967   D. not here

6. 974,274
      −264,502

A. 609,700   B. 709,702
C. 709,772   D. 710,772

7. $6 \times 14 = \blacksquare$

A. 48   B. 64
C. 84   D. 102

8. $56 \div 7 = \blacksquare$

A. 5   B. 6
C. 7   D. 8

9. Estimate the product of 3×738.

A. 210   B. 2,100
C. 2,800   D. 4,100

10. $4 \times 170 = \blacksquare$

A. 480   B. 680
C. 800   D. 2,250

11. Susan buys 4 tickets to the arts and crafts show. Each ticket costs $3.76. How much does Susan spend?

A. $15.00   B. $15.04
C. $15.24   D. $15.76

12. The rodeo arena holds 274 people. The arena is full for 3 shows each day. How many people watch the rodeo each day?

A. 682 people   B. 802 people
C. 822 people   D. 8,802 people

MULTIPLYING
BY 2-DIGIT NUMBERS

Did you know . . .

. . . that in the United States we use over 65 billion aluminum cans a year? By recycling one can, you can save enough energy to run a TV for 3 hours!

Talk About It

To earn money and help save energy, Marcus's class has collected 78 pounds of aluminum cans. The recycling center pays $0.40 per pound for aluminum. How can Marcus find how much money the class will earn for the cans?

Newspaper
Only Please

Recycling aluminum cans helps keep our environment clean. The Boys' Club filled 30 bags with cans. Each bag held 100 cans. How many cans did the Boys' Club collect?

- You can count by hundreds.   Count to 30 hundreds.
  100, 200, 300, . . .

- You can multiply 30 by 100.

Factors   Product
30 × 1 = 30
30 × 10 = 300
30 × 100 = 3,000

Think: Use a basic fact and look for a pattern in the zeros.

$$\begin{array}{r} 100 \\ \times\ 30 \\ \hline 3{,}000 \end{array}$$

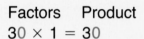
three zeros   three zeros

What relationship do you notice between the factors and the product?

So, the Boys' Club collected 3,000 cans.

More Examples

You can use a basic fact and mental math to find products.

A. Basic fact: $1 \times 4 = 4$

$10 \times 4 = 40$
$100 \times 4 = 400$
$100 \times 40 = 4{,}000$

B. Basic fact: $3 \times 6 = 18$

$3 \times 60 = 180$
$30 \times 60 = 1{,}800$
$30 \times 600 = 18{,}000$

C. Basic fact: $5 \times 8 = 40$

$5 \times 80 = 400$
$50 \times 80 = 4{,}000$
$500 \times 800 = 400{,}000$

Check for Understanding

Complete. Use a basic fact to help you.

1. $10 \times 9 = \blacksquare$
   $100 \times 9 = \blacksquare$
   $100 \times 90 = \blacksquare$

2. $2 \times 60 = \blacksquare$
   $20 \times 60 = \blacksquare$
   $20 \times 600 = \blacksquare$

3. $4 \times 50 = \blacksquare$
   $40 \times 50 = \blacksquare$
   $400 \times 500 = \blacksquare$

Find the product.

4. $40 \times 10 = \blacksquare$

5. $300 \times 90 = \blacksquare$

6. $4{,}000 \times 70 = \blacksquare$

Practice

Copy and complete. Use a basic fact to help you.

7. $4 \times 20 = $ ■
$40 \times 20 = $ ■
$40 \times 200 = $ ■

8. $10 \times 7 = $ ■
$100 \times 7 = $ ■
$100 \times 70 = $ ■

9. $6 \times 80 = $ ■
$60 \times 80 = $ ■
$600 \times 800 = $ ■

10. $90 \times 5 = $ ■
$900 \times 5 = $ ■
$900 \times 50 = $ ■

Find the product.

11. $\begin{array}{r} 70 \\ \times 10 \\ \hline \end{array}$

12. $\begin{array}{r} 3,000 \\ \times \quad 400 \\ \hline \end{array}$

13. $\begin{array}{r} 9,000 \\ \times \quad 80 \\ \hline \end{array}$

14. $\begin{array}{r} 500 \\ \times 700 \\ \hline \end{array}$

15. $\begin{array}{r} 40,000 \\ \times \quad 600 \\ \hline \end{array}$

16. $\begin{array}{r} 100 \\ \times \quad 80 \\ \hline \end{array}$

17. $\begin{array}{r} 5,000 \\ \times \quad 600 \\ \hline \end{array}$

18. $\begin{array}{r} 20 \\ \times 90 \\ \hline \end{array}$

19. $\begin{array}{r} 800 \\ \times 300 \\ \hline \end{array}$

20. $\begin{array}{r} 70,000 \\ \times \quad 90 \\ \hline \end{array}$

Use mental math to complete the table.

×	100	200	300	400	500	600	700	800	900	1,000
21. 300	30,000	60,000	■	■	■	■	■	■	■	■

Mixed Applications

22. The recycling center collects about 800 aluminum cans in one day. At this rate, about how many cans will be collected in 10 days?

23. The P.T.A. sends a newsletter each month except for June and July. It sends 300 newsletters per month. How many newsletters will be sent during the year?

Use the table to answer Exercises 24–25.

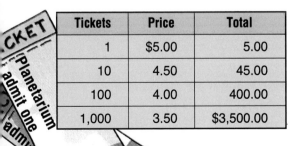

Tickets	Price	Total
1	$5.00	5.00
10	4.50	45.00
100	4.00	400.00
1,000	3.50	$3,500.00

24. **Analyze Data** What is the difference in the cost of a ticket when you buy 1 ticket and when you buy 10 tickets?

25. What is the relationship between the number of tickets bought and the price of an individual ticket?

When you multiply multiples of 10, what pattern helps you find the product?

WRAP
U P . . .

ESTIMATING PRODUCTS

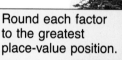

FIRE ALERT Save Our Forests

During the 28 days of February, in Georgia alone, a daily average of 225 fires burned out of control. We _must_ prevent forest fires!

Rob and Liz are working on a science project about forests. They want to estimate about how many acres of Georgia forest burned in February. Rob estimated 4,000 acres and Liz estimated 6,000 acres.

Rob and Liz each used a different method of estimation.

Rob used front-end estimation.   **Liz used rounding.**

$$\begin{array}{r} 225 \rightarrow \quad 200 \\ \times\ 28 \rightarrow \times\ \ 20 \\ \hline 4,000 \end{array}$$ Multiply the front-end digits of each factor.

$$\begin{array}{r} 225 \rightarrow \quad 200 \\ \times\ 28 \rightarrow \times\ \ 30 \\ \hline 6,000 \end{array}$$ Round each factor to the greatest place-value position.

Use a calculator to find the exact number.

Press: [2] [8] [×] [2] [2] [5] [=] [　　6300.]

Talk About It

▶ Whose estimate is more reasonable? Explain.

Another Example

Front-End Estimation   **Rounding**

$$\begin{array}{r} \$4.39 \rightarrow \quad 4.00 \\ \times\ \ 23 \rightarrow \times\ \ 20 \\ \hline \$80.00 \end{array}$$

$$\begin{array}{r} \$4.39 \rightarrow \\ \times\ \ 23 \rightarrow \end{array}$$ rounded to the nearest dollar $$\begin{array}{r} 4.00 \\ \times\ \ 20 \\ \hline \$80.00 \end{array}$$ or rounded to the nearest ten cents $$\begin{array}{r} 4.40 \\ \times\ \ 20 \\ \hline \$88.00 \end{array}$$

Use a calculator to find the exact answer.

• Which estimate is more reasonable? Why?

Check for Understanding

Estimate by using both methods. Use a calculator to find the exact answer. Then circle the more reasonable estimate.

1. $\begin{array}{r} 88 \\ \times 69 \\ \hline \end{array}$ 2. $\begin{array}{r} 47 \\ \times 39 \\ \hline \end{array}$ 3. $\begin{array}{r} 172 \\ \times\ 21 \\ \hline \end{array}$ 4. $\begin{array}{r} 392 \\ \times\ 53 \\ \hline \end{array}$ 5. $\begin{array}{r} \$4.88 \\ \times\ \ 29 \\ \hline \end{array}$

Practice

Estimate.

6. $12 \times 77 = $ ▨

7. $49 \times 25 = $ ▨

8. $54 \times 86 = $ ▨

9. $104 \times 37 = $ ▨

10. $422 \times 71 = $ ▨

11. $69 \times 338 = $ ▨

12. $418 \times 88 = $ ▨

13. $783 \times 41 = $ ▨

14. $5.81
  $\times$ 17

15. $2.72
  $\times$ 44

16. $1.36
  $\times$ 99

17. $8.13
  $\times$ 87

18. $1.23
  $\times$ 45

Choose the answers for Exercises 19–20 from the box.

19. Which amounts are closest to one dollar?

20. Which amounts are closest to one dime?

| $0.15 | $1.17 | $1.05 |
| $0.08 | $0.91 | $0.19 |

Mixed Applications

21. Making Choices A terrarium set is on sale for $19.57. Separately, the container costs $9.99, the rocks cost $3.85, and the plants cost $6.19. Which is the better buy, the set or the individual pieces?

22. Ramon bought 18 tickets to a wildlife tour. Each ticket cost $11. Estimate how much Ramon spent.

NUMBER SENSE • ESTIMATION

Write the letter of the most reasonable answer.

23. The tallest tree in the United States is a redwood tree that is found in California. It is about 360 feet tall. That is about as tall as a

a. skyscraper. **b.** mountain. **c.** flagpole.

24. Rounded to the nearest ten, the height of the giant sequoia tree is 280 ft. What is the range of exact heights that the tree can be?

a. 200–300 ft **b.** 275–284 ft **c.** 270–290 ft

Which method of estimation, front-end or rounding, usually provides an estimate nearer to the actual product?

WRAP
UP...

MULTIPLICATION
Multiples of 10

Recycled paper is made into grocery bags to be used at a supermarket. The bags come in packages of 75. How many bags are in 40 packages?

Multiply. $40 \times 75 = n$ You can use n instead of ▧ for a missing number.

Step 1	**Step 2**
Multiply by the ones. Place a zero in the ones place.	Multiply by the tens.

Step 1

$$\begin{array}{r} 75 \\ \times 40 \\ \hline 0 \end{array} \leftarrow 0 \times 75$$

Step 2

$$\begin{array}{r} \overset{2}{75} \\ \times \quad 40 \\ \hline 3{,}000 \end{array} \leftarrow 4 \text{ tens} \times 75$$

So, there are 3,000 bags in 40 packages.

Another Method

$40 \quad \times 75 = n$

$10 \times 4 \times 75 = n$

$10 \times \quad 300 \quad = n$

$\quad 3{,}000 \quad = n$

Talk About It

▶ How can you rename a number so that it includes a multiple of 10?

▶ How does multiplying by a multiple of 10 help you use mental math to find the product?

Check for Understanding

Copy and complete. Then find the value of n.

1. $20 \quad \times 75 = n$

$10 \times$ ▧ $\times 75 = n$

$10 \times$ ▧ $= n$

2. $50 \quad \times 26 = n$

▧ $\times 5 \times 26 = n$

$10 \times$ ▧ $= n$

3. $80 \quad \times 31 = n$

$10 \times 8 \times$ ▧ $= n$

$10 \times$ ▧ $= n$

Find the product.

4. $\begin{array}{r} 89 \\ \times 30 \\ \hline \end{array}$
5. $\begin{array}{r} 105 \\ \times \ 40 \\ \hline \end{array}$
6. $\begin{array}{r} 711 \\ \times \ 70 \\ \hline \end{array}$
7. $\begin{array}{r} 237 \\ \times \ 30 \\ \hline \end{array}$
8. $\begin{array}{r} 519 \\ \times \ 60 \\ \hline \end{array}$
9. $\begin{array}{r} 672 \\ \times \ 90 \\ \hline \end{array}$

Practice

Copy and complete. Then find the value of *n*.

10. $25 \times 50 = n$

$25 \times 5 \times \blacksquare = n$

$\blacksquare \times 10 = n$

11. $30 \times 15 = n$

$\blacksquare \times 3 \times 15 = n$

$10 \times \blacksquare = n$

12. $20 \times 42 = n$

$\blacksquare \times 2 \times 42 = n$

$10 \times \blacksquare = n$

Complete each table.

Rule: Multiply by 50				
Input	43	36	76	19
Output	▦	▦	▦	▦
	13.	**14.**	**15.**	**16.**

Rule: Multiply by 30				
Input	27	68	94	53
Output	▦	▦	▦	▦
	17.	**18.**	**19.**	**20.**

Find the product.

21. 44
      ×60

22. 23
      ×50

23. 14
      ×70

24. 96
      ×20

25. 19
      ×30

Find the value of *n*.

26. $n \times 30 = 90 \times 20$

27. $40 \times n = 10 \times 20$

28. $30 \times 100 = n \times 50$

Mixed Applications

29. Mrs. Meeks buys grocery bags for her craft shop. The grocery store will sell her a package of bags for $2.47. How much will 20 packages of bags cost?

30. **Logical Reasoning** Mr. Lewis drives a truck every other Monday during April and May. If his first workday is April 2, what will be his fifth workday?

CALCULATOR

31. On a calculator, press [5] [0] [+] [5] [0].

Press [=] until the display shows [900.]. How many times did you press [=]? What happened each time you pressed [=]? What multiplication sentence will give you the same answer?

Why does the product of 47×30 end in zero?

W R A P
U P ...

More Practice, Lesson 6.3, page H54

183

Loud noises annoy people and can cause damage to hearing. Suppose you had to make a speech about noise pollution. How could you best use the information at the right for your speech?

You can make a graph to display information.

► **UNDERSTAND**

What are you asked to find?

What type of information is given?

► **PLAN**

What strategy can you use to solve the problem?

Making a bar graph is a good strategy. A bar graph organizes and clearly displays information so that it can be seen as you make your speech.

What will the bar graph show?

The bar graph will show the noise level of each activity and indicate whether the noise level is acceptable, annoying, or damaging.

► **SOLVE**

How can you make the graph?

Count to determine the number of rows and columns needed. Label the bottom of the graph with the types of noises. Label the left side of the graph by tens from 0 to 150. Always begin at 0. Color the bars in the acceptable range blue. Color the bars in the annoying range yellow and the bars in the damaging range red. Make a color key to identify each color.

This bar graph will clearly display the information to the audience while you are making your speech.

► **LOOK BACK**

How can you check to see whether your graph is correct?

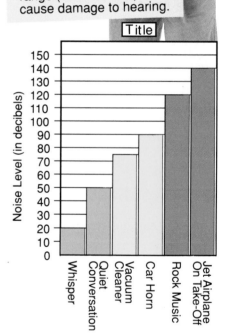

Environment Update

Noises are measured in units called decibels. The noise level of a whisper (20 decibels) or of quiet conversation (50 decibels) is acceptable. A vacuum cleaner (75 decibels) or a car horn (90 decibels) has an annoying effect on hearing. Frequent exposure to rock music (120 decibels) or a jet airplane taking off at close range (140 decibels) could cause damage to hearing.

Title

Noise Level (in decibels)

150 140 130 120 110 100 90 80 70 60 50 40 30 20 10 0

Whisper · Quiet Conversation · Vacuum Cleaner · Car Horn · Rock Music · Jet Airplane On Take-Off

Color Key
☐ acceptable
☐ annoying
☐ damaging

HINT: The numbers on the left side of the graph must be equally spaced.

WHAT IF... ... you made a table to display the information? Which would be better for your speech, the table or the bar graph? Why?

Apply

(1) Use the table to copy and complete the bar graph about the environmental workshop.

Students Attending Workshop

Grade	Number of Students
Third	25
Fourth	60
Fifth	35
Sixth	50

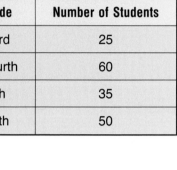

I need:
Label
Scale
Title

(2) Several classes at Carver School collected paper to be recycled. Use the information in the table to make a bar graph.

Paper for Recycling

Class	Pounds Collected
Mrs. Ward	42
Mrs. Hart	24
Mr. Betts	38
Miss Lin	46

Mixed Applications ➤ **STRATEGIES**
- Find a Pattern
- Make a Graph
- Write a Number Sentence
- Make a Table

Choose a strategy and solve.

(3) Sumter School had 117 entries in the "Save the Planet" poster contest. Lovett School had 98 entries in the same contest. How many entries did the two schools have in the contest?

(4) Jo wants to buy a fan that costs $15.75. She saves $0.25 the first week and doubles the amount saved each week. In how many weeks will she have enough money to buy the fan?

(5) Abby, Bess, and Chris competed in an obstacle course. Abby earned 26 points, Bess earned 35 points, and Chris earned 18 points. How can this data be displayed?

(6) Darren collected 18 bottles for recycling. Maeve collected 3 times as many bottles. How many bottles did Maeve collect?

More Practice, Lesson 6.4, page H55

EXPLORING
Two-Digit Factors

Paper is one of the most commonly recycled materials. The members of the Girls' Club tied 25 bundles of newspapers for recycling. Each bundle contained 37 newspapers. How many newspapers did they bundle?

Multiply. $25 \times 37 = n$

| $20 \times 30 = 600$ | $5 \cdot 30 = 150$ |
| $20 \times 7 = 140$ | $5 \times 7 = 35$ |

WORK TOGETHER

Building Understanding

Use graph paper to make a rectangle that is 37 squares long by 25 squares wide.

• How can you count to find how many squares there are in all?

Now divide the rectangle into smaller rectangles so that you can count the squares more quickly.

> Follow these steps:
> 1. Count off 30 squares along the length. Draw a line down the rectangle.
> 2. Count off 20 squares along the width. Draw a line across.
> 3. Find the number of squares in each smaller rectangle. Then add the numbers together.
> This method is called finding **partial products.**

There is a shorter way of doing what you just did with the model.

Partial Products

$$
\begin{array}{r}
37 \\
\times\ 25 \\
\hline
35 \leftarrow (5 \times 7) \\
150 \leftarrow (5 \times 30) \\
140 \leftarrow (20 \times 7) \\
+600 \leftarrow (20 \times 30) \\
\hline
925
\end{array}
$$

Shorter Way

$$
\begin{array}{r}
\overset{3}{37} \\
\times\ 25 \\
\hline
185 \\
+740 \\
\hline
925
\end{array}
$$

$> (5 \times 37) \rightarrow$

$> (20 \times 37) \rightarrow$

Talk About It

► Look at the four numbers added together. What part of the model does each number stand for?

► Compare the two ways shown. What is the same? What is different?

So, the Girl's Club bundled 925 newspapers.

Making the Connection

Use a model to find partial products. Solve.

1.

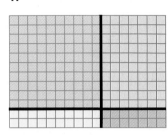

$(2 \times 7 = 14)$
$(2 \times 10 = 20)$
$(10 \times 7 = 70)$
$(10 \times 10 = 100)$

2.

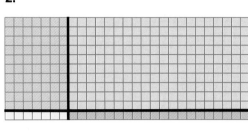

$(1 \times 7 = 7)$
$(1 \times 20 = 20)$
$(10 \times 7 = 70)$
$(10 \times 20 = 200)$

3.

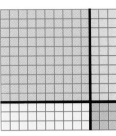

$(3 \times 3 = 9)$
$(10 \times 3 = 30)$
$(3 \times 10 = 30)$
$(10 \times 10 = (100)$

Use graph paper to make a model for each number sentence.
Divide the rectangle into smaller rectangles. Solve.

4. $11 \times 20 = n$

5. $24 \times 32 = n$

6. $19 \times 41 = n$

Checking Understanding

Solve using partial products. Then solve using the shorter way.

7. $18 \times 13 = n$

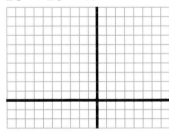

8. $14 \times 11 = n$

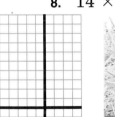

Use graph paper to make a model for each number sentence. Solve.

9. $15 \times 22 = n$

10. $26 \times 11 = n$

11. $30 \times 19 = n$

12. $20 \times 18 = n$

Write a number sentence. Solve.

13. Abe delivers newspapers 5 days a week. He delivers 42 newspapers each day. How many newspapers does he deliver in 2 weeks?

14. Mr. Hubbard arranges chairs into 16 rows of 24 in each row and 22 rows of 32 in each row. How many chairs are there in all?

An oil spill is harmful to wildlife that lives in or near the water. Volunteers often must clean the oil from birds. If each of 34 volunteers cleans 36 birds, how many birds are cleaned?

Estimate.   Front-end: 30 × 30 = 900
                 Rounding: 30 × 40 = 1,200

Multiply.   34 × 36 = *n*

Step 1	**Step 2**	**Step 3**
Think of 34 as 30 + 4, or 3 tens and 4 ones. Multiply by 4 ones.	Multiply by 30, or 3 tens.	Add the products.
$$\begin{array}{r} 2 \\ 36 \\ \times\ 34 \\ \hline 144 \end{array}$$ **Think:** $$\begin{array}{r} 36 \\ \times\ 4 \\ \hline 144 \end{array}$$	$$\begin{array}{r} 1 \\ 2 \\ 36 \\ \times\ 34 \\ \hline 144 \\ 1080 \end{array}$$ **Think:** $$\begin{array}{r} 36 \\ \times\ 30 \\ \hline 1,080 \end{array}$$	$$\begin{array}{r} 1 \\ 2 \\ 36 \\ \times\ 34 \\ \hline 144 \\ +1,080 \\ \hline 1,224 \end{array}$$

So, 1,224 birds are cleaned.
Since 1,224 is close to the rounded estimate, the answer is reasonable.

More Examples

A.
$$\begin{array}{r} 1 \\ 1 \\ 63 \\ \times\ 45 \\ \hline 315 \\ +2,520 \\ \hline 2,835 \end{array}$$
Think: $$\begin{array}{r} 63 \\ \times\ 5 \\ \hline 315 \end{array} + \begin{array}{r} 63 \\ \times\ 40 \\ \hline 2520 \end{array}$$

B.
$$\begin{array}{r} 6\ 5 \\ 8\ 7 \\ \$0.98 \\ \times\ 79 \\ \hline 8\ 82 \\ +\ 68\ 60 \\ \hline \$77.42 \end{array}$$
Think: $$\begin{array}{r} 98 \\ \times\ 9 \\ \hline 882 \end{array} + \begin{array}{r} 98 \\ \times\ 70 \\ \hline 6860 \end{array}$$

Write the answer as a money amount.

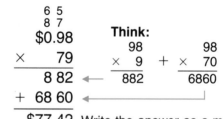

Check for Understanding

Estimate first. Then find the product.

1. $\begin{array}{r} 12 \\ \times 24 \end{array}$	2. $\begin{array}{r} 27 \\ \times 55 \end{array}$	3. $\begin{array}{r} 38 \\ \times 62 \end{array}$	4. $\begin{array}{r} 96 \\ \times 71 \end{array}$	5. $\begin{array}{r} 24 \\ \times 56 \end{array}$	6. $\begin{array}{r} 45 \\ \times 38 \end{array}$

Practice

Estimate first. Then find the product.

7. 16
    ×22

8. 28
    ×13

9. 36
    ×42

10. 57
    ×18

11. 80
    ×39

12. 47
    ×34

Find the product.

13. 79
    ×11

14. 66
    ×34

15. 55
    ×46

16. 19
    ×15

17. 74
    ×53

18. 92
    ×31

19. $13 \times 39 = n$

20. $62 \times 46 = n$

21. $82 \times 50 = n$

22. $45 \times 33 = n$

Mixed Applications

23. Miss Boatman has 27 students in her science class. In February each student worked 12 hours as a volunteer at the animal rescue center. How many hours did all the students work?

24. One container holds 85 soda cans or 65 bottles. The Lee Road School collected 18 containers full of cans to take to the recycling center. How many cans did the school collect?

25. **Logical Reasoning** To save money and fuel, Mr. Orr took a bicycle trip for his vacation. He rode 35 miles each day for 12 days, rested 2 days, and then rode 27 miles each day for 10 days. How far did Mr. Orr travel?

MIXED REVIEW

Find the product or quotient.

1. 6
    ×5

2. 9
    ×9

3. 5
    ×4

4. 8
    ×5

5. 2
    ×7

6. 3
    ×8

7. 4
    ×9

8. 9
    ×0

9. $48 \div 8 = n$

10. $36 \div 9 = n$

11. $63 \div 7 = n$

12. $27 \div 3 = n$

13. $40 \div 5 = n$

When multiplying 23×56, what two problems do you compute to find the product?

WRAP
UP...

Graphs help you find data to solve problems.

Use the bar graph to answer Exercises 1–4.

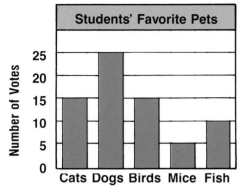

Students' Favorite Pets

Number of Votes: 0, 5, 10, 15, 20, 25

Cats Dogs Birds Mice Fish

1. Which kind of pet is the most popular?

2. How many students like fish best?

3. Which two pets are equally popular?

4. How many more students like dogs than like fish?

Use the table for Exercises 5–6.

5. How many more books does Lee Road Library have than Parkway Library?

6. How many books do Southwest and East Grove libraries have altogether?

Library	Number of Books
Parkway	5,937
Lee Road	8,311
Southwest	4,699
East Grove	12,578

Write the value of the digit 3 in each number.

7. 24,300   8. 130   9. 403,275   10. 2,398,675

11. 43   12. 3,705,211   13. 31,487   14. 37,099,201

Find the sum or difference.

15. 372
    +128

16. 8,037
    +9,578

17. 3,604
    − 495

18. 3,779
     314
   + 47

19. 251
     68
     94
   +479

Find the product or quotient.

20. $7 \times 9 = $ ▮   21. $45 \div 5 = $ ▮   22. $8 \times 4 = $ ▮   23. $56 \div 7 = $ ▮

24. 24
   × 5

25. 56
   × 9

26. 243
   × 2

27. 4,739
   ×   4

28. 2,085
   ×   3

Spotlight ON PROBLEM SOLVING

Check the Solution for Reasonableness

When a problem is solved, the solution should be reasonable.

Terry and Marge collected 47 glass bottles for recycling. If they received $0.02 per bottle when they took them to a recycling center, how much money did they receive? Which is the most reasonable answer, $1.94, $0.94, or $0.84?

Talk About It

Work with a partner and discuss the questions below.

a. Which is the most reasonable answer for the amount of money received for the recycled glass bottles? How do you know?

b. How can you decide whether an answer to a problem is reasonable?

Decide whether each answer is reasonable. If an answer is not reasonable, correct it. Provide at least one additional answer. Use your calculator.

1. The 4-H Club was selling tree seedlings for $0.10 each. Freedom School bought one seedling for each of its 642 students. **They paid $64.20 for the seedlings.**

2. Sally bought birdseed. It cost $4.25 per bag. She paid with a $10 bill. **She received $2.50 in change.**

3. The fourth graders held a mulch sale. They sold truckloads of mulch for $10.00 a load. One Saturday they sold 28 truckloads. **At the end of the day, the total amount earned was $200.00.**

4. Ellen's class surveyed restaurants to see whether their disposable cups and dishes were plastic foam or paper. The students visited 50 restaurants. **They found that 26 restaurants, or about half of those surveyed, use paper.**

Many lumber companies plant tree seedlings to replace the trees that have been cut down. A lumber company planted 12 rows with 188 seedlings in each row. How many seedlings were planted?

Estimate. Front-end: $10 \times 100 = 1,000$
Rounding: $10 \times 200 = 2,000$

Multiply. $12 \times 188 = n$

Step 1 Multiply the ones.	**Step 2** Multiply the tens.	**Step 3** Add.
$\begin{array}{r} {\scriptstyle 1\,1} \\ 188 \\ \times\ \ 12 \\ \hline 376 \end{array}$ ← 2×188	$\begin{array}{r} {\scriptstyle 1\,1} \\ 188 \\ \times\ \ \ 12 \\ \hline 376 \\ 1,880 \end{array}$ ← 10×188	$\begin{array}{r} {\scriptstyle 1\,1} \\ 188 \\ \times\ \ 12 \\ \hline 376 \\ +1,880 \\ \hline 2,256 \end{array}$

The lumber company planted 2,256 seedlings. Since 2,256 is close to the rounded estimate, the answer is reasonable.

More Examples

A.
$$\begin{array}{r} {\scriptstyle 4} \\ {\scriptstyle 2} \\ \$4.07 \\ \times\quad\ 64 \\ \hline 16\ 28 \\ +\ 244\ 20 \\ \hline \$260.48 \end{array}$$
$16\ 28$ ← 4×407
$244\ 20$ ← 60×407

B.
$$\begin{array}{r} {\scriptstyle 3} \\ {\scriptstyle 3} \\ 650 \\ \times\quad\ 76 \\ \hline 3\ 900 \\ +45\ 500 \\ \hline 49,400 \end{array}$$
$3\ 900$ ← 6×650
$45\ 500$ ← 70×650

Check for Understanding

Estimate the product.

1. $\begin{array}{r} 465 \\ \times\ 56 \\ \hline \end{array}$
2. $\begin{array}{r} 601 \\ \times\ 12 \\ \hline \end{array}$
3. $\begin{array}{r} 550 \\ \times\ 25 \\ \hline \end{array}$

Find the product.

4. $\begin{array}{r} 632 \\ \times\ 21 \\ \hline \end{array}$
5. $\begin{array}{r} 424 \\ \times\ 15 \\ \hline \end{array}$
6. $\begin{array}{r} 133 \\ \times\ 33 \\ \hline \end{array}$

Practice

Estimate the product.

7. 622
   × 49

8. 378
   × 62

9. 416
   × 88

10. 675
    × 64

11. 821
    × 39

Find the product.

12. 188
    × 29

13. 470
    × 62

14. 843
    × 55

15. 685
    × 59

16. 914
    × 47

17. 188
    × 67

18. 216
    × 29

19. 479
    × 81

20. 214
    × 77

21. 191
    × 52

Mixed Applications

22. Each week Mr. Montoya travels 230 miles to and from his job at a paper mill. How many miles does he travel in 16 weeks?

23. Pine seedlings are packed 12 to a box. How many seedlings are in 144 boxes?

24. **Number Sense** Mrs. Davis connects 12 garden hoses. Each hose is 50 feet long. Estimate the length of the connected hoses.

25. Mr. Almon will landscape 12 apartment buildings. He buys 168 junipers and 135 boxwoods for each building. How many plants does he need?

MIXED REVIEW

Write each number in two other ways.

1. 43,279

2. 800 + 40 + 5

3. 106,711

4. nine hundred seventeen

Write the time for each clock in two different ways.

5.

6.

7.

8.

When do you need an estimate of a product?

USING MULTIPLICATION

Conserving water is an important step in protecting our environment. You can save 15 gallons of water each day by taking a 5-minute shower instead of a bath. If you shower every day, how much water will you save in a year?

Since there are 365 days in a year, you can multiply 365 by 15.

Estimate. $20 \times 400 = 8{,}000$

Multiply. $15 \times 365 = n.$

Step 1 Multiply the ones.	**Step 2** Multiply the tens.	**Step 3** Add.
$\begin{array}{r} {\scriptstyle 3\,2} \\ 365 \\ \times\ \ \ 15 \\ \hline 1{,}825 \end{array}$ ← 5 × 365	$\begin{array}{r} {\scriptstyle 3\,2} \\ 365 \\ \times\ \ \ 15 \\ \hline 1{,}825 \\ 3{,}650 \end{array}$ ← 10 × 365	$\begin{array}{r} {\scriptstyle 3\,2} \\ 365 \\ \times\ \ \ 15 \\ \hline 1{,}825 \\ +3{,}650 \\ \hline 5{,}475 \end{array}$

So, you will save 5,475 gallons of water in a year.

Talk About It

▶ Why is your estimate greater than the exact answer?

▶ If each student in your class takes a shower instead of a bath each day for a year, how much water will the class save?

▶ If about 40 gallons of water are used for a bath, about how many gallons are used for a 5-minute shower?

Check for Understanding

Estimate. Then find the product.

1. $30 \times 687 = n$
2. $37 \times 5{,}038 = n$
3. $56 \times 11{,}099 = n$

4. $\begin{array}{r} 106 \\ \times\ \ 96 \\ \hline \end{array}$
5. $\begin{array}{r} 586 \\ \times\ \ 32 \\ \hline \end{array}$
6. $\begin{array}{r} 2{,}877 \\ \times\ \ \ \ 41 \\ \hline \end{array}$
7. $\begin{array}{r} 70{,}432 \\ \times\ \ \ \ \ \ 83 \\ \hline \end{array}$
8. $\begin{array}{r} 13{,}224 \\ \times\ \ \ \ \ \ 11 \\ \hline \end{array}$

Practice

Estimate. Then find the product.

9. 204
× 18

10. 183
× 32

11. 3,931
× 68

12. 30,699
× 72

13. 17,098
× 19

14. 403
× 29

15. 878
× 33

16. 313
× 76

17. 3,134
× 12

18. 21,650
× 33

19. $20 \times 593 = n$

20. $49 \times 3,609 = n$

21. $81 \times 20,005 = n$

Copy and complete the table, using the data given.

	Club	Hours per Month	Total Hours per Year	Amount Earned
	Boys' Club	12	144	$36.00
22.	Girls' Club	15	■	■
23.	Ecology Club	25	■	■
24.	County 4-H Club	20	■	■
25.	Concerned Citizens' Club	32	■	■

Club Earnings at Environmental Center (at $0.25 an hour)

Mixed Applications

26. Rona bought 12 bottles of water. Each bottle cost $2.37. How much did Rona spend in all?

27. There are 12 watercoolers. Each cooler contains 10 gallons of water. How many gallons of water are in all the coolers?

28. During April, May, and June, Mr. Prioletti installed 18 sprinkler systems. He installed the same number each month. How many systems did he install each month?

29. Logical Reasoning Mrs. Olsen earned $190 last week and spent $64. The week before, she earned $214 and spent $98. How much did she save in the two weeks?

How do you use the regrouped digit in a multiplication problem?

More Practice, Lesson 6.8, page H56

PROBLEM Solving

An apple costs $0.15, and an orange costs $0.12. Mary spent $1.47 for apples and oranges. How many apples did Mary buy? How many oranges did she buy?

You can solve some problems by making a guess and then checking to see whether the guess is correct.

▶ **UNDERSTAND**

What are you asked to find?

What facts are given?

▶ **PLAN**

What can you do if you do not know how to begin solving the problem?

You can guess an answer.

▶ **SOLVE**

How can you solve the problem?

Guess 1 apple and 1 orange. Multiply to find the total cost. Continue guessing and checking until you get $1.47 as the total cost.

Guess	Apples	Oranges	Total	Notes
1	1 × $0.15	1 × $0.12	$0.27	too low
2	4 × $0.15	3 × $0.12	$0.96	still too low
3	5 × $0.15	5 × $0.12	$1.35	close
4	5 × $0.15	6 × $0.12	$1.47	just right

So, Mary bought 5 apples and 6 oranges.

▶ **LOOK BACK**

How can you check your answer?

WHAT IF... . . . you guess 6 apples and 5 oranges? Would the total amount spent be less than or greater than $1.47?

Connection, pages 446–447

Apply

1 The difference between two numbers is 2. Their product is 99. Find the two numbers.

2 Jake had 12 checkers. He made two stacks. One stack had 2 more checkers than the other. How many checkers were in each stack?

3 There were 24 people who sat in the front row at a concert. There were 6 more children than adults. How many children sat in the front row?

4 I am a three-digit number with digits that are all the same. When you multiply me by this digit, the product is 1,776. What number am I?

Mixed Applications	STRATEGIES	• Make a Table • Find a Pattern • Write a Number Sentence • Draw a Picture

Choose a strategy and solve.

5 Barry likes to collect postcards. He pays $1.00 for each set of 4 postcards and $0.30 for each additional postcard. How much will Barry pay for 15 postcards?

6 The Ecology Club earns $0.40 for each pound of aluminum cans they collect. If they collect 29 pounds of cans, how much money will the club earn?

7 Seth planted a row of trees. He planted a dogwood in front of a maple. He planted an oak between the maple and redbud. Write the names of the trees in the order Seth planted them.

8 Glenda planted three kinds of flowers in a flower garden. What color will the next flower be?

WRITER'S CORNER

9 Use the table to write two word problems about buying gardening equipment. Write the problems so that their solutions require multiplication or addition. Exchange with a partner. Solve.

Flower Box Nursery		
Item	Number per Box	Total Boxes
Gloves	24 pairs	16
Goggles	18 pairs	10
Hat	12	12
Spade	36	24
Watering can	8	15

Some cities require that trash be separated so that items such as aluminum cans and glass can be recycled. If a hardware store sells 13 trash cans at $11.95 each, what is the total amount of the sale?

Estimate. $10 \times \$12.00 = \$120.00$

Multiply. $13 \times \$11.95 = n$

Multiply amounts of money the same way you multiply whole numbers.

$$
\$11.95 \rightarrow
\begin{array}{r}
\overset{2\,1}{1\,195} \\
\times \quad 13 \\
\hline
3\,585 \\
+11\,950 \\
\hline
15\,535
\end{array}
\quad \text{or} \quad
\begin{array}{r}
\overset{2\,1}{\$11.95} \\
\times \quad 13 \\
\hline
35\,85 \\
+\,119\,50 \\
\hline
\$155.35
\end{array}
$$

Write the product in dollars and cents.

$15\,535 \rightarrow \$155.35$

So, the total amount of the sale is $155.35.

Talk About It

▶ Is the estimate greater than or less than the product? Why?

▶ How do you know where to place the dollar sign and decimal point in the answer?

Another Method

Use a calculator to find the product. $13 \times \$11.95 = n$

Press: ⬚1 ⬚3 ⬚× ⬚1 ⬚1 ⬚. ⬚9 ⬚5 ⬚= [155.35] , or $155.35.

Check for Understanding

Find the product. Use a calculator.

1. $63.68
    × 14

2. $35.66
    × 63

3. $92.50
    × 78

4. $73.95
    × 42

5. $89.03
    × 27

6. $43 \times \$0.79 = n$

7. $41 \times \$13.49 = n$

8. $35 \times \$58.98 = n$

Practice

Find the product. You may use a calculator.

9. $0.34
 × 12

10. $0.99
 × 15

11. $45.19
 × 20

12. $60.98
 × 18

13. $39.95
 × 50

14. $14.88
 × 13

15. $27.31
 × 33

16. $19.50
 × 25

17. $26.62
 × 41

18. $0.89
 × 90

19. $18 × \$0.58 = n$

20. $75 × \$1.27 = n$

21. $\$4.55 × 24 = n$

22. $36 × \$2.13 = n$

23. $\$15.25 × 12 = n$

24. $32 × \$1.19 = n$

25. $(\$25.42 + \$18.58) × 50 = n$

26. $(\$12.49 + \$2.88) × 19 = n$

Mixed Applications

Use the table to solve Exercises 27–30.

27. Find the cost of 10 brooms.

28. Find the cost of 24 packages of sponges and 12 mops.

29. Suppose you buy 2 kitchen trash cans and 4 boxes of plastic liners. The sales tax is $0.69. Find the total amount you pay.

30. If you buy one of each item listed, how much will you spend?

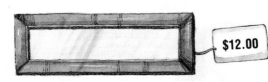

"Clean-Up" Special!	
ITEM	PRICE
Kitchen trash bags	$2.94 per box
Kitchen trash cans	$4.07 each
Plastic liners	$1.69 per box
Deodorizers	$2.19 each
Brooms	$4.38 each
Mops	$3.11 each
Sponges	$0.77 per package

MAKING CHOICES

31. Suppose you have $64 to spend on 6 picture frames. List all possible combinations of frames you can buy.

$4.00 $12.00 $8.00

To estimate the cost of several items at the store, should you overestimate or underestimate each item?

W R A P
U P . . .

Vocabulary Check

Choose a word from the box to complete each sentence.

estimate
graph
guess
multiple
n
pattern
product

Estimate first so you can check the answer for reasonableness.

1. The answer to a multiplication problem is the ? .
   (pages 180, 182)

2. You can make a ? to display information. *(page 184)*

3. To multiply multiples of 10, use a basic fact and follow the ? of zeros. *(page 178)*

4. You can ? a product by rounding each factor to its greatest place-value position and then multiplying. *(page 180)*

5. You can solve some problems by making a ? and then checking to see if it is correct. *(page 196)*

6. If $10 \times 5 = 50$, then 50 is a ? of 10. *(page 182)*

7. You can use ? instead of ▥ to represent a missing number. *(page 182)*

Concept Check

Complete. Use a basic fact to help you. *(page 178)*

8. $10 \times 5 = $ ▥
   $100 \times 5 = $ ▥
   $100 \times 50 = $ ▥

9. $5 \times 70 = $ ▥
   $50 \times 70 = $ ▥
   $50 \times 700 = $ ▥

10. $3 \times 90 = $ ▥
    $30 \times 90 = $ ▥
    $300 \times 900 = $ ▥

Estimate the product. Round each number to its greatest place-value position. *(page 180)*

11. $10 \times \$3.12 = n$ 12. $\$0.98 \times 20 = n$ 13. $50 \times \$49.95 = n$ 14. $\$2.16 \times 40 = n$

Solve using partial products. Then solve using the shorter way. *(page 186)*

15. $11 \times 17 = n$

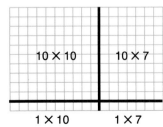

16. $21 \times 12 = n$

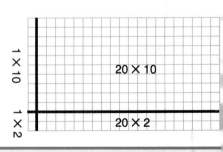

Skill Check

Complete the table. Look for a pattern. *(page 178)*

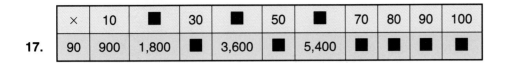

×	10	■	30	■	50	■	70	80	90	100
17. 90	900	1,800	■	3,600	■	5,400	■	■	■	■

×	100	200	300	400	500	600	700	800	900	1,000
18. 400	■	■	■	■	■	■	■	■	■	■

Estimate. Find the product. *(page 180)*

19.	**20.**	**21.**	**22.**	**23.**	**24.**	**25.**
49	13	97	293	$1.13	$4.79	$12.29
×21	×80	×56	× 19	× 45	× 12	× 18

Find the product. *(page 190)*

26.	**27.**	**28.**	**29.**	**30.**	**31.**	**32.**
67	39	14	27	117	288	$5.11
×13	×42	×83	×52	× 30	× 11	× 68

Find the product. You may use a calculator. *(page 198)*

33. $90 \times \$312.14 = n$

34. $688 \times 20 = n$

35. $40 \times 417 = n$

Problem-Solving Check *(pages 184, 196)*

36. A bran muffin cost $0.55, and a blueberry muffin cost $0.79. Ann spent $5.12. How many muffins of each kind did she buy?

37. Mr. Pham has 2 sons. The sum of their ages is 15. The product of their ages is 56. How old is each son?

38. Hill County Schools held an art contest. There were 38 entries from Bailey School, East School had 23 entries, Oak School had 50 entries, and Park School had 15 entries. Make a bar graph to display this data.

39. The students in Mrs. Carr's class voted on their favorite foods. Use the data to make a bar graph: chicken nuggets, 4 votes; burgers, 6 votes; pizza, 11 votes; tacos, 7 votes.

Use a basic fact and look for a pattern in the zeros.

Copy and complete each table.

1.

×	10	20	30	40	50	60	70	80	90	100
40	▪	▪	▪	▪	▪	▪	▪	▪	▪	▪

2.

×	100	200	300	400	500	600	700	800	900	1,000
20	▪	▪	▪	▪	▪	▪	▪	▪	▪	▪

Estimate the product.

3. 29
    ×13

4. 32
    ×49

5. 279
    × 83

6. 411
    × 19

7. 34
    ×59

8. 413
    × 28

9. 68
    ×15

10. $1.84
    ×   33

11. $5.34
    ×   62

Find the product.

12. 46
     ×15

13. 73
     ×20

14. 55
     ×84

15. 96
     ×30

16. 21
     ×75

17. 132
     × 64

18. 524
     × 18

19. $3.48
     ×   94

20. $2.51
     ×   16

21. $6.77
     ×   25

Solve.

22. Mrs. Lei has 2 daughters. The sum of their ages is 19. The product of their ages is 84. How old is each girl?

23. Pencils cost $0.25 each. Crayons cost $1.50 per box. Dwayne spent $2.25. How many of each item did he buy?

24. There are 9 students who have brown hair, 4 students with black hair, 6 students with blond hair, and 2 students who have red hair. Use the information to make a bar graph.

25. Mr. Huff's class voted on their favorite pets. Use this data to make a bar graph: 4 votes for birds, 11 votes for dogs, and 8 votes for cats.

Protect Our Wildlife

Scientists estimate that we are losing three species of wildlife every day and that by the twenty-first century, we will be losing several hundred species a day. For example, in Louisiana the black bear is threatened, and in the northwestern United States the spotted owl is endangered. Work with your teammates to create a poster and write a report about a threatened or an endangered species.

Decide

✔ Make a list of sources where you could find information about endangered and threatened species.

✔ Decide on a kind of species you would like to learn about.

✔ Find out whether there are any endangered species in your area.

✔ Choose one species to research.

✔ Make a list of the information you want to include on your poster and in a report.

Do

✔ Design a poster that is colorful, appealing, and informative about the threatened loss of the species.

✔ Include a sketch or a picture of the species.

✔ Write a brief report about the species, and include important data, such as its size, appearance, and location.

Share

✔ Present your report to the class. Display the poster and the report on the bulletin board.

Talk About It

• Can you think of a way to save the species you studied?

• What facts did you find that were surprising?

• How is multiplication used to find the total number of species that might be lost from 1991 to the year 2000?

extend your thinking

ACTIVITY....
Multiplication Race

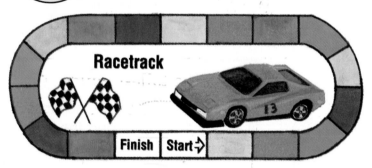

Racetrack

Finish | Start →

○ Play the game with one, two, or three
○ classmates. Each player will need a marker
○ and ten cards labeled with the digits 0–9. The
○ group will need a calculator.
○
○ Each player places a marker on START on the
○ racetrack, shuffles his or her ten cards, places
○ them facedown, and draws four cards. The
○ first player then calls either "high" or "low"
○ to tell players to form 2 two-digit factors that
○ equal either the greatest or the least product
○ possible.
○
○ Each player uses the calculator to check the
○ product. The player with the greatest (or the
○ least) product that is correct wins the round
○ and moves his or her marker one space along
○ the racetrack.
○
○ The second player begins the second round.
○ The first player to reach the FINISH line is the
○ winner.

Number Puzzles
Find the missing digits.

1.
$$\begin{array}{r} 2\blacksquare \\ \times\ 19 \\ \hline 2\blacksquare5 \\ +2\blacksquare0 \\ \hline 4\blacksquare5 \end{array}$$

2.
$$\begin{array}{r} \blacksquare7 \\ \times\ \blacksquare6 \\ \hline \blacksquare22 \\ +\ 37\blacksquare \\ \hline 59\blacksquare \end{array}$$

3.
$$\begin{array}{r} 14\blacksquare \\ \times\ 3\blacksquare \\ \hline 43\blacksquare \\ +438\blacksquare \\ \hline 4,81\blacksquare \end{array}$$

4.
$$\begin{array}{r} 4\blacksquare6 \\ \times\ \blacksquare8 \\ \hline 35\blacksquare8 \\ +9\blacksquare0 \\ \hline 1,\blacksquare4\blacksquare8 \end{array}$$

Logical Reasoning

Van has four times as many marbles as Kevin. Jana has twice as many marbles as Van. Rounded to the nearest ten, the number of marbles Jana has is 30. How many marbles does each person have?

Write the letter of the correct answer.

1. Which is the value of the digit 8 in 128,765?

A. 8   B. 8,000
C. 800,000   D. 8,000,000

2. Round 43,720 to the nearest thousand.

A. 40,000   B. 43,000
C. 44,000   D. 45,000

3.
```
  80
 −27
```

A. 57   B. 63
C. 67   D. not here

4.
```
  4,067
 +2,792
```

A. 6,759   B. 6,859
C. 7,859   D. 7,869

5. What time will it be in 2 hours 10 minutes?

A. 1:30   B. 3:30
C. 3:40   D. 4:30

6. Which is the tallest building?

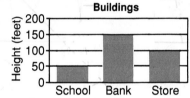

A. school   B. store
C. bank   D. not here

7. Find the value of *n*.
$64 \div 8 = n$

A. $n = 8$ B. $n = 9$
C. $n = 10$ D. $n = 11$

8.
```
  351
×   5
```

A. 1,555   B. 1,655
C. 1,755   D. 2,755

9.
```
  62
×40
```

A. 248   B. 2,480
C. 24,800   D. not here

10.
```
 $3.25
×   28
```

A. $91.00   B. $91.60
C. $92.00   D. $92.60

11. There are 16 baseball cards in a package. Joan bought 6 packages of baseball cards. How many cards did she buy?

A. 22 cards   B. 96 cards
C. 66 cards   D. 86 cards

12. Jody earned $2 on Monday, $4 on Tuesday, and $6 on Wednesday. If the pattern continues, how much will he earn on Thursday?

A. $4   B. $6
C. $8   D. $10

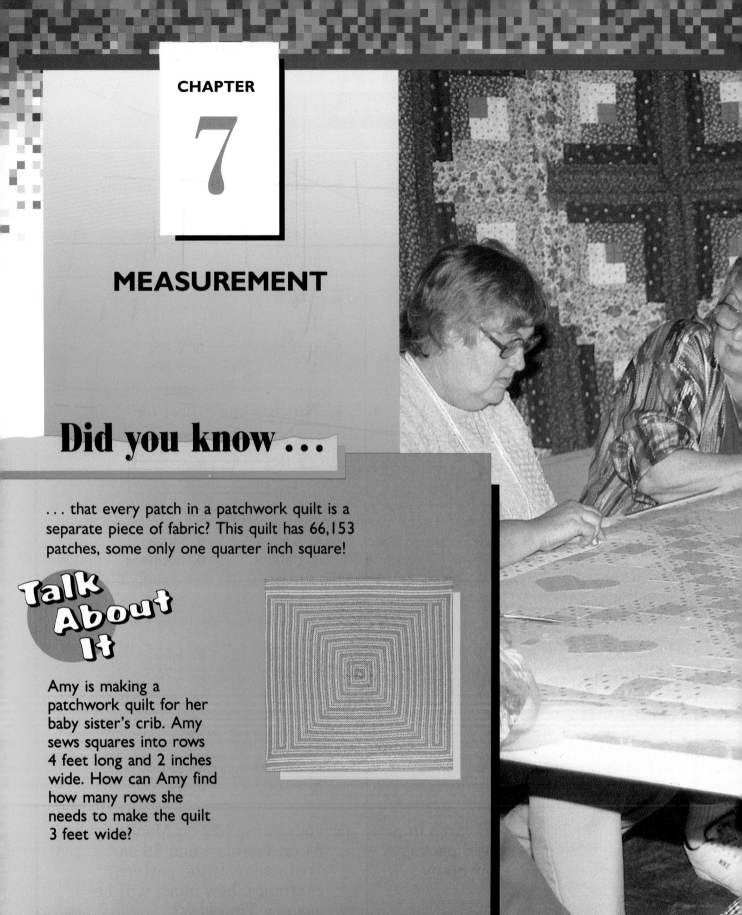

Did you know ...

... that every patch in a patchwork quilt is a separate piece of fabric? This quilt has 66,153 patches, some only one quarter inch square!

Talk About It

Amy is making a patchwork quilt for her baby sister's crib. Amy sews squares into rows 4 feet long and 2 inches wide. How can Amy find how many rows she needs to make the quilt 3 feet wide?

EXPLORING

Units of Measure

All measurement systems use standard units. The centimeter in the metric system and the inch in the customary system are standard units. A nonstandard unit can be anything you want it to be.

Suppose a unit of measure was called a "blip" and looked like this. ├────┤

WORK TOGETHER

Building Understanding

Use paper and pencil, a centimeter ruler, an inch ruler, and string to measure length.

Make a blip ruler.

Show marks from 1 to 10 blips. Match the string to the ribbon on this page. Use the blip ruler to measure the string.

Talk About It
▶ How many blips long is the string?

▶ Why do you think a measurement system needs standard units?

The **centimeter** is a unit of length in the metric system.

1 centimeter (cm)

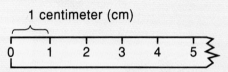

The **inch** is a unit of length in the customary system.

1 inch (in.)

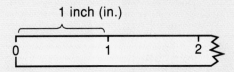

Measure the string by using the centimeter ruler. Measure the string by using the inch ruler.

Talk About It
▶ About how many centimeters long is the string?

▶ How many inches long is the string?

Making the Connection

Work with a partner. Invent your own unit and give it a name. Make a ruler using your unit. Measure the length of each object in your unit and in inches. Record your measurements.

1. a book
2. a window
3. a desk
4. your finger
5. a sheet of paper
6. a pencil

Checking Understanding

Find the length of each in centimeters, inches, blips, and your units. Use rulers and string.

7. a pencil
8. a crayon
9. your shoe
10. a paper towel
11. the chalkboard
12. a door

Solve.

13. If you measure the length of a bookmark in centimeters, inches, and blips, which measurement will have the most units?

14. **Logical Reasoning** Compare the unit you invented, the centimeter, the inch, and the blip. Place them in order from shortest to longest.

15. **Making Decisions** Holly needs 120 cm of ribbon to put a border around a picture. One piece of ribbon is 85 cm long, and another piece is 43 cm long. Is this enough ribbon for the border? Explain your answer.

16. **Analyze Data** Choose an everyday item to be your "mystery object." Use your string and ruler to find its length. Write the length and three related clues about the object. Exchange with a partner, and find each other's mystery object.

More Practice, Lesson 7.1, page H58

Many animals live in and around lakes. These pictures of some lake animals will help you think about metric units for measuring length.

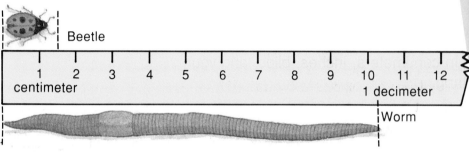

Beetle

1 centimeter 2 3 4 5 6 7 8 9 10 11 12 1 decimeter

Worm

Talk About It

▶ About how long is the beetle?

▶ Name some other living creatures that are about 1 centimeter long.

▶ About how long is the worm?

▶ Name some other living creatures that are about 1 decimeter long.

Here is a table of metric units.

Metric Units	
10 centimeters (cm)	= 1 decimeter (dm)
10 decimeters (dm)	= 1 meter (m)
100 centimeters (cm)	= 1 meter (m)
1,000 meters (m)	= 1 kilometer (km)

A **centimeter** is about the width of your index finger.

| 1 cm |

A **decimeter** is about the width of an adult's hand.

| 1 dm |

Talk About It

▶ Which unit is equal to 10 centimeters? 100 centimeters?

▶ Which unit would be most appropriate to measure the length of your desk?

▶ How is the metric system similar to our number system?

▶ Measure the width of this book, using your index finger. What unit can you use for nearly the same measurement?

A **meter** is about the distance from one hand to the other when your arms are stretched out.

A **kilometer** is about how far you can walk in 15 minutes.

Talk About It

▶ If you and a partner stretch your arms out with fingers touching, about how far is this?

▶ If students were lined up next to each other with arms stretched out, about how many students will be needed to measure 1 kilometer?

▶ If you walk for 30 minutes, about how many kilometers will you walk? meters?

▶ Which unit (cm, dm, m, or km) would you use to measure the height of a tree?

> This pencil is 12 cm long. I am 1 dm long. Which is longer?

Check for Understanding

Name the longer unit.

1. 1 cm or 1 dm   2. 1 km or 1 m   3. 1 dm or 1 m   4. 1 cm or 1 km

Use your index finger to measure each.

5.   6.

7.

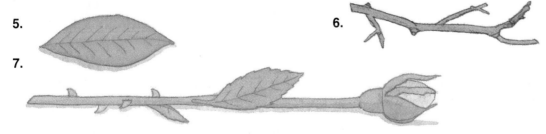

Choose the appropriate unit of measure. Write *cm, dm, m,* or *km.*

8. length of a ladybug   9. distance a car travels in 1 hour

10. width of a door   11. length of the classroom

Practice

Choose the more reasonable answer.

12.
    a. 3 cm   b. 30 cm

13.
    a. 500 cm   b. 5 cm

14.
    a. 10 dm   b. 1 dm

Choose the appropriate unit of measure. Write *cm, dm, m,* or *km.*

15. width of a table 16. height of a classroom wall 17. height of a garbage can

Draw a line of each length.

18. 5 cm   19. 1 dm   20. 12 cm   21. 2 dm

Name the longer unit.

22. 4 dm or 4 cm   23. 5 m or 5 cm   24. 700 dm or 700 km   25. 2 km or 2 m

Mixed Applications

26. Sue walks dogs in groups of 4. She walks 5 groups a day. How many dogs does she walk in a day?

27. Mr. Cruz drove 57 km to Elk City and 72 km to St. Cloud. Estimate the total distance that he drove.

28. Patti walked 1 km on a hike. Then she walked 500 m farther to a new trail. Pam walked 2 km on a hike. Who walked farther? How many meters farther?

29. **Logical Reasoning** Haley has 3 times as many rocks in her collection as Heidi. Lori has 5 more rocks than Heidi. Eric has 3 fewer rocks than Lori. Eric has 9 rocks. How many rocks does Haley have?

VISUAL THINKING

30. Without measuring, list the pictures in order from the shortest ribbon to the longest ribbon. Write only the letters.

a.

b.

c.

d.

How are a centimeter, a decimeter, and a meter related?

WRAP UP...

Once upon a time, there was a very rude dolphin. It kicked up the sand at the bottom of the ocean. It crushed the seaweed. It disturbed the fish that were trying to sleep.

1. One day the dolphin decided to chase the schools of baby fish. It chased 7 schools of 30 fish each. How many fish did the dolphin chase?

2. The parents of the fish did not like having their babies chased. So, 72 parents went to King Neptune to complain. The king would talk only to groups of 8. How many groups of parents talked to the king?

3. King Neptune called on his shark police. He had 7 sharks on each of 9 teams. How many sharks in all were on the king's police teams?

4. The sharks were not successful in stopping the rude dolphin. So, the fish went to Ocean Court to complain. They sat in 30 rows of 50 fish to a row. How many fish went to Ocean Court?

5. The dolphin was embarrassed and felt ashamed. It made 87 apology speeches each day for 9 days. How many apology speeches did it make altogether?

6. After the apology speeches, all the fish in the ocean heard about the dolphin. They came to a grand party in his honor. There were 56 flounders, 245 tunas, 27 crabs, and King Neptune himself. How many sea creatures attended the party?

These pictures of the things that Ryan found in his desk will help you think about customary units for measuring length.

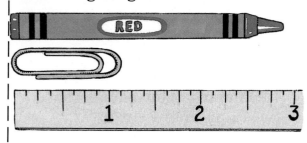

Talk About It

▶ About how long is the paper clip? ▶ About how long is the crayon?

Here is a table of customary units.

Customary Units	
12 inches (in.)	= 1 foot (ft)
3 feet	= 1 yard (yd)
36 inches	= 1 yard
5,280 feet	= 1 mile (mi)
1,760 yards	= 1 mile

An **inch** is about the length of your thumb from the first knuckle to the tip.

1 in.

A **yard** is about the length of a baseball bat.

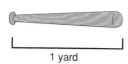

1 yard

A **foot** is about the length of a man's shoe.

1 foot

A **mile** is about the distance you can walk in 20 minutes.

Check for Understanding

Name the longer unit.

1. 1 in. or 1 ft

2. 1 mi or 1 yd

3. 1 yd or 1 in.

Choose the appropriate unit of measure. Write *in.*, *ft*, *yd*, or *mi*.

4. The length of a football field is 100 _?_ .

5. The distance across Florida is 150 _?_ .

6. The length of your pencil is 6 _?_ .

7. The man is 6 _?_ tall.

8. The width of the paper is 9 _?_ .

9. It is 3 _?_ from my house to school.

Practice

Choose the appropriate unit of measure. Write *in.*, *ft*, *yd*, or *mi*.

10. The distance from floor to chalkboard is about 3 _?_ .

11. Mrs. McBee bought 3 _?_ of fabric to make a dress.

12. The distance from home to the grocery store is about 3 _?_ .

Name the longer unit.

13. 2 yd or 2 ft

14. 72 in. or 72 ft

15. 5,000 mi or 5,000 ft

16. 1 yd or 1 mi

17. 10 yd or 10 ft

18. 33 ft or 33 in.

Mixed Applications

19. Nathan rides his bike 5,000 ft to school. Teri rides 1 mi to school. Who rides the greater distance?

20. **Number Sense** Miss Carter wants to measure the school playground. Which would be the more appropriate measuring tool, a ruler or a yardstick?

Use the table for Exercises 21–23.

21. How many miles is it from Chicago to Washington, D.C.?

22. Which cities are less than 500 mi from Chicago?

23. Name the city whose distance from Chicago is about four times greater than the distance from Chicago to Kansas City.

Road Mileage from Chicago, Illinois	
City	**Number of Miles**
Seattle, WA	2,013
New Orleans, LA	912
Omaha, NE	459
Boston, MA	963
Kansas City, MO	499
Washington, DC	671
Houston, TX	1,067

LANGUAGE ARTS CONNECTION

Write a sentence about math, using each underlined word.

24. Nan's cat sleeps at the <u>foot</u> of her bed.

25. Through the deep snow, the car <u>inches</u> its way forward.

26. Becoming a teenager is a <u>milestone</u> in a person's life.

27. Mr. Murphy's <u>yard</u> was flooded after the heavy rain.

Why is the system of measuring length by using inches, feet, and yards called the customary system?

More Practice, Lesson 7.3, page H58

Nicki, Dawn, and Paul are comparing their heights. At 52 inches, Nicki is 6 inches taller than Paul. Paul is 3 inches shorter than Dawn. How tall is Dawn?

Sometimes you can draw a picture to solve a problem.

▶ **UNDERSTAND**

What are you asked to find?

What facts are given?

▶ **PLAN**

What strategy can you use to solve the problem?

You can *draw a picture* to compare the heights.

▶ **SOLVE**

How can you solve the problem?

Draw a number line showing 40 to 60 inches. Be sure to mark the units at equal intervals.

Mark a point on the number line to show each person's height. Start with Nicki's height, 52 inches.

Count down 6 spaces and stop at 46, Paul's height.

From there, count up 3 spaces to 49, Dawn's height.

So, Dawn is 49 inches tall.

▶ **LOOK BACK**

What other strategy can you use to solve the problem?

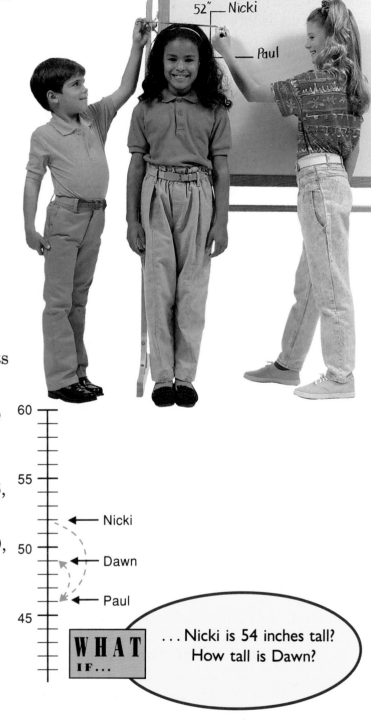

WHAT IF... ... Nicki is 54 inches tall? How tall is Dawn?

Apply

Draw a picture to solve.

(1) Katy placed her eggs into an egg carton. Every other egg is yellow. One egg is blue, one is pink, and four are green. The eggs are placed in horizontal rows. How are the eggs arranged?

(2) Mrs. Sims lives in a four-room apartment. The rooms are in a line. The bedroom is next to the kitchen. The dining room is between the kitchen and the living room. Which room is the farthest from the living room?

(3) Rex, Logan, Pete, and Jules live on the left side of Vine Street. Pete lives next to Jules. Logan lives next to Pete. Jules and Rex live next to each other. In what order are their homes?

(4) The maple tree is taller than the pine tree. The oak is taller than the maple. The height of the spruce is between the heights of the maple and the oak. Which tree is the shortest?

Mixed Applications ➤ **STRATEGIES**   • Work Backward   • Write a Number Sentence   • Draw a Picture   • Guess and Check

Choose a strategy and solve.

(5) Bev and Alice collect seashells. Bev has 75 more shells than Alice. Together they have 211 shells. How many shells does each have?

(6) Aunt Bet gave Ada some money for her birthday. Ada spent $5 on bowling. Then Fletch paid Ada the $10 he owed her. Ada then had $15. How much money did Ada receive from Aunt Bet?

(7) Anita has 3 in. of red fabric, 3 ft of blue fabric, and 3 yd of green fabric. She wants to make a belt. Which fabric is closest to the length that she will need?

(8) Van bought 3 pounds of apples and 6 oranges. Apples sell for 89¢ a pound, and oranges are 3 for 69¢. How much did Van spend in all?

WRITER'S CORNER

(9) Write a paragraph describing a room in your home. Include information that tells exactly where windows, doors, closets, and furniture are located in the room. Exchange with a partner. Have your partner draw a diagram of the room by using your description.

EXPLORING

Measuring Perimeter

The distance around a figure is called the **perimeter.**

WORK TOGETHER

Building Understanding

Use geometric shapes, string, and a metric ruler to find perimeters.

Estimate the perimeter of a large triangle in centimeters.

To find the perimeter of the triangle, cut the string to fit exactly around the outside edge of the triangle. Measure the string using the metric ruler.

Talk About It
- ▶ What is the perimeter of the triangle in centimeters?
- ▶ How close was your estimate to the perimeter?
- ▶ How can you use addition to find the perimeter of the triangle?

Write a number sentence that shows how you can use addition to find the perimeter of each figure below.

A.
5 dm
5 dm   5 dm
5 dm

B.
9 ft
6 ft   6 ft
9 ft

C.
4 yd
4 yd   4 yd
4 yd   4 yd
4 yd

D.
30 cm
36 cm
24 cm

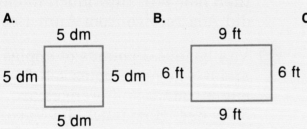

Talk About It
- ▶ If the sides of a figure are all the same length, how can you use multiplication to find the perimeter?
- ▶ What two ways can you use to find the perimeter of a rectangle?
- ▶ How can you use a calculator to find perimeter?

Making the Connection

Different shapes can have the same perimeter. Sonny wants to make a rectangular pen for his rabbit with 24 feet of fencing.

1. On graph paper, draw pictures of the different pens Sonny can make.

2. If each side is measured in whole units, how many different shapes of rectangular pens can Sonny make?

Checking Understanding

Work with a partner. Use an inch ruler and a string to find the perimeter of each.

3. a calendar   4. a box lid   5. a poster   6. your math book

Write a number sentence to find the perimeter of each figure.

7.
3 cm
1 cm
1 cm
2 cm
3 cm

8.

9.
3 cm
3 cm   3 cm
3 cm   3 cm
3 cm

Solve. You may use a calculator.

10. Each side of a square measures 11 in. Find the perimeter of the square.

11. How many feet of fencing are needed to enclose a rectangular pen that is 14 ft by 10 ft?

12. Marie drew a rectangle. The length of each shorter side was 4 cm. The length of each longer side was 7 cm. Find the perimeter.

13. **Logical Reasoning** What happens to the perimeter of a square when the lengths of all sides double? triple? (HINT: Use graph paper.)

LOGICAL REASONING

For each figure, find the length that is not given. You may use a calculator.

14. perimeter: 48 cm

12 cm   12 cm
12 cm

15. perimeter: 70 cm
25 cm
10 cm   10 cm

16. perimeter: 26 units
5
1
4
4   4
1
5

1. Jean bought a book for $16 and paints for $9. Later her father gave her $5. Then she had $8. How much money did she have before she went shopping?

2. Missy has two cousins. The sum of their ages is 13. The product of their ages is 36. How old is each cousin?

Tell how much time has elapsed.

3.  Starting Time   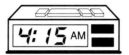 Ending Time

4.  Starting Time    Ending Time

Use the grid to write the ordered pair for each shape.

5. ■

6. ●

7. ▲

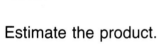

The first digit shows how many spaces to the right.

Estimate the product.

8.	9.	10.	11.	12.
59	432	6,734	38	213
× 4	× 7	× 6	×12	× 23

Find the product.

13.	14.	15.	16.	17.
1,354	63	85	432	213
× 3	×15	×20	× 17	× 23

18.	19.	20.	21.	22.
2,065	918	5,167	$5.67	$2.78
× 20	× 83	× 31	× 35	× 23

Copy and complete the table.

23.

×	100	200	300	400	500	600	700	800	900	1,000
60	■	■	■	■	■	■	■	■	■	■

Spotlight ON
PROBLEM SOLVING

Understand
Plan
Solve
Look Back

Draw Conclusions

You can use information from a situation to draw conclusions. Read the situation.

Ms. Jamison measured the height of her fourth graders. The shortest student in the class was 94 cm tall. The tallest student was 125 cm tall. There were 30 students in Ms. Jamison's class.

Talk About It

Can each conclusion be drawn from the information given? Write *yes*, *no*, or *maybe*.

a. All of Ms. Jamison's students were over 1 meter tall.

b. Most of Ms. Jamison's students were over 1 meter tall.

c. Twenty-nine of Ms. Jamison's students were over 1 meter tall.

d. The tallest student in the class was over 1 meter tall.

e. All of the students were over 90 centimeters tall.

f. The difference between the tallest and shortest students in Ms. Jamison's class was 31 centimeters.

Apply

Can the underlined conclusion be drawn from the information given? Write *yes*, *no*, or *maybe*.

 Marsha used 1 cup of milk for a recipe. Her mother tripled the recipe for a party. <u>Marsha's mother used 3 cups, or 24 ounces, of milk.</u>

 Dave has grown 4 inches since the last time he was measured. He now measures 4 feet 6 inches tall. <u>The last time Dave was measured he was more than 4 feet tall.</u>

 John takes 5 milliliters of medicine once a day. <u>He takes less than 30 milliliters a week.</u>

EXPLORING

Customary Units of Capacity

The customary units for measuring capacity are **teaspoon (t)**, **tablespoon (tbsp)**, **ounce (oz)**, **cup (c)**, **pint (pt)**, **quart (qt)**, and **gallon (gal)**.

WORK TOGETHER

Building Understanding

Work with a group. Use an empty lunch milk carton to explore capacity.

Fill the empty milk carton with water and pour the water into a gallon container.

Talk About It

▶ How many half-pint cartons of water are needed to fill the gallon container?

▶ Estimate how many quart containers you can fill with the gallon of water. Now, pour the water into the quart containers. How many quarts equal 1 gallon?

▶ How close was your estimate?

Customary Units to Measure Liquid

3 teaspoons (tsp)	= 1 tablespoon (tbsp)
8 fluid ounces	= 1 cup (c)
2 cups	= 1 pint (pt)
2 pints	= 1 quart (qt)
▨ quarts	= 1 gallon (gal)

Talk About It

▶ If you poured 3 pints from A to B, how many pints would be in each container?

▶ How many cups equal a pint?

▶ Now, how many cups would be in A and B?

▶ If you poured 1 gallon from D to C, how many gallons would be in each?

▶ How many quarts would be in each?

Look at the pictures.

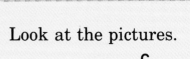

A.	B.	C.	D.
5 pints	3 pints	1 gallon	5 gallons

Making the Connection

You need to know how to measure capacity when using a recipe.

Suppose you are making fruit punch. You have only a cup to use for measuring. The punch bowl holds 1 gallon. The recipe calls for 1 quart of orange juice, 3 pints of pineapple juice, and 3 pints of grapefruit juice.

1. How many cups of juice will you use in all?

2. Will the punch bowl be large enough for the entire recipe?

3. What are three things that you can buy by the pint? by the quart? by the gallon?

Checking Understanding

Choose the appropriate unit of measure. Write *tsp, tbsp, c, pt, qt,* or *gal.*

4.

5.

6.

7.

8.

9.

Solve.

10. A recipe makes 2 quarts of soup and serves 8 people. If you want to serve soup to 12 people, how many more cups will you need? How many pints will you need?

11. Lou made chili sauce to freeze. He has enough sauce to fill six 2-quart freezer bags. How many gallons of sauce will he freeze?

MIXED REVIEW

Find the product.

| 1. $0.79 × 5 | 2. $0.99 × 8 | 3. $2.08 × 3 | 4. $12.55 × 4 | 5. $19.95 × 6 |

| 6. 40 ×15 | 7. 90 ×28 | 8. 18 ×65 | 9. 37 ×74 | 10. 183 × 12 |

Beth and Gary are making blueberry muffins for the fourth-grade picnic. The recipe calls for 4 cups of blueberries. The blueberries come in 1-pint containers. How many pints are needed to triple the recipe?

Sometimes you need to use more than one step to solve a problem.

▶ **UNDERSTAND**

What are you asked to find?

What facts are given?

▶ **PLAN**

What steps must you take to solve the problem?

You must answer two questions, so you need two steps.

Step 1. How many cups of blueberries are needed if you triple the recipe?

Step 2. How many pints does that equal?

▶ **SOLVE**

How can you solve the problem?

Answer the two questions.

Step 1. Multiply to find how many cups of blueberries are needed. $3 \times 4 = 12$ cups

Step 2. Since there are 2 cups in 1 pint, divide 12 by 2 to find how many pints are in 12 cups. $12 \div 2 = 6$ pints

So, Beth and Gary need 6 pints of blueberries.

▶ **LOOK BACK**

How can you check your answer?

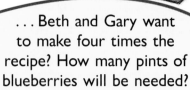

. . . Beth and Gary want to make four times the recipe? How many pints of blueberries will be needed?

Apply

Use more than one step to solve.

1 Olivia bought apples, oranges, and bananas. Her total was $5.16, including $0.29 tax. She paid $2.19 for the apples, and $0.79 for the bananas. How much did she pay for the oranges?

2 Sara works as a bagger at a grocery store. She works 3 hours on each Tuesday and Thursday afternoon and 5 hours on Saturday. If she is paid $4 an hour, how much does she earn in one week?

3 Gabe and Ted have made lemonade for the picnic. They use a cup to fill a gallon jug. Gabe pours 8 cups and Ted pours 4 cups. How many cups are left to pour?

| Mixed Applications | STRATEGIES | • Work Backward • Guess and Check • Write a Number Sentence • Make a Table |

Choose a strategy and solve.

4 The people at the picnic ate 188 hamburgers and hot dogs. They ate 10 more hot dogs than hamburgers. How many hamburgers did they eat?

5 Rusty bought a $5 gift. Next, he spent half of his remaining money on a T-shirt. Then, he paid $3 for lunch. After lunch he had $15 left. How much money did he have to start?

Organize this information into a table, and use it to answer Exercises 6–9.

Four fourth-grade classes attended the picnic. Class 4A had 24 students, Class 4B had 26 students, Class 4C had 27 students, and Class 4D had 22 students. There were 15 parents and 4 teachers attending the picnic.

6 How many students attended the picnic?

7 How many adults attended the picnic?

8 How many people attended the picnic in all?

9 How many more students attended the picnic than adults?

CAPACITY
Metric Units

The **milliliter (mL)** and the **liter (L)** are metric units of capacity. This picture will help you understand the relationship between these units.

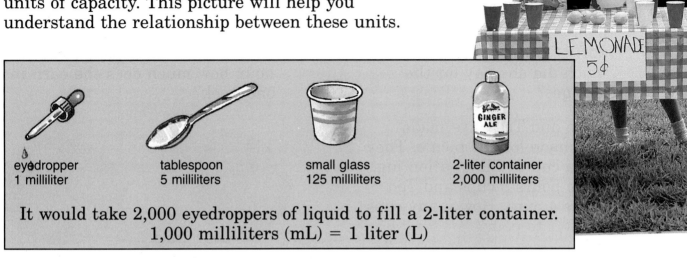

eyedropper 1 milliliter	tablespoon 5 milliliters	small glass 125 milliliters	2-liter container 2,000 milliliters

It would take 2,000 eyedroppers of liquid to fill a 2-liter container.
1,000 milliliters (mL) = 1 liter (L)

Talk About It

▶ Suppose you had to use the eyedropper to fill the tablespoon. How many eyedroppers would you use?

▶ Suppose you had to fill an aquarium. Which container would you use?

▶ Give two examples of when you can use metric units of capacity.

Name the objects in order from the one with the least capacity to the one with the greatest capacity.

Check for Understanding

Choose the appropriate unit of measure. Write *mL* or *L*.

1. a bottle of maple syrup
2. a fish bowl
3. white glue
4. a bathtub of water
5. a glass of lemonade
6. juice from 1 orange

Practice

Choose the appropriate unit of measure. Write *mL* or *L.*

7. a bucket of water

8. a baby bottle

9. a jug of grape juice

10. a bottle of shampoo

11. a bathroom sink

12. a hot-water heater

Write the correct measure.

13.

300 mL or 300 L

14.

3 mL or 3 L

15.

40 mL or 40 L

Choose the most reasonable measurement.

16. The gas tank of a car holds __?__ .　　**a.** 60 mL　　**b.** 30 L　　**c.** 180 L

17. A punch bowl holds __?__ of punch.　　**a.** 6 L　　**b.** 6 mL　　**c.** 60 mL

18. Risa used __?__ of suntan lotion.　　**a.** 5 mL　　**b.** 5 L　　**c.** 200 mL

19. The tank truck held __?__ of milk.　　**a.** 2 mL　　**b.** 2 L　　**c.** 2,000 L

Mixed Applications

20. A blue pitcher holds 800 mL. A green pitcher holds 4 L. Which pitcher holds more?

21. Fritz and Andre went on an all-day hike. They each had 750 mL of water. How much water did they have in all?

22. The soccer team is having a car wash. It takes 80 liters of water to wash 1 car. How many liters of water does it take to wash 10 cars?

23. Flora lives 1,072 km from the beach. John lives 987 km from the beach. Who lives closer to the beach?

EVERYDAY MATH CONNECTION

24. Jim and Mike are planning the food for a camping trip. They need 450 mL of milk for one recipe, 260 mL of milk for a second recipe, and 325 mL of milk for a third recipe. Will 1 L of milk be enough? Explain.

What metric container for capacity do you see most often in the grocery store?

WRAP
UP...

MASS
Metric Units

> The **mass** of an object tells how much it weighs.

The **gram (g)** and the **kilogram (kg)** are metric units of mass.

1,000 grams = 1 kilogram

The mass of a large paper clip is about 1 gram.

The mass of this book is about 1 kilogram.

The mass of a penny is about 3 grams.

The mass of an orange is about 300 grams.

The mass of a bicycle is about 16 kilograms.

Talk About It

▶ Hold your book in one hand and a pencil in the other hand. Which has the greater mass?

▶ What are two objects that have about the same mass?

▶ Which is larger, the marble or the table-tennis ball?

▶ Which has the greater mass?

▶ Does the larger object always have the greater mass? Why or why not?

Check for Understanding

Choose the appropriate unit to weigh each item. Write *g* or *kg*.

1.

2.

3.

4.

Practice

Choose the appropriate unit to weigh each item. Write *g* or *kg*.

5.    6.   7.   8.

Choose the more reasonable measurement.

9. a can of soup
   312 g or 312 kg

10. a brick
    1 g or 1 kg

11. a dime
    2 g or 2 kg

12. a truck
    2,000 g or 2,000 kg

Mixed Applications

13. Leanne bought 5 boxes of cereal. Each box weighs 400 grams. How many kilograms do all the boxes weigh?

14. Penny needs 4 balls of yarn to make mittens. Each ball weighs 4 ounces and costs 50¢ an ounce. How much will the yarn cost?

15. **Number Sense** Choose the weights from the tags to complete these sentences: Mera went grocery shopping. She bought one _?_ package of cream cheese, a _?_ box of cereal, a _?_ chicken, and a _?_ turkey.

16. **Find Data** Some school supplies are sold by the **gross,** which is 12 dozen. Find the weights of 1 pencil, 1 eraser, and 1 piece of chalk. Use these weights to find the weight of a gross of each item. You may use a calculator to help you. Make a table to record the data.

HEALTH CONNECTION

The labels on most packaged foods contain nutrition information. The amounts of nutrients are sometimes given in grams. Use the nutrition information to answer Exercises 17–19.

17. How many grams of protein are in 3 bags of pretzels?

18. How many grams of carbohydrates are consumed if you eat only half of the pretzels?

19. Explain why it may be important to list how many grams of fat or cholesterol there are.

PRETZELS
Nutritional Information
Calories   150
Protein   3 g
Carbohydrate   22 g
Fat   0 g
Cholesterol   0 mg

Why do you think nutrition information is given most often in grams, not ounces?

WRAP UP...

WEIGHT
Customary Units

Carl and his classmates like to race miniature cars. Carl compared his toy car to his mother's new car.

The **ounce (oz), pound (lb),** and **ton (T)** are customary units used to measure weight.

16 ounces (oz) = 1 pound (lb)
2,000 pounds = 1 ton (T)

A small toy car weighs about 1 ounce.

A remote-control toy car weighs about 1 pound.

A full-size car weighs about 1 ton.

Talk About It

▶ Name something that weighs an ounce or less.

▶ Name something that weighs about a pound.

▶ Name something that weighs about a ton.

Use a calculator to change units. Carl stores his cars in a carrying case that weighs 3 pounds. How many ounces are in 3 pounds?

Since 16 ounces equal 1 pound, multiply by 16. **Press:** 3 × 1 6 = 48.

So, there are 48 ounces in 3 pounds.

Check for Understanding

Choose the appropriate unit of measure. Write *oz, lb,* or *T.*

1. 2. 3.

Write the letter of the appropriate estimate for each.

4. a school bus
   a. about 2 T
   b. about 20 lb

5. a pair of shoes
   a. about 2 T
   b. about 2 lb

6. a pencil
   a. about 1 oz
   b. about 1 lb

Practice

Choose the appropriate unit of measure. Write *oz*, *lb*, or *T*.

7.

8.

9.

10.

Choose the more reasonable measurement.

11.

$1\frac{1}{2}$ oz or $1\frac{1}{2}$ lb

12.

2 oz or 2 lb

13.

3 oz or 3 lb

14.

1 lb or 1 T

Complete. You may use a calculator.

15. 4 lb = ▉ oz

16. 2 T = ▉ lb

17. 32 oz = ▉ lb

18. 1 lb 3 oz = ▉ oz

Mixed Applications

19. Each medal for the field-day events weighs 2 oz. There are 72 medals in a box. The empty box weighs 12 oz. How much do the medals and the box weigh?

20. Mr. Tims has 258 packages of raisins. Each package weighs 5 oz. What is the total weight of the raisins? Write your answer, using *lb* and *oz*.

21. **Estimation** If every student in your class climbed onto a big scale, about how much would they weigh?

22. Which container of juice is the better buy?

SCIENCE CONNECTION

Gravity is the pulling force we feel from large objects, such as the earth and the moon. A fourth grader who weighs 60 lb on the earth would weigh only about 10 lb on the moon. Gravity is weaker on the moon because the moon is smaller and has less mass than the earth.

23. Would a 1-ton truck on Earth weigh more than or less than it would on the moon?

24. Divide your weight by 6 to find about how much you would weigh on the moon.

List these objects in order from lightest to heaviest: bus, bicycle, motorcycle, skateboard.

WRAP UP...

Mrs. Doyle has a recipe for spaghetti sauce. It calls for 2 quarts of tomato sauce and 9 teaspoons of oregano. How many cups of tomato sauce will Mrs. Doyle use? How many tablespoons of oregano will she use?

When you change larger units to smaller units, you multiply.

number of quarts		cups in 1 quart		total cups
2	×	4	=	8

Since there are 4 cups in 1 quart, Mrs. Doyle will use 8 cups of tomato sauce.

When you change smaller units into larger units, you divide.

number of teaspoons		teaspoons in 1 tablespoon		total tablespoons
9	÷	3	=	3

Since there are 3 teaspoons in 1 tablespoon, Mrs. Doyle will use 3 tablespoons of oregano.

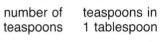

You can use a calculator when changing larger units.

A. How many feet are in 23 miles?

number of miles	feet in 1 mile	total feet
23	× 5,280	= 121,440 ft

Press:

B. How many yards are in 288 feet?

number of feet	feet in 1 yard	total yards
288	÷ 3	= 96 yd

Press:

Check for Understanding

Write *multiply* or *divide* to tell how you change the units.

1. feet to inches
2. pounds to ounces
3. feet to yards
4. cups to pints

Complete. Use a calculator.

5. 180 ft = ■ yd
6. 35 lb = ■ oz
7. 68 gal = ■ qt
8. 6,000 lb = ■ T

Practice

Write *true* or *false* for each statement.

9. When you change inches to feet, you divide.

10. When you change tons to pounds, you divide.

11. There are 12 quarts in 3 gallons.

12. Thirty-six inches are equal to 2 yards.

Complete. You may use a calculator.

13. ■ cups = 3 quarts   14. 600 feet = ■ yards   15. 32 ounces = ■ pounds

Mixed Applications

16. April is making waffles. She has a gallon of milk. The recipe calls for 1 cup of milk. How many cups of milk will she have left after she makes the waffles?

17. Jacob bought 2 lb of peanuts at the baseball game. He shared them equally with 3 friends. How many ounces of peanuts did each person receive?

18. **Logical Reasoning** Bryan used a 2-ft piece of wood to make a rack for hanging brushes. He hammered a nail every 2 in. How many nails did he use?

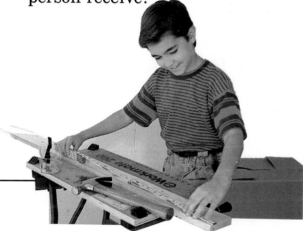

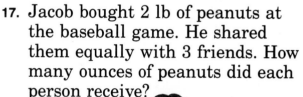

MIXED REVIEW

Use mental math to find the product.

1. $36 \times 100 = n$ 2. $10 \times 895 = n$ 3. $1,000 \times 4,374 = n$ 4. $100 \times 90 = n$

Estimate the sum or difference, using front-end digits.

5. 800	6. 3,894	7. 502	8. 26,683	9. 14,005
−263	+3,592	−147	+18,894	− 8,235

How can you change a division problem to make it easier to compute mentally?

WRAP UP...

CHAPTER REVIEW

Vocabulary Check

Choose a word from the box to complete each sentence.

centimeter
decimeter
foot
inch
kilometer
mass
meter
mile
perimeter
yard

I can choose standard or nonstandard units to measure something.

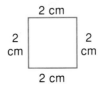

1. The gram (g) and the kilogram (kg) are metric units of __?__ . *(page 228)*

2. The distance around a figure is called the __?__ . *(page 218)*

3. You can walk a __?__ in about 20 min. *(page 214)*

4. A __?__ is about the length of a baseball bat. *(page 214)*

5. The length of a man's shoe is about a __?__ . *(page 214)*

6. The length of your thumb from the first knuckle to the tip is about an __?__ . *(page 214)*

7. A __?__ is the distance you can walk in about 15 min. *(page 210)*

8. The distance from one hand to the other when your arms are stretched out is about a __?__ . *(page 210)*

9. A __?__ is about the width of your index finger. *(page 210)*

10. The width of an adult's hand is about a __?__ . *(page 210)*

Concept Check

Choose the appropriate unit of measure. Write *cm, dm, m,* or *km.* *(page 210)*

11. length of a fly

12. width of a door

13. height of a classmate

14. distance a truck travels in 2 hr

15. length of your classroom

Name the longer unit. *(pages 210, 214)*

16. 1 ft or 1 in.

17. 1 cm or 1 m

18. 1 yd or 1 in.

19. 1 mi or 1 yd

Write a number sentence to find the perimeter of each figure. Solve. *(page 218)*

20.

2 cm
2 cm   2 cm
2 cm

21.

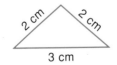

2 cm   2 cm
3 cm

22.

4 cm
1 cm

Choose the appropriate unit of measure. Write *c, pt, qt,* or *gal.* (page 222)

23. 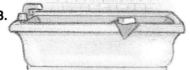 **24.**  **25.**

Choose the more reasonable measurement. (page 226)

26. a kitchen sink
17 L or 17 mL

27. a straw
6 mL or 6 L

28. a bottle of lotion
30 L or 30 mL

Skill Check

Find the length of each in centimeters. (page 208)

29.  **30.**  **31.**

Find the perimeter of each. (page 218)

32.   **33.** 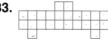 **34.**   **35.**

Choose the better estimate of mass or weight for each. (pages 228, 230)

36.

3 kg or 3 g

37.

300 g or 300 kg

38.

4,000 lb or 4,000 T

Complete. You may use a calculator. (pages 230, 232)

39. 18 lb = ▨ oz

40. 50 lb = ▨ oz

41. 2 lb 9 oz = ▨ oz

Problem-Solving Check (pages 216, 224)

42. Ron, Darryl, and Jack are comparing their ages. Ron is older than Jack but younger than Darryl. Darryl is older than Jack. Who is the youngest?

43. A recipe for 1 loaf of strawberry bread calls for 4 cups of strawberries. Strawberries come in 1-pint containers. How many pints of strawberries are needed to make 3 loaves?

CHAPTER TEST

Name the longer unit.

1. 1 m or 1 km **2.** 80 cm or 8 m **3.** 1 mi or 2,000 yd **4.** 60 in. or 9 ft

5. 1 cm or 1 in. **6.** 4 ft or 4 yd **7.** 10 yd or 10 mi **8.** 2 dm or 2 m

Choose the appropriate unit of measure. Write *cm, dm, m,* or *km.*

9. height of a tree **10.** length of your arm **11.** distance from Ohio to Utah **12.** width of your math book

Find the perimeter of each in centimeters.

13.

14.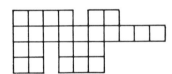

15.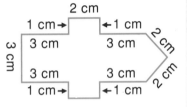

Write a number sentence to find the perimeter of each figure. Solve.

16.

17.

18.

Choose the more reasonable measurement.

19. cheeseburger 180 g or 180 kg **20.** library book 1 g or 1 kg **21.** kitten 10 lb or 10 oz **22.** bulldozer 4 T or 400 lb

Solve.

23. Marge is taller than Pam. Oren is taller than Marge. Sylvia's height is between Marge's and Oren's heights. Who is the shortest?

24. Ralph spent $5.28 for wood, $1.97 for glue, and $2.74 for paint. How much change did he receive from a $20.00 bill?

25. Kelly decorated T-shirts. She put 6 bows on each of 5 shirts. She put 4 bows on each of 3 shirts. How many bows did she use?

I can draw a picture to solve a problem.

Where Is It?

N
W   E
S

A compass identifies direction. A compass rose appears on all maps and shows the directions north, south, east, and west. With your teammates, create a map of your classroom.

☐ Measure distances to the nearest meter, and draw objects in the correct places on your map.

☐ Let 1 unit length on the grid = 1 m on the map.

Decide

☐ Talk about how you can use graph paper, a compass, and a meterstick to make a classroom map.

Do

☐ Work with your teammates.

☐ Make a dot in the middle of a sheet of graph paper. Label it WE ARE HERE.

☐ Hold the compass level, and turn it until the needle points north. Draw a compass rose in the upper right corner of your paper, and record the directions.

☐ Point to objects that are north, south, east, and west.

Share

☐ Show your map. With other teams, compare distances of objects from the center dot.

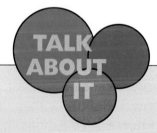

TALK ABOUT IT

• How can you use your map to imagine the distance from one end of the classroom to the other?

• In your everyday activities, what other metric measurements have you noticed?

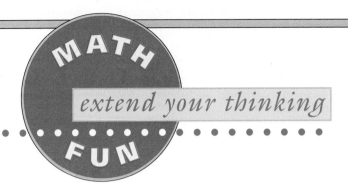

MATH FUN

extend your thinking

Activity

Crazy Measures

Find the "crazy measures" in the chart. Record the letters of the crazy measures. Then unscramble the letters to write a word that describes how well you completed this activity.

HINT: There are 9 crazy measures.

_ _ _ _ _ _ _ _ _

L A paper clip weighs 1 kg.	B An apple tree is 4 m high.	C Michael Jordon is 10 ft tall.	N A building is 1 m high.	J A pickup truck weighs 2 T.
T Joe's foot is 8 ft long.	G The chef made 20 qt of potato soup.	H Mary Kathryn's waist is 26 in. around.	E A baseball bat is 10 in. long.	E A tree is 10 km tall.
E A dog stands 5 ft high.	A A pencil is 5 in. long.	L Antarctica is 6,000 yd away.	D A window is 1 m wide.	X This book weighs 3 oz.

Challenge

Logical Reasoning

1. Mineral water comes in 3-pint, 2-quart, and 1-gallon bottles. What is the least number of bottles that will contain exactly 29 pints?

2. Cheese comes in 10-oz, 1-lb, and $1\frac{1}{2}$-lb packages. What is the least number of packages that will contain exactly 84 oz of cheese?

Make Decisions

Which would you buy? Explain your decision.

1. a. one 2-lb package of cheese for $3.89
   b. three 10-oz packages of cheese for $3.75

2. a. one 64-oz container of juice for $1.99
   b. two 32-oz containers for $2.09

3. a. two gallons of milk for $4.38
   b. four quarts of milk for $5.60

CUMULATIVE REVIEW

Write the letter of the correct answer.

1. $39 + 45 + 16 + 92 =$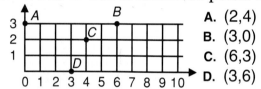

    A. 192   **B.** 193

    C. 195   **D.** not here

2. Estimate the difference.
$3,291 - 1,873 =$

    A. 2,000   **B.** 3,000

    C. 4,000   **D.** 6,000

3. Which is the standard form for four million, seven hundred sixty-nine thousand, three hundred five?

    A. 4,305,769   **B.** 4,350,769

    C. 47,693,005   **D.** not here

4. Which fact is missing from this family of facts?
$9 \times 6 = 54$ $54 \div 6 = 9$
        $6 \times 9 = 54$

    A. $9 - 6 = 3$ **B.** $6 + 9 = 15$

    C. $54 \div 9 = 6$ **D.** $54 \times 6 = 324$

5. What time is shown on the clock?

    A. 3:43

    B. 3:45

    C. 4:15

    D. 9:17

6. What is the location of point B?

    A. (2,4)

    B. (3,0)

    C. (6,3)

    D. (3,6)

7. $5,000 \times 40 =$

    A. 2,000   **B.** 20,000

    C. 200,000   **D.** not here

8.
$$
\begin{array}{r}
\$289.67 \\
\times \quad\quad 9 \\
\hline
\end{array}
$$

    A. $1,807.03   **B.** $1,989.66

    C. $2,607.03   **D.** $2,703.07

9. Find the perimeter.

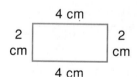

    A. 12 cm

    B. 14 cm

    C. 18 cm

    D. 21 cm

10. 8 lb 12 oz = ▨ oz

    A. 72   **B.** 108

    C. 138   **D.** 140

11. Mrs. Amos paid $15,488.00 for her car. The first year she spent $286.19 on repairs. The second year she spent $413.05 on repairs. How much more did she spend on repairs the second year?

    A. $126.86   **B.** $273.14

    C. $699.24   **D.** $14,734.99

12. Bud has $327 in his bank account. Last week he withdrew $100. Two weeks ago he withdrew $45. How much was in his account before he withdrew any money?

    A. $182   **B.** $218

    C. $272   **D.** $472

8

DIVIDING
BY 1-DIGIT NUMBERS

Did you know ...

... that laser light is as useful as it is beautiful? Over 4,000 telephone calls at a time can be sent through one glass fiber thinner than a human hair.

After the laser show at the science museum, Terry called his uncle George to tell him about it. The call lasted for 3 minutes and cost $0.75. How can Terry find how much the call cost per minute if each minute cost the same?

EXPLORING

Patterns in Division

You can use *n* instead of ■ to show a missing number.

Newspapers communicate the news from around the world. Joey helps his brother deliver newspapers. They have 80 newspapers wrapped into 4 equal bundles. How many newspapers are in each bundle?

Divide. $80 \div 4 = n$ $4\overline{)80}$

dividend   divisor   quotient

WORK TOGETHER

Building Understanding

Use place-value materials to model the problem. There are 8 tens in 80, so you can use 8 longs. Draw 4 circles. Put an equal number of longs into each circle.

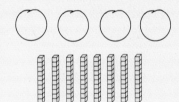

Use place-value materials.

a. $4 \div 2 = n$

b. $40 \div 2 = n$

c. $400 \div 2 = n$

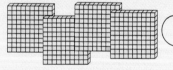

Talk About It

▶ Why were 4 circles used?

▶ How many longs did you put in each circle?

▶ What number do the longs represent? So, how many newspapers are in each bundle?

▶ Write a number sentence to show what you did.

Talk About It

▶ How can you use multiplication to find the quotient?

▶ What is the basic division fact for each problem?

▶ What pattern do you see in the quotients?

242

Making the Connection

Look for patterns in division.

Example   Place Value

	Place-Value Chart			
	Thousands	**Hundreds**	**Tens**	**Ones**
$2\overline{)8}$ → 8 ones ÷ 2 = →				4
$2\overline{)80}$ → 8 tens ÷ 2 = →			4	0
$2\overline{)800}$ → 8 hundreds ÷ 2 = →		4	0	0
$2\overline{)8,000}$ → 8 thousands ÷ 2 = →	4	0	0	0

Rewrite each problem to show place value as in the example. Then record the quotient on a place-value chart like the one above.

1. $2\overline{)6}$
   $2\overline{)60}$
   $2\overline{)600}$
   $2\overline{)6,000}$

2. $9 \div 3 = n$
   $90 \div 3 = n$
   $900 \div 3 = n$
   $9,000 \div 3 = n$

3. $5\overline{)10}$
   $5\overline{)100}$
   $5\overline{)1,000}$
   $5\overline{)10,000}$

4. $12 \div 4 = n$
   $120 \div 4 = n$
   $1,200 \div 4 = n$
   $12,000 \div 4 = n$

5. Look at the place-value chart in the example. As each quotient was written on the chart, did the value of the digit 4 increase or decrease?

6. As the number of zeros in the dividend increases, what happens to the number of zeros in the quotient? Why are the zeros necessary?

Checking Understanding

Using what you have learned, tell how many digits there will be in each quotient.

7. $6\overline{)600}$

8. $2\overline{)12,000}$

9. $4\overline{)20}$

10. $5\overline{)2,000}$

Complete the pattern.

11. $\overset{7}{5\overline{)35}}$ $\overset{70}{5\overline{)350}}$ $\overset{\blacksquare\blacksquare\blacksquare}{5\overline{)3,5\,0\,0}}$

12. $\overset{6}{8\overline{)48}}$ $\overset{60}{8\overline{)480}}$ $\overset{\blacksquare\blacksquare\blacksquare}{8\overline{)4,8\,0\,0}}$

Find the quotient. Then multiply each dividend by 10, 100, and 1,000 to make a pattern.

13. $6\overline{)42}$

14. $9\overline{)27}$

15. $3\overline{)18}$

16. $8\overline{)32}$

17. $6\overline{)54}$

Multiplication and Division

Copies of messages can be sent within minutes by using a facsimile machine (fax). Mr. Hunt wants to fax 43 pages of a report to his Miami office. If his fax machine will send 6 pages per minute, how long will it take to fax the report to Miami?

Divide. $43 \div 6 = n$ $6\overline{)43}$

dividend   divisor   quotient

Think of the missing factor in a multiplication problem.

$43 \div 6 = n, n \times 6 = 43$

Think: $6 \times 6 = 36 \longrightarrow$ not close enough
$7 \times 6 = 42 \longrightarrow$ close
$8 \times 6 = 48 \longrightarrow$ over

$$\begin{array}{r} 7\,r1 \\ 6\overline{)43} \\ -42 \\ \hline 1 \end{array}$$

So, $43 \div 6 = 7$ remainder 1.

Mr. Hunt can fax his report in a little more than 7 minutes.

More Examples

A. $35 \div 8 = n$

Think: $3 \times 8 = 24 \longrightarrow$ not close enough
$4 \times 8 = 32 \longrightarrow$ close
$5 \times 8 = 40 \longrightarrow$ over

$$\begin{array}{r} 4\,r3 \\ 8\overline{)35} \\ -32 \\ \hline 3 \end{array}$$

So, $35 \div 8 = 4$ r3.

B. $67 \div 9 = n$

Think: $6 \times 9 = 54 \longrightarrow$ not close enough
$7 \times 9 = 63 \longrightarrow$ close
$8 \times 9 = 72 \longrightarrow$ over

$$\begin{array}{r} 7\,r4 \\ 9\overline{)67} \\ -63 \\ \hline 4 \end{array}$$

So, $67 \div 9 = 7$ r4.

Check for Understanding

Copy and complete.

1. $20 \div 6 = n$

Think: $2 \times 6 = 12$
$3 \times 6 = 18$
$4 \times 6 = 24$

2. $29 \div 5 = n$

Think: $4 \times 5 = n$
$5 \times 5 = n$
$6 \times 5 = n$

3. $35 \div 4 = n$

Think: $7 \times 4 = n$
$8 \times 4 = n$
$9 \times 4 = n$

Practice

Copy and complete.

4. $25 \div 6 = n$

    Think: $3 \times 6 = 18$
                   $4 \times 6 = 24$
                   $5 \times 6 = 30$

5. $32 \div 5 = n$

    Think: $5 \times 5 = n$
                   $6 \times 5 = n$
                   $7 \times 5 = n$

6. $30 \div 9 = n$

    Think: $2 \times 9 = n$
                   $3 \times 9 = n$
                   $4 \times 9 = n$

Use multiplication to find the quotient.

7. $26 \div 5 = n$ **8.** $75 \div 9 = n$ **9.** $38 \div 4 = n$ **10.** $51 \div 8 = n$

11. $3\overline{)29}$ **12.** $2\overline{)19}$ **13.** $6\overline{)32}$ **14.** $4\overline{)23}$ **15.** $8\overline{)68}$ **16.** $5\overline{)47}$

Use this division example for Exercises 17–20.
Write the number for each part of the division problem named. $8\overline{)52}^{\,6\,r4}$

17. divisor   **18.** quotient   **19.** dividend   **20.** remainder

Mixed Applications

21. The quotient is 5, and the divisor is 6. The dividend is 34. I am the remainder. What number am I?

22. If you divide me by 9, the remainder is 4. I am a multiple of 10. What two-digit number am I?

23. Barry types for Ms. Griff. He can type 9 pages per hour. How many pages can he type in 6 hours?

24. Mr. Simms gives an oral quiz to one student at a time. Each quiz takes 8 minutes. How many students can he quiz in 1 hour? How many minutes will be left?

25. Write a Question Mrs. Rosen has 23 reports to be typed. She has 3 secretaries. It takes 1 hour to type each report, and she needs the reports in 8 hours. Exchange with a classmate to solve.

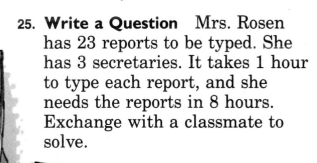

What is the largest remainder you can have when you divide by 8?

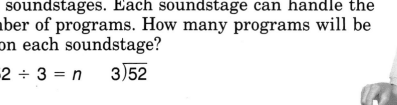

WHBJ-TV produces 52 children's programs per season on their 3 soundstages. Each soundstage can handle the same number of programs. How many programs will be produced on each soundstage?

Divide. $52 \div 3 = n$ $3\overline{)52}$

WORK TOGETHER

Building Understanding

Use place-value materials to model the problem. Record the numbers as you complete each step.

Step 1
Draw 3 circles. Show 52 as 5 tens and 2 ones.

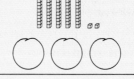

Record:

$3\overline{)52}$

Step 2
Place an equal number of tens into each circle.

Record:

$$\begin{array}{r} 1 \\ 3\overline{)52} \\ -3 \\ \hline 2 \end{array}$$

← 1 ten in each group
← 3 tens used
← 2 tens left

Step 3
Regroup the 2 tens left over into ones.

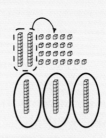

Record:

$$\begin{array}{r} 1 \\ 3\overline{)52} \\ -3\downarrow \\ \hline 22 \end{array}$$ Bring down ones.

Step 4
Place an equal number of ones into each circle.

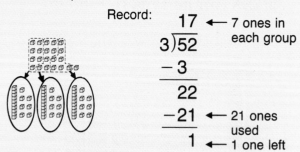

Record:

$$\begin{array}{r} 17 \\ 3\overline{)52} \\ -3 \\ \hline 22 \\ -21 \\ \hline 1 \end{array}$$

← 7 ones in each group

← 21 ones used
← 1 one left

Talk About It

▶ In Step 2, why did you put only 1 ten in each circle?

▶ Why did you have to regroup the 2 tens left over?

▶ Why must you bring down the ones before you can divide again?

▶ After Step 4, how many blocks are in each circle? So, how many programs will be produced on each soundstage?

Making the Connection

You can model division with money as you did with place-value materials.

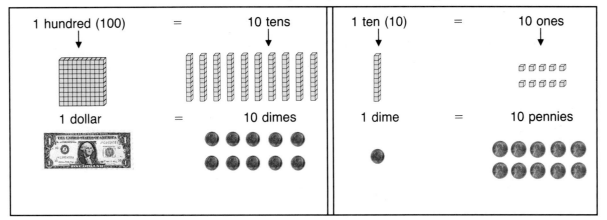

Example

$3.24 \div 2 = n$

$=$1.62$ $= 1.62

So, $3.24 \div 2 = 1.62.

Use play money to model each problem. Solve.

1. $4.66 \div 2 = n$ **2.** $7.20 \div 3 = n$

Checking Understanding

Use place-value materials to model each problem. Record the numbers as you complete each step.

3. $2\overline{)46}$ **4.** $3\overline{)48}$ **5.** $2\overline{)38}$ **6.** $3\overline{)42}$

Use play money to model each problem. Solve.

7. $5.00 \div 2 = n$ **8.** $9.75 \div 3 = n$ **9.** $8.12 \div 4 = n$

More Practice, Lesson 8.3, page H62   **247**

ESTIMATING QUOTIENTS

Julianne and Juanita communicate with each other by sending messages on their computers. During summer vacation they sent about 4 messages per day for a total of 152 messages. For about how many days did they send computer messages?

Estimate. $152 \div 4 = n$ $4\overline{)152}$

One way to estimate is to look for compatible numbers. **Compatible numbers** are numbers that are easy to work with mentally.

Change the dividend to the nearest number that can be easily divided by 4.

$$
4\overline{)152} \quad \rightarrow \quad
\begin{array}{l} \text{Think of a} \\ \text{basic fact.} \\ 3 \times 4 = 12 \\ 4 \times 4 = 16 \end{array}
\quad \rightarrow \quad
\begin{array}{l} \text{Change the} \\ \text{dividend.} \\ 40 \\ 4\overline{)160} \end{array}
$$

So, they sent messages on about 40 days.

Talk About It

▶ How many digits are in the quotient of $4\overline{)16}$?

▶ How many digits are in the quotient of $4\overline{)160}$?

▶ Why was 152 changed to 160?

Check for Understanding

Choose the letter of the best estimate. Write the method you used.

1. $2\overline{)134}$ a. 50   b. 30   c. 60   d. 70

2. $6\overline{)59}$ a. 10   b. 40   c. 9   d. 12

Estimate the quotient.

3. $3\overline{)268}$ 4. $5\overline{)207}$ 5. $8\overline{)490}$ 6. $3\overline{)133}$

Practice

Choose the letter of the best estimate. Write the method you used.

7. $2\overline{)181}$ **a.** 70   **b.** 80   **c.** 90   **d.** 100

8. $5\overline{)263}$ **a.** 40   **b.** 45   **c.** 50   **d.** 60

9. $6\overline{)411}$ **a.** 60   **b.** 70   **c.** 80   **d.** 90

Estimate the quotient. Look for compatible numbers.

10. $4\overline{)203}$ 11. $4\overline{)197}$ 12. $9\overline{)259}$ 13. $7\overline{)418}$ 14. $5\overline{)312}$

15. $822 \div 9 = n$ 16. $458 \div 5 = n$ 17. $621 \div 7 = n$ 18. $178 \div 6 = n$

Mixed Applications

19. Val is transferring 243 files to diskettes. She can put 8 files on each diskette. About how many diskettes will she use?

20. In a film about polar bears, walruses, rabbits, and seals, the producer wants each animal's segment to be the same. The film will last 82 minutes. About how long will each segment be?

21. **Number Sense** If the divisor increases and the dividend remains the same, what happens to the quotient?

MIXED REVIEW

Write the customary unit that completes each sentence.

1. An _?_ is about the length of your thumb from the first knuckle to the tip.

2. A _?_ is about the distance you can walk in 20 minutes.

3. A _?_ is about the length of a baseball bat.

4. A _?_ is about the length of a man's shoe.

Name the longer unit.

5. 1 in. or 1 ft   6. 5 mi or 5 yd   7. 230 ft or 230 yd

Explain how to find the length of an object in yards if you know its length in feet.

WRAP UP...

PROBLEM *Solving*

Megan, James, Kim, and Christy are standing in line to use the telephone. James is behind Megan and in front of Kim. Megan is behind Christy and in front of James. In what order are the children standing in line?

Understand
Plan
Solve
Look Back

Choosing a strategy is an important part of making a plan to solve a problem. Sometimes, you can use different strategies to solve the same problem.

Strategy: Act It Out

Ask four classmates to pretend to be Megan, James, Kim, and Christy. You can move them around according to the directions in the problem until they are in the correct order.

The correct order of the children standing in line is Christy, Megan, James, and Kim.

Strategy: Draw a Picture

Draw a straight line. Use stick figures to show each person's place in line. Show James behind Megan and in front of Kim. Show Christy in front of Megan.

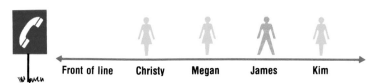

Front of line   Christy   Megan   James   Kim

Now you can see that the order of the children standing in line is Christy, Megan, James, and Kim.

WHAT IF... . . . Gilbert is in front of Christy? In what order are the children standing?

250

Choose a strategy and solve.
Complete the table for Exercises 1–3.

Use the table for Exercises 4–5.

Telephone Equipment Damaged			
Equipment	**Total**	**Damaged**	**Working**
(1) Fax machines	15	7	■
(2) Telephones	45	■	45
(3) Computers	9	■	0

(4) What is the total number of damaged pieces of equipment?

(5) Which kind of equipment was least damaged?

(6) Tara called her friend in Cleveland. They talked for 14 minutes. The first 3 minutes cost $1.00. Each minute after that cost $0.23. How much did she pay for the call?

(7) Bart has 14 telephone numbers in his address book. There are 6 more local numbers than long-distance numbers. How many long-distance numbers are there?

Use the digits 1–9 on the number pad for Exercises 8–10.

(8) Add the digits across each row on the number pad. Look for a pattern in the sums. What is it?

(9) Now add the digits in each column. What is the pattern in the sums?

(10) What pattern do you see for any line of 3 digits that passes through the center digit?

WRITER'S CORNER

Global Telephone Company Rates						
Long Distance from Dover	**Weekday**		**Evening**		**After 11 P.M. & Sat., Sun.**	
	First Min	**Each Extra Min**	**First Min**	**Each Extra Min**	**First Min**	**Each Extra Min**
To Ashford	$0.40	$0.28	$0.26	$0.18	$0.16	$0.11
To Wilmouth	$0.51	$0.37	$0.33	$0.24	$0.25	$0.20
To York	$0.35	$0.23	$0.26	$0.24	$0.18	$0.13

(11) Use the table to write three word problems. Exchange with a classmate and solve.

DIVIDING
Two-Digit Numbers

A fourth-grade class makes collages to show different ways to communicate. The 5 groups cut pictures from 65 magazines. If they share the magazines equally, how many can each group use?

Divide. $65 \div 5 = n$ $5\overline{)65}$

Step 1	Step 2	Step 3	Step 4
Decide where to place the first digit in the quotient.	Divide the tens. $5\overline{)6}$ **Think:** $5 \times n \approx 6$ $\approx$ means *is about.*	Bring down the ones. Divide. $5\overline{)15}$ **Think:** $5 \times n \approx 15.$	Check the answer by multiplying.
■ There are $5\overline{)65}$ enough tens.	$\begin{array}{r} 1 \\ 5\overline{)65} \\ -5 \\ \hline 1 \end{array}$ Multiply. 1×5 Subtract. $6 - 5$ Compare the remainder to the divisor. $1 < 5$	$\begin{array}{r} 13 \\ 5\overline{)65} \\ -5\downarrow \\ \hline 15 \\ -15 \\ \hline 0 \end{array}$ Multiply. 5×3 Subtract. $15 - 15$ Compare. $0 < 5$	$\begin{array}{r} 13 \leftarrow \text{quotient} \\ \times\ 5 \leftarrow \text{divisor} \\ \hline 65 \\ +\ 0 \leftarrow \text{remainder.} \\ \hline 65 \leftarrow \text{dividend} \end{array}$ Add the So, the quotient is correct.

So, each group uses 13 magazines.

Talk About It

▶ How can you decide where to place the first digit in the quotient?

▶ Why is it necessary to compare the remainder to the divisor in Steps 2 and 3?

Check for Understanding

Copy each problem. Draw a ■ where the first digit in the quotient should be placed.

1. $6\overline{)36}$
2. $8\overline{)93}$
3. $4\overline{)56}$
4. $5\overline{)28}$

Find the quotient. Check by multiplying.

5. $86 \div 6 = n$
6. $77 \div 2 = n$
7. $5\overline{)70}$
8. $7\overline{)87}$

Practice

Copy each problem. Draw a ■ where the first digit in the quotient should be placed.

9. $5\overline{)25}$ **10.** $7\overline{)82}$ **11.** $8\overline{)66}$ **12.** $2\overline{)43}$ **13.** $4\overline{)87}$

Find the quotient. Check by multiplying.

14. $2\overline{)64}$ **15.** $4\overline{)60}$ **16.** $6\overline{)76}$ **17.** $8\overline{)95}$ **18.** $3\overline{)92}$ **19.** $4\overline{)59}$

20. $52 \div 4 = n$ **21.** $48 \div 3 = n$ **22.** $79 \div 5 = n$ **23.** $26 \div 2 = n$ **24.** $44 \div 3 = n$

Mixed Applications

25. Darren's group cut out 82 pictures of computers. Darren put the pictures into 7 equal piles. How many pictures were in each pile? How many pictures were left over?

26. Logical Reasoning Bea's group of 4 members cut out 59 pictures for the collage. Bea cut out 3 more pictures than the others, who each cut out the same number. How many pictures did each other member cut out?

27. Analyze Data The table shows a daily schedule of the time the students worked on their collages. For how long did they work each day?

	Tuesday	Wednesday	Thursday
Start	1:10 P.M.	2:00 P.M.	1:30 P.M.
Finish	2:30 P.M.	3:15 P.M.	2:20 P.M.

 CALCULATOR

Copy these exercises. Use your calculator to choose the

, , , or key for each ◯.

Write the correct sign for the ◯.

28. $35 \bigcirc 5 \bigcirc 5 = 2$ **29.** $28 \bigcirc 4 \bigcirc 4 = 11$

30. $36 \bigcirc 4 \bigcirc 3 = 27$ **31.** $3 \bigcirc 4 \bigcirc 6 = 2$

When you check division by multiplication, what do you do with the remainder?

WRAP UP...

Use the data for Exercises 1–3.

Telephone Numbers

Kimmie
556-2383

Suzette
766-8492

Chelsea
353-8051

LaWanda
766-6379

1. The girls played a game using their telephone numbers. First, each girl wrote her seven-digit number in standard form. Kimmie's was 5,562,383. Write the other numbers in standard form.

2. Then each girl subtracted her seven-digit number from each number that was greater than her own. Which girl had to do the most subtraction?

3. Which girl did not have to do any subtraction problems? Why?

Write two different names for each.

4. 420 5. 810 6. 9,700 7. 2,800 8. 1,200

Find the sum or difference.

9. 396
   +119

10. 245
    − 98

11. 400
    −168

12. $12.83
    + 49.95

13. 6,983
    −2,094

Find the product.

14. 69
    × 7

15. 55
    × 8

16. 84
    × 6

17. 945
    × 3

18. 265
    × 5

19. 326
    × 2

Choose the appropriate unit for each.

20. amount of cheese on 100 pizzas   a. oz   b. lb   c. T
21. length of 100 skateboards placed end-to-end   a. in.   b. yd   c. mi
22. amount of water used to wash an elephant   a. pt   b. qt   c. gal

Write the time using A.M. or P.M. to tell when each event ends.

23. The wildlife film begins at 10:45 A.M. and lasts for 2 hours.

24. Dave and Nancy's wedding began at 11:30 A.M. and lasted 35 minutes.

Spotlight ON
PROBLEM SOLVING

Understand
Plan
Solve
Look Back

✓ ✓ ✓ Check the Solution ✓ ✓ ✓

You need to check your solution to a problem to see whether it answers the question and whether it makes sense.

✓ Matthew's hobby is collecting postcards from around the world. He has 100 postcards that he wants to place into 2 albums with the same number of pages. He places 5 postcards on each page to fill the albums. How many pages are in each album?

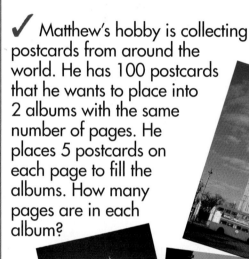

Talk About It

Solution:

$$\begin{array}{r} 20 \\ 5\overline{)100} \\ -10 \\ \hline 000 \\ -000 \\ \hline 000 \end{array}$$

He will use 20 pages.

✓ Does the solution make sense?

✓ Does the solution answer the question?

Correct Solution:

$$\begin{array}{r} 20 \\ 5\overline{)100} \\ -10 \\ \hline 000 \end{array} \qquad \begin{array}{r} 10 \\ 2\overline{)20} \end{array}$$

Each album has 10 pages. This solution answers the question and makes sense.

Apply

Read each problem. Write *yes* or *no* to tell whether the solution makes sense and answers the question. Correct the incorrect solutions.

1. Lisa had 27 stickers. She gave 13 to her cousin. She gave 3 to her sister. How many stickers did she have left?
Solution: Lisa gave away 16 stickers in all.

2. Ira buys 6 rolls of film for his camera. Each roll costs $3.16. How much change does he get from $20.00?
Solution: He gets $1.04 in change.

3. Marty had 20 pencils. She shared them with 4 classmates. How many pencils did each person have?
Solution: Each person had 5 pencils.

A satellite dish can receive signals from communications satellites out in space. There are 131 satellite dishes to be divided equally among 6 stores. How many satellite dishes will each store receive?

Estimate. $120 \div 6 = 20$ **Think:** $6 \times 2 = 12$

Divide. $131 \div 6 = n$ $6\overline{)131}$

Step 1	**Step 2**	**Step 3**
Decide where to place the first digit in the quotient.	Divide the tens. $6\overline{)13}$ **Think:** $6 \times n \approx 13$.	Bring down the ones. Divide. $6\overline{)11}$ **Think:** $6 \times n \approx 11$.
$\overset{no}{\text{X}}$ $6\overline{)131}$ You *cannot* divide 1 by 6. Not enough hundreds yes ▪ $6\overline{)131}$ You *can* divide 13 by 6. There are enough tens.	$\begin{array}{r} 2 \\ 6\overline{)131} \\ -12 \\ \hline 1 \end{array}$ Multiply. 6×2 Subtract. $13 - 12$ Compare. $1 < 6$	$\begin{array}{r} 21 \ r5 \\ 6\overline{)131} \\ -12\!\downarrow \\ \hline \ \ 11 \\ -\ 6 \\ \hline 5 \end{array}$ Multiply. 6×1 Subtract. $11 - 6$ Compare. $5 < 6$ Write the remainder next to the quotient.

Each store will receive 21 satellite dishes.
There will be 5 left over.

• Is your answer reasonable? How do you know?

Check for Understanding

Copy each problem. Draw a ▪ where the first digit in the quotient should be placed.

1. $5\overline{)412}$ 2. $6\overline{)918}$ 3. $4\overline{)448}$ 4. $8\overline{)789}$

Find the quotient. Check by multiplying.

5. $356 \div 9 = n$ 6. $233 \div 2 = n$ 7. $6\overline{)597}$ 8. $4\overline{)362}$

Practice

Copy each problem. Draw a ■ where the first digit in the quotient should be placed.

9. $4\overline{)522}$ **10.** $6\overline{)453}$ **11.** $8\overline{)795}$ **12.** $5\overline{)548}$ **13.** $6\overline{)924}$

Find the quotient. Check by multiplying.

14. $455 \div 5 = n$ **15.** $635 \div 8 = n$ **16.** $348 \div 4 = n$ **17.** $841 \div 7 = n$

18. $4\overline{)389}$ **19.** $8\overline{)762}$ **20.** $9\overline{)439}$ **21.** $7\overline{)198}$

Mixed Applications

22. During the last 6 months 252 customers had cable television installed in their homes. The same number of customers had cable installed each month. How many customers had cable installed each month?

23. The Satellite Equipment Company shipped 75 cables, 125 receivers, and 30 satellite dishes to 5 stores. If the equipment was divided equally, how many pieces of equipment did each store receive?

24. Logical Reasoning Joe made 15 telephone calls. Sally made twice as many calls as Carol. Carol made 5 more calls than Joe. How many telephone calls did Sally make?

SCIENCE CONNECTION

HINT: $time\overline{)miles}^{speed}$

One millisecond equals one thousandth of a second. Which signal has the faster speed? Divide, and compare the quotients.

25. A signal relayed by Alpha satellite takes 6 milliseconds to travel 570 miles.

26. A signal relayed by Beta satellite takes 9 milliseconds to travel 828 miles.

How can you predict the number of digits in the quotient?

WRAP UP...

ZEROS IN THE QUOTIENT

The Woodside School sent fliers home to communicate information about a Parent/Teacher meeting. There were 321 fliers divided equally among 3 grade levels. How many fliers did each grade level receive?

Estimate. $300 \div 3 = 100$

Divide. $321 \div 3 = n$ $3\overline{)321}$

Use place-value materials to model the example.

Step 1	Step 2	Step 3	Step 4
Decide where to place the first digit in the quotient.	Divide the hundreds. $3\overline{)3}$ Then multiply.	Bring down the tens. Divide. $3\overline{)2}$	Bring down the ones. Divide. $3\overline{)21}$
$3\overline{)321}$ **Think:** You can divide 3 hundreds by 3.	$\begin{array}{r} 1 \\ 3\overline{)321} \\ -3 \\ \hline 0 \end{array}$ Multiply. 3×1 Subtract. $3 - 3$ Compare. $0 < 3$	$\begin{array}{r} 10 \\ 3\overline{)321} \\ -3{\downarrow} \\ \hline 02 \\ -0 \\ \hline 2 \end{array}$ Write a zero in the quotient.	$\begin{array}{r} 107 \\ 3\overline{)321} \\ -3 \\ \hline 02 \\ -0{\downarrow} \\ \hline 21 \\ -21 \\ \hline 0 \end{array}$ Multiply. 3×7 Subtract. $21 - 21$ Compare. $0 < 3$

So, each grade level received 107 fliers.

- What place-value materials show the quotient?

- Why is there a 0 in the tens place of the quotient?

Check for Understanding

Copy each problem. Draw a ■ where the first digit in the quotient should be placed.

1. $8\overline{)808}$ **2.** $3\overline{)345}$ **3.** $9\overline{)899}$ **4.** $5\overline{)655}$

Estimate. Then find the quotient.

5. $4\overline{)412}$ **6.** $6\overline{)780}$ **7.** $8\overline{)864}$ **8.** $7\overline{)840}$

Practice

Copy each problem. Draw a ■ where the first digit in the quotient should be placed.

9. $4\overline{)432}$ **10.** $5\overline{)528}$ **11.** $5\overline{)502}$ **12.** $7\overline{)702}$ **13.** $9\overline{)927}$

Estimate. Then find the quotient.

14. $5\overline{)525}$ **15.** $8\overline{)869}$ **16.** $6\overline{)604}$ **17.** $5\overline{)603}$ **18.** $7\overline{)728}$

19. $108 \div 1 = n$ **20.** $655 \div 6 = n$ **21.** $938 \div 9 = n$ **22.** $838 \div 8 = n$

Complete. Use mental math to find n.

23. If $800 \div 8 = 100$, then $801 \div 8 = n$.

24. If $500 \div 5 = 100$, then $504 \div 5 = n$.

25. If $600 \div 2 = 300$, then $601 \div 2 = n$.

26. $707 \div 7 = n$ **27.** $205 \div 2 = n$ **28.** $332 \div 3 = n$

Mixed Applications

Complete the table. Use the table for Exercises 29–30.

29. Order from least to greatest the news shows by the number of minutes spent on them each week.

30. How many minutes did WHBJ spend on news shows last week?

WHBJ: Time Spent On News Last Week			
Kind of News	Number of Shows	Minutes on Each Show	Total Minutes
Local	12	13	■
State	■	4	148
National	14	11	■
World	■	7	147

MIXED REVIEW

Name the longer unit.

1. 1 cm or 1 dm   **2.** 5 yd or 5 mi   **3.** 1 cm or 1 in.   **4.** 6 km or 6 m

Complete. You may use a calculator.

5. 3 yd = ■ ft   **6.** 4,000 lb = ■ T   **7.** 2 lb = ■ oz   **8.** 2 gal = ■ qt

Why is it important to put a zero in this quotient? $7\overline{)714}$ 102

DIVIDING
with Money

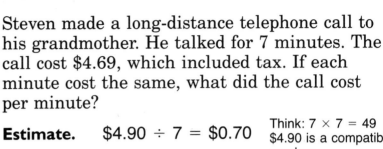

Steven made a long-distance telephone call to his grandmother. He talked for 7 minutes. The call cost $4.69, which included tax. If each minute cost the same, what did the call cost per minute?

Estimate. $4.90 ÷ 7 = $0.70   Think: 7 × 7 = 49
$4.90 is a compatible number.

Divide money the same as you divide whole numbers.

$$7)\overline{\$4.69} \rightarrow \begin{array}{r} 67 \\ 7)\overline{469} \\ -42\downarrow \\ \hline 49 \\ -49 \\ \hline 0 \end{array}$$

← Since there are no dollars, write $0.67.

So, Steven's call cost $0.67 per minute.

- Is the answer reasonable?

Another Example   Divide: $0.63 ÷ 9 = n

$$9)\overline{\$0.63} \rightarrow \begin{array}{r} 7 \\ 9)\overline{63} \\ -63 \\ \hline 0 \end{array}$$ Divide as you would whole numbers.

$$\begin{array}{r} \$0.07 \\ 9)\overline{\$0.63} \end{array}$$ Line up the dollar signs and the decimal points. Since there are no dollars and no dimes, write $0.07.

Try these examples with a calculator.

A. **Press:**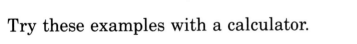

B. **Press:**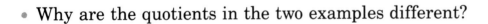

- Why are the quotients in the two examples different?

Check for Understanding

Find the quotient. You may use a calculator.

1. $5)\overline{\$5.55}$ **2.** $4)\overline{\$1.72}$ **3.** $8)\overline{\$0.72}$ **4.** $7)\overline{\$5.45}$ **5.** $6)\overline{\$3.66}$

Practice

Find the quotient. Check by multiplying.

6. $6\overline{)\$5.10}$ 7. $4\overline{)\$4.36}$ 8. $3\overline{)\$0.24}$ 9. $8\overline{)\$9.92}$

10. $5\overline{)\$6.30}$ 11. $7\overline{)\$4.27}$ 12. $4\overline{)\$1.84}$ 13. $2\overline{)\$9.32}$

14. $\$9.00 \div 5 = n$ 15. $\$0.56 \div 4 = n$ 16. $\$5.21 \div 9 = n$ 17. $\$7.77 \div 7 = n$

Mixed Applications

Use the table for Exercises 18–19.

Measurements		
12 in. = 1 ft	8 oz = 1 c	2 pt = 1 qt
3 ft = 1 yd	2 c = 1 pt	4 qt = 1 gal

18. For the party, Lisa decorated the room with ribbon that cost $1.62 a yard. How much did the ribbon cost per foot?

19. The punch cost $6.88 per gallon. How much did the punch cost per quart?

20. Each 2-foot-long submarine sandwich cost $10.38. How much did each sub cost per foot?

21. The cheese cost $5.45 per pound. How much did 2 pounds cost?

22. **Write a Question** The telephone company is offering many bargains during Customer Appreciation Week. Use the information in the table to write a problem. Exchange with a classmate and solve.

Customer Appreciation Week Telephone Rates		
Length of Call	To (State)	Total Cost of Call
6 min	Georgia	$0.89
4 min	Texas	$1.22
9 min	Hawaii	$4.38

CALCULATOR

You can use a calculator to help you find the remainder.

$239 \div 5 = 47$ r ■

Multiply. [5] [×] [4] [7] [=]   [235.]

Subtract. [2] [3] [9] [−] [2] [3] [5] [=]   [4.]

Find each remainder.

23. $472 \div 6 = 78$ r ■   24. $391 \div 7 = 55$ r ■   25. $106 \div 4 = 26$ r ■

How is dividing money like dividing whole numbers?

WRAP
UP...

PROBLEM Solving

Choose the Method

Leslie has a paper route. She delivers 1,491 newspapers a week. If she delivers the same number of newspapers each day, how many does she deliver per day?

You can solve a problem by using objects, paper and pencil, a calculator, or mental math.

▶ **UNDERSTAND**

What are you asked to find?

What facts are given?

▶ **PLAN**

How can you solve the problem?

You can analyze all methods and choose the most appropriate one for this problem.

▶ **SOLVE**

Choose one of the following methods.

Method	Example	Think:
Mental math	Use with small numbers and multiples of 10; 100; 1,000; and so on.	It would be difficult to find the answer to this problem mentally.
Objects	Use objects to act out the situation.	The number is so large that acting it out would be difficult, too.
Paper and pencil	Use when a calculator is not available and the problem is too difficult to solve mentally.	You could use paper and pencil if you have them.
Calculator	Use with large numbers or when you need an answer quickly.	You can use a calculator if you have one.

Because this problem has large numbers, use a calculator.

Press: 1 4 9 1 ÷ 7 =   213.

7 days in a week

Leslie delivers 213 newspapers per day.

▶ **LOOK BACK**

How can you check your answer?

WHAT IF... ...Leslie delivered 200 papers each day? Which method of computation would you use to find how many she delivered in a week?

262

Apply

Write which method you would use to solve the problem. Solve.

1 Erik's job is to fill the city's 200 newspaper vending machines. Each machine holds 60 papers. How many papers must be loaded onto Erik's truck each day?

2 Erik was paid $425 for one week's work and $287 for another week's work. He receives $8 an hour. How many hours did he work in the 2 weeks?

Mixed Applications | **STRATEGIES** | • Guess and Check • Write a Number Sentence • Work Backward • Draw a Picture • Act It Out

Choose a strategy and solve.

3 Perry surveyed 223 people to find how they usually learn news. There were 85 people who watch news on TV. There were 54 people who hear news on radio. The rest of the people surveyed read news in newspapers. What is the most popular way of getting the news?

4 The mayor posed for news photos with 4 council members. The mayor was in the middle. Ms. Drew stood next to the mayor. Mr. Burke was at the left end. Mr. Ashe stood between the mayor and Mr. Burke. Where did Mrs. Vigoda stand?

5 Francie works in the newsroom after school. On Tuesday she typed for 1 hour and 22 minutes. She took a 15-minute break. Then she did filing for 1 hour and 8 minutes. She went home at 5:45. At what time did she get to work?

6 Kelsey used 43 rolls of film taking sports action photos for the *Herald* in March. There are 36 pictures on each roll. Did he take more than 1,400 photos?

SOCIAL STUDIES CONNECTION

7 In 1833 the New York *Sun* was sold on street corners by newsboys for 6¢. To sell more papers, the *Sun*'s owner lowered the price to a penny. Suppose that Billy sold 264 papers a day before the price was changed. How many papers would he have to sell at 1¢ to bring in the same amount of money as before?

EXPLORING
Averages

Estimate the average number of telephone calls that you make in a week.

Susan and Joanne recorded the number of telephone calls that they made on five different days.

Day	Susan	Joanne
Sat.	3	4
Sun.	7	3
Mon.	4	5
Tues.	6	4
Wed.	5	4

WORK TOGETHER

Building Understanding

Work in a group. Use connecting cubes to explore finding the median, range, and average of a set of numbers.

Build five stacks of cubes to represent the number of calls that Susan made on each of the five days.

Now, arrange the stacks in order from the shortest to the tallest.

Talk About It
▶ How many cubes are in the middle stack? You have just found the **median** of this set of numbers.

▶ How many cubes are in the shortest stack? in the tallest stack?

▶ What is the difference between the number of cubes in the shortest stack and the number of cubes in the tallest stack? You have just found the **range** of this set of numbers.

Now, connect all of the cubes together. Then, separate them into five *equal* stacks.

Talk About It
▶ How many cubes were in each stack the first time that you built stacks?

▶ How many cubes are in each stack now that you have rearranged them? You have just found the **average** of a set of numbers.

▶ Write two number sentences to show how you can find an average.

▶ Find the average number of calls that Joanne made during the five days by repeating the same procedure.

264

Making the Connection

Play this game of "Averages." Place all of the connecting cubes in a pile in the center of the table. Have each member of the group take a turn.

1. With your eyes closed, grasp as many connecting cubes as you can with one hand.
2. Make a stack with your cubes.
3. After everyone has had a turn, find the average number of cubes that each member could grasp in one hand.
4. Compare your group's average with the other groups' averages.

Checking Understanding

Use connecting cubes to explore finding the average. The data in the table tells how long Sammy talked to several people on the telephone. Let one connecting cube stand for one minute.

Sammy's Calls	
Name	**Number of Minutes**
John	10
Tina	4
Mr. Holt	3
Shawn	7
Chet	6

5. How many stacks did you make?

6. Write a number sentence to show how many cubes you used in all.

7. Arrange the cubes in equal stacks. How many cubes are in each stack?

8. What is the average length of Sammy's calls?

9. Write a number sentence to show how you found the average.

CALCULATOR

Use a calculator to find averages. Add each set of numbers. Then divide the sum by the number of addends. This is the average of that set of numbers.

sum
↓

Example: Press: (2) (+) (7) (+) (5) (+) (8) (+) (3) (=) [25.]

Then press: (÷) (5) (=) [5.] ← average

Find the average for each set of numbers. Follow the example above.

10. 10, 23, 16, 11, 15

11. 53, 68, 47, 32

12. 14, 18, 16, 22, 20

MEDIAN, RANGE, AND AVERAGE

Miss Alverez communicates with her students about their progress in math class. She records their test scores and then has them each find their own average score. Find Marley's average score.

You can use division to find the average of a set of numbers. First, add the numbers. Then, count the addends and divide by the number of addends. The quotient is the average.

Add.

```
   87
   95
   85
  100
+  93
─────
  460
```

Divide.

```
        92 ← average
   5)460
    − 45
    ─────
      10
    −10
    ─────
       0
```

So, Marley's average score is 92.

Math Test Scores

Date	Marley	Alex	Amado
9/17	87	76	72
9/24	95	82	95
10/1	85	87	100
10/8	100	95	85
10/15	93	90	88
Average			

• The **median** is the middle number in a set of data when you order the numbers from least to greatest. What is Marley's median score?

• The **range** is the difference between the greatest number and the least number. What is the range of Marley's scores?

More Examples

A. Find Alex's median, range, and average scores.

```
   76        86     median–87
   82     5)430     range–19
   87      − 40     average–86
   95        30
+  90       −30
─────       ────
  430         0
```

B. Find Amado's median, range, and average scores.

```
   72        88     median–88
   95     5)440     range–28
  100      − 40     average–88
   85        40
+  88       −40
─────       ────
  440         0
```

Check for Understanding

Find the median, range, and average for each set of numbers.

1. 5, 8, 9, 6, 7

2. 11, 9, 12, 8, 15

3. 43, 37, 43, 38, 39

Practice

Find the median, range, and average for each set of numbers.

4. 1, 20, 6

5. 35, 21, 49

6. 84, 98, 60, 70, 78

7. 4, 8, 12, 16, 20

8. 28, 36, 60, 10, 41

9. 100, 96, 85, 72, 87

Find the average for each set of test scores.

10. 83, 87, 91, 95

11. 100, 65, 93, 84, 90, 96

Mixed Applications

12. Write 5 numbers from 1 to 20. Exchange with a classmate and find the median, range, and average of the numbers.

13. Measure the height in inches of four classmates. Find the median, range, and average of the measures. Compare your results.

14. Find the median, range, and average of the data in the graph.

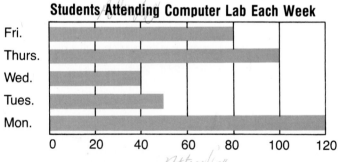

Students Attending Computer Lab Each Week

15. Mrs. Kuhn's class earns points for completed assignments. For every 25 points earned, Mrs. Kuhn awards the class a treat. At the end of the year, the class had earned 165 points. How many treats did they receive?

PATTERNS, RELATIONS, AND FUNCTIONS

16. Look at the calendar. Find the median and average for the dates in each full week of the month. What pattern do you notice? Why does this pattern occur?

Sun	Mon	Tues	Wed	Thu	Fri	Sat
						1
2	3	4	5	6	7	8
9	10	11	12	13	14	15
16	17	18	19	20	21	22
23	24	25	26	27	28	

February

Example:

median

$$2 + 3 + 4 + 5 + 6 + 7 + 8 = 35$$

$$7\overline{)35} \quad \begin{array}{c} 5 \end{array} \leftarrow \text{average}$$

Explain in your own words what *average* means.

WRAP UP...

Vocabulary Check

Choose a word from the box to complete each sentence.

average
compatible
dividend
divisor
median
quotient
range
remainder

Read each problem carefully.

1. The number to be divided is the __?__ . *(pages 242, 244)*

2. The amount left over when you find the quotient is called the __?__ . *(page 244)*

3. The answer to a division problem is called the __?__ . *(pages 242, 244)*

4. After you move blocks to make different stacks equal, the number of blocks in each stack is the __?__ . *(page 264)*

5. To change the dividend to the nearest number that can be divided easily is to estimate by using __?__ numbers. *(page 248)*

6. The middle number in a set of numbers that has been arranged in order is the __?__ . *(pages 264, 266)*

7. The dividend is divided by the __?__ . *(pages 242, 244)*

8. The difference between the least number and the greatest number is the __?__ . *(pages 264, 266)*

Concept Check

Draw place-value materials and circles to model these problems. *(page 242)*

9. $6 \div 2 = n$

10. $60 \div 2 = n$

11. $600 \div 2 = n$

Use connecting cubes to model each problem. Move the cubes to help you find the median, range, and average for each set. *(page 264)*

12.

Median: ■
Range: ■
Average: ■

13.

Median: ■
Range: ■
Average: ■

14.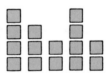

Median: ■
Range: ■
Average: ■

15.

Median: ■
Range: ■
Average: ■

Choose the letter of the best estimate. *(page 248)*

16. $3\overline{)260}$ **a.** 60   **b.** 70   **c.** 90   **d.** 100

17. $6\overline{)419}$ **a.** 60   **b.** 70   **c.** 80   **d.** 90

Skill Check

Estimate. Then find the quotient. *(pages 248, 256)*

18. $4\overline{)80}$ **19.** $9\overline{)83}$ **20.** $6\overline{)239}$ **21.** $7\overline{)345}$ **22.** $4\overline{)176}$

23. $322 \div 3 = n$ **24.** $412 \div 2 = n$ **25.** $752 \div 8 = n$ **26.** $217 \div 7 = n$

Find the quotient. Check by multiplying. *(pages 252, 260)*

27. $5\overline{)64}$ **28.** $2\overline{)33}$ **29.** $8\overline{)91}$ **30.** $6\overline{)79}$

31. $5\overline{)\$6.82}$ **32.** $6\overline{)\$7.21}$ **33.** $2\overline{)\$3.19}$ **34.** $4\overline{)\$4.39}$

Find the average for each set of numbers. *(pages 264, 266)*

35. $56, 65, 38, 47, 59$ **36.** $154, 175, 149, 167, 160$

Problem-Solving Check

Write **a, b, c,** or **d** to show the method of computation you used. Solve. *(pages 250, 262)*

a. mental math   **b.** objects   **c.** paper and pencil   **d.** calculator

37. There are 17 math books in one stack. Three other stacks have 11 books, 16 books, and 8 books. Can Sherman make 4 equal stacks?

38. There are 22 science books in one stack and 48 science books in another stack. Can George make 2 equal stacks?

39. There are 69 employees that work at the WRJH television station. There are twice as many women as men. How many employees are women? How many are men?

40. Five members of the Computer Club stood in a row. Bobby was in the middle. Thalia stood next to Bobby. Joel was at the right end. Sylvia stood between Bobby and Joel. Where was Tom?

Write the number of digits that will be in each quotient.

1. $4\overline{)400}$ **2.** $6\overline{)30}$ **3.** $7\overline{)1,400}$ **4.** $6\overline{)360}$

Use the division problem for Exercises 5–7. Write the number for each part of the division problem named.

$$\begin{array}{r} 7 \\ 6\overline{)42} \end{array}$$

5. quotient   **6.** dividend   **7.** divisor

Use multiplication to find the quotient.

8. $54 \div 7 = n$ **9.** $37 \div 6 = n$ **10.** $52 \div 9 = n$

> Make sure the problem number matches the problem that you copy.

Estimate the quotient.

11. $3\overline{)19}$ **12.** $4\overline{)26}$ **13.** $5\overline{)39}$ **14.** $7\overline{)44}$

Find the quotient.

15. $6\overline{)64}$ **16.** $8\overline{)172}$ **17.** $8\overline{)\$0.56}$ **18.** $51 \div 6 = n$

Find the median, range, and average for each.

19. $36, 43, 32$ **20.** $82, 69, 89, 84, 91$ **21.** $64, 68, 76, 60, 72$

Solve. Write **a, b, c,** or **d** to show the method of computation you used.

     a. mental math   **b.** objects   **c.** paper and pencil   **d.** calculator

22. Steve served dinner to 4 guests. He had 63 shrimp to share equally among the guests and himself. How many did each person receive? Were any left over? If so, how many?

23. Rosie packed 916 lamps. Each box contained 9 lamps. How many boxes did Rosie use to pack all the lamps? Were all the boxes full? If not, how many lamps were placed in the last box?

24. Four students are in line at an exhibit. Ad is in front of Nora. Fletch is behind Cynthia. Cynthia is in front of Fletch but behind Nora. Who is second in line?

25. Ariel and Celia worked on the computer for 25 minutes altogether. Ariel worked 5 minutes longer than Celia. For how long did Celia work?

Teamwork PROJECT
P-R-O-J-E-C-T

Hold the Phone

Suppose you have just been given permission to buy a telephone for your own room. You may select the model and style you want. HOLD ON! In addition to paying for any long-distance calls, you will have to pay for the monthly service charges. IT'S NOT OVER YET! For a year, you will have to make monthly payments on the cost of the telephone. Work as a team to find the estimated cost of having your own telephone.

DECIDE

Decide where you will go or what you will read in order to select a telephone.

Look in a local telephone directory to get information on service and rates.

DO
Interview an adult to find how much the telephone service usually costs each month.

Prepare a sample telephone bill to estimate what you think the monthly cost of your telephone will be. This is your estimated cost.

SHARE
Compare your group's estimated cost with those of other groups.

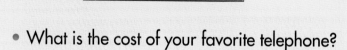

Talk About It

• What is the cost of your favorite telephone?

• What is the cost of extra features on a telephone?

• How does the cost of long-distance calls compare with the cost of local calls?

• To what cities or areas can you make free calls, or calls without long-distance charges?

• Can you earn enough money each month to pay for a telephone in your room? Name some ways you can earn this money.

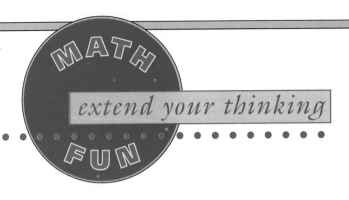

MATH FUN *extend your thinking*

Activity

Pick 'n Spin

Divisibility rules can help you decide whether one number is divisible by another. One whole number is divisible by another whole number if there is no remainder in the quotient.

DIVISIBILITY RULES

If a number is an even number, it is divisible by 2.

If the sum of the digits of a number is divisible by 3, then the number is divisible by 3.

If the digit in the ones place of a number is 0 or 5, then the number is divisible by 5.

If a number ends in 0, it is divisible by 10.

- To play this game, write a different three-digit number on each of 25 cards. Also, make a spinner with sections labeled 2, 3, 5, and 10.

- On each turn, pick a card and spin the spinner. Predict whether the dividend from the card is divisible by the divisor from the spinner. Use the divisibility rules to help you.

- Find the quotient by using a calculator. If you predicted correctly, you win the number of points equal to the divisor. The first player to score 35 points wins.

Challenge

Number Puzzles

From the eight numbers below, find four pairs of factors with a product of 180. You may use a calculator.

30, 2, 5, 90, 4, 36, 6, 45

From the ten numbers below, find five pairs of numbers with a quotient of 24.

7, 72, 4, 6, 96, 120, 144, 5, 3, 168

Everyday Math

Work in a group. Keep a record of the number of hours of television that each member of your group watches in one week.

1. Find the median, range, and average of the number of hours of television watched by your group.

2. Compare your group's data with the other groups' data.

3. Find a class average.

Write the letter of the correct answer.

1. Which is another name for 5,620?

    A. 20 tens   **B.** 56 tens

    C. 60 tens   **D.** 562 tens

2. What is the missing ordinal number? 2nd, 4th, 6th, 8th, _?_, 12th

    A. 9th   **B.** 10th

    C. 11th   **D.** 13th

3. In what form is this data shown?

Daily High Temperatures

Degrees (°F) 86 82 78 74 70 0

Sun. Mon. Tues. Wed. Thurs. Fri. Sat.

    A. line graph   **C.** table

    B. bar graph   **D.** pictograph

4. Which is the correct multiplication sentence for this array?

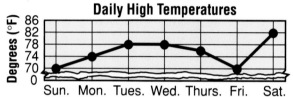

    A. $12 \div 2 = 6$

    B. $2 \times 6 = 12$

    C. $3 \times 4 = 12$

    D. $6 + 6 = 12$

5. Which is a fact in the same fact family as $3 \times 8 = 24$?

    A. $24 \div 3 = 8$ **B.** $24 \div 2 = 12$

    C. $8 \times 2 = 16$ **D.** not here

6. Which is the best estimate? $4 \times 69 = \blacksquare$

    A. 76   **B.** 280

    C. 320   **D.** 2,800

7. Find the value of n. $24 \times 63 = n$

    A. 152   **B.** 1,052

    C. 1,302   **D.** 1,512

8. Which unit could be used to measure the length of a cat's tail?

    A. cm   **B.** m

    C. km   **D.** not here

9. What is the average of 24, 17, 19, 16?

    A. 8   **B.** 18

    C. 19   **D.** 76

10. Find the value of n. $167 \div 3 = n$

    A. 53   **B.** 55

    C. 55 r2   **D.** 83 r2

11. The baker made 965 biscuits. If he puts 9 biscuits in each box, how many boxes can he fill?

    A. 17 boxes   **B.** 103 boxes

    C. 107 boxes   **D.** 117 boxes

12. Tess and Tamika began cleaning their room at 11:20 A.M. They were finished in 2 hours and 5 minutes. At what time did they finish?

    A. 1:25 A.M.   **B.** 1:25 P.M.

    C. 2:25 P.M.   **D.** 12:25 P.M.

9

GEOMETRY

Did you know ...

... that Spaceship Earth™ in Epcot Center™ at Walt Disney World™ is a three-dimensional figure called a geodesic dome? .

Talk About It

Spaceship Earth™ took 2 years and 2 months to build, and is made of 1,450 triangular panels. It appears to be a sphere, but is made with triangular panels. How can you find out if all of the panels are congruent? Explain your answer.

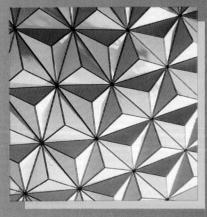

©The Walt Disney Company

EXPLORING

Geometry

Flat Matt was just like any other fourth grader except that he was flat. Sometimes it was difficult for Matt to be a two-dimensional person in a three-dimensional world. Everywhere he looked he saw objects with depth, and he had no depth.

Matt was studying geometry one day when he learned that he was a "plane figure." This made Matt curious! He looked up the words *plane* and *plane figure* in a dictionary.

> A **plane** is a flat surface that goes on and on in all directions.

> A **plane figure** is a flat shape that is all in one plane.

"Gee," exclaimed Matt, "I guess I *am* a plane figure!"

- What makes Matt the same as his classmates? What makes Matt different?

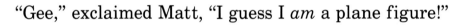

WORK TOGETHER

Building Understanding

Use patterns for three-dimensional, or solid, figures. Make models of these solid figures.

 cone

 cube

 cylinder

 pyramid

 rectangular prism

You can trace around one face of a solid figure to make a plane figure. Trace around one face of your cube.

 Talk About It

▶ What shape did you draw?

▶ Is your drawing a plane figure? How do you know?

▶ What part of a solid figure is a plane figure?

▶ Name some examples of plane figures and solid figures.

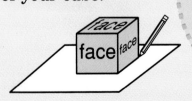

276

Making the Connection

Trace around your solid models to draw these plane figures.

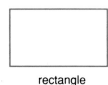

triangle   rectangle   circle   square

1. Which solid figure did you use to draw the triangle?

2. Which solid figure did you use to draw the rectangle?

3. Which solid figure did you use to draw the circle?

4. Which solid figure did you use to draw the square?

Checking Understanding

Write whether each is a picture of a *plane* figure or a *solid* figure.

5.   6.    7. 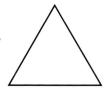   8.

Name the solid figure represented by each.

9.   10.   11.   12.

13.   14.   15.   16.

VISUAL THINKING

17. Which piece is missing? Write **a, b, c,** or **d.**

a.   b.

c.   d.

EXPLORING

Plane Figures and Polygons

Some plane figures are polygons.

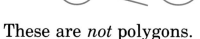

These are polygons.   These are *not* polygons.

WORK TOGETHER

Building Understanding

Use string to model some different plane figures. Cut a piece of string about six feet long. Lay the string on a flat table or a desktop. Make sure that the ends do not touch. This is an **open figure.**

Talk About It

▶ How can you make a **closed figure** with the string?

▶ How do you know that the string forms a plane figure?

Now, tie the ends of the string. Have three people in the group each hold a point on the string and stretch it tight. Each point shows where two sides meet and is called a **vertex.**

Talk About It

▶ What is the figure that you made? Is it a closed figure?

▶ Is the figure a plane figure? How do you know?

▶ If one person lifts a point up, will the figure be in a different plane?

▶ Is the figure a polygon? How do you know?

▶ What makes a polygon different from other plane figures?

▶ Why is a curve, an angle, or a circle not a polygon?

Connection, pages 440–441

Making the Connection

A **polygon** is a closed plane figure with straight sides called line segments. Use your string to make a model of each polygon below. Then make two different examples of each type of polygon and draw them.

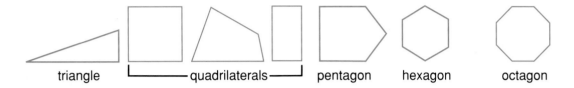

triangle — quadrilaterals — pentagon — hexagon — octagon

Write *true* or *false* for each statement.

1. A quadrilateral can be a rectangle, a square, or any figure with four straight sides.

2. The point where the sides meet is the vertex.

3. A circle is a polygon.

4. All plane figures are polygons.

Checking Understanding

Write *yes* or *no* to tell whether the figure is a polygon. Give a reason for your answer.

5.
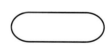

6.

7.
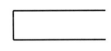

8.

Name each figure.

9.
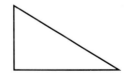

10.
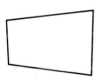

11.

12.

13. a polygon with four sides

14. a quadrilateral with four equal sides

15. This is a nogylop. The head is a hexagon. The nose is a square. Draw a different nogylop. Make the arms and legs rectangles, and the body a square. Add eyes, ears, a mouth, and a hat.

16. Write a paragraph that describes how you think the nogylop got its name.

More Practice, Lesson 9.2, page H66

EXPLORING

Area

Area is the number of square units needed to cover a flat surface.

Imagine that you are putting tiles on the wall behind the bathtub. How many tiles are needed to fill the area?

WORK TOGETHER

Building Understanding

Use this picture and square pieces to explore area.

First, estimate how many tiles you will need.

Then, make a model of the wall by filling the area using square pieces.

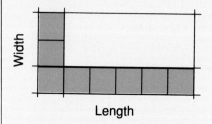

Width

Length

Look at each example. Find the area. Tell what method you used.

Talk About It

▶ How many rows of square units did you make in your model?

▶ How many square units are in each row?

▶ How can you find the number of square units in the area?

▶ Write a multiplication number sentence to show how to find the area of your model.

▶ How close was your estimate to the actual area?

a.

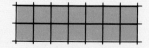

b.

    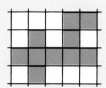

Area can be measured by using different units.

The **square centimeter (sq cm)** is a metric unit for measuring area.

A.

Width

Length

This is 1 square centimeter.

2 rows
3 in a row

Area: 6 sq cm

The **square inch (sq in.)** is a customary unit for measuring area.

B.

Width

Length

This is 1 square inch.

1 row
2 in a row

Area: 2 sq in.

Making the Connection

You can find the area of an irregular surface by counting the square units. Count the number of whole squares first. Then look at the parts of squares and estimate how many whole squares they would make.

Talk About It

▶ What number sentence shows how to multiply to find area in Example A? in Example B?

▶ Give an example of when you cannot use multiplication to find area. Tell another way you could find area.

Find the area in square units.

1.
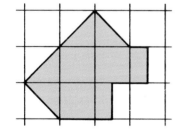

2.

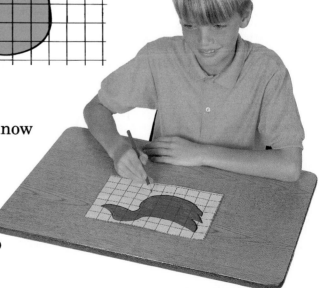

3. In what situation might you need to know the area of an irregular surface?

4. Trace an outline of your hand onto centimeter graph paper. Estimate the area of your tracing. Then count to find how close the actual number is to your estimate.

How many square units are in each figure? (= 1 square unit)

5.

6.

7.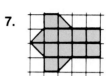

8. Name two ways you can find the area of a figure.

Checking Understanding

On graph paper, draw a model for each area given.

9. 32 square units   10. 14 square units   11. 63 square units

Find the area in square units. Write a multiplication number
sentence for Exercises 16–19.

12.   13. 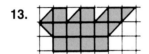   14. 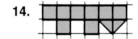   15.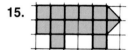

16.   17. 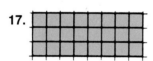   18. 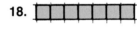   19.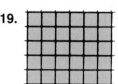

Use the figures a.–d. for Exercises 20–21. Write the letters of the correct answers.
Remember: Perimeter is the distance around a figure.

20. Which figures have the same
    area but different perimeters?

21. Which figures have the same
    perimeter but different areas?

a.    b. 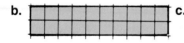   c.   d.

22. Which is larger, a figure that is
    3 square centimeters or one that
    is 3 square inches?

23. Which is larger, a figure that is
    10 square inches or one that is
    10 square centimeters?

Solve each problem.

One night Flat Matt had a wonderful dream. He dreamed he could fly and he traveled to a faraway land. Flat people were everywhere!

1. Flat Matt stopped to ask directions to the park. Flat Sara said to go 1,590 feet west, then 2,677 feet north, and 569 feet northwest. How many feet did Flat Matt have to go?

2. At the park there were picnic tables for groups of 12. There were 87 tables. How many flat people could sit at the picnic tables?

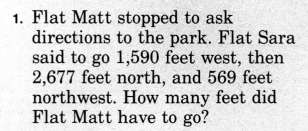

3. The flat people's president ordered the children's games to begin. There were 288 children who signed up for volleyball. If there were 9 teams, how many flat children were on each team?

4. At the stand-on-your-head contest, a great commotion was heard. Rex, a three-dimensional player, was winning. Everyone was shouting that it was not fair. Write a sentence to tell why you think the flat people objected to Rex winning the contest.

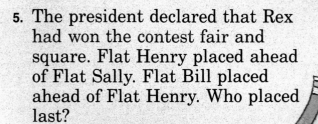

5. The president declared that Rex had won the contest fair and square. Flat Henry placed ahead of Flat Sally. Flat Bill placed ahead of Flat Henry. Who placed last?

6. By the end of his visit, Flat Matt was homesick. You see, at home he was the only flat person and that made him feel special. He left at 10:45 A.M. and arrived home at 11:50 A.M. the next day. In his dream, how long did the trip home take?

Flat Matt is helping his dad install new carpet in their living and dining rooms. He made a diagram of the rooms and recorded the measurements. How many square feet of carpet do they need?

Sometimes it takes more than one step to solve a problem.

▶ UNDERSTAND

What are you asked to find?

What facts are given?

▶ PLAN

How can you solve the problem?

The first step is to find the length of the two rooms together.

15 feet + 10 feet = 25 feet
    ↑   ↑
living room   dining room

▶ SOLVE

Now, how can you find the total amount of carpet needed?

You need to find the area in square feet of the two rooms. You can multiply the total length by the width.

25 feet × 12 feet = 300 square feet

So, Flat Matt and his dad need 300 square feet of carpet.

▶ LOOK BACK

How can you check your answer?

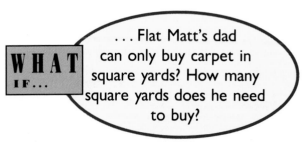

WHAT **IF...** ...Flat Matt's dad can only buy carpet in square yards? How many square yards does he need to buy?

HINT: 9 sq ft are in 1 sq yd.

284

Apply

1 Flat Matt's dad travels 20 miles to work each day. How many miles does he travel in 10 days if he goes to work and back each day?

2 Flat Matt's Aunt Dot is the school librarian at Flatland School. She earns $9.60 an hour. She works 7 hours a day, 5 days a week. How much does she earn in 2 weeks?

3 Flat Matt talked long distance on the telephone for 15 minutes. The rate for the first minute was $0.43. The rate for each additional minute was $0.15. What was the total cost of the call?

4 On Thursday 15 cartons of tacks were delivered to Jasper's Hardware Store. There were 12 boxes of tacks in each carton. On Friday 12 cartons were delivered, with 10 boxes in each carton. How many boxes of tacks were delivered on both days?

Mixed Applications ➔ **STRATEGIES** • Draw a Picture • Guess and Check • Write a Number Sentence • Find a Pattern

Choose a strategy and solve.

5 The area of a floor is 20 square yards. The length of the floor is 5 yards. What is the width of the floor?

6 Carter mailed 4 packages. The postage on each one was $2.65. The postage on a fifth package was $4.37. What was the total postage?

7 Flat Matt and his dad checked carpet prices at two different stores. At Carpet City the price was $720. At Carpet Warehouse the price was $645. How much money did Flat Matt and his dad save by buying the carpet at Carpet Warehouse?

8 Flat Matt wants to put a wallpaper border around his room. His room is 14 feet long and 10 feet wide. How many feet of border will Flat Matt need?

WRITER'S CORNER

9 Imagine that you are Flat Matt. Write three sentences describing the advantages or disadvantages of being a two-dimensional person in a three-dimensional world.

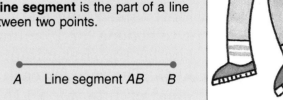

Flat Matt is making toothpick models of polygons. The side of a polygon is a line segment. How many sides are in Flat Matt's model?

A **line** is straight and has no endpoints. It goes on and on in both directions. The arrows show that the line continues.

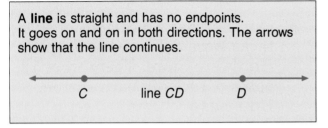

C   line CD   D

A **line segment** is the part of a line between two points.

A   Line segment AB   B

There are three line segments in Flat Matt's model.

Talk About It

▶ How many line segments are in a square?

▶ What do you call the point where two line segments meet?

▶ Can a toothpick be used to make a model of a line? Why or why not?

▶ Name a polygon that can be made with eight toothpicks.

A **ray** is part of a line and has one endpoint. A ray is straight and goes on and on in one direction.

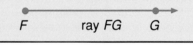

F   ray FG   G

You can show a line, a line segment, and a ray by using your arms.

a. Stretch your arms out to the side with your hands open, and imagine they stretch out forever. This shows a **line**.

b. Stretch your arms out to the side with your fists clenched. Your clenched fists represent the points. This shows a **line segment**.

c. Stretch your arms out to the sides with one fist clenched and one hand open. What figure does this represent?

Check for Understanding

Identify each figure. Write *line segment, line,* or *ray.*

1.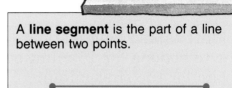

2.

3.

4.

Use toothpicks to model each figure.

5. rectangle   6. pentagon   7. hexagon   8. octagon

Practice

Identify each figure. Write *line segment, line,* or *ray.*

9.
10.
11.
12.

Draw each figure.

13. ray QR

14. line JK

15. line segment RS

Decide whether the figure is a line segment. Write *yes* or *no.*

16.
17.
18.
19.

Mixed Applications

20. Draw four endpoints as shown. What is the greatest number of line segments you can draw using these endpoints? • •

  • •

21. Copy the diagram as shown. Connect the endpoints to make a closed figure. Find the perimeter and area of the figure.

  • •
  • • •
  • •
  • • •

22. The model castle has 3 floors with 10 doors on each floor, 2 floors with 12 doors on each floor, and 1 floor with 11 doors. How many doors are in the castle?

23. Three friends are in a play. Kay has 4 times as many lines as Lyle. Claire has 7 more lines than Kay. Claire has 47 lines. How many lines does Lyle have?

MIXED REVIEW

Find the quotient.

1. $3\overline{)240}$ **2.** $5\overline{)565}$ **3.** $8\overline{)429}$ **4.** $6\overline{)\$3.24}$ **5.** $4\overline{)5,967}$

Find the average of each set of numbers.

6. $27, 28, 29$ **7.** $88, 70, 94$ **8.** $52, 65, 80, 95$ **9.** $100, 95, 84, 76, 90$

How are line segments, lines, and rays the same? How are they different?

More Practice, Lesson 9.5, page H67

287

EXPLORING

Angles

An **angle** is formed by two rays that have the same endpoint. The endpoint is called the **vertex**. The vertex of angle *ABC* is endpoint *B*.

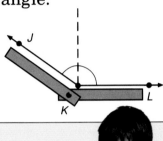
This is the sign for an angle.
vertex

A **right angle** forms a square corner.	An **acute angle** is less than a right angle.	An **obtuse angle** is greater than a right angle.

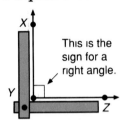
This is the sign for a right angle.

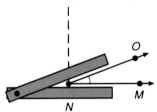

WORK TOGETHER

Building Understanding

Use two cardboard strips and a fastener to explore angles.

Attach the two cardboard strips at one end with the fastener. You can move the cardboard strips to help you draw different angles. Draw an example of each kind of angle.

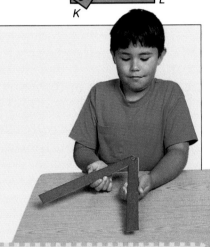

Talk About It

▶ Which angle is a right angle? How do you know?

▶ Which angle is an acute angle? How do you know?

▶ Which angle is an obtuse angle? How do you know?

▶ How can you check an angle to see whether it is a right angle?

Use your sense of touch to identify angles. Close your eyes. Have your partner form an angle with the cardboard strips. Follow the angle with your finger. Tell whether the angle is right, acute, or obtuse.

288

Connection, pages 442–443

Making the Connection

You can see angles everywhere. Write whether each example is a *right,* an *acute,* or an *obtuse* angle.

1.
2.
3.
4.
5.

6. Draw a picture of something that has a right angle. Outline the angle on your drawing.

7. Draw a picture of something that has an acute angle. Outline the angle on your drawing.

8. Draw a picture of something that has an obtuse angle. Outline the angle on your drawing.

Checking Understanding

Write whether each example is a *right,* an *acute,* or an *obtuse* angle.

9.
10.
11.

12.
13.
14.
15.

Find the number of right angles in each.

16. E
17. H
18. T
19. F
20. L

CHALLENGE

Study the figure to answer Exercises 21–23.

21. How many triangles can you find?

22. How many polygons can you find?

23. How many angles can you find?

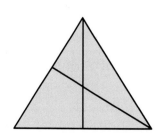

I can use logical reasoning and mental math.

Use the table for Exercises 1–2.

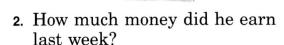

Money Jimmy Earned Last Week			
	Baby-Sitting	Walking the Dog	Raking the Lawn
Hourly Wage	$1.50	$1.00	$1.25
Hours Worked	7	4	4

1. How much money did Jimmy earn last week for babysitting?

2. How much money did he earn last week?

3. Evelyn arranged her four bears. She put Brownie on the left end. She put Blackie on Panda's right. She put Pinkie between Panda and Brownie. Which bear is on the right end?

4. On Tuesday, February 17, Toby realized that in 8 days it would be his birthday. What will be the day and date of his birthday?

Write a division fact for each model.

5.

6.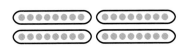

7.

8.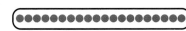

9.

10.

Find the quotient.

11. $4\overline{)366}$ 12. $7\overline{)439}$ 13. $2\overline{)199}$ 14. $7\overline{)215}$ 15. $6\overline{)625}$

Choose the more reasonable unit of measure.

16. the weight of 100 horses

    oz or ton

17. the food a dolphin eats in one day

    lb or ton

18. the length of a door key

    in. or ft

19. the thickness of a math book

    cm or dm

Spotlight ON PROBLEM SOLVING

Understand
Plan
Solve
Look Back

Analyze Data

Sometimes data must be analyzed and compared to solve a problem.

Glen wants to build a pen for his dog. He has 36 meters of fencing. He wants the pen to be in the shape of a rectangle, and he wants the area to be as large as possible.

Talk About It

Work with a partner. Answer the questions about Glen's dog pen.

- What will be the perimeter of Glen's dog pen?

- Make a list of the length, width, and area of each dog pen Glen could build.

- How many different rectangles could he create with 36 meters of fencing?

- What is the smallest area a dog pen with a 36-meter perimeter can have? the largest?

- Will the longest dog pen have the most area?

- Write a sentence to explain the relationship between the perimeter and the area of a figure.

- Based on your analysis, what size and shape should Glen make the dog pen?

Apply

Analyze the information provided. Solve.

1. The bus from town to the mall runs every 25 min. Stacey and her friend missed the 11:05 A.M. bus. So, they went to the library and stayed there until noon. When can they next take a bus to the mall?

2. The price of a radio that Carmen wants to buy has been going up by $1.25 every 3 months. The price is now $60. What was the price 9 months ago?

Use your imagination to think about the railroad tracks. They go on farther than you can see. The two tracks may appear to meet in the distance, but they do not. What do you know about the relationship of these two lines?

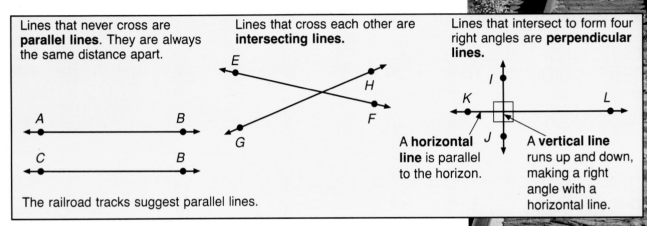

Lines that never cross are **parallel lines.** They are always the same distance apart.

The railroad tracks suggest parallel lines.

Lines that cross each other are **intersecting lines.**

Lines that intersect to form four right angles are **perpendicular lines.**

A **horizontal line** is parallel to the horizon.

A **vertical line** runs up and down, making a right angle with a horizontal line.

With straws, make models to demonstrate parallel, intersecting, and perpendicular line segments. Draw a picture of each model, and label it.

Talk About It

▶ How did you place the straws to show parallel line segments?

▶ How did you place the straws to show intersecting line segments?

▶ How did you place the straws to show perpendicular line segments?

▶ How are the intersecting and perpendicular models alike? How are they different?

Check for Understanding

Write *parallel, intersecting,* or *perpendicular* for each figure.
HINT: Some figures may have more than one answer.

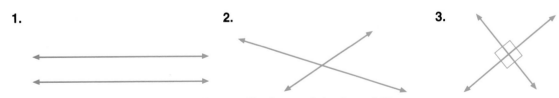

1.

2.

3.

4. Draw a polygon that has all three kinds of line segments.

Practice

5. On graph paper, draw a sketch of your classroom.

6. Find five examples of parallel line segments in your classroom sketch. Outline them in red.

7. Find five examples of perpendicular line segments in your classroom sketch. Outline them in blue.

Write whether each picture suggests *intersecting lines, parallel lines, perpendicular lines,* or *rays.*

 8.

9.

10.

Draw the line segments that are described.

11. intersecting

12. parallel

13. perpendicular

Mixed Applications

14. The 24 students in Mr. Murphy's class purchased tickets to the railroad museum. Each ticket cost $3.75. How much did the tickets cost for the whole class?

15. When Tamara took her dog for a walk, the light was red at every other corner. The first light was red. At the fifth corner, was the light red or green?

VISUAL THINKING

Use the figures for Exercises 16–19.

a.   b.   c.   d.   e.

16. How many pairs of perpendicular line segments are in the square?

17. How many pairs of parallel line segments are in the octagon?

18. How many pairs of perpendicular line segments are in the triangle?

19. Which polygon has no parallel or perpendicular line segments?

How are parallel, intersecting, and perpendicular lines the same? How are they different?

EXPLORING

Circles

A **circle** is a simple closed curve that is named by a point in its center. All points on the circle are the same distance from the center.

WORK TOGETHER

Building Understanding

Have each member in your group take turns making an imaginary circle.

a. Choose a spot on the floor to be the center for all of the circles.

b. Hold your arm out straight and make one complete turn while the other members observe your circle.

c. After each member has made a circle, write the members' names in order from the one who made the smallest circle to the one who made the largest circle.

d. Write how you will explain to the other groups how you ordered the circles.

Use a paper clip and two pencils to explore circles. Draw point *A* on your paper for the center of circle *A*. Place one pencil on point *A* inside one end of the paper clip and hold it still. Place the second pencil inside the other end and draw the circle.

Talk About It

▶ How many centers can your circle have?

▶ What other methods can you use to draw a circle?

▶ Is a circle a polygon? Why or why not?

  Idea Bank, page 454, Exercises 1–2

Making the Connection

Choose one of the methods discussed
on page 294, and draw a circle.

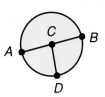

circle C
diameter AB
radii CA, CB, CD

A **radius** is a line segment from the center to any point on the circle. The word for more than one radius is *radii*.	A **diameter** is a line segment that passes through the center and has its endpoints on the circle.

Use your centimeter ruler to measure the radius and the diameter
of your circle. Label the center and three points on the circle.

1. What is the name of your circle?

2. How many centimeters long is the diameter? the radius?

Checking Understanding

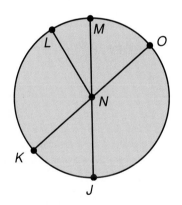

Copy and complete. Use the drawing for Exercises 3–7.

3. Line segment *LN* is a __?__ .

4. The center of this circle is __?__ .

5. Line segment *JM* is a __?__ .

6. Line segment *NJ* is a __?__ .

7. Points *K* and *O* are the endpoints of a __?__ of the circle.

MIXED REVIEW

Find the product or quotient.

1. 12 × 3	2. 68 × 4	3. 207 × 5	4. 896 × 20	5. 734 × 53

6. 4)‾16‾   7. 5)‾42‾   8. 3)‾45‾   9. 7)‾2,100‾   10. 8)‾3,064‾

EXPLORING

Congruent and Similar Figures

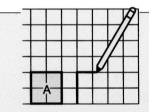

The figures in each pair are congruent and similar.

Congruent figures have the same shape and size.

Similar figures have the same shape. They may or may not have the same size.

The figures in each pair are similar but not congruent.

WORK TOGETHER

Building Understanding

Use graph paper and a ruler to explore congruent and similar figures.

Draw two square figures that are each two squares long by two squares wide. Label them **A** and **B**. Draw a third square figure that is three squares long by three squares wide. Label it **C**.

Talk About It

▶ Which figures are congruent?

▶ Which figure is similar but not congruent to figure **A**?

▶ If two figures are congruent, are they always similar?

▶ Do congruent figures also have congruent angles?

Copy this picture onto centimeter graph paper.

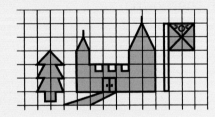

▶ Is your picture congruent to the one in the book? Why or why not?

▶ Is your picture similar to the one in the book? How do you know?

Trace each figure. Draw one figure that is congruent and one that is similar but not congruent for each.

a.

b.

c.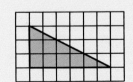

d.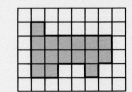

Making the Connection

1. Are the trees in this picture congruent or similar? Are real trees similar to each other?

2. How can you explain your answer in Exercise 1?

Write whether each pair of figures is *congruent*, *similar*, or *both*.

3.

4.

5.

Checking Understanding

Write whether each pair of figures is *congruent*, *similar*, or *both*.

6.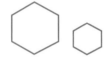

7.

8.

9.

10. On graph paper, draw a simple tile design inside a square. Then enlarge the square so that the second design is two times the size of the first one.

11. Draw another design. Ask a partner to reduce the design by half.

ART CONNECTION

In geometry, patterns of polygons like the ones shown here are called **tessellations**. Some polygons will tessellate and some will not. Some polygons with all sides congruent and all angles congruent can be used to make these patterns.

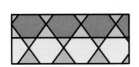 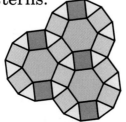

12. Give some examples of tessellations in your classroom or at home. What kinds of polygons are used?

13. Draw a rectangle that is 6 inches by 10 inches. Then trace copies of the patterns on page H87 to make a tessellation that covers the rectangle. Complete and color the design.

Samantha is making a mosaic trivet with ceramic tiles. She can choose from red, blue, and yellow squares and triangles. She must choose a design and tell the art teacher which tiles she needs.

Sometimes you can *make a model* to solve a problem.

▶ **UNDERSTAND**

What are you asked to do?

What facts are given?

▶ **PLAN**

How can you solve the problem?

You can use pattern blocks to make a model of the mosaic. The design must tessellate.

▶ **SOLVE**

How can making a model help you choose a design?

Arrange and rearrange red, blue, and yellow square and triangle pattern blocks until you find the design you like best. The model will help you visualize how the mosaic will look.

Here are some possible designs.

Samantha decided to make her mosaic look like the second model from the left. She will need 8 blue and 4 red square tiles and 4 blue and 4 yellow triangle tiles.

▶ **LOOK BACK**

How could you draw a picture to solve the problem?

WHAT IF... ...Samantha uses only blue and yellow tiles in the shape of hexagons and triangles? What design can she make?

Apply

The students in Ms. Ivey's class are making a patchwork quilt. They can use squares, triangles, or hexagons on each quilt square. They can choose from yellow, green, blue, and white fabric. Each student will design one quilt square.

(1) Amelia wants to design a square with red and blue triangles and a yellow hexagon. Use shapes to show what her design might look like.

(2) Wesley wants to design a square using green hexagons and yellow squares. Use shapes to show what his design might look like.

Mixed Applications ➤ STRATEGIES
- Use Estimation • Work Backward
- Act It Out • Write a Number Sentence

Choose a strategy and solve.

(3) Nell made 4 patchwork quilts. She made 2 quilts with 576 squares each. The other 2 had 144 squares each. How many squares were used in the 4 quilts?

(4) Elaine and Mitzi made necklaces from old buttons. Elaine used 235 buttons, and Mitzi used 269. How many buttons did the girls use?

(5) Merrill wants to buy a sweatshirt that costs $15.95, a bandanna that costs $3.99, and a headband that costs $6.00. About how much change will she receive from $30.00?

(6) On Thursday Barney earned some money for mowing a lawn. On Friday he spent $3.50. On Saturday he spent $7.75. He then had $3.75 left. How much money did he have to start with?

(7) When Jamal got his allowance, he spent $5 of it right away. The next day his sister paid him $4 she owed him. If Jamal now has $9, how much was his allowance?

(8) Mrs. Andino sold 9 quilts at a crafts show. She received a total of $1,575 for the quilts. What was the average price of each quilt?

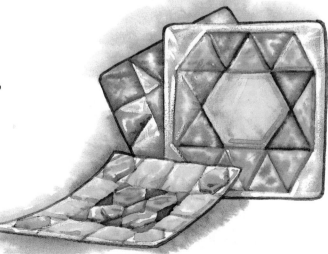

SYMMETRY

One day Flat Matt went to answer the doorbell, and the door flew open and pressed him against the wall! He folded along his line of symmetry. It took a week for him to flatten out!

A figure is **symmetric** if it can be folded so that its two parts match exactly. The line along the fold is the **line of symmetry**.

Fold a sheet of paper exactly in half. Draw a shape that begins and ends on the folded line. Cut out the shape and open it.

Talk About It

▶ Are the two parts of your figure congruent? How do you know?

▶ Can you fold your figure along a different line of symmetry?

▶ How many lines of symmetry does your figure have?

▶ Name three things in your environment that are symmetric and three things that are not symmetric.

Check for Understanding

Trace, cut out, and fold each figure to tell whether the blue line is a line of symmetry. Write *yes* or *no*.

1.

2.

3.

4.

5.
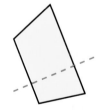

6.
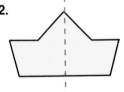

7.

8.

 Connection, pages 444–445

Practice

How many lines of symmetry does each figure have?

9.

10.

11.

12.

Is the blue line a line of symmetry? Write *yes* or *no*.

13.

14.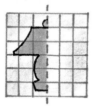

15.

16.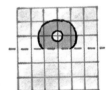

17.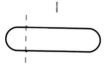

18.

19.

20.

Copy each drawing. Then draw the other half of the figure to show that it has two symmetric parts.

21.

22.

23.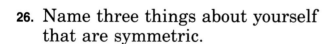

24.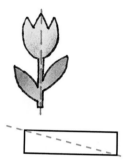

Mixed Applications

25. Make a "mystery shape" by folding a sheet of paper exactly in half and drawing a shape. Exchange folded papers with a partner, and predict what that shape will be. Check by cutting out and unfolding it.

26. Name three things about yourself that are symmetric.

27. Name something in the classroom that is *not* symmetric. How do you know?

28. Daryl collected 58 insects for a school project. He needs a total of 100 insects. How many more does he need?

29. **Analyze Data** Make a list of ten flat classroom items. Decide whether each is symmetric. Arrange the data in a table. Share the information with your class.

Which has more lines of symmetry, a circle or a square?

WRAP
U P...

EXPLORING

Slides, Flips, and Turns

You can move a figure to many different positions.

a. 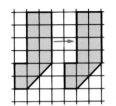 slide

b. 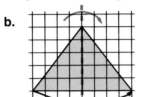 flip

c. 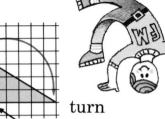 turn

vertex

WORK TOGETHER

Building Understanding

Use graph paper to explore slides, flips, and turns.

Draw a large triangle on the graph paper, and cut it out. Trace it onto a new sheet of graph paper.

- Slide it to the right, and trace it.

- Flip it over a line, and trace it.

- Turn the figure around a vertex. Trace it.

Talk About It

Which one of your tracings shows a slide? a flip? a turn? How do you know?

▶ When you moved the figure, what did you notice about the size and shape of the figure?

▶ Are your tracings of the figure congruent? How do you know?

▶ Can a figure be moved in more than one way? Explain.

▶ In which move did the top of the figure stay at the top?

Making the Connection

You can slide, flip, and turn a figure to make a tesselation. Use pattern blocks. Trace one block. Then move it and trace it again. Be sure the figures are touching. Continue to tessellate the figures until you have made a design.

Example

Use each figure to make a tessellation.

1.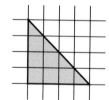

2.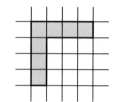

3.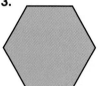

Checking Understanding

Trace each figure. Draw a flip, turn, and slide for each. Show flip lines and direction arrows.

4.

5.

6.

Tell how each polygon was moved. Write *slide*, *flip*, or *turn*.

7.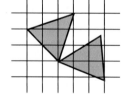

8.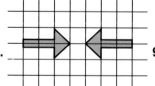

9.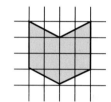

10.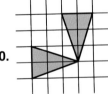

Solve.

11. Imagine that you walk around the block. How many right-hand turns would you have to make to return to your original position? Draw a picture to show your solution.

12. Chanda made pancakes for breakfast. She flipped them five times. Did they end up on the same side as they began?

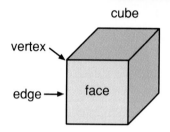

cube

vertex

edge → face

Solid shapes have three dimensions.
They are length, width, and height.
Name three solid shapes in your classroom.

Use paper, scissors, a ruler, tape, crayons, and
the patterns from pages H90–H94 to build a
model city.

Trace the pattern. Cut on the solid lines. Fold on
the broken lines. Before you use tape to make
each shape, draw and color the windows, doors,
bricks, and so on to make the shape look like a
building. Arrange the buildings to create your
city.

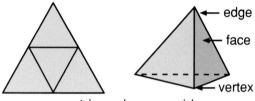

edge
face
vertex

triangular pyramid

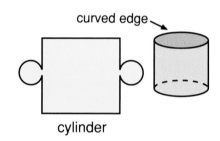

curved edge

cylinder

Talk About It

▶ How is an edge different from a face?

▶ How is a cube different from one of its faces?

▶ How many faces and edges does a sphere
have?

▶ Which shapes can make a building?

Which shapes can make a roof?

▶ Which shapes can combine to form new shapes?

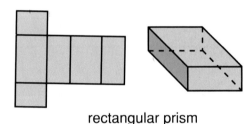

rectangular prism

cone

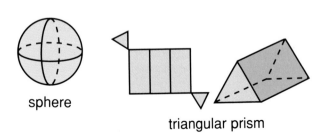

sphere

triangular prism

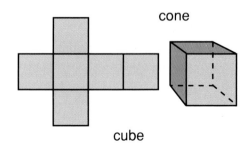

cube

Check for Understanding

Solve each riddle.

1. Two of my faces are circles. What am I?

2. I have no faces or edges. What am I?

3. All of my six faces are congruent. What am I?

4. I have one vertex and one face. What am I?

Practice

Copy and complete the table.

Figure		Flat Faces	Vertices	Straight Edges	Curved Edges	Curved Faces
	cube	6	8	12	0	0
5.	triangular pyramid	■	■	■	■	■
6.	rectangular prism	■	■	■	■	■
7.	sphere	■	■	■	■	■
8.	cylinder	■	■	■	■	■
9.	cone	■	■	■	■	■
10.	triangular prism	■	■	■	■	■

Mixed Applications

Jan folded the pattern along the dotted lines to make a solid figure. Use the figure to answer Exercises 11–14.

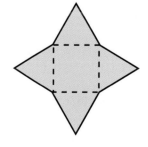

11. How many faces are triangles?

12. What kind of polygon is the other face?

13. How many faces does the solid figure have?

14. What solid figure did Jan make?

15. Eden's math test scores are 85, 92, 81, and 98. What is her math test average?

How are a square and a cube alike?
How are they different?

WRAP UP...

EXPLORING

Volume

Volume is the measure of the space inside a solid figure.

WORK TOGETHER

Building Understanding

Use connecting cubes to explore volume. Make a model of this rectangular prism. Let 1 connecting cube equal 1 cubic unit.

1 connecting cube = 1 cubic unit

First, estimate how many connecting cubes you will need.

How many cubes will make 1 row?

How many rows will make 1 layer?

How many layers will fill the rectangular prism?

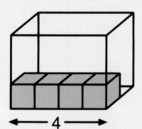

4

This is the length.

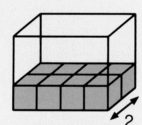

2

This is the width.

3

This is the height.

Talk About It

► Besides counting, how else can you find the total number of cubes needed to fill the rectangular prism?

► Write a multiplication number sentence to find volume.

► How close was your estimate to the actual volume of the rectangular prism?

Making the Connection

Now, use 18 connecting cubes. Make as many different-shaped prisms as you can. Record the length, width, and height in a table.

Example

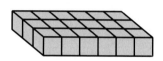

Measuring Volume			
Length	Width	Height	Volume
9	2	1	18 cubic units

1. What is the volume of each model you made?

2. If the length of one model is 18 units, what are the other two measurements?

3. If a prism is 2 units in length, 6 units in width, and 4 units in height, what is the volume?

Find the volume in cubic units.

4.

5.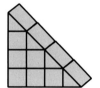

6.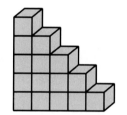

7.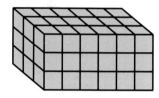

8. For which figures can you use multiplication to find the volume?

Checking Understanding

Find the volume. Use connecting cubes to help you.

9.

10.

11.

12.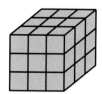

13.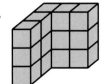

14.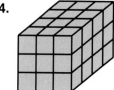

Write a multiplication sentence to find the volume of each.

15.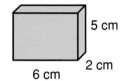
5 cm
2 cm
6 cm

16.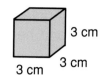
3 cm
3 cm
3 cm

17.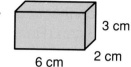
3 cm
2 cm
6 cm

18.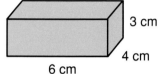
3 cm
4 cm
6 cm

19.
3 cm
1 cm
5 cm

20.
1 cm
3 cm
4 cm

Copy and complete this table for rectangular prisms.

	Length	Width	Height	Volume
21.	2 cm	3 cm	1 cm	
22.	5 cm	3 cm	2 cm	
23.	3 cm	2 cm		18 cubic cm
24.	4 cm		1 cm	8 cubic cm
25.		4 cm	3 cm	60 cubic cm

LOGICAL REASONING

In the metric system, volume and capacity are related. A volume of 1 cubic centimeter (cc) can hold 1 milliliter (mL) of water.

26. Complete the table of equivalent measures.

Volume of Container	Capacity
1 cc	1 mL
10 cc	10 mL
100 cc	mL
1,000 cc	mL

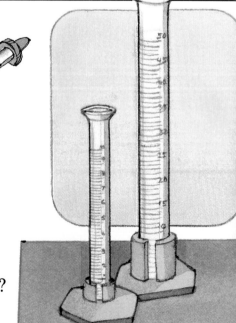

27. How many milliliters are in 3,000 cubic centimeters?

More Practice, Lesson 9.14, page H69

Geometric figures can be one-dimensional, two-dimensional, or three-dimensional. Sort the figures in the picture by drawing them in a table.

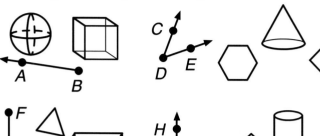
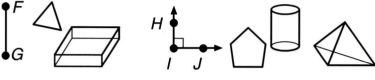

One-Dimensional	Two-Dimensional	Three-Dimensional
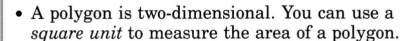	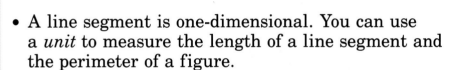	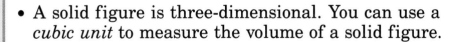

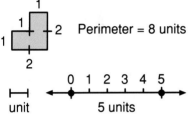

Perimeter = 8 units

5 units

square unit   8 square units

cubic unit   6 cubic units

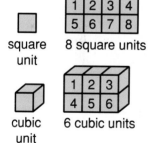

• A line segment is one-dimensional. You can use a *unit* to measure the length of a line segment and the perimeter of a figure.

• A polygon is two-dimensional. You can use a *square unit* to measure the area of a polygon.

• A solid figure is three-dimensional. You can use a *cubic unit* to measure the volume of a solid figure.

Check for Understanding

1. In what other way can you sort the figures?

2. What two dimensions do you use to find the area of a rectangle?

3. What three dimensions do you use to find the volume of a rectangular prism?

4. What are some units you can use to measure length?

5. What are some units you can use to measure area?

6. What are some units you can use to measure volume?

CHAPTER REVIEW

Vocabulary Check

Choose a word or words from the box to complete each sentence.

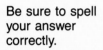

acute angle
diameter
intersecting
obtuse angle
parallel
perpendicular
plane figure
radius
similar
solid figures

Be sure to spell your answer correctly.

1. A closed, flat shape that is all on one plane is a ? .
   (page 276)

2. An ? is less than a right angle. *(page 288)*

3. An ? is greater than a right angle. *(page 288)*

4. Lines that never cross and are always the same distance apart are ? . *(page 292)*

5. Lines that cross each other to form right angles are ? . *(page 292)*

6. All lines that cross each other are ? . *(page 292)*

7. A line segment from the center to any point on a circle is a ? . *(page 294)*

8. A line segment that passes through the center of a circle and has its endpoints on that circle is a ? . *(page 294)*

9. Figures that have the same shape but may not be the same size are ? . *(page 296)*

10. Length, width, and height are dimensions of ? . *(page 304)*

Concept Check

Write *yes* or *no* to tell whether the figure is a polygon. *(page 278)*

11.   12.   13.   14.   15.

Write whether each figure is a *right*, an *acute*, or an *obtuse* angle. *(page 288)*

16.   17.   18.   19.   20.

Write *parallel*, *intersecting*, or *perpendicular* for each figure. *(page 292)*

21.   **22.**   **23.**   **24.**

How many lines of symmetry does each figure have? *(page 300)*

Tell how each polygon was moved. Write *slide, flip,* or *turn.* *(page 302)*

25.   **26.**   **27.**   **28.**   **29.**   **30.**

Find the volume in cubic units. *(page 306)*

31.  **32.** 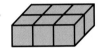 **33.**

Skill Check

Identify each figure. *(pages 276, 278, 286, 288, and 304)*

34.  **35.** 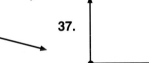 **36.**   **37.** 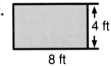 **38.**

Find the area in square units. *(page 280)*

39.   **40.** 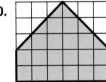 **41.** 6 ft **42.** 4 ft 8 ft

Problem-Solving Check *(pages 284, 298)*

43. Mr. Gober wants to put vinyl floor covering in his kitchen. The vinyl costs $1.25 per sq ft. The kitchen measures 11 ft by 13 ft. How much does the floor covering cost?

44. Make a model of a cube using toothpicks and clay. Let each toothpick be an edge. How many toothpicks did you use?

CHAPTER TEST

Write the letter of the word or words that describe each example. Each letter may be used only once.

Make sure the letter matches the correct picture.

1.
2.
3.
4.
5.
6.
7.
8.
9.
10.

a. right angle
b. congruent figures
c. diameter
d. intersecting lines
e. line segment
f. parallel lines
g. perpendicular lines
h. radius
i. ray
j. similar figures

Identify each figure.

11.
12.
13.
14.
15.

Is the blue line a line of symmetry? Write *yes* or *no*.

16.
17.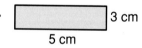

Tell how each polygon was moved. Write *slide, flip,* or *turn*.

18.
19.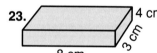

Find the area in square units.

20.
21. 3 cm
5 cm

Find the volume in cubic units.

22.
23. 4 cm 3 cm 8 cm

Solve the problem by making a model.

24. Owen wants to carpet a bedroom and a closet. The bedroom is 14 ft by 15 ft, and the closet is 3 ft by 8 ft. How many square feet of carpet will he need?

25. Noell wants to make a tile design. She has red, blue, and yellow squares and triangles. Make a design and tell how many of each color shape she needs.

Ancient Puzzles

A tangram is an ancient Chinese puzzle. The word may have come from *tang* from the T'ang dynasty, a great family of rulers in Chinese history. *Gram* means "something drawn or written." The seven pieces of a tangram fit together to make a square.

Look at the tangram shapes in the border on this page. How many of these figures can you make? Create a tangram design to decorate your classroom.

Decide

Discuss how you can use the tangram pattern to make a design. Choose the design you want to make.

Do

Work as a team.

Trace the tangram pattern on page H95.

Cut out all seven pieces, and color them.

Glue the pieces in the design you chose onto a sheet of colored paper.

Cut around the design.

Punch a hole at the top of the design, and loop a ribbon through the hole.

Hang your design on display in the classroom.

Share

Show your designs. Compare the different shapes of each design. Identify the shapes of other teams.

Talk About It

- How many different kinds of polygons can you find in your tangram design?

- How many triangles can you find in your tangram design?

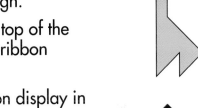

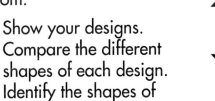

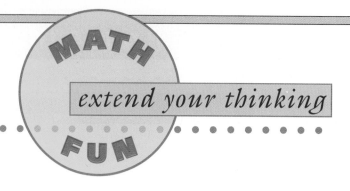

Activity

Find Areas

The area of each small square is 1 square unit.

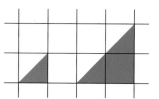

1. What is the area of the blue triangle?　　2. What is the area of the green triangle?

3. Find the area of each figure below in square units.

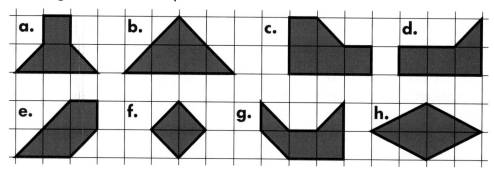

4. Use centimeter graph paper, and draw as many figures as you can with an area of 6 square centimeters.

Challenge

Logical Reasoning

Think about how the first two figures are related. Then draw the figure that completes the sentence.

1. ○ is to ● as ☐ is to ? .

2. ▲ is to △ as ▮ is to ? .

3. ◈ is to ◆ as ◑ is to ? .

4. ⬛ is to ☐ as ▲ is to ? .

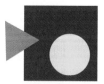

Visual Thinking

Which patterns can be folded to make a cube?

1.

2.

3.

4.

Write the letter of the correct answer.

1.
46,894
+69,897

A. 105,681 **B.** 116,781
C. 116,791 **D.** 156,421

2.
$500.00
− 299.95

A. $200.05 **B.** $211.15
C. $300.05 **D.** $399.95

3.
$12.14
× 32

A. $377.98 **B.** $387.48
C. $388.48 **D.** $396.48

4. What is the perimeter?

A. 30 ft
B. 31 ft
C. 57 ft
D. not here

5 ft 7 ft 1 ft 4 ft 3 ft 9 ft

5. Which is the best estimate of the length?

A. about 1 cm **B.** about 2 cm
C. about 4 cm **D.** about 5 cm

6. 2 km = ■ m

A. 20 **B.** 200
C. 2,000 **D.** not here

7. 3)500

A. 20 **B.** 159 r23
C. 166 r2 **D.** 173 r1

8. Which is the average?
88, 75, 60, 93

A. 76 **B.** 79
C. 84 **D.** 86

9. Which is an obtuse angle?

A. **B.**

C. **D.**

10. Which figure is *not* a polygon?

A. **B.**

C. **D.**

11. Sid bought a poster for $12.19. Lew bought a photo cube for $10.17. Hank bought a cassette for $10.59. Who received the most change back from $15.00?

A. Hank **B.** Lew
C. Sid **D.** Trina

12. The postage on a letter was 98¢. The postal rate was 29¢ for the first ounce and 23¢ for each additional ounce. How much did the letter weigh?

A. 2 oz **B.** 3 oz
C. 4 oz **D.** 5 oz

10

UNDERSTANDING FRACTIONS AND MIXED NUMBERS

Did you know . . .

. . . that fitness is for everyone? Most sports and games now have special rules so that people with disabilities can join in the fun, too!

Shawn has come in first in 3 of his last 15 hundred-meter dashes. How can he find what fraction of the races he has won?

EXPLORING
Fractions

Miss Allen's class is planning a bulletin board on health and fitness. Joel's group worked on the exercise part, and the other groups worked on food, sleep, and checkups. If the bulletin board is divided into equal parts, what fraction of it is Joel's group going to make?

WORK TOGETHER

Building Understanding

Use paper to make a model of the bulletin board.

Fold the paper exactly in half, keeping the fold on the short side. Fold it in half again. Open the paper. Shade one part.

A fraction names one or more equal parts of a whole or part of a group. You can read a fraction as:

one fourth
one out of four $\frac{1}{4}$
one divided by four

Make another model. Use four pieces of paper. Shade one piece.

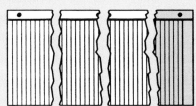

Talk About It
▶ How do you know that all the parts are equal?

▶ How many parts are shaded?

▶ How many total parts are there?

▶ What fraction can you write that names the shaded part?

▶ So, on what fraction of the bulletin board is Joel's group working?

Talk About It
▶ How is the second model like the first model? How is it different?

▶ Why can you describe $\frac{1}{4}$ as 1 out of 4?

▶ Why can you describe $\frac{1}{4}$ as 1 divided by 4?

Use paper to make two models for each fraction, one to show an equal part of a whole and one to show part of a group.

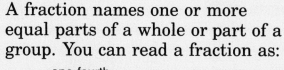

a. $\frac{1}{8}$ b. $\frac{1}{2}$ c. $\frac{3}{4}$

Share your models with your classmates. Have them name the fraction for the unshaded part.

Making the Connection

The same fraction can represent different amounts.

1. Morgan and Melissa each colored $\frac{1}{2}$ of a poster green. Did they both color the same amount of paper? Why or why not?

2. Which is larger, $\frac{1}{3}$ of Figure A or $\frac{1}{3}$ of Figure B?

 A.   **B.**

3. Which is smaller, $\frac{1}{4}$ of Figure A or $\frac{1}{4}$ of Figure B?

A.    **B.**

Checking Understanding

Write *part of a whole* or *part of a group* to describe the shaded part of each figure.

4. $\frac{1}{6}$ 5. $\frac{2}{6}$ 6. $\frac{1}{3}$ 7. $\frac{3}{9}$

8. Write the letters of the figures that show eighths.

a.   **b.**   **c.**   **d.**

Fold paper, and shade the part for each fraction.

9. $\frac{3}{8}$ 10. $\frac{4}{12}$ 11. $\frac{1}{4}$ 12. $\frac{7}{16}$

13. Sandy says that each of the colors of her drawing shows thirds. Is she correct? Why or why not?

14. Is it possible that $\frac{1}{2}$ of your allowance is more than $\frac{1}{2}$ of your friend's allowance? Explain.

After the soccer game, Ami, Ted, and Sara shared a small pizza equally. What fraction of the pizza did each person eat?

A fraction names an equal part of a whole.

each person's part ⟶ 1 ⟵ numerator
total equal parts ⟶ 3 ⟵ denominator **Read:** one third

So, each person ate $\frac{1}{3}$ of the pizza.

Talk About It

▶ How can you explain that $\frac{1}{3}$ is 1 divided by 3?

▶ What fraction names the whole pizza?

More Examples

A.

$\frac{1}{5}$ is shaded.
What fraction is
not shaded?

B.

$\frac{3}{4}$ is shaded.
What fraction is
not shaded?

C.

$\frac{3}{3}$ is shaded. What
fraction is not shaded?
($\frac{3}{3}$ = 1 whole)

Check for Understanding

Write a fraction for the shaded part.

1.

2.

3.

4.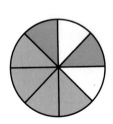

Use the circle at the right to answer Exercises 5–7.

5. How much of the figure is red?

6. How much of the figure is not red or blue?

7. How many eighths are in 1 whole?

Practice

Write a fraction for the shaded part.

8.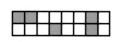

9.

10.

11.

Use the rectangle at the right to answer Exercises 12–15.

12. How much of the figure is blue?

13. How much of the figure is not green or blue?

14. How much of the figure is not blue, green, or purple?

15. How many twelfths are in 1 whole?

Draw a figure, and shade part of it to show the fraction.

16. $\frac{4}{6}$

17. $\frac{3}{5}$

18. $\frac{6}{8}$

19. $\frac{2}{3}$

20. $\frac{8}{10}$

Write the letter of the fraction for the shaded part of each figure.

a. $\frac{3}{4}$ b. $\frac{7}{10}$ c. $\frac{1}{2}$ d. $\frac{4}{6}$

21.

22.

23.

24.

Mixed Applications

25. Sol ordered a pizza with 8 equal slices. He ate 4 slices. What fraction of the pizza was not eaten?

26. The soccer game began at 5:15. It lasted 1 hour and 8 minutes. At what time did the game end?

27. **Logical Reasoning** Ms. Craft asked her students to draw a picture of fourths. This is Keifer's picture. Is it correct? Why or why not?

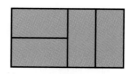

Explain why $\frac{4}{4}$ equals 1 whole.

In physical education class, 7 students can each do 50 sit-ups without stopping. If 4 of the students are girls, what fraction of them are girls?

A fraction can name a part of a group.

number of girls ⟶ $\frac{4}{7}$ ⟵ numerator

total number of students ⟶ ⟵ denominator

Read: four sevenths

So, $\frac{4}{7}$ of the students are girls.

Talk About It

▶ Is $\frac{4}{7}$ the same as 4 out of 7? Explain.

▶ What fraction of the students are boys?

More Examples

A.

$\frac{2}{5}$ are shaded.
What fraction is
not shaded?

B.

$\frac{3}{9}$ are shaded.
What fraction is
not shaded?

C.

$\frac{4}{4}$ are shaded. What
fraction is not shaded?
($\frac{4}{4}$ = 1 group)

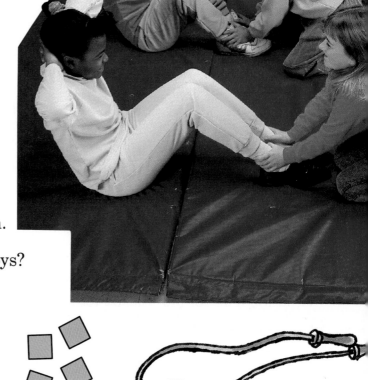

Check for Understanding

Write a fraction for the shaded part.

1.

2.

3.

4.

Draw a picture of a group, and shade part of it to show the fraction.

5. $\frac{2}{3}$

6. $\frac{4}{5}$

7. $\frac{1}{10}$

8. $\frac{3}{6}$

Practice

Write a fraction for the shaded part.

9.

10.

11.

12.

13.

14.

15.

16.

Draw a picture of a group, and shade part of it to show the fraction.

17. $\frac{4}{9}$ 18. $\frac{5}{5}$ 19. $\frac{3}{6}$ 20. $\frac{10}{12}$ 21. $\frac{6}{8}$ 22. $\frac{2}{10}$

Write the fraction.

23. Eight of the dozen eggs were eaten.

24. All of the twenty seats were taken.

25. None of the six bowling lanes were used.

Mixed Applications

26. Zeke did 50 sit-ups. Yan did 37 sit-ups. How many more sit-ups did Zeke do than Yan?

27. Wayne purchased a jump rope for $5.95, a pedometer for $12.19, and ankle weights for $8.94. How much change did he receive from $30.00?

VISUAL THINKING

Study the set of objects below. Write a fraction for the part of the group that is described.

28. foods

29. items to read

30. red items

31. sports gear

32. items that are not blue

What does the denominator represent when the fraction names part of a group?

WRAP UP...

EXPLORING

Finding a Fraction of a Number

A balanced diet includes a selection of foods from each of the four basic food groups. For a health project, Emmitt and Eve are recording the foods they eat.

WORK TOGETHER

Building Understanding

Of the 12 foods that Emmitt ate today, one fourth were dairy products. How many dairy products did Emmitt eat today?

You know the 12 foods are divided into 4 equal groups. You need to find how many foods are in 1 of these groups.

Find $\frac{1}{4}$ of 12.

Use counters to show the total number of foods. Separate the counters into 4 equal groups.

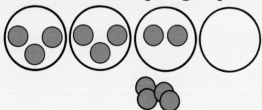

Of the 16 foods that Eve ate today, two fourths were dairy and vegetable products. How many dairy and vegetable products did Eve eat today?

You know the 16 foods are divided into 4 equal groups. You need to find how many of the 16 foods are in 2 of these groups.

Find $\frac{2}{4}$ of 16.

Use counters to show the total number of foods. Separate the counters into 4 equal groups.

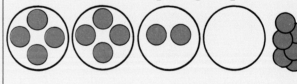

Talk About It
▶ How many counters do you need for the total number of foods?

▶ How many counters are in *one* group?

▶ How many dairy products did Emmitt eat?

Talk About It
▶ How many counters do you need for the total number of foods?

▶ How many counters are in *two* groups?

▶ How many dairy and vegetable products did Eve eat?

324

Making the Connection

Use counters and number sentences to find a fraction of a number.

Find $\frac{3}{5}$ of 20.

Step 1 Use the denominator. Divide 20 counters into 5 equal groups to find the number in each group.	**Step 2** Use the numerator. Multiply the number in each group (4) by the number of groups (3).
Record:	Record:
$20 \div 5 = 4$	$3 \times 4 = 12$
total number → total number of groups → number in each group	number of groups → number in each group → counters

So, $\frac{3}{5}$ of 20 = 12.

- How can you use division and multiplication to find the fraction of a number?

Use counters to find the fraction of each number. Record what you did.

1. $\frac{1}{5}$ of 20
2. $\frac{2}{3}$ of 9
3. $\frac{3}{4}$ of 32
4. $\frac{4}{5}$ of 30

Checking Understanding

Use the pictures to help you complete Exercises 5–7.

5.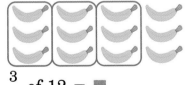
$\frac{3}{4}$ of 12 = ■

6.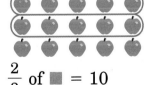
$\frac{2}{3}$ of ■ = 10

7.
$\frac{■}{■}$ of 9 = 3

Use counters to model each exercise. Record what you did.

8. $\frac{2}{3}$ of 27
9. $\frac{4}{9}$ of 36
10. $\frac{5}{7}$ of 14
11. $\frac{3}{5}$ of 20

12. Draw counters to model a fraction of a number. Exchange drawings with a partner. Write the fraction that is modeled.

13. If $\frac{1}{4}$ of 24 is 6, which of the following problems have an answer that is less than 6? Tell why.
a. $\frac{1}{4}$ of 22 b. $\frac{1}{4}$ of 25 c. $\frac{1}{4}$ of 32

More Practice, Lesson 10.4, page H71

Janis, Val, Tom, and Calvin had a lemonade stand at the big race. At the end of the day, they shared the profit. There were 5 one-dollar bills, 1 quarter, 2 dimes, and 3 pennies in the cash box. How much profit did each person receive?

Sometimes you can solve a problem by *acting it out*.

▶ **UNDERSTAND**

What are you asked to find?

What information is given in the problem?

▶ **PLAN**

What strategy can you use to solve the problem?

You can use play money to act out the situation.

Count the money and trade.

Place the money into 4 equal groups.

▶ **SOLVE**

How can you solve the problem?

Count the total amount of money. Try different combinations of bills and coins. Trade 1 one-dollar bill for 3 quarters, 2 dimes, and 5 pennies. Place the money into 4 equal groups. Count one group.

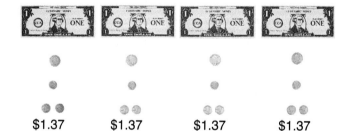

$1.37 $1.37 $1.37 $1.37

So, each person earned $1.37 profit.

▶ **LOOK BACK**

What other method could you use to solve the problem?

WHAT IF...

...there were only two people to share the profit? Would each person receive more or less money?

Apply

Solve each problem by acting it out.

1 Maya's teacher took the 27 students in her class to a health fair. While they were there, $\frac{2}{3}$ of the class had their pulse taken. How many students had their pulse taken?

2 Ira's class is divided into groups of 5 for a health project on vitamins and minerals. There are 5 groups. How many students are in Ira's class?

Mixed Applications ➤ | **STRATEGIES** • Work Backward • Act It Out • Guess and Check • Use Estimation • Write a Number Sentence

Choose a strategy and solve.

3 Jacob's mother has 7 quarters in her car to pay tolls for the drive to the fair. How much money does she have for the tolls?

4 Meta threw away $\frac{2}{3}$ of her sweat socks because they had holes in them. She had 18 socks in all. How many socks did she throw away?

5 Doris arrived at the school 14 minutes after the bus had left for the fair. She arrived at the school at 3:30 P.M. What time did the bus leave the school?

6 Ernie folded a sheet of paper in half several times. When he opened it up, it showed 16 squares. How many times did Ernie fold the paper?

7 Bess recorded the number of calories she consumed in 2 weeks. She recorded 11,361 calories the first week and 12,790 calories the second week. Estimate how many calories Bess consumed in the 2 weeks by rounding to the nearest hundred.

8 Mr. Bailey took a group of 66 students to the fair. There were a dozen more girls than boys. How many of the students were girls?

WRITER'S CORNER

9 Use the information in the box to write a problem. Exchange with a partner and solve.

165 Fourth-Grade Students
Number of boys = $\frac{1}{3}$ of total
Number of girls = $\frac{2}{3}$ of total

EXPLORING

Equivalent Fractions

Mary and Martha ordered oranges at Nature's Snack Bar. Mary ate $\frac{1}{2}$ of her orange, and Martha ate $\frac{2}{4}$ of her orange. Who ate more of her orange?

Equivalent fractions name the same number.

WORK TOGETHER

Building Understanding

Use fraction bars to explore equivalent fractions.

Make fraction bars by cutting paper into strips.

Fold a sheet of paper in half two times along the shorter side. Open and cut along the folds so that you have four equal strips of paper.

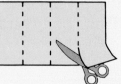

Label a strip 1 whole. Fold the next strip exactly in half. Label each part $\frac{1}{2}$. Fold another strip in half twice. Label the parts $\frac{1}{4}$. Fold the last strip in half three times. Label each part $\frac{1}{8}$.

> **Talk About It**
> ▶ What fractions tell how many halves, fourths, and eighths are in each strip?
>
> ▶ Are the fractions you named equivalent fractions?

Compare the fraction bars for $\frac{1}{2}$ and $\frac{2}{4}$. Place the fraction bar for halves above the fraction bar for fourths. Shade one of the halves.

$\frac{1}{2}$	$\frac{1}{2}$

$\frac{1}{4}$	$\frac{1}{4}$	$\frac{1}{4}$	$\frac{1}{4}$

> **Talk About It**
> ▶ How many fourths are the same as one half? Shade the fourths.
>
> ▶ Are $\frac{2}{4}$ and $\frac{1}{2}$ equivalent? Explain.
>
> ▶ So, who ate more of her orange?

Use your fraction bars to complete these equivalent fractions.

$\frac{1}{4}$	$\frac{1}{4}$	$\frac{1}{4}$	$\frac{1}{4}$		$\frac{1}{2}$		$\frac{1}{2}$	

$\frac{1}{8}$	$\frac{1}{8}$	$\frac{1}{8}$	$\frac{1}{8}$	$\frac{1}{8}$	$\frac{1}{8}$	$\frac{1}{8}$	$\frac{1}{8}$	$\frac{1}{8}$	$\frac{1}{8}$	$\frac{1}{8}$	$\frac{1}{8}$	$\frac{1}{8}$	$\frac{1}{8}$	$\frac{1}{8}$	$\frac{1}{8}$

a. $\frac{1}{4} = \frac{\blacksquare}{8}$ **b.** $\frac{1}{2} = \frac{\blacksquare}{8}$

328

Making the Connection

Use counters to find equivalent fractions of a group.

Examples   A. Use 9 counters to make 9 equal groups.

$\frac{6}{9} = \frac{\blacksquare}{3}$ B. Use 9 counters to make 3 equal groups. ⊂••⊃⊂••⊃⊂••⊃

1. Write a fraction to show how many groups in Example A equal 6 counters.

2. Write a fraction to show how many groups in Example B equal 6 counters.

3. What is the equivalent fraction for $\frac{6}{9}$?

Find the equivalent fraction. Use counters.

4. $\frac{1}{3} = \frac{\blacksquare}{6}$

5. $\frac{1}{3} = \frac{\blacksquare}{15}$

6. $\frac{1}{5} = \frac{\blacksquare}{10}$

7. $\frac{3}{12} = \frac{\blacksquare}{4}$

Checking Understanding

Write the letter of the figure that shows an equivalent fraction.

8.    a.    b. 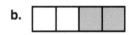   c.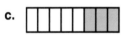

9.   a.   b.   c.

Write two equivalent fractions for each.

10. $\frac{2}{3}$ 11. $\frac{1}{8}$ 12. $\frac{3}{4}$ 13. $\frac{1}{2}$ 14. $\frac{2}{5}$ 15. $\frac{3}{8}$

Solve.

16. Merle sleeps 8 hours a day. What fraction of the day does he sleep?

17. Lenny's age is $\frac{1}{2}$ the age of Zeb. Lena's age is $\frac{2}{3}$ the age of Zeb. Zeb is 18 years old. How old are Lenny and Lena?

MIXED REVIEW

Find the product.

1. 59×7

2. 306×8

3. $1,217 \times 23$

Find the quotient.

4. $5\overline{)105}$

5. $9\overline{)252}$

6. $8\overline{)280}$

---

1. In a football game, the Wolves scored 14 more points than the Bears. If the Bears scored 13 points, how many points did the Wolves score?

2. The Youth Center sold boxes of fruit bars for $2.00. They made $0.50 for each box sold. If Jan sold 6 boxes, Tom sold 9 boxes, and Susan sold 8 boxes, how much money did they make?

3. Allison crosses First Avenue 4 times each day. How many times does she cross it in a week? in a year?

4. Jessica buys a shirt for $18.99 and a bracelet for $12.50. How much change does she receive from $40.00?

Some problems take more than 1 step to solve.

Write in order from least to greatest.

5. 29,334; 31,996; 28,051; 6,125

6. 8,654; 18,472; 14,872; 18,676

7. 557; 598; 549; 581; 535

8. 1,010; 1,001; 1,101; 1,000; 1,100

Find the perimeter of each figure.

9.
3 m 3 m
3 m 3 m

10.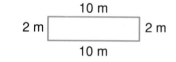
10 m
2 m [   ] 2 m
10 m

11.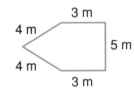
3 m
4 m
5 m
4 m
3 m

12.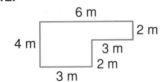
6 m
2 m
4 m
3 m
2 m
3 m

Find the area of each figure.

13.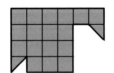

14.

15.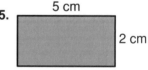
5 cm
2 cm

16.
2 cm

Write whether each figure shows *intersecting*, *parallel*, or *perpendicular* lines.

17.

18.

19.

20.

Spotlight ON

PROBLEM SOLVING

« Check the Solution for Reasonableness »

Sometimes you need to check an answer for reasonableness. You need to check that it answers the question and is properly labeled.

Todd had an operation. So, he goes to physical therapy each week to build strength in his knees. His therapy includes 10 minutes of stretching, 5 minutes of riding a stationary bicycle, 2 minutes on a balance beam, 5 minutes of using a trampoline, and 6 minutes on a weight machine. About how much time does Todd spend in therapy? What fraction of Todd's therapy time is spent riding a stationary bicycle and using a balance beam?

Talk About It

Work with a partner. Answer each of the following questions.

- What is an appropriate estimate of the amount of time Todd spends in therapy?

- How should the estimate be labeled?

- Is $\frac{1}{3}$ of the therapy time a reasonable answer to the problem's second question? If not, what is a reasonable answer to this question?

- If Todd goes to therapy five times a week, about how many hours does he spend there in a week?

Apply

Solve. Check that the answer is reasonable, that it answers the question, and that its label is correct.

1. Tom completed 55 sit-ups, 5 chin-ups, 15 push-ups, and 10 leg-lifts. How many exercises did he complete? What fraction of Tom's exercises were push-ups, leg-lifts, and chin-ups?

2. Dot walks the same distance every day. Each week she walks 14 miles. How many miles does she walk on Saturday and Sunday?

   HINT: $\frac{\text{weekend days}}{\text{days of the week}} \rightarrow \frac{2}{7}$ of $14 = \square$

331

FRACTIONS
Simplest Form

Sleep is an important part of a good fitness plan. Chandra sleeps 8 hours, or $\frac{8}{24}$, of the day. What is another fraction that is equivalent to $\frac{8}{24}$ that names the part of the day Chandra sleeps?

Use a strip of paper the same length as 1 whole fraction bar. Divide it into 24 equal sections, and shade 8 of them.

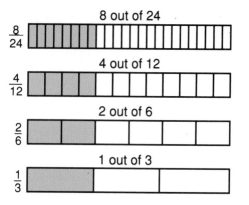

• What fraction piece did you find?

The fractions $\frac{8}{24}$ and $\frac{1}{3}$ are equivalent. The simplest form of $\frac{8}{24}$ is $\frac{1}{3}$.

So, Chandra sleeps $\frac{1}{3}$ of the day.

You can find the simplest form of a fraction by dividing by a common factor.

$$\frac{8 \div 2}{24 \div 2} = \frac{4}{12}$$ 2 is a factor of 8 and 24. 2 is a common factor.

$$\frac{4 \div 4}{12 \div 4} = \frac{1}{3}$$ 4 is a factor of 4 and 12. 4 is a common factor.

A fraction is in **simplest form** when the numerator and denominator have no common factor greater than 1.

More Examples

A. $\frac{3 \div 3}{12 \div 3} = \frac{1}{4}$

3 is a common factor of 3 and 12.

B. $\frac{1}{7}$

The only common factor is 1. So, this is the simplest form.

C. $\frac{3}{8}$

The only common factor is 1. So, this is the simplest form.

D. $\frac{6 \div 2}{10 \div 2} = \frac{3}{5}$

2 is a common factor of 6 and 10.

Check for Understanding

Complete.

1.

$$\frac{2}{4} = \frac{\blacksquare}{2}$$

2.

$$\frac{2}{6} = \frac{\blacksquare}{\blacksquare}$$

3.

$$\frac{2}{8} = \frac{\blacksquare}{\blacksquare}$$

4.

$$\frac{3}{9} = \frac{\blacksquare}{\blacksquare}$$

Practice

Complete.

5.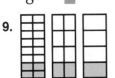

$$\frac{2}{8} = \frac{1}{\blacksquare}$$

6.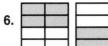

$$\frac{4}{8} = \frac{\blacksquare}{4}$$

7.

$$\frac{6}{8} = \frac{\blacksquare}{4}$$

8.

$$\frac{4}{12} = \frac{\blacksquare}{3}$$

9.

$$\frac{4}{16} = \frac{\blacksquare}{8} = \frac{1}{\blacksquare}$$

10.

$$\frac{10}{\blacksquare} = \frac{\blacksquare}{6}$$

11.

$$\frac{\blacksquare}{\blacksquare} = \frac{\blacksquare}{\blacksquare}$$

12.

$$\frac{\blacksquare}{\blacksquare} = \frac{\blacksquare}{\blacksquare}$$

13. $\dfrac{6}{9} = \dfrac{6 \div 3}{9 \div 3} = \dfrac{\blacksquare}{\blacksquare}$

14. $\dfrac{12}{14} = \dfrac{12 \div 2}{14 \div 2} = \dfrac{\blacksquare}{\blacksquare}$

15. $\dfrac{4}{12} = \dfrac{4 \div 4}{12 \div 4} = \dfrac{\blacksquare}{\blacksquare}$

16. Look at the fractions at the right. Write those that are in simplest form.

$$\frac{3}{8} \quad \frac{2}{4} \quad \frac{5}{9} \quad \frac{9}{16} \quad \frac{4}{6}$$
$$\frac{9}{12} \quad \frac{13}{16} \quad \frac{2}{6} \quad \frac{4}{5} \quad \frac{6}{10}$$

Write each fraction in simplest form.

17. $\dfrac{8}{18}$ **18.** $\dfrac{12}{36}$ **19.** $\dfrac{10}{24}$ **20.** $\dfrac{9}{12}$ **21.** $\dfrac{6}{10}$ **22.** $\dfrac{14}{16}$

23. Explain how you know that seventy-five cents is three fourths of a dollar.

24. Explain how you know that one quarter of an hour is fifteen minutes.

EVERYDAY MATH CONNECTION

Copy and complete the table. You may use an analog clock to help you.

	Activity	Fraction of Hour	Simplest Form	Number of Minutes
25.	Watching cartoons	$\blacksquare$	$\dfrac{1}{2}$	30
26.	Baking biscuits	$\dfrac{15}{60}$	$\blacksquare$	15
27.	Watching a videotape	$\dfrac{50}{60}$	$\blacksquare$	50
28.	Eating a light breakfast	$\blacksquare$	$\dfrac{1}{6}$	10

Hint: 1 hr = 60 min

How can you test whether a fraction is in simplest form?

WRAP UP...

The scout troop planned a hike to earn their physical fitness pins. There were 24 hikers in all, and $\frac{1}{6}$ of them were leaders. How many of the hikers were leaders?

Understand
Plan
Solve
Look Back

Choosing a strategy is an important part of problem solving. Sometimes you can use different strategies to solve the same problem.

Strategy: Make a Model

Use counters to make a model of the problem. You need to find how many are in 1 group out of a total of 6 groups. Find $\frac{1}{6}$ of 24.

Separate the 24 counters into 6 equal groups.

Now you can count to find how many counters are in 1 group.

So, 4 of the hikers were leaders.

Strategy: Draw a Picture

Draw stick figures to represent the 24 hikers. Circle 6 equal groups of the figures. Count the number of figures in 1 group. Find $\frac{1}{6}$ of 24.

So, 4 of the hikers were leaders.

WHAT IF... . . . there were 8 leaders? What fraction in simplest form would represent the number of leaders?

334

Choose a strategy and solve.

1. Helga buys eggs in a carton of 24. If she uses $\frac{5}{6}$ of the eggs to make breakfast, how many eggs are left?

I can guess and check to solve a problem.

2. Tony, his sister, and his brother have to share $180 equally. How much money will each of them receive?

3. Tim can buy 3 granola bars for $1. How many can he buy for $16?

4. Mrs. Lopez made 3 loaves of banana bread for her 3 sons to take on their hike. She cut each loaf into 9 slices. If the boys shared the bread equally, how many slices did each boy receive?

5. The scout troop returned from the park at 6:15 P.M. They had spent 7 hours hiking, $\frac{1}{2}$ hour eating lunch, and 1 hour traveling to and from the park. What time did they leave to go hiking?

6. Ramey buys a box of bandages for $2.59, a can of insect spray for $5.88, and a package of garbage bags for $3.63. If he has $20.00 to spend, will he have enough to buy a canteen for $7.99?

7. Luke's backpack is twice as heavy as Sam's. Together the backpacks weigh 18 pounds. How much does Luke's backpack weigh?

8. Bill's mother baked 4 more apple than carrot muffins. She baked 16 muffins altogether. What fraction shows the number of carrot muffins she baked?

The scout troop made a graph to show the change in temperature as they hiked. Use the graph for Exercises 9–11.

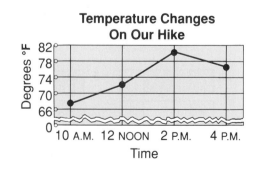

Temperature Changes On Our Hike

9. At what time was the temperature the highest?

10. At what time was the temperature the lowest?

11. Find the average temperature.

COMPARING FRACTIONS

Shelby and Jodi are members of the swim team. Shelby practices every day for $\frac{3}{4}$ hour. Jodi practices every day for $\frac{2}{4}$ hour. Who practices for a longer time?

Use fraction bars to compare fractions with like and unlike denominators.

Like fractions have the same denominators.	**Unlike fractions** have different denominators.
Compare $\frac{3}{4}$ and $\frac{2}{4}$.	Compare $\frac{1}{3}$ and $\frac{4}{6}$.
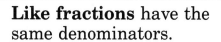	
To compare like fractions, compare the numerators.	To compare unlike fractions, find equivalent fractions with the same denominator. Then compare numerators.
$3 > 2$	$4 > 2$ and $\frac{4}{6} > \frac{2}{6}$
So, $\frac{3}{4} > \frac{2}{4}$, or $\frac{2}{4} < \frac{3}{4}$.	So, $\frac{4}{6} > \frac{1}{3}$, or $\frac{1}{3} < \frac{4}{6}$.
Shelby practices longer.	

Talk About It

▶ Compare $\frac{2}{5}$ and $\frac{2}{7}$. How can you tell which fraction is greater?

 Fifths

 Sevenths

Check for Understanding

Write *like* or *unlike* to describe each pair of fractions. Then compare, using <, >, or = for ●. Use fraction bars to help you.

1.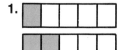

$\frac{1}{5}$ ● $\frac{2}{5}$

2.

$\frac{3}{12}$ ● $\frac{1}{6}$

3.

$\frac{2}{4}$ ● $\frac{3}{8}$

4.

$\frac{3}{4}$ ● $\frac{1}{4}$

5.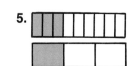

$\frac{3}{9}$ ● $\frac{1}{3}$

Practice

Write the fraction for the shaded part of each figure. Then compare, using <, >, or =.

6.

7.

8.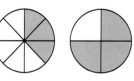

Write *like* or *unlike* to describe each pair of fractions. Then compare, using <, >, or = for ●.

9.

$\frac{3}{8}$ ● $\frac{5}{8}$

10.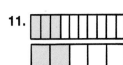

$\frac{1}{4}$ ● $\frac{1}{2}$

11.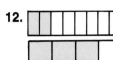

$\frac{3}{10}$ ● $\frac{2}{5}$

12.

$\frac{2}{8}$ ● $\frac{3}{4}$

13.

$\frac{5}{9}$ ● $\frac{2}{3}$

Mixed Applications

14. Tom drinks juice after practice. He drank $\frac{2}{3}$ cup on Monday and $\frac{1}{2}$ cup on Tuesday. On which day did he drink more juice?

15. Cindy swam for $\frac{1}{2}$ hour on Sunday, $\frac{1}{4}$ hour on Monday, and $\frac{3}{4}$ hour on Tuesday. On which day did she swim for the longest time?

Use the table for Exercises 16–17.

Event	Number of Swimmers
100-meter breaststroke	168
100-meter butterfly	96
100-meter freestyle	210
100-meter backstroke	114

16. How many more swimmers competed in the freestyle than in the butterfly?

17. What was the total number of participants in the four events?

VISUAL THINKING

Decide whether each picture represents about $\frac{1}{2}$. Write *yes* or *no*.

18.

19.

20.

21.

Is $\frac{5}{8}$ less than or greater than $\frac{1}{2}$? How do you know?

WRAP UP...

EXPLORING
Mixed Numbers

A **mixed number** is made up of a whole number and a fraction.

WORK TOGETHER

Building Understanding

Play Mixed Number Jumble to explore mixed numbers.

Make fraction circles for halves, thirds, fourths, fifths, sixths, eighths, tenths, and twelfths. Cut them into fractional pieces, label them, and "jumble" them up.

This game is for 2 to 3 players.

1. Deal out all of the fractional pieces, one at a time, from the top of the pile.

2. Build the greatest mixed number that you can name. You may discard unused pieces.

3. Remember: you can use equivalent fractions. $\frac{1}{2} = \frac{2}{4}$

4. The player who makes the greatest mixed number wins.

When a fraction's numerator is greater than its denominator, you can write a mixed number.

Make three more fraction circles and cut them into fourths. Make a model to show $\frac{10}{4}$.

Talk About It

▶ How many whole circles can you make with $\frac{10}{4}$?

▶ What fraction is left?

▶ What mixed number can you write for $\frac{10}{4}$?

▶ What is your age as a mixed number?

Making the Connection

When the numerator is greater than the denominator, you can divide to write a mixed number.

Example $\frac{7}{5}$ is the same as 7 divided by 5. → 7 ÷ 5

$$5\overline{)7}\ \overset{1\ \text{r}2}{} = 1\frac{2}{5}$$

Write each fraction as a mixed number. Draw a model of the mixed number.

1. $\frac{6}{5}$ 2. $\frac{9}{2}$ 3. $\frac{11}{5}$ 4. $\frac{17}{4}$ 5. $\frac{23}{7}$ 6. $\frac{46}{9}$

Checking Understanding

Use the figures at the right to complete Exercises 7–10.

7. How many whole figures are shaded?

8. Each figure is divided into how many equal parts?

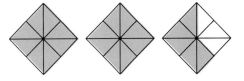

9. How many parts of the third figure are shaded?

10. What mixed number describes the picture?

Draw a picture to show each mixed number or fraction.

11. $\frac{8}{6}$ 12. $3\frac{2}{3}$ 13. $\frac{12}{5}$ 14. $2\frac{2}{4}$ 15. $\frac{9}{2}$

Write a mixed number for each picture.

16.

17.

18.

19.

20.

21.

Vocabulary Check

Choose a word or words from the box to complete each sentence.

denominator
equivalent
fraction
like
mixed
numerator
simplest form
unlike

When the numerator is larger than the denominator, I can make a mixed number.

1. A _?_ names a part of a whole or a part of a group. *(page 318)*

2. In the fraction $\frac{3}{7}$, the 3 is the _?_. *(pages 320, 322)*

3. The total number of equal parts or objects in a fraction is the _?_. *(pages 320, 322)*

4. Fractions that name the same number are _?_. *(page 328)*

5. When a fraction is in _?_, the numerator and denominator have no common factor greater than 1. *(page 332)*

6. _?_ fractions have the same denominators. *(page 336)*

7. _?_ fractions have different denominators. *(page 336)*

8. A _?_ number is made up of a whole number and a fraction. *(page 338)*

Concept Check

Write *part of a whole* or *part of a group* to describe the shaded part of each figure. *(page 318)*

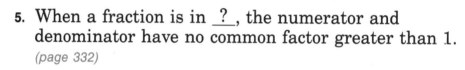

9.   10.   11.   12.

Write a fraction for the shaded part. *(pages 320, 322)*

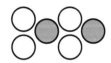 

13.   14.   15.   16.

Draw a figure, and shade part of it to show the fraction. *(page 320)*

Use counters to model each. Record what you did. *(page 324)*

17. $\frac{3}{5}$ 18. $\frac{7}{10}$ 19. $\frac{2}{7}$ 20. $\frac{4}{5}$ of 20   21. $\frac{1}{3}$ of 15

Complete. *(page 332)*

22.

$$\frac{6}{8} = \frac{\blacksquare}{4}$$

23.

$$\frac{4}{\blacksquare} = \frac{\blacksquare}{2}$$

24.

$$\frac{\blacksquare}{\blacksquare} = \frac{\blacksquare}{\blacksquare}$$

25.

$$\frac{\blacksquare}{\blacksquare} = \frac{\blacksquare}{\blacksquare}$$

Compare by using <, >, or = for ●. *(page 336)*

26.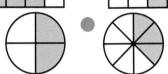

27.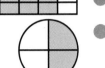

Draw a picture to show each mixed number or fraction. *(page 338)*

28. $2\frac{3}{4}$ **29.** $\frac{8}{6}$ **30.** $\frac{9}{5}$

Skill Check

Write a fraction for the shaded part. *(pages 320, 322)*

31.   **32.**   **33.**    **34.**

Write two equivalent fractions for each. *(page 328)*

35. $\frac{1}{2}$ **36.** $\frac{2}{3}$ **37.** $\frac{3}{4}$

Write each fraction in simplest form. *(page 332)*

38. $\frac{3}{12}$ **39.** $\frac{12}{24}$ **40.** $\frac{14}{16}$

Complete. *(page 324)*

41. $\frac{3}{7}$ of $21 = \blacksquare$ **42.** $\frac{2}{5}$ of $25 = \blacksquare$ **43.** $\frac{4}{9}$ of $18 = \blacksquare$

Write each fraction as a mixed number. *(page 338)*

44. $\frac{5}{3}$ **45.** $\frac{3}{2}$ **46.** $\frac{7}{4}$ **47.** $\frac{8}{5}$

Problem-Solving Check *(pages 326, 334)*

48. There are 24 students in Bob's class. Mr. Burton took $\frac{2}{3}$ of them to a workshop. How many students went to the workshop?

49. Lola's class is divided into teams of 4 for competition. There are 7 teams. How many students are in Lola's class?

First I read the directions. Then I study the model.

Write *part of a whole* or *part of a group* for the shaded part of each figure.

1.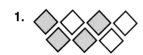
2.
3.

Write a fraction for the shaded part.

4.
5.
6.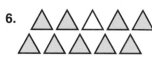

7.
8.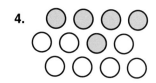
9.

Complete.

10. $\dfrac{6}{7}$ of $28 = $ ■

11. $\dfrac{3}{5}$ of $30 = $ ■

12. $\dfrac{5}{8}$ of $56 = $ ■

Compare using $<$, $>$, or $=$ for ●.

13. $\dfrac{2}{3}$ ● $\dfrac{3}{6}$

14. $\dfrac{3}{4}$ ● $\dfrac{4}{8}$

Write a mixed number for each picture.

15.
16.
17.
18.

Choose a strategy and solve.

19. Miss Lake has 30 students in her class. She gave a fitness test to $\dfrac{2}{3}$ of them on Friday. How many students did she test on Friday?

20. Al, Bill, Kris, and Dee had a juice stand. They shared the profit of $20.60 equally. How much of the profit did each person receive?

Happy Trails

Whether you are walking, running, biking, hiking, or riding horseback, it is always good to use a marked trail. It often leads to interesting places, and it is usually away from heavy traffic. Imagine that you and your teammates are members of the parks-and-recreation committee. Work together to plan a bicycle trail in your community.

 ## Decide

☐ Research interesting places where the trail should go.

☐ Discuss approximately how long the trail should be and how long it should take to ride it.

☐ Decide where to get a map of the community, for marking your trail.

☐ Discuss a way to show distances on the map.

 ## Do

☐ Mark your trail on the map.

☐ Include the total distance and the distances for parts of the trail.

☐ Highlight places of interest.

 ## Share

☐ Show your map to the other teams. Tell why your bicycle trail is interesting.

Talk About It

- How can you share the plans for your trail with your community leaders?

- Which parts of the trail are hardest to follow? How could you mark them?

- How could you mark points along your trail at $\frac{1}{4}$, $\frac{1}{2}$, and $\frac{3}{4}$ of the total distance?

- How can using fractions help you make a map?

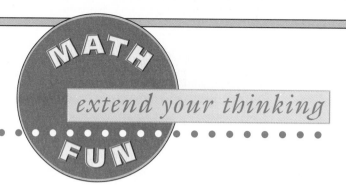

extend your thinking

Activity

Equivalent-Fraction Concentration

Prepare a set of 36 number cards. Write one of the following fractions on each of 12 cards:

$\frac{1}{2}$, $\frac{2}{3}$, $\frac{1}{4}$, $\frac{2}{5}$, $\frac{3}{5}$, $\frac{4}{5}$, $\frac{1}{6}$, $\frac{1}{8}$, $\frac{3}{8}$, $\frac{5}{8}$, $\frac{3}{10}$, and $\frac{7}{10}$.

For each of these 12 fractions, write 2 equivalent fractions on the remaining 24 cards.

Play the game with a partner. Shuffle all the cards. Place them facedown, forming a 4 × 9 array. A player selects two cards, turns them faceup, and shows them to the other player. If the fractions are equivalent, the two cards match and the player keeps them and continues playing. If the two cards do not match, they are placed back on the table facedown, and the other player has a turn.

When all the cards have been matched, the player with the most matches is the winner.

Challenge
Visual Thinking

1. Find four different ways to divide this figure into 4 equal parts.

2. Study the shapes in the box below.

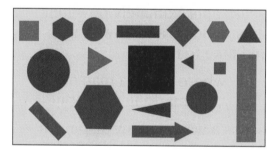

Write a fraction that tells what part of the group is *not* blue, square, or rectangular.

Challenge
Everyday Math

1. There are 7 coins. $\frac{2}{7}$ are nickels. The rest are dimes. How much money is this altogether?

2. There are 8 coins. $\frac{1}{8}$ are quarters, $\frac{3}{8}$ are dimes, and the rest are nickels. How much money is this altogether? .

CUMULATIVE REVIEW

Write the letter of the correct answer.

1. Which of the following is another name for 20 tens?

   A. 20   B. 200
   C. 2,000   D. 20,000

2. Which is 4,297 rounded to its greatest place-value position?

   A. 4,000   B. 4,200
   C. 4,300   D. 5,000

3. Estimate the sum.
   289 + 314 + 107 + 477 = ■

   A. 900   B. 1,180
   C. 1,200   D. 1,400

4. Estimate the difference.
   8,412 − 1,905 = ■

   A. 2,000   B. 4,000
   C. 6,000   D. 8,000

5. Find the elapsed time.

   12:35   4:50

   A. 4 hr   B. 4 hr 15 min
   C. 4hr 25 min   D. 5 hr

6.   3,456
    ×   4

   A. 12,064   B. 12,824
   C. 13,024   D. not here

7. Find the perimeter.

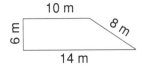

   A. 28 m
   B. 38 m
   C. 60 m
   D. 3,360 m

8. Find the area.

   A. 8 square units
   B. 16 square units
   C. 20 square units
   D. 24 square units

9. Find the average.
   100, 68, 96, 84, 77

   A. 32   B. 81
   C. 84   D. 85

10. Which fraction is equivalent to $\frac{3}{4}$?

    A. $\frac{3}{8}$ B. $\frac{4}{7}$

    C. $\frac{4}{6}$ D. $\frac{6}{8}$

11. Jerry bought a sweatshirt and jeans for $53.45. The jeans cost $28.50. How much did the sweatshirt cost?

    A. $24.95   B. $25.95
    C. $75.15   D. $81.95

12. Monte bought 3 cans of tennis balls for $9.19 and new tennis shoes for $37.95. How much change did he receive from $50.00?

    A. $2.86   B. $2.96
    C. $13.86   D. $47.14

USING FRACTIONS
AND EXPLORING PROBABILITY

Did you know . . .

. . . that the game of marbles has been played for at least 5,000 years? Children have used round stones, nuts, or glass spheres to play marbles.

Kerry has 4 red marbles and 8 blue marbles in his marble bag. Suppose he reaches in and takes out 1 marble without looking. How can he find the probability of picking a blue marble?

Estimating Fractions

Aaron's baseball team has just completed the 8th inning of a game. There are 9 innings in the game. So, $\frac{8}{9}$ of the game has been completed. Has the game just started, is it close to halfway, or is it almost over?

WORK TOGETHER

Building Understanding

Use pictures and a model to estimate fractions.

Trace this fraction model and label it as shown. Cut out the tracing.

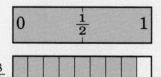 ← model

Match your model to the models below to see whether the shaded parts are closer to 0, $\frac{1}{2}$, or 1.

| 0 | $\frac{1}{2}$ | 1 |

$\frac{8}{9}$

Talk About It

► How do you line up the model with the picture?

► How do you know that $\frac{8}{9}$ is closer to 1 than to 0 or $\frac{1}{2}$?

► So, if $\frac{8}{9}$ of the game has been completed, has the game just started, is it close to halfway, or is it almost over?

Use your model to estimate the shaded part of each. Write *about* 0, *about* $\frac{1}{2}$, or *about* 1.

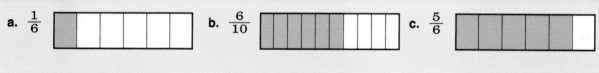

a. $\frac{1}{6}$ b. $\frac{6}{10}$ c. $\frac{5}{6}$

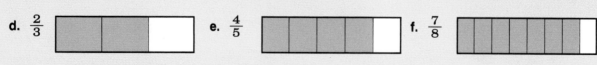

d. $\frac{2}{3}$ e. $\frac{4}{5}$ f. $\frac{7}{8}$

Making the Connection

Rounding fractions to 0, $\frac{1}{2}$, or 1 can help
you estimate sums and differences.

Examples

Estimate. $\frac{3}{4} + \frac{4}{6} =$ 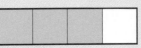	Estimate. $\frac{5}{8} - \frac{1}{10} =$ 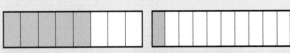
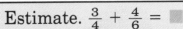	
Think: $\frac{3}{4}$ is close to 1, and $\frac{4}{6}$ is close to $\frac{1}{2}$. $1 + \frac{1}{2} = 1\frac{1}{2}$ Record: $\frac{3}{4} + \frac{4}{6}$ is about $1\frac{1}{2}$.	**Think:** $\frac{5}{8}$ is close to $\frac{1}{2}$, and $\frac{1}{10}$ is close to 0. $\frac{1}{2} - 0 = \frac{1}{2}$ Record: $\frac{5}{8} - \frac{1}{10}$ is about $\frac{1}{2}$.

Use your model to estimate each sum or difference.
Draw a picture to show your estimate.

1. $\frac{2}{3} + \frac{5}{6} =$

2. $\frac{8}{10} - \frac{1}{5} =$

3. $\frac{1}{4} + \frac{5}{8} =$

4. $\frac{9}{10} + \frac{4}{8} =$

Checking Understanding

Use your fraction model to estimate the shaded part of each.
Write *about* 0, *about* $\frac{1}{2}$, or *about* 1.

5. $\frac{1}{8}$
6. $\frac{10}{16}$
7. $\frac{5}{6}$

Use your model to estimate each sum or difference. Draw a
picture to show your estimate.

8. $\frac{1}{3} + \frac{4}{9} =$

9. $\frac{6}{10} + \frac{7}{8} =$

10. $\frac{2}{3} - \frac{1}{6} =$

11. $\frac{3}{4} - \frac{3}{8} =$

VISUAL THINKING

An **analogy** is a statement that
compares properties of two objects.
Complete each analogy by drawing
the missing figure.

Example ◖ is to ◗ as ◖ is to ◗.

12. ▲ is to ▼ as ↓ is to _?_.

13. 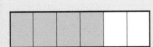 is to ◈ as ⊕ is to _?_.

14. ▤ is to ▤ as ▦ is to _?_.

EXPLORING

Adding Fractions with Like Denominators

Fizzle is a game of fractions. Jamie scored $\frac{2}{8}$ point, and his teammate scored $\frac{5}{8}$ point. They want to find their team score.

WORK TOGETHER

Building Understanding

Use fraction circles to explore adding fractions with like denominators.

Trace 1 whole fraction circle.

a. (1 whole)

Place 2 eighth pieces on the circle.

b. $\frac{2}{8}$

Think: Record:

2 eighths $\frac{2}{8}$

Then add 5 more eighths pieces to the circle.

c. $\frac{5}{8}$

$+ 5 \text{ eighths} \quad + \frac{5}{8}$

■ eighths $\quad \dfrac{\blacksquare}{8}$

Talk About It

▶ What fraction did you write to record the first 2 eighth pieces?

▶ What fraction did you write to record the next 5 eighth pieces?

▶ How many eighths did you place on the circle in all? What is the team's score?

Find each sum by making a model with fraction circles. Draw a picture of each model, and record your work as in the first activity.

a. $\frac{1}{8} + \frac{4}{8} = \blacksquare$ 　　**b.** $\frac{2}{4} + \frac{1}{4} = \blacksquare$

Talk About It

▶ What do you notice about the denominators of the addends and the sum?

▶ How did you find the sum of the fractions?

▶ What rule can you write for adding fractions when the denominators are the same?

Idea Bank, page 454, Exercise 6

Making the Connection

You can add fractions with like denominators by adding the numerators.

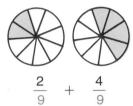

$$\frac{2}{9} + \frac{4}{9}$$

Check the denominators.
Denominators are the same.

$$\frac{2}{9} + \frac{4}{9}$$

Add the numerators.

Record: Write the sum over the denominator.

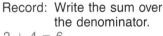

$2 + 4 = 6$

$$\frac{2}{9} + \frac{4}{9} = \frac{6}{9}$$

Find the sum. Use fraction pieces.

1. $\dfrac{6}{8} + \dfrac{1}{8} = \dfrac{\blacksquare}{\blacksquare}$

2. $\dfrac{2}{5} + \dfrac{1}{5} = \dfrac{\blacksquare}{\blacksquare}$

3. $\dfrac{7}{10} + \dfrac{2}{10} = \dfrac{\blacksquare}{\blacksquare}$

Checking Understanding

Use fraction pieces to find the sum. The sum may be written in simplest form.

4.

$$\frac{2}{8} + \frac{4}{8} = \frac{\blacksquare}{\blacksquare}$$

5.

$$\frac{7}{8} + \frac{1}{8} = \frac{\blacksquare}{\blacksquare}$$

6. $\dfrac{4}{10} + \dfrac{2}{10} = \dfrac{\blacksquare}{\blacksquare}$

7. $\dfrac{9}{12} + \dfrac{1}{12} = \dfrac{\blacksquare}{\blacksquare}$

8. $\dfrac{2}{9} + \dfrac{4}{9} = \dfrac{\blacksquare}{\blacksquare}$

Write the letter of the number sentence that helps you add the fraction pieces. Draw a picture of each sum.

9.

10.

a. $\dfrac{3}{8} + \dfrac{2}{8} = \dfrac{5}{8}$

b. $\dfrac{7}{12} + \dfrac{4}{12} = \dfrac{11}{12}$

c. $\dfrac{2}{5} + \dfrac{3}{5} = \dfrac{5}{5}$, or 1

d. $\dfrac{1}{6} + \dfrac{3}{6} = \dfrac{4}{6}$, or $\dfrac{2}{3}$

11.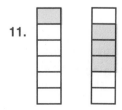

12.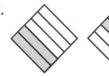

More Practice, Lesson 11.2, page H74

351

Subtracting Fractions with Like Denominators

Bobby and Lea are playing a board game called Strategy. If Bobby covers $\frac{9}{10}$ of the board, he will win the game. He has already covered $\frac{7}{10}$ of the board. What fraction of the board does he still need to cover to win the game?

WORK TOGETHER

Building Understanding

Use fraction bars to explore subtracting fractions with like denominators.

Trace 1 whole fraction bar.

1 whole

Place 9 tenth pieces on the bar.

$$\frac{9}{10}$$

Think:	Record:
9 tenths	$\frac{9}{10}$

Then take away 7 tenth pieces.

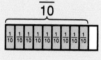

$$\frac{7}{10}$$

$-$ 7 tenths	$-\frac{7}{10}$
■ tenths	$\frac{\blacksquare}{10}$

Find each difference by making a model with fraction bars. Draw a picture of each model, and record your work as in the first activity.

a. $\frac{6}{10} - \frac{4}{10} = \frac{\blacksquare}{\blacksquare}$

b. $\frac{7}{8} - \frac{1}{8} = \frac{\blacksquare}{\blacksquare}$

Talk About It

▸ What fraction did you write to record the first 9 tenth pieces?

▸ What fraction did you write to record the next 7 tenth pieces?

▸ How many tenth pieces were left after you subtracted 7? So, what fraction of the board does Bobby still need to cover to win the game?

Talk About It

▸ What do you notice about the denominators in each problem?

▸ How did you find the difference of the fractions?

▸ What rule can you write for subtracting fractions when the denominators are the same?

Making the Connection

You can subtract fractions with like denominators by subtracting the numerators.

Record: Write the difference over the denominator.

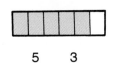

$$\frac{5}{6} - \frac{3}{6}$$

Check the denominators.
Denominators are the same.

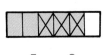

$$\frac{5}{6} - \frac{3}{6}$$

Subtract the numerators.

$5 - 3 = 2$

$$\frac{5}{6} - \frac{3}{6} = \frac{2}{6}$$

Find the difference. Use fraction pieces.

1. $\dfrac{4}{5} - \dfrac{1}{5} = \dfrac{\blacksquare}{\blacksquare}$

2. $\dfrac{7}{9} - \dfrac{2}{9} = \dfrac{\blacksquare}{\blacksquare}$

3. $\dfrac{4}{8} - \dfrac{3}{8} = \dfrac{\blacksquare}{\blacksquare}$

Checking Understanding

Use fraction pieces to find the difference. The difference may be written in simplest form.

4. $\dfrac{5}{6} - \dfrac{3}{6} = \dfrac{\blacksquare}{6}$

5. $\dfrac{12}{16} - \dfrac{6}{16} = \dfrac{\blacksquare}{\blacksquare}$

6. $\dfrac{7}{9} - \dfrac{4}{9} = \dfrac{\blacksquare}{\blacksquare}$

7. $\dfrac{8}{9} - \dfrac{5}{9} = \dfrac{\blacksquare}{\blacksquare}$

8. $\dfrac{11}{14} - \dfrac{9}{14} = \dfrac{\blacksquare}{\blacksquare}$

9. $\dfrac{11}{12} - \dfrac{5}{12} = \dfrac{\blacksquare}{\blacksquare}$

10. $\dfrac{15}{16} - \dfrac{11}{16} = \dfrac{\blacksquare}{\blacksquare}$

11. $\dfrac{12}{15} - \dfrac{6}{15} = \dfrac{\blacksquare}{\blacksquare}$

12. $\dfrac{9}{9} - \dfrac{6}{9} = \dfrac{\blacksquare}{\blacksquare}$

13. $\dfrac{8}{10} - \dfrac{6}{10} = \dfrac{\blacksquare}{\blacksquare}$

14. $\dfrac{10}{12} - \dfrac{2}{12} = \dfrac{\blacksquare}{\blacksquare}$

MIXED REVIEW

Write three equivalent fractions for each.

1. $\dfrac{1}{4}$

2. $\dfrac{1}{2}$

3. $\dfrac{2}{3}$

4. $\dfrac{3}{4}$

5. $\dfrac{1}{3}$

Write each fraction in simplest form.

6. $\dfrac{20}{40}$

7. $\dfrac{18}{24}$

8. $\dfrac{12}{20}$

9. $\dfrac{16}{18}$

10. $\dfrac{6}{9}$

PROBLEM Solving

Strategy • Make a Model

Jamal made a game with a spinner. Each player spins to find the two colors that he or she can use on the gameboard. Each player wants the two colors that together cover the largest part of the spinner. Do any two colors cover more than half of the spinner?

Sometimes you can *make a model* to solve a problem.

▶ **UNDERSTAND**

What are you asked to find?

What information is given in the problem?

▶ **PLAN**

How can you make it easier to estimate?

You can make a model by tracing the spinner and coloring the sections on your model to match the spinner. Cut out the sections, and rearrange them so that the same colors are next to each other.

▶ **SOLVE**

How can you solve the problem?

Look at the model, and mentally estimate whether any two colors cover more than half of the spinner. Record *yes* or *no* for each two colors.

Two colors that cover more than half of the spinner are green and red.

▶ **LOOK BACK**

How can you check your answer?

Examples	yes	no
blue/yellow		x
red/blue		x
green/white		x

> . . . Jamal spins and gets blue and white? About what fraction of the spinner is blue and white?

WHAT IF...

354

Apply

Make a model to solve.

1 Ronald colored $\frac{1}{2}$ of a large square blue and $\frac{1}{4}$ of the square red. How much of the square did he color?

2 Kay poured $\frac{1}{4}$ cup of milk and $\frac{2}{3}$ cup of water into a mixing bowl. About how much liquid did she pour into the bowl?

Mixed Applications

| STRATEGIES | • Use Estimation • Act It Out • Write a Number Sentence • Draw a Picture • Guess and Check |

Choose a strategy and solve.

3 Roger is 13 years old. Simeon is 15 years younger than twice Roger's age. How old is Simeon?

4 Stuart placed 24 colored cubes in each of 6 bags. How many cubes did he use?

Use the pictures for Exercises 5–7.

5 Lars wants to buy a calculator, a ruler, a paint set, and a stapler. He bought only two of these and spent $9.14. Which items did he buy?

6 Estimate the cost of all the items.

7 Babs has $15.00. What three combinations of items can she buy?

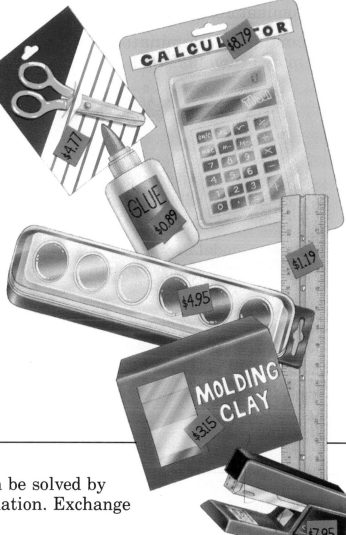

WRITER'S CORNER

8 Create your own problem that can be solved by making a model. Use your imagination. Exchange problems with a partner. Solve.

EXPLORING

Finding a Common Denominator

Mike and April both like to play Monopoly®. When two or more people have the same interest, they have something *in common*.

- Look at the picture. What else do Mike and April have in common?

- What do the numbers 2 and 4 have in common?

When adding or subtracting fractions with different denominators, you need to find a *common denominator*.

A **common denominator** is a common multiple of two or more denominators.

WORK TOGETHER

Building Understanding

Use fraction pieces to find the common denominator of two fractions.

Show a model of one half piece and a model of three fourth pieces.

$\frac{1}{2}$ and $\frac{3}{4}$

Use fraction pieces to change unlike fractions into like fractions.

Make a model of the unlike fractions. Then trade fraction pieces to make like fractions.

$\frac{2}{3}$ and $\frac{5}{6}$
unlike denominators

$\frac{\blacksquare}{\blacksquare}$ and $\frac{\blacksquare}{\blacksquare}$
like denominators

Talk About It

▶ How can you trade the half piece for fourth pieces? Write the new fraction for $\frac{1}{2}$.

▶ What is the common denominator? How do you know?

Talk About It

▶ What fraction pieces did you trade each third piece for?

▶ What is the common denominator of thirds and sixths?

▶ What are the like fractions that you made?

356

Making the Connection

Changing *unlike* fractions into *like* fractions makes them
easy to add and subtract.

Add.

$\frac{1}{4}$ and $\frac{2}{8}$ are
equivalent
fractions.

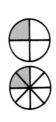

$\frac{1}{4} + \frac{1}{8}$

$\downarrow \quad \downarrow$

$\frac{2}{8} + \frac{1}{8} = \frac{3}{8}$

$\frac{1}{2}$ and $\frac{2}{4}$ are
equivalent
fractions.

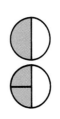

Subtract.

$\frac{1}{2} - \frac{1}{4}$

$\downarrow \quad \downarrow$

$\frac{2}{4} - \frac{1}{4} = \frac{1}{4}$

Use fraction pieces to find the sum or difference.

1. $\frac{1}{2} + \frac{1}{8}$

2. $\frac{2}{3} - \frac{1}{6}$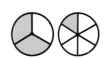

Checking Understanding

Use fraction pieces to find the common denominator.

3. $\frac{1}{8}$ and $\frac{2}{4}$

4. $\frac{2}{6}$ and $\frac{1}{3}$

5. $\frac{1}{10}$ and $\frac{2}{5}$

Use fraction pieces to change unlike fractions into like fractions.

6. $\frac{3}{8}$ and $\frac{1}{4}$

7. $\frac{1}{9}$ and $\frac{1}{3}$

8. $\frac{7}{8}$ and $\frac{2}{4}$

Use fraction pieces to find the sum or difference.

9. $\frac{2}{4} + \frac{1}{8} = n$
10. $\frac{2}{3} + \frac{1}{6} = n$
11. $\frac{5}{6} - \frac{1}{3} = n$
12. $\frac{6}{8} - \frac{1}{2} = n$

13. Hugh ate $\frac{1}{3}$ of the pizza, and
Tina ate $\frac{1}{6}$ of it. How much did
they eat altogether?

14. Bill had $\frac{6}{10}$ of the Monopoly®
properties. He sold $\frac{1}{5}$. What
fraction of the properties does
Bill have left?

MIXED REVIEW

Write whether each set of fractions is *like* or *unlike*.

1. $\frac{1}{4}$ and $\frac{3}{4}$
2. $\frac{5}{6}$ and $\frac{2}{3}$
3. $\frac{1}{7}$ and $\frac{2}{4}$
4. $\frac{3}{8}$ and $\frac{1}{8}$

Use mental math to find the sum or difference.

5. $\frac{3}{4} + \frac{1}{4} = n$
6. $\frac{5}{10} + \frac{3}{10} = n$
7. $\frac{8}{9} - \frac{2}{9} = n$
8. $\frac{7}{12} - \frac{3}{12} = n$

More Practice, Lesson 11.5, page H75

ADDING AND SUBTRACTING
with Unlike Denominators

At Windermere School the soccer field covers $\frac{3}{8}$ of the playground, and the baseball field covers $\frac{1}{4}$ of the playground. What fraction of the playground is covered by the two game fields? How much more of the playground is used for the soccer field?

Add. $\frac{3}{8} + \frac{1}{4}$

Step 1	**Step 2**
The denominators are different. Find an equivalent fraction with a common denominator.	Add the numerators.
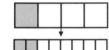	$\frac{3}{8}$ $\frac{2}{8}$ $\frac{3}{8} + \frac{2}{8} = \frac{5}{8}$

Subtract. $\frac{3}{8} - \frac{1}{4}$

Step 1	**Step 2**
The denominators are different. Find an equivalent fraction with a common denominator.	Subtract the numerators.
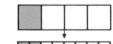	$\frac{1}{4}$ $\frac{3}{8} - \frac{2}{8} = \frac{1}{8}$

So, $\frac{5}{8}$ of the playground is covered by the soccer field and the baseball field. The soccer field covers $\frac{1}{8}$ more of the playground than the baseball field.

Check for Understanding

Find the sum or difference. Use fraction pieces to help you.

1. $\frac{3}{4} - \frac{1}{2}$ 2. $\frac{1}{6} + \frac{1}{3}$ 3. $\frac{5}{6} - \frac{1}{3}$ 4. $\frac{3}{8} + \frac{2}{4}$

Practice

Copy and complete. Use fraction pieces to help you.

5. $\dfrac{1}{3} \rightarrow \dfrac{\blacksquare}{6}$
$+\dfrac{4}{6} \rightarrow \dfrac{\blacksquare}{6}$
$\overline{\qquad \dfrac{\blacksquare}{6}}$

6. $\dfrac{1}{4} \rightarrow \dfrac{\blacksquare}{8}$
$+\dfrac{3}{8} \rightarrow \dfrac{\blacksquare}{8}$
$\overline{\qquad \dfrac{\blacksquare}{8}}$

7. $\dfrac{9}{10} \rightarrow \dfrac{\blacksquare}{\blacksquare}$
$-\dfrac{1}{2} \rightarrow \dfrac{\blacksquare}{\blacksquare}$
$\overline{\qquad \dfrac{\blacksquare}{\blacksquare}}$

8. $\dfrac{6}{9} \rightarrow \dfrac{\blacksquare}{\blacksquare}$
$-\dfrac{1}{3} \rightarrow \dfrac{\blacksquare}{\blacksquare}$
$\overline{\qquad \dfrac{\blacksquare}{\blacksquare}}$

Use fraction pieces to find the sum or difference.

9.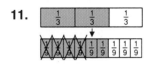

$\dfrac{1}{2} + \dfrac{3}{10} =$

$\dfrac{5}{10} + \dfrac{3}{10}$

10.

$\dfrac{3}{4} - \dfrac{1}{8} =$

$\dfrac{6}{8} - \dfrac{1}{8}$

11.

$\dfrac{2}{3} - \dfrac{4}{9} =$

$\dfrac{6}{9} - \dfrac{4}{9}$

12.

$\dfrac{1}{2} + \dfrac{2}{6} =$

$\dfrac{3}{6} + \dfrac{2}{6}$

Find the sum or difference. Use fraction pieces to help you.

13. $\dfrac{2}{3} + \dfrac{1}{6}$

14. $\dfrac{4}{8} - \dfrac{1}{4}$

15. $\dfrac{4}{16} + \dfrac{1}{4}$

16. $\dfrac{1}{3} - \dfrac{1}{9}$

Mixed Applications

17. Marty walked $\dfrac{5}{10}$ mile and Sue walked $\dfrac{4}{5}$ mile. Who walked farther? How much farther?

18. There are 268 fourth and fifth graders on the playground. There are 143 fifth graders. How many fourth graders are there?

19. Marta rode $\dfrac{1}{3}$ mile to school, $\dfrac{5}{12}$ mile to the store, and then $\dfrac{3}{4}$ mile home. How far did Marta ride?

20. **Number Sense** Which has the greater sum?

    a. $\dfrac{5}{6} + \dfrac{1}{3}$ or $\dfrac{5}{6} + \dfrac{2}{3}$

    b. $\dfrac{3}{8} + \dfrac{1}{4}$ or $\dfrac{3}{8} + \dfrac{3}{4}$

What denominator would you use to subtract $\dfrac{4}{8} - \dfrac{7}{24}$? Why?

Use the graph for Exercises 1–3.

Games Won This Season	
Aggies	✔ ✔ ✔ ✔
Bruins	✔ ✔ ✔
Tigers	✔ ✔ ✔ ✔ ✔
Terriers	✔ ✔
Each ✔ stands for 3 games.	

1. Which team won the most games this season?

2. Were more games won by the Terriers or by the Bruins?

3. Which two teams won a total of 18 games?

Solve each problem if possible. Write whether there is *too much* or *too little* information.

4. On Monday 55 people ate lunch at Tony's Grill. Tony cooked more than 150 hamburgers that day. On Tuesday 95 people ate lunch at Tony's. How many people ate lunch there on Monday and Tuesday?

5. Roberto is making a game for his math class. The length of the gameboard is 60 centimeters. What is the area of the gameboard?

To find area, I can count square units or multiply length times width.

Copy and complete.

6. $1 \text{ ft} = \blacksquare \text{ in.}$

7. $3 \text{ ft} = \blacksquare \text{ in.}$

8. $1 \text{ mi} = \blacksquare \text{ ft}$

Find the quotient.

9. $273 \div 4 = n$

10. $585 \div 5 = n$

11. $778 \div 7 = n$

Find the average of each set of numbers.

12. 12, 16, 40, 32

13. 90, 73, 100, 88, 99

Write each fraction in simplest form.

14. $\frac{8}{12}$

15. $\frac{3}{9}$

16. $\frac{5}{10}$

17. $\frac{6}{8}$

Write each fraction as a mixed number.

18. $\frac{10}{3}$

19. $\frac{8}{5}$

20. $\frac{12}{7}$

21. $\frac{20}{9}$

Copy and complete.

22. $\frac{1}{3}$ of $12 = \blacksquare$

23. $\frac{4}{5}$ of $15 = \blacksquare$

24. $\frac{7}{8}$ of $24 = \blacksquare$

Spotlight ON PROBLEM SOLVING

Solve the Problem in Another Way

Sometimes a problem can be solved in more than one way. As you become comfortable as a problem solver, you will recognize more solution strategies. Work in a group. Solve this problem. Share your method with other groups.

Sara created a story about a class of students. The class has 24 students. One half of the students are girls. One half of the girls are ten years old. How many girls are ten years old?

Talk About It

a. How many different methods were used to solve the problem?

b. What does the problem ask?

c. How many students are in the class?

d. What fraction of the class are girls?

e. How many girls are in the class? How did you find this number?

f. What fraction of the girls are ten years old?

g. How many girls are ten years old? How did you find this number?

Apply

Solve each problem in more than one way. Share solutions with your classmates.

1. The PTA sponsored a puppet show for students from kindergarten through fifth grade. The PTA paid one third of the regular cost of $60 per class. If there was one class from each grade, how much did the PTA pay for the show?

2. Jamie's new toolbox measures 2 feet long, 2 feet wide, and 1 foot high. His old toolbox was $\frac{1}{2}$ of each new dimension. What were the dimensions in inches of the old toolbox?

Wade's class made a game with squares. Wade's team made $3\frac{1}{4}$ squares, and Marlena's team made $4\frac{2}{4}$ squares. How many squares did the teams make?

Add. $3\frac{1}{4} + 4\frac{2}{4}$

You can use fraction pieces to make a model to solve the problem.

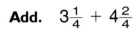

Talk About It

▶ How many whole pieces are in the model?

▶ How can you add the fraction pieces?

So, the teams made $7\frac{3}{4}$ squares for the game.

Another Example   The students colored $2\frac{1}{4}$ of the $7\frac{3}{4}$ squares blue. How many of the squares are not blue?

Subtract the fractions first.

Then subtract the whole numbers.

Use your fraction pieces.

$$7\frac{3}{4}$$
$$-2\frac{1}{4}$$
$$\blacksquare\frac{2}{4}$$

$\rightarrow$

$$7\frac{3}{4}$$
$$-2\frac{1}{4}$$
$$5\frac{2}{4}, \text{ or } 5\frac{1}{2}$$

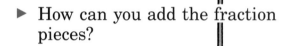

So, $5\frac{1}{2}$ of the squares are not blue.

> Remember: When the denominators are the same, add or subtract the numerators.

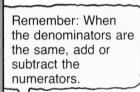

Check for Understanding

Draw fraction pieces to make a model. Solve.

1. $2\frac{3}{5} + 4\frac{1}{5} = \blacksquare$ 2. $3\frac{7}{9} - 1\frac{2}{9} = \blacksquare$ 3. $5\frac{6}{12} + 3\frac{5}{12} = \blacksquare$ 4. $4\frac{3}{4} - 2\frac{1}{2} = \blacksquare$

Practice

Draw fraction pieces to make a model. Solve.

5. $3\frac{1}{2}$
$+2\frac{3}{4}$
_____

6. $1\frac{7}{8}$
$-1\frac{1}{4}$
_____

7. $3\frac{5}{9}$
$+1\frac{2}{3}$
_____

8. $4\frac{5}{6}$
$-2\frac{1}{3}$
_____

9. $6\frac{1}{10}$
$+2\frac{5}{10}$
_____

Find the sum or difference. You may write your answer in simplest form.

10.

$1\frac{3}{6} + 2\frac{2}{6}$

11.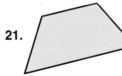

$7\frac{4}{5} - 2\frac{1}{5}$

12.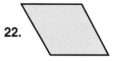

$7\frac{5}{6} - 4\frac{3}{6}$

13.

$5\frac{6}{8} - 2\frac{3}{8}$

14. $3\frac{11}{12}$
$-1\frac{6}{12}$
_____

15. $9\frac{9}{10}$
$-5\frac{3}{10}$
_____

16. $12\frac{5}{6}$
$-\ 9\frac{2}{6}$
_____

17. $10\frac{9}{16}$
$+\ 8\frac{3}{16}$
_____

18. $6\frac{6}{9}$
$+9\frac{1}{9}$
_____

Mixed Applications

19. Wade has $\frac{3}{4}$ yard of fabric. If he uses $\frac{1}{8}$ yard to cover a cardboard square, how many squares can he cover?

20. Luke cut out 52 squares to use for his math game. He colored $\frac{1}{2}$ of the squares blue and the rest of the squares red. How many squares are red?

VISUAL THINKING

What fraction of the whole hexagon is each piece?

21.

22.

23.

24.

Describe how to add or subtract mixed numbers.

WRAP
UP...

CONNECTING FRACTIONS AND MEASUREMENT

Sam and Tyrone are playing tiddledywinks. On the game-winning move, both players' game pieces missed the cup. So, they decided that the person whose game piece landed closest to the cup would win the game. Who won the game?

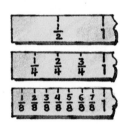

Sam measured his game piece as $2\frac{3}{8}$ inches from the cup. Tyrone measured his game piece as $2\frac{5}{8}$ inches from the cup. Whose piece is closer? How much closer?

So, Sam won the game by $\frac{2}{8}$ inch.

More Examples

A.

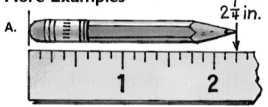

$2\frac{1}{4}$ in.

B.

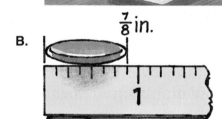

$\frac{7}{8}$ in.

Talk About It

▶ When might you need to measure to a fraction of a unit?

▶ Why does measuring the game piece to the nearest $\frac{1}{8}$ inch come closer to the exact measurement than measuring to the nearest $\frac{1}{4}$ inch?

Check for Understanding

Use a customary ruler to measure each.

1.

2.

3.

Practice

Use a customary ruler to measure each to the nearest unit. Use
$\frac{1}{2}$ inch, $\frac{1}{4}$ inch, and $\frac{1}{8}$ inch.

4.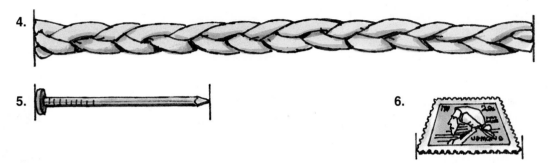

5.

6.

7. length of an unsharpened pencil

8. width of your math book

Name an object that measures about

9. $\frac{7}{8}$ inch long.

10. 1 inch wide.

11. $8\frac{1}{2}$ inches wide.

Use a customary ruler for Exercises 12–13.

12. Measure the distance from the floor to the top of your desk.

13. Draw a line segment that is $2\frac{3}{4}$ inches long.

Mixed Applications

14. Colin made a square gameboard. Each side is $10\frac{1}{8}$ inches long. What is the perimeter of the gameboard?

15. On some rulers an inch is divided into 16 equal parts. Each part is $\frac{1}{16}$ inch. How many sixteenths of an inch are in $3\frac{1}{2}$ inches?

16. Mick and Forrest played a round of carpet golf. On the last hole, they measured to see whose golf ball was closer. Mick's was $8\frac{1}{2}$ feet away from the hole, and Forrest's was $7\frac{7}{8}$ feet away. Whose ball was closer to the hole? How much closer?

17. **Number Sense** Use the lengths given on the game cards to make this sentence reasonable: The length $3\frac{7}{8}$ inches is large compared to ■, small compared to ■, and about the same as ■.

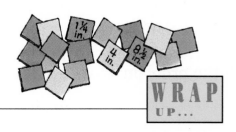

Which would give a more accurate measurement: the nearest $\frac{1}{2}$ inch or $\frac{1}{8}$ inch?

WRAP UP...

PROBLEM *Solving*

Jenny is playing Astro-Race, a video game. She must choose a vehicle and a color. How many different combinations of choices does she have?

Sometimes you can *make an organized list* to help you solve a problem.

▶ **UNDERSTAND**

What are you asked to find?

What information is given in the problem?

▶ **PLAN**

How can you *make an organized list* to help you solve the problem?

You can start with the first color and list all the vehicles that color.

▶ **SOLVE**

How can you solve the problem?

Continue listing the colors with all possible vehicles.

Choice	Color	Vehicle
1.	red	van
2.	red	car
3.	red	plane
4.	red	boat
5.	blue	van
6.	blue	car

Then you can count all the possible choices.

So, Jenny has 12 choices.

▶ **LOOK BACK**

What other method can you use to solve the problem?

WHAT IF... ...the vehicles also come in yellow? How many choices does Jenny have?

Apply

Make an organized list to solve.

(1) Dave has three T-shirts: a red one, a blue one, and a green one. He also has three pairs of shorts. The colors of the shorts are yellow, white, and black. List the different combinations of T-shirts and shorts he can wear.

(2) Use the digits 2, 4, and 6. List all the three-digit numbers you can make with 4 in the hundreds place. You may use each digit only once in the same number.

Mixed Applications → **STRATEGIES** • Draw a Picture • Make an Organized List • Guess and Check • Use Estimation

Choose a strategy and solve.

(3) Use the digits 1, 3, 7, and 8. List all the four-digit numbers you can make with 7 in the tens place without repeating any digits in the same number.

(4) Tickets for a football game cost $3.75 each. If you give the ticket seller $4.00, what combinations of coins might you receive in change, not including pennies?

(5) Choose one multiple of 10 to use as a divisor. Then write and solve five division problems that each have a remainder of 1.

(6) Al and Antoine worked on a science project together. Al spent $4.96 and Antoine spent $5.87. Did they spend more than or less than $10.00 altogether?

(7) Blair wants to take a picture of his classmates Aleck, Bev, and Candy. In how many different ways can Blair line them up?

(8) Cindy collects bottle caps. Every time she collects 50 caps, she buys a new container. She has 400 caps. How many containers does she have?

EXPLORING

Probability

Paula invented a game called Probability. On the spinner, red is worth 100, blue 75, green 50, and yellow 25. Each player spins three times and records the score. What is the probability the spinner will land on red?

Probability is the chance that a given event will occur.

WORK TOGETHER

Building Understanding

Use a spinner to explore probability.

Make a spinner with cardboard and a paper clip. Take turns spinning three times, and record the scores.

Talk About It

▸ Is the spinner divided into equal parts?

▸ How many colors are on the spinner? These are the **possible outcomes.**

▸ How many red parts are on the spinner?

The probability of landing on red is 1 out of 4. You can write probability as a fraction.

$$\frac{1}{4} \begin{array}{l} \leftarrow \text{ red part} \\ \leftarrow \text{ total number of parts} \end{array}$$

• What is the probability of landing on blue? on green? on yellow?

Write the letters of your first name on separate pieces of paper, and place them facedown. Record a fraction that tells the probability of each letter being chosen.

Example   S U S A N

S has 2 chances out of 5, or $\frac{2}{5}$.

U, A, and N each have 1 chance out of 5, or $\frac{1}{5}$.

Talk About It

▸ How many letters are in your name? These are the **possible outcomes.**

▸ What fraction did you write for each letter?

▸ If one letter occurs more than once, is there a greater probability that you will choose that letter rather than the other letters? Why?

Making the Connection

You can make predictions based on probability.

Use paper squares numbered 1, 2, 2, 3, 3, and 3. Put the squares into a paper bag. Each student will draw one square and replace it on each of 10 turns. Each student should predict whether a 1, 2, or 3 will be drawn most often. Record your predictions and results.

1. How did the predictions compare to the actual draws?

2. What is the probability of drawing a 3?

3. Repeat the procedure, having each student take 30 turns. How did the prediction compare to the actual draws?

Checking Understanding

Look at the colored cubes in the bag. Find the probability of picking each color.

4. red   5. yellow   6. blue   7. green   8. orange

Write the probability of the outcome when a number cube with the numbers 1 to 6 on it is tossed.

9. the number 6   10. the number 2   11. a number greater than 3

Solve.

12. There are 12 marbles in a box. There are 3 red marbles and 9 blue marbles. If you pick up a marble without looking, what are the chances of getting a blue marble?

13. **Mental Math** Choose from a drawer in which there are 5 white shirts, 2 striped shirts, 6 blue shirts, and 3 red shirts. What is the probability of choosing a blue shirt? a striped shirt?

14. A spinner has equal sections: 2 yellow, 1 red, and 2 green. What is the probability of spinning green? yellow? red?

15. Joe has a penny, a nickel, and 3 dimes in his pocket. Which type of coin is he most likely to pull out of his pocket?

The Hill Valley Chess Team must choose a uniform. The shirt can be red, striped, or white. The slacks can be blue or green. What are all the possible combinations from which the team members can choose? List all the possibilities.

You can make a tree diagram to see all of the possibilities.

Tree Diagram

Shirts	**Slacks**	**Possibilities**
red	blue	→ red shirt, blue slacks
	green	→ red shirt, green slacks
striped	blue	→ striped shirt, blue slacks
	green	→ striped shirt, green slacks
white	blue	→ white shirt, blue slacks
	green	→ white shirt, green slacks

Talk About It

▶ If team members choose a red shirt, how many different uniforms can they make?

▶ If they choose blue slacks, how many different uniforms can they make?

▶ How many possible uniforms are there in all?

▶ You found that with 3 shirts and 2 pairs of slacks there are 6 possible combinations. Can you think of a mathematical way to find all possible combinations?

Check for Understanding

1. Jodie's sister works at the Snack Shop. She can wear a white or brown top and a white, brown, or plaid skirt. Draw a tree diagram, and list all the possible uniforms she can wear.

2. Sari, Jeremy, and Cassie are in a play. They can choose the order in which they speak. List their names in all possible orders of speaking.

Practice

Make a tree diagram of all possible combinations for Exercises 3–6.

3. A T-shirt shop sells T-shirts with an emblem printed on the front. You can choose a seal, a whale, or a shark. You can choose a small, medium, large, or extra-large size.

4. A sandwich shop offers egg-salad, tuna-salad, and chicken-salad sandwiches. Each sandwich can be made with rye, whole-wheat, or white bread.

5. Grace has 4 sweaters and 3 skirts. She can wear a blue, a green, a white, or a red sweater and a blue, a white, or a striped skirt.

6. Lavida wants to order a plate of pasta with sauce for lunch. She can choose from 3 types of pasta and 3 types of sauce.

Mixed Applications

7. The letters *A, E, I, O,* and *U* are vowels. What fraction of the letters in the name *Michael Jordan* are vowels? What fraction of the letters in your own name are vowels?

8. Darla walked $\frac{3}{10}$ mile to the library. Then she walked $\frac{1}{5}$ mile from the library to school. How far did she walk in all?

Each chess set contains pawns, rooks, bishops, knights, kings, queens, and a gameboard.
Use the table for Exercises 9–10.

How many knights are

9. in 7 chess sets?

10. in 2,581 chess sets?

Number of Chess Sets	Number of Knights
2	8
10	40
7	■
2,581	■

Explain why a tree diagram can be more useful than just multiplying to find all possible combinations.

WRAP UP...

CHAPTER REVIEW

Vocabulary Check

Choose a word or words from the box to complete each sentence.

add
denominator
numerators
organized list
possible
  outcomes
tree diagram

I can use my fraction pieces to help me solve problems.

1. When you add fractions with like denominators, __?__ the numerators and write the sum over the __?__. *(page 350)*

2. If you use a spinner to explore probability, the colors on the spinner are the __?__. *(page 368)*

3. When denominators are the same, you can subtract the __?__ to find the difference. *(page 352)*

4. You can use a __?__ to see all the possibilities. *(page 370)*

5. You can make an __?__ to help you choose from several different choices. *(page 366)*

Concept Check

Use fraction bars to estimate the shaded part for each.
Write *about* 0, *about* $\frac{1}{2}$, or *about* 1. *(page 348)*

6.

7.

8.

Use fraction pieces to find the common denominator. *(page 356)*

9.

$\frac{2}{9}$ and $\frac{1}{3}$

10.

$\frac{3}{8}$ and $\frac{1}{4}$

11.

$\frac{1}{3}$ and $\frac{1}{6}$

Use fraction pieces to find the sum or difference. *(pages 350, 356)*

12. $\frac{5}{8} + \frac{1}{8}$

13. $\frac{3}{10} + \frac{5}{10}$

14. 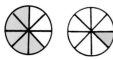 $\frac{5}{6} - \frac{2}{3}$

15. $\frac{3}{4} - \frac{4}{8}$

Draw a picture to show each number sentence. Solve. *(page 356)*

16. $\dfrac{1}{6} + \dfrac{2}{3} = \dfrac{\blacksquare}{\blacksquare}$

17. $\dfrac{1}{5} + \dfrac{5}{10} = \dfrac{\blacksquare}{\blacksquare}$

18. $\dfrac{3}{6} + \dfrac{1}{2} = \dfrac{\blacksquare}{\blacksquare}$

Draw fraction pieces to make a model. Solve. *(page 362)*

19. $2\dfrac{1}{4} + 1\dfrac{3}{4}$

20. $1\dfrac{2}{9} + 2\dfrac{4}{9}$

21. $3\dfrac{7}{8} - 2\dfrac{1}{8}$

22. $3\dfrac{5}{6} - 1\dfrac{1}{6}$

Use a customary ruler to measure each line segment. *(page 364)*

23. •————————•

24. •————————————————————————•

Skill Check

Find the sum or difference. You may write your answer in simplest form. *(pages 350, 352, 356, 358, 362)*

25. $\dfrac{1}{5} + \dfrac{3}{5} = \dfrac{\blacksquare}{\blacksquare}$

26. $\dfrac{2}{6} + \dfrac{4}{6} = \dfrac{\blacksquare}{\blacksquare}$

27. $\dfrac{4}{8} + \dfrac{2}{8} = \dfrac{\blacksquare}{\blacksquare}$

28. $\dfrac{7}{12} - \dfrac{3}{12} = \dfrac{\blacksquare}{\blacksquare}$

29. $\dfrac{12}{16} - \dfrac{4}{16} = \dfrac{\blacksquare}{\blacksquare}$

30. $\dfrac{6}{9} - \dfrac{1}{3} = \dfrac{\blacksquare}{\blacksquare}$

31. $\begin{array}{r} 2\dfrac{3}{8} \\ + 1\dfrac{2}{8} \\ \hline \end{array}$

32. $\begin{array}{r} 7\dfrac{2}{5} \\ + 1\dfrac{1}{5} \\ \hline \end{array}$

33. $\begin{array}{r} 9\dfrac{6}{8} \\ - 5\dfrac{4}{8} \\ \hline \end{array}$

34. $\begin{array}{r} 8\dfrac{3}{4} \\ - 4\dfrac{1}{4} \\ \hline \end{array}$

Look at the colored cubes. Find the probability of picking each color. *(page 368)*

35. red

36. blue

37. not green

Problem-Solving Check *(pages 354, 366)*

38. When Nate works at Cozy Kids, he wears a T-shirt and shorts. He has a white, a red, a yellow, and a navy T-shirt, and navy, white, red, and khaki shorts. How many different outfits can he wear?

39. There are 2 red checkers and 2 black checkers on the table. Ricco takes 3 checkers. What colors could they be?

CHAPTER TEST

Estimate what fraction of each bar is shaded. Write *about* 0, *about* $\frac{1}{2}$, or *about* 1.

1.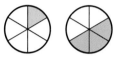

2.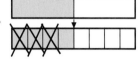

Finding a common denominator helps me add and subtract fractions.

Find the sum or difference. You may write your answer in simplest form.

3.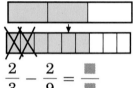

$$\frac{1}{6} + \frac{3}{6} = \frac{\blacksquare}{\blacksquare}$$

4.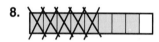

$$\frac{1}{2} - \frac{3}{8} = \frac{\blacksquare}{\blacksquare}$$

5.

$$\frac{5}{16} + \frac{1}{4} = \frac{\blacksquare}{\blacksquare}$$

6.

$$\frac{2}{3} - \frac{2}{9} = \frac{\blacksquare}{\blacksquare}$$

7.

$$\frac{1}{8} + \frac{2}{4} = \frac{\blacksquare}{\blacksquare}$$

8.

$$\frac{8}{9} - \frac{5}{9} = \frac{\blacksquare}{\blacksquare}$$

Use a customary ruler to measure each line segment.

9. •————————•

10. •————————•

11. •————————————•

Solve.

12. Ed can choose 1 balloon and 1 flag. Make a tree diagram to show all the possible combinations.

13. Jo wants soup and a sandwich for lunch. She can order either tomato or chicken soup, and she can order either a turkey or tuna sandwich. List all the possible combinations she can order for lunch.

14. Abby, Bob, and Chris are giving speeches. They can choose the order in which they speak. List their names in all possible arrangements, or orders, of speaking.

15. Phil made a spinner with 8 sections. He made 3 sections red, 1 section blue, 2 sections green, and 2 sections yellow. Which two colors together cover more than $\frac{1}{2}$ of the spinner?

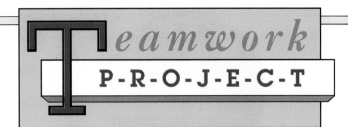

Teamwork P-R-O-J-E-C-T

MAKE A GAME

You and your teammates are challenged to invent a game that can be played in small groups. You must include various fractions in your game. Work with your teammates to create a game you would enjoy playing.

DECIDE

Talk about the types of games you could create. Select a type of game you could play using available materials.

Talk about different things you can do with fractions.

Decide what materials would be needed.

Discuss a theme for the game.

Talk About It

Are the rules easy to understand?

What is the scoring method?

Does the game take too much time? too little time?

What required parts are included in the game?

Write a sentence to explain the object of the game.

What are some interesting features of the game?

Does the game require equal participation of the players?

How could the game be improved?

What skills are required to play the game?

DO

Write the rules for the game. Prepare a sketch of the playing field or gameboard, if one is needed. Label all parts.

SHARE

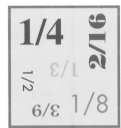

Present your game to the other teams. Each team should play another team's game.

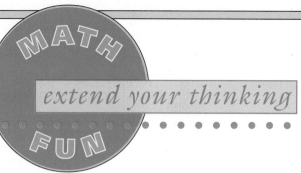

Activity

ADDITION TIC
TAC
TOE

To play this game, you will need two spinners, a tic-tac-toe grid, and an answer sheet.

Work with a partner. The first player spins both spinners and finds the sum of the two fractions. The second player then checks the sum with the answer sheet. (The answer sheet should contain answers for all the addition problems that use the numbers on the spinners as addends.)

If the sum is correct, the first player writes an X on any space on the grid. If the answer is incorrect, the second player has a turn. The second player writes an O on the grid for each correct answer. The winner is the first player to get three X's or three O's in a row—horizontally, vertically, or diagonally.

Challenge

Number Puzzles

Use fraction pieces to model an addition problem with each mixed number as the sum. Use numbers less than 1 as the addends.

1. $1\frac{3}{8}$ 2. $1\frac{5}{12}$

3. $1\frac{5}{7}$ 4. $1\frac{7}{9}$

5. $1\frac{2}{5}$ 6. $1\frac{4}{6}$

7. $1\frac{4}{11}$ 8. $1\frac{4}{10}$

Everyday Math

One gallon of lemonade can be made with the following ingredients.

$1\frac{1}{4}$ cups sugar

1 tablespoon lemon peel

$1\frac{3}{4}$ cups lemon juice

$3\frac{1}{4}$ quarts water

How much of each ingredient would you use to make 2 gallons of lemonade?

Write the letter of the correct answer.

1. $26 + 32 + 44 = n$

   A. 92   **B.** 102
   C. 112   **D.** 122

2.   842
   −786

   A. 56   **B.** 144
   C. 156   **D.** 166

3. Which names the polygon?

   A. hexagon
   B. pentagon
   C. octagon
   D. quadrilateral

4. Which figure is similar to ▢

   A. ▭   **B.** ▢

   C. ▽   **D.** ⬡

5. Ann's foot is about 20 ■ long.

   A. centimeters   **B.** decimeters
   C. meters   **D.** kilometers

6. $3{,}000 \text{ g} = ■ \text{ kg}$

   A. 3   **B.** 300
   C. 300,000   **D.** not here

7. $5{,}406 \times 7 = n$

   A. 35,842   **B.** 37,842
   C. 38,242   **D.** 38,424

8. $5\overline{)509}$

   A. 10 r4   **B.** 11 r4
   C. 101 r4   **D.** 101 r9

9. Which fraction is equivalent to $\frac{2}{3}$?

   A. $\frac{6}{8}$ **B.** $\frac{4}{8}$

   C. $\frac{6}{9}$ **D.** $\frac{2}{6}$

10. Which names a decimal for $\frac{7}{10}$?

   A. 0.07   **B.** 0.7
   C. 7.0   **D.** not here

11. Bananas are $0.33 per pound. Apples are $0.65 per pound. How much will it cost to buy 5 pounds of bananas and 7 pounds of apples?

   A. $1.65   **B.** $4.55
   C. $6.20   **D.** $11.76

12. Nora bought 12 packages of baseball cards for $7.08 and 2 baseballs for $7.96. How much did each package of baseball cards cost?

   A. $0.59   **B.** $0.66
   C. $0.69   **D.** not here

CHAPTER 12

UNDERSTANDING DECIMALS

Did you know ...

... Mary Lou Retton was the first American gymnast to win an All-Around gold medal at the Olympics? She scored a perfect 10.00 in vault.

Paige's goal is to perform at the Olympics one day. At today's qualifying meet, she has scored 8.6 on vault, 7.95 on beam, and 9.2 on bars. She needs a score of 34.00 to qualify. How can Paige find the score she needs to make on floor exercise to qualify?

EXPLORING

Decimals

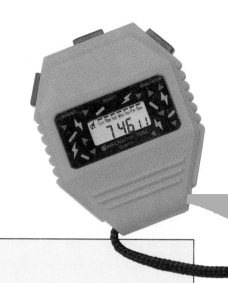

Greg Foster ran the 60-meter hurdles race in $7\frac{46}{100}$ seconds. You can write $7\frac{46}{100}$ as a decimal.

A **decimal** is a number that uses place value and a decimal point to show tenths, hundredths, and so on.

WORK TOGETHER

Building Understanding

Use graph paper to model decimals.

Draw three figures that are 10 squares by 10 squares each.

A. Color one figure, and label it one whole.

B. Color one row of ten squares in the next figure, and label it one tenth.

C. Color one square in the last figure, and label it one hundredth.

Read: one
Write: 1 or 1.0

Read: one tenth
Write: $\frac{1}{10}$ or 0.1

Read: one hundredth
Write: $\frac{1}{100}$ or 0.01

Talk About It
▶ What whole number does model A represent?

▶ What parts of the whole do models B and C represent?

Make a model of $7\frac{46}{100}$ on your graph paper.

Talk About It
▶ How many whole figures will you need to draw?

▶ How many squares out of 100 squares can you color to show $\frac{46}{100}$?

▶ What decimal can you write for your model?

 Idea Bank, page 454, Exercise 4

Making the Connection

You can use money to model decimals.

100 cents   10 cents   1 cent

A.   **B.**   **C.**

Read: one dollar   **Read:** one dime   **Read:** one penny
Write: $1.00   **Write:** $0.10   **Write:** $0.01

1. Which of the graph-paper models shows the same amount as one dollar? one dime? one penny?

2. Which of the graph-paper models shows $\frac{1}{10}$ of a dollar? $\frac{1}{100}$ of a dollar?

3. Use play money to model $0.47. Now make a graph-paper model of $0.47.

4. Use play money to model $3.67. Now make a graph-paper model of $3.67.

Checking Understanding

Tell whether the shaded part of the model shows *tenths* or *hundredths*.

5.   6.   7.   8.

On graph paper, draw a model for each decimal.
Then write each decimal in words.

9. 0.25   10. 0.59   11. 1.15   12. 2.38   13. 4.09

Write the letter of the decimal that matches each model.

14.   15.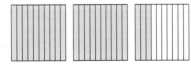

16.   17.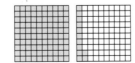

a.	2.3
b.	1.12
c.	0.65
d.	0.4

Write each as a decimal.

18. nine tenths   19. forty-two hundredths   20. one and three tenths

RELATING FRACTIONS TO DECIMALS

Carrie and her dad went to see Magic Johnson play basketball. They sat in 2 seats of Section B. Each section had 100 seats with 10 seats in a row. Write a fraction and a decimal to show one row in Section B. Write a fraction and a decimal to show 2 seats in Section B.

Model	Fraction	Decimal

$\frac{1}{10}$

Ones	Tenths	Hundredths
0	1	
0	0	2

$\frac{2}{100}$

0 means that → ↑ decimal
there are no ones. point

You can write a mixed number as a decimal.

Model	Mixed Number	Decimal

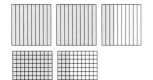

$2\frac{3}{10}$

Ones	Tenths	Hundredths
2	3	
1	3	4

$1\frac{34}{100}$

You can divide the numerator by the denominator to show a fraction as a decimal.

Find the decimal for $\frac{4}{10}$.

Press: (4) (÷) (1) (0) (=) [0.4]

Now, find a decimal for $\frac{40}{100}$. How is the decimal on the calculator different from the decimal you would write on a place-value chart?

Check for Understanding

Write a fraction or a mixed number and a decimal for each.

1.
2.
3.
4.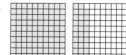

Practice

Write a fraction or a mixed number and a decimal for each.

5.

6.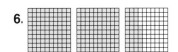

7.

8.

Write the decimal. Use a calculator to help you.

9. $\dfrac{9}{10}$

10. $\dfrac{59}{100}$

11. $\dfrac{27}{100}$

12. $\dfrac{2}{10}$

13. $\dfrac{7}{100}$

14. four tenths

15. two and nine hundredths

16. fifteen hundredths

Mixed Applications

Use the table for Exercises 17–19.

17. How much greater was the attendance in 1991 than in 1988?

18. Order the attendance totals from greatest to least.

19. What was the average attendance from 1988 through 1991? You may wish to use a calculator.

Gold City Stadium	
Year	**Attendance**
1988	236,987
1989	227,014
1990	234,879
1991	240,312

20. Scott's basketball team has scored 100 points so far this season. Scott scored 13 of these points. Write a fraction and a decimal to show Scott's points.

21. Tiffany spent $0.40 of her $1.00 allowance. Draw a model to show what part of $1.00 she spent. Write a fraction for your model.

MIXED REVIEW

Find the sum or difference. You may write each in simplest form.

1. $\dfrac{4}{8} + \dfrac{2}{8} = \dfrac{\blacksquare}{\blacksquare}$

2. $\dfrac{11}{12} - \dfrac{3}{12} = \dfrac{\blacksquare}{\blacksquare}$

3. $\dfrac{1}{10} + \dfrac{3}{10} = \dfrac{\blacksquare}{\blacksquare}$

Compare. Use $<$, $>$, or $=$ for ●.

 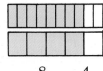 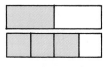 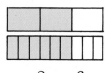 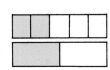

4. $\dfrac{6}{12}$ ● $\dfrac{4}{12}$

5. $\dfrac{8}{10}$ ● $\dfrac{4}{5}$

6. $\dfrac{1}{2}$ ● $\dfrac{3}{4}$

7. $\dfrac{2}{3}$ ● $\dfrac{6}{9}$

8. $\dfrac{2}{5}$ ● $\dfrac{1}{2}$

How can you write a decimal for $\frac{2}{5}$?

Felipe and his dad went to see a Miami Dolphins football game. Felipe bought popcorn for $1.20 and a drink for $0.95. His dad gave him $1.50 more. Felipe had $2.35 left at the end of the game. How much did he have at the start of the game?

Sometimes, you can *work backward* to solve a problem.

▶ **UNDERSTAND**

What are you asked to find?

What information is given?

▶ **PLAN**

What can you do to find how much money Felipe had at the start of the game?

Write a number sentence to show how he spent his money. Use a ▇ for the amount he had at the start of the game.

▇ − $1.20 − $0.95 + $1.50 = $2.35

▶ **SOLVE**

How can you solve the problem?

Now, you can use the strategy *work backward* to find the missing amount.

Begin with the $2.35 that Felipe had left.

Work backward using opposite operations.

Subtract the $1.50 that his dad gave him. Add the $1.20 and $0.95 that he spent on popcorn and a drink.
$2.35 − $1.50 + $0.95 + $1.20 = $3.00

So, Felipe had $3.00 at the start of the game.

▶ **LOOK BACK**

How can you check your answer?

WHAT IF... . . . Felipe's dad gave him $3.00? How does that change the amount he had to start?

Apply

Solve by *working backward*.

1 Lara gave half her football cards to Bela. Then she gave 8 cards to T.J. and 5 cards to Adam. Lara had 6 cards left. How many cards did Lara have at the start?

2 Chin spent half his money for a ticket to a football game. Then he spent half of what was left on a snack. He had $4 left. How much money did Chin have at the start?

Mixed Applications ➤ **STRATEGIES** • Write a Number Sentence • Find a Pattern • Work Backward • Draw a Picture

Choose a strategy and solve.

3 Moriah has a box 8 cm wide and 11 cm long. If the volume is 264 cubic cm, what is the height of the box?

4 The average weight of 11 professional football players is 225 lb. Is their combined weight more than or less than one ton?

5 Walton School has four football teams. The Eagles have won more games than the Bulldogs. The Lions have won more than the Wildcats. The Lions have won 2 fewer than the Bulldogs. Which team has won the most games?

6 A game ticket and popcorn cost a total of $12. The ticket cost 5 times as much as the popcorn. How much did the popcorn cost?

7 Draw the next domino.

EQUIVALENT DECIMALS

Leon said there was two tenths of a second left on the stopwatch. Mia said there was 20 hundredths of a second left. Who was correct?

Work together. Use decimal squares to model equivalent decimals.

Equivalent Decimals		**Not Equivalent Decimals**	
0.2	0.20	0.3	0.03
two tenths 2 out of 10	twenty hundredths 20 out of 100	three tenths 3 out of 10	three hundredths 3 out of 100

0.2 and 0.20 are equivalent decimals.

Equivalent decimals are different names for the same amount.

So, Leon and Mia were both correct.

More Examples

0.4	0.40	1.1	1.10
four tenths 4 out of 10	forty hundredths 40 out of 100	one and one tenth 1 whole and 1 out of 10	one and ten hundredths 1 whole and 10 out of 100

Check for Understanding

Write two equivalent decimals for the shaded part of each model.

1.   2.    3.    4.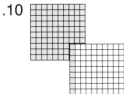

Write an equivalent decimal for each.

5. 0.60   **6.** 2.3   **7.** 3.40   **8.** 0.7

Practice

Write two equivalent decimals for the shaded part of each model.

9.   10.   11. 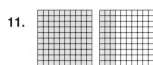   12.

Tell whether the decimals are equivalent. Write *yes* or *no*.

13. 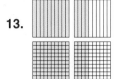   14. 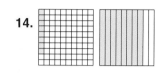   15.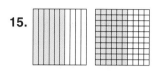

16. 15.3 and 15.03   17. 5.9 and 5.90   18. 6.20 and 6.2   19. 3.13 and 3.31

Write an equivalent decimal for each.

20. 0.80   21. 9.7   22. 5.60   23. 0.3

Mixed Applications

24. Marion said that $0.50 is 50 hundredths of a dollar. Seth said that $0.50 is 5 tenths of a dollar. Why are both statements correct?

25. **Number Sense** Write all the four-digit whole numbers that have only 0 and 1 as digits.

VISUAL THINKING

Look at the decimal squares. Write the letter of the picture that shows a decimal that is equivalent to the one shown.

26.   a.   b.   c.

27.   a.   b.   c.

28.   a.   b. (vertical bars)   c. (grid)

Why are the decimals 14.06 and 14.60 not equivalent?

DECIMALS
Comparing and Ordering

At a gymnastics meet, Brandy Johnson scored 9.93 on vault and 9.85 on floor exercise. Which score was higher?

Scores	
Vault	9.93
Bars	9.82
Beam	9.40
Floor Exercise	9.85

Models can help you compare decimals.

9.93

9.85

You can also compare numbers on a place-value chart.

First line up the decimal points. Begin with the digits on the left, and compare the digits in each place. Find the first place where the digits are different. You have found the larger number.

Ones	Tenths	Hundredths
Ones are the same.	Compare tenths.	
9	9	3
9	8	5
Since, 9 > 8, then 9.93 > 9.85.		

Line up the decimal points.

The vault score of 9.93 was higher.

Now, order all four of Brandy's scores from greatest to least.

Use a number line to help you.

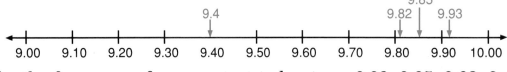

So, the four scores from greatest to least are 9.93, 9.85, 9.82, 9.40.

Check for Understanding

Compare. Use <, >, or = for ●.

1. 8.95 ● 9.85   **2.** 22.03 ● 22.03   **3.** 1.93 ● 1.57   **4.** 0.61 ● 0.68

Order the decimals from greatest to least.

5. 3.5, 3.7, 2.9, 3.2   **6.** 18.11, 14.09, 18.23, 16.13, 16.29   **7.** 8.06, 8.00, 8.60

Practice

Compare. Use <, >, or = for ●.

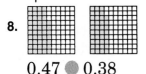 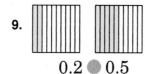 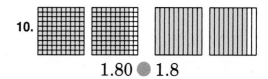

8. 0.47 ● 0.38   9. 0.2 ● 0.5   10. 1.80 ● 1.8

11. 0.25 ● 0.5   12. 0.20 ● 0.2   13. 0.9 ● 0.19   14. 0.4 ● 0.40   15. 0.70 ● 0.07

Order the decimals from greatest to least.

16. 0.76, 0.67, 0.70, 1.76

17. 2.3, 3.2, 2.03, 3.02, 20.3

18. 0.19, 0.91, 1.19, 1.09

19. 4.3, 2.4, 4.56, 0.04, 4.03

> How can I find the highest score?

Mixed Applications

Use the table for Exercises 20–24.

20. Does Corie or Miko have the higher score?

21. Does Shari or Tara have the higher score?

22. Whose score was higher than Shari's but lower than Miko's?

23. Order the scores from highest to lowest.

24. Whose score was thirty-two and five tenths?

Gymnastics Team B All-Around Scores	
Tara	29.75
Shari	31.83
Corie	32.50
Miko	33.25
Nedra	30.95

CALCULATOR

You can compare fractions by changing them into decimals. Divide the numerator by the denominator to find each decimal.

> Remember:
> $\frac{3}{4}$ means 3 ÷ 4.
> $\frac{4}{5}$ means 4 ÷ 5.

Example

Compare $\frac{3}{4}$ and $\frac{4}{5}$.

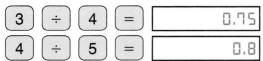

| 3 | ÷ | 4 | = | 0.75 |
| 4 | ÷ | 5 | = | 0.8 |

Line up the decimal points. Compare the tenths. 7 < 8 So, 0.75 < 0.8, and $\frac{3}{4} < \frac{4}{5}$.

Use a calculator to change each fraction to a decimal. Compare, using <, >, or = for ●.

25. $\frac{3}{5}$ ● $\frac{12}{25}$

26. $\frac{32}{40}$ ● $\frac{4}{5}$

27. $\frac{12}{16}$ ● $\frac{19}{25}$

Is 43.67 < 43.76? Why?

DECIMALS
Estimating and Rounding

At the 1988 Olympics, Matt Biondi swam the 50-meter freestyle event in 22.14 seconds.

At the Wade County Swim Meet, these times were recorded by four swimmers in the 9–11 age group. What are the boys' times to the nearest whole number?

You can use rounding to estimate.

- Look at the tenths digit.

- Round to the next higher whole number if the digit is 5 or more.

- Round to the same whole number if the digit is less than 5.

50-Meter Freestyle	
Jason	28.12 seconds
Cal	27.84 seconds
Doug	28.23 seconds
Stan	27.92 seconds

In 28.12, the 1 is less than 5, so round to 28 seconds.

You can show how close the decimals are to the nearest whole number by using a number line.

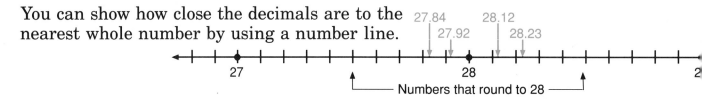

So, all four boys swam the 50-meter freestyle in about 28 seconds.

Talk About It

▶ Use the number line to find the least number that rounds to 28.

▶ If you wanted to know who won the race, what place values would you compare?

Check for Understanding

Round each number to the nearest whole number. Draw a number line for Exercises 1, 3, and 5.

1. 4.9   **2.** 8.2   **3.** 56.8   **4.** 15.1   **5.** 0.9

Practice

6. Use the number line to choose the numbers from the box that round to 6.0.

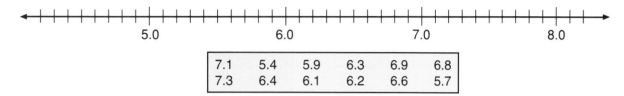

| 7.1 | 5.4 | 5.9 | 6.3 | 6.9 | 6.8 |
| 7.3 | 6.4 | 6.1 | 6.2 | 6.6 | 5.7 |

Round each decimal to the nearest whole number.
Draw a number line for Exercises 7, 11, and 16.

7. 7.1   8. 9.5   9. 1.8   10. 3.6   11. 4.4

12. 5.9   13. 2.4   14. 0.77   15. 1.08   16. 26.32

Write the numbers from the box that round to the given number.

23.99	24.8	25.09
25.12	23.9	24.5
24.49	26.1	25.50

17. 24   18. 25   19. 26

Mixed Applications

Use the table for Exercises 20–23.

20. Was the winning time faster in 1976 or in 1988?

21. When rounded to the nearest whole number, which winning times round to 55 sec?

22. Order the winning times from fastest to slowest.

23. Which year had the fastest winning time?

24. In the backstroke event, Lee finished before Sue. Deb finished after Lee but before Ann. Who finished first?

Olympic Winning Times Women's 100–Meter Freestyle (Swimming)	
Year	Time
1976	55.65 sec
1980	54.76 sec
1984	55.92 sec
1988	54.93 sec

HINT: The fastest time is the least number.

Explain how rounding decimals is like rounding whole numbers.

REVIEW AND MAINTENANCE

Use the graph for Exercises 1–3.

1. In which month did Joe earn the least amount of money?

2. How much more did Joe earn in May than in January?

3. If Joe mowed 3 lawns in April, how much did he charge to mow each lawn?

4. Brenda, Mona, and Dennis lined up from shortest to tallest for a picture. Dennis stood between Brenda and Mona. Brenda stood at Dennis's left. Mona was the shortest. Who was the tallest?

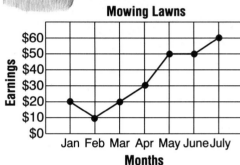

I can use this graph to solve the problems.

Mowing Lawns

Find the volume of each in cubic units.

5.   6.   7.   8.

Find the quotient.

9. $5\overline{)248}$ 10. $6\overline{)351}$ 11. $4\overline{)823}$ 12. $2\overline{)457}$ 13. $7\overline{)229}$

Write a fraction for the shaded part.

14.   15.   16.   17.

Find the sum or difference. You may write your answer in simplest form.

18. $\dfrac{2}{5} + \dfrac{1}{5}$ 19. $\dfrac{7}{8} - \dfrac{3}{8}$ 20. $\dfrac{5}{12} + \dfrac{1}{12}$ 21. $\dfrac{11}{32} - \dfrac{3}{32}$

22. $\begin{array}{r} 3\frac{8}{10} \\ -1\frac{4}{10} \\ \hline \end{array}$ 23. $\begin{array}{r} 6\frac{3}{5} \\ +2\frac{1}{5} \\ \hline \end{array}$ 24. $\begin{array}{r} 12\frac{6}{8} \\ -9\frac{2}{8} \\ \hline \end{array}$ 25. $\begin{array}{r} 5\frac{3}{6} \\ +2\frac{1}{6} \\ \hline \end{array}$

Spotlight ON
PROBLEM SOLVING

Understand
Plan
Solve
Look Back

Make Predictions

Cobra Swim Meet	
Boys' 50-m Freestyle	
Nick	33.43
Matt	34.21
Jody	34.53
Girls' 50-m Freestyle	
Sarah	33.20
Heather	34.23
Jamie	36.79
Boys' 100-m Individual Medley	
Nick	1:26.26
Chris	1:26.32
Brett	1:27.40
Girls' 100-m Individual Medley	
Sarah	1:29.15
Stacey	1:30.02
Mary	1:30.93

You can use data that has been collected to make predictions about future events.

Talk About It

a. At the next swim meet, which swimmers are most likely to swim the 50-m freestyle race in less than 33 seconds?

b. Would you predict that the next time Sarah swims the 100-m individual medley race, she can swim the race in 1 minute? Explain.

c. If Brett swam the 100-m individual medley race again, is it likely that his time would be faster than 1 min 30 sec? Explain.

Apply

Solve each problem by reviewing the sports information and making predictions. You may use a calculator.

1. John's basketball statistics for the year show that he has taken 93 shots and made 29. Predict whether John will make his next shot. Explain.

2. In 100 at-bats, a Little League baseball player made 3 home runs, 2 triples, 3 doubles, and 14 singles. She also walked 12 times. How many times did the player make an out? Predict whether she will get a hit or make an out the next time she is at bat.

ESTIMATING
Sums and Differences

Wayne Gretzky plays professional ice hockey.

Kenny Goetz plays ice hockey for the local boys' club. Every Friday he rides his bicycle 1.73 miles to school, 1.86 miles from school to practice, and 2.2 miles from practice to home. About how many miles does Kenny ride altogether?

Estimate. $1.73 + 1.86 + 2.2$

Kenny estimated the distance in two different ways.

Front-End Digits
Add the front-end digits only.

$$
\begin{array}{rcr}
1.73 & \rightarrow & 1 \\
1.86 & \rightarrow & 1 \\
+2.20 & \rightarrow & +2 \\
\hline
& & 4
\end{array}
$$

Rounding
Round to the nearest whole number.

$$
\begin{array}{rcr}
1.73 & \rightarrow & 2 \\
1.86 & \rightarrow & 2 \\
+2.20 & \rightarrow & +2 \\
\hline
& & 6
\end{array}
$$

So, Kenny rides his bicycle between 4 and 6 miles.

Talk About It

▶ Use a calculator to find the exact answer. Is the answer between your estimates? Why or why not?

▶ Why is the front-end estimate a low estimate?

▶ How can you estimate the difference of $9.03 - 3.8$ in two different ways?

Check for Understanding

Estimate the sum or difference by using front-end digits.

1. 2.14	2. 5.12	3. 5.27	4. 8.97	5. 7.05
$+5.87$	-0.45	$+9.86$	-3.08	$+9.20$

Estimate the sum or difference by rounding to the nearest whole number.

6. $7.03 - 4.5 = n$ 7. $3.21 + 4.29 + 6.1 = n$ 8. $9.07 + 3.26 + 7.8 = n$

Practice

Estimate the sum or difference by using front-end digits.

9. 6.03
    $+2.91$

10. 7.15
    -5.72

11. 1.97
    $+9.25$

12. 9.09
    -4.88

13. 5.09
    $+1.76$

Estimate by rounding to the nearest whole number.

14. $9.14 - 2.7 = n$

15. $6.1 + 2.9 + 8.3 = n$

16. $9.05 + 9.88 + 6.5 = n$

Estimate the sum or difference by using either method.

17. 9.01
    -8.31

18. 2.08
    9.19
    $+6.23$

19. 0.98
    2.12
    $+3.75$

20. 2.10
    3.93
    $+1.07$

21. 4.1
    1.6
    $+2.3$

22. 6.88
    -3.79

23. 9.07
    -4.88

24. 3.95
    -3.10

25. 9.99
    $+1.18$

26. 6.73
    -3.06

Mixed Applications

27. Each week Joe has hockey practice from 3:30 to 5:00 on Monday, Wednesday, and Friday. How many hours does Joe have hockey practice each week?

28. The distance around a triangular exercise field is 36.25 m. Each of 2 sides is 14.6 m long. What is the length of the third side?

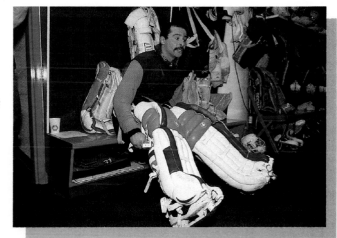

29. Miss Blount earned $276 one week and $339 the next. Then she spent $417 for an exercise machine. Estimate the amount of money she had left from these earnings to put in the bank.

30. Mickey is walking to the hockey rink, which is 1.3 km from his home. He has walked 0.6 km. How much farther must he walk?

Why is the estimate of a sum using front digits always less than or equal to an estimate found by rounding?

W R A P
U P . . .

EXPLORING
Adding and Subtracting Decimals

WORK TOGETHER

Building Understanding

Use centimeter graph paper to explore adding and subtracting decimals.

Add 0.23 + 0.77.

Cut out a model of 0.23 by using one 10-by-10 grid. Cut out a model of 0.77, using one 10-by-10 grid.

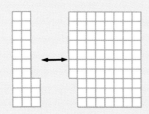

$$0.23 + 0.77 = \blacksquare$$

Subtract 1.00 − 0.28.

Cut out a model to show 1.00 − 0.28.

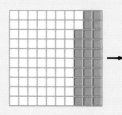

$$1.00 - 0.28 = \blacksquare$$

Talk About It
▶ How can you use the model to show the sum of 0.23 + 0.77?

▶ What is the sum of 0.23 + 0.77?

▶ Write a number sentence to show what you did.

▶ If you add two decimals that are both less than 0.5, will the sum be less than or greater than 1?

Make three more models with addends whose sum is 1.00.

Talk About It
▶ How can you use the model to find the difference of 1.00 − 0.28?

▶ What is the difference of 1.00 − 0.28?

▶ Write a number sentence to show what you did.

Make three more models to show subtracting a decimal from 1.00.

Making the Connection

To help keep the digits aligned, it is important to make the number of decimal places equivalent. Then you can add and subtract decimals in the same way you add and subtract whole numbers.

Add. $2.3 + 4.56 + 7.03 = n$

Since $2.3 = 2.30$, you can place a zero to line up the digits in each place-value position. So, the sum is 13.89.

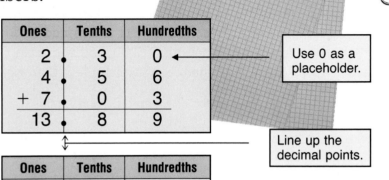

Use 0 as a placeholder.

Line up the decimal points.

Subtract. $4 - 2.46 = n$

Since $4 = 4.00$, you can use zeros to line up the digits in each place-value position. So, the difference is 1.54.

Ones	Tenths	Hundredths
	9	
3	$\cancel{10}$	10
$\cancel{4}$	$\cancel{0}$	$\cancel{0}$
-2	4	6
1	5	4

Use 0 as a placeholder.

Show each problem on a place-value chart. Solve.

1. $72.3 + 6.34 + 12.03 = n$
2. $15.63 - 12.8 = n$
3. $8.1 - 4.6 = n$

Checking Understanding

Find the sum and difference for each pair of models.

4.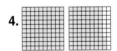
5.
6.

Use graph paper to draw models for each problem. Solve. Check students' models.

7. $0.36 + 0.23 = n$
8. $1.29 - 0.15 = n$
9. $1.55 + 0.45 = n$

Show each problem on a place-value chart. Solve. Check students' charts.

10. $5.8 - 2.9 = n$
11. $3.0 - 1.7 = n$
12. $4.15 + 2.05 = n$

CHALLENGE

Place the missing decimal point in each addend.

13. $1234 + 56 = 17.94$
14. $17 + 162 = 3.32$
15. $603 + 205 = 26.53$

Brittany and her mother are going to a figure-skating exhibition featuring Olympian Debi Thomas. Brittany's mother does not want to spend over $100, so Brittany estimates their expenses. The tickets are priced at $18.25 each, their lunch will be about $20.00, and the train trip will cost $17.75 each. Will their expenses be less than or greater than $100?

You can *use estimation* to help you solve a problem.

▶ **UNDERSTAND**

What are you asked to find?

What information is given?

▶ **PLAN**

What strategy can you use to solve the problem?

You can estimate the cost mentally.

▶ **SOLVE**

How can you solve the problem?

List all of the expenses. Since each one is close to $20.00, you can multiply 5 × $20.00.

Brittany's show ticket	$18.25
Her mother's show ticket	18.25
Lunch..	20.00
Brittany's train ticket	17.75
Her mother's train ticket	+ 17.75

$$\begin{array}{r} 20 \\ \times\ \ 5 \\ \hline \$100 \end{array}$$

So, Brittany estimated their expenses will be less than or close to $100.

▶ **LOOK BACK**

How can you check your estimate?

WHAT IF... ... Brittany had used front-end digits to estimate? How would the estimate change?

Apply

Use estimation to solve.

(1) On Saturday Rhoda rode her bicycle 4.57 km from her home to the skating rink. Then she rode 6.69 km from the rink to the park and 2.8 km from the park back home. About how many km did she ride?

(2) Jarvis wants to buy some new music tapes to use for skating routines. He has $25.00. Can he buy 3 tapes if each one costs $7.89?

Mixed Applications → **STRATEGIES**
- Use Estimation • Write a Number Sentence
- Make an Organized List • Guess and Check
- Make a Model

Choose a strategy and solve.

(3) Jana bought a leotard for $18.28 and tights for $9.83. About how much change did she receive from $30.00?

(4) Lila wants to take either gymnastics, ice-skating, or swimming lessons one day each week. All the lessons are offered on Tuesdays and Thursdays. How many choices does she have for the lessons?

(5) Gene, Leo, and Karin have skating practice after school. Gene practiced for 10 min less than Leo, and half as long as Karin. Karin practiced for 90 min. For how long did Leo practice?

(6) The skating arena will seat 680 people. If 489 tickets have been sold and 35 tickets have been given away, how many tickets are still unsold?

WRITER'S CORNER

(7) Create a word problem about taking a trip. The problem should involve estimation and adding or subtracting decimals. Use 274 mi as the solution.

ADDING DECIMALS

Jackie Joyner-Kersee won the heptathlon event in the 1988 Olympics. This event includes a 100-m hurdles race, a high jump, a shot put, a 200-m run, a long jump, a javelin throw, and an 800-m run.

Runner	Time (sec)
Tasha	10.15
Jan	9.5
Carmen	8.9
Anna	10.04

Tasha, Jan, Carmen, and Anna won the relay race at their school track meet. What was their total winning time for this event?

Estimate.   Rounding: 10 + 10 + 9 + 10 = 39

Add.   10.15 + 9.5 + 8.9 + 10.04 = *n*.

Step 1	**Step 2**	**Step 3**
Line up the decimal points. Write an equivalent decimal if needed.	Add the hundredths. Add the tenths. Regroup if needed.	Add the whole numbers. Write the decimal point between ones and tenths.
	1	1 1
10.15	10.15	10.15
9.50	9.50	9.50
8.90	8.90	8.90
+10.04	+10.04	+10.04
	59	38.59

So, the winning time for the relay race was 38.59 seconds. The estimate of 39 was close to 38.59, so your answer is reasonable.

Use a calculator to find the sum of 6.90 and 13.84.

Talk About It

▶ Do you need to enter the 0 in 6.90 to get a correct answer? Why or why not?

▶ How is adding decimals like adding whole numbers? How is it different?

Check for Understanding

Estimate first, and then find the sum. You may use a calculator.

	1.	2.	3.	4.	5.
	6.7	5.2	17.2	25.55	3.4
	+9.3	+12.43	+ 8.33	+ 7.3	+42.16

Practice

Find the sum. You may use a calculator.

6. 0.73
+0.09

7. 17.4
+ 3.5

8. 2.57
+0.89

9. 0.63
+9.68

10. 38.9
+62.1

11. 3.9
+4.7

12. 0.73
+2.91

13. 12.75
+30.99

14. 0.76
9.11
+3.63

15. 2.85
9.01
+6.07

16. $0.40 + 1.92 + 6 = n$
17. $2.54 + 3 + 0.27 = n$
18. $1.87 + 4 + 3.95 = n$

Find the sums by adding across, down, and diagonally.

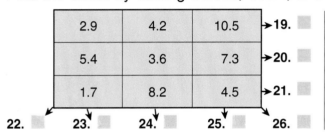

2.9	4.2	10.5	→**19.**
5.4	3.6	7.3	→**20.**
1.7	8.2	4.5	→**21.**

22. **23.** **24.** **25.** **26.**

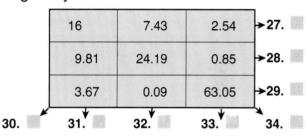

16	7.43	2.54	→**27.**
9.81	24.19	0.85	→**28.**
3.67	0.09	63.05	→**29.**

30. **31.** **32.** **33.** **34.**

Mixed Applications

35. Four teammates ran in a relay race. Their times were 34.21 sec, 33.05 sec, 35.12 sec, and 29.90 sec. What was their total time?

36. Number Sense There are some mistakes in this ad for a sports store. Copy the ad and make the necessary corrections.

37. Analyze Data Thomas had $35.00 to spend at the All-Around Sports Sale. He bought 3 different items. Write all the possible combinations of items.

| **ALL-AROUND SPORTS** |
| **★ ★ ★ ★ S A L E ★ ★ ★ ★** |
| Track Shoes $2995/pr |
| Sweatbands $316/pkg. |
| Socks $1.88/pr. |
| Towels $275/ea. |
| Mini Trampoline $3999/ea. |

MIXED REVIEW

Tell how much time has elapsed.

1.

Find the sum or difference.

2. 500
−256

3. 4,623
−1,738

4. 395
−187

When you use a calculator, what possible mistakes can you make?

WRAP UP...

SUBTRACTING DECIMALS

Bonnie Blair set a world record in speed skating at the 1988 Olympics. She skated 500 meters in 39.10 seconds. For how many seconds less than 1 minute did Bonnie skate?

Estimate.   60 − 40 = 20 seconds
Subtract.   60 − 39.10 = n

HINT: There are 60 seconds in 1 minute.

Step 1	**Step 2**	**Step 3**
Line up the decimal points. Write an equivalent decimal if needed.	Subtract the hundredths. Regroup 6 tens as 5 tens 10 ones. Regroup 10 ones as 9 ones 10 tenths. Subtract the tenths.	Subtract the whole numbers. Write the decimal point between the ones and the tenths in the answer.
$\begin{array}{r} 60.00 \\ -39.10 \\ \hline \end{array}$	$\begin{array}{r} 9 \\ 5\ \cancel{10}\ 10 \\ \cancel{60}.\cancel{00} \\ -39.10 \\ \hline 90 \end{array}$	$\begin{array}{r} 9 \\ 5\ \cancel{10}\ 10 \\ \cancel{60}.\cancel{00} \\ -39.10 \\ \hline 20.90 \end{array}$

So, Bonnie's time was 20.90 seconds less than 1 minute.

Talk About It

▶ Compare the answer to your estimate. Is the answer reasonable?

▶ How is subtracting decimals like subtracting whole numbers? How is it different?

▶ When you subtract decimals on a calculator, do you need to add the missing zeros?

Check for Understanding

Find the difference.

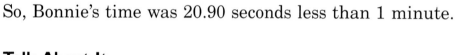

1. $4.5 - 3.97 = n$

2. $15.07 - 9.6 = n$

3. $6.2 - 1.08 = n$

4. $\begin{array}{r} 5.7 \\ -0.9 \\ \hline \end{array}$

5. $\begin{array}{r} 11.05 \\ -\ 9.6 \\ \hline \end{array}$

6. $\begin{array}{r} 7.2 \\ -3.67 \\ \hline \end{array}$

7. $\begin{array}{r} 1.92 \\ -1.08 \\ \hline \end{array}$

8. $\begin{array}{r} 4.63 \\ -2.75 \\ \hline \end{array}$

Practice

Find the difference. You may use a calculator.

9. 12.67
  −10.34

10. 27.25
   −16.73

11. 45.00
   −19.39

12. 15.05
   − 9.19

13. 99.10
   −65.88

14. 10.00
   − 9.17

15. 9.8
   −7.9

16. 13.96
   − 8.87

17. 2.04
   −0.46

18. 17.08
   −13.69

19. $6.8 - 2.9 = n$

20. $5 - 4.7 = n$

21. $23.01 - 12.90 = n$

Mixed Applications

22. Tory's time for 400 m was 59.58 sec. Krystle's time was 57.06 sec. How much faster was Krystle's time?

23. Three members of the Cookville track team each ran 50 m. Their times were 8.13 sec, 8.56 sec, and 8.02 sec. List the times in order from least to greatest.

24. Eighty-two out of one hundred students watched the Olympic Games. What decimal tells the part of the group that watched the games?

25. The men's world speed-skating record for 500 m is 36.03 sec. The women's record is 39.10 sec. Estimate the difference in the records.

NUMBER SENSE • LOGICAL REASONING

Copy and complete the addition problems, using the numbers 2, 4, 5, 6, and 9 only once. Use a zero in each problem.

26.
□.□ □
+ □.□ □
――――――
 8.9 9

27.
□.□ □
+ □.□ □
――――――
12.0 5

28.
□.□ □
+ □.□ □
――――――
 8.0 0

How many times do you regroup to subtract $18 - 2.35$?

WRAP UP...

Vocabulary Check

Choose a word or words from the box to complete each sentence.

decimal
decimal points
equivalent
    decimals
estimate
hundredths
mixed number
tenths

If I forget what a word means, I can look back in the chapter.

1. When adding or subtracting decimals, you must line up the __?__. *(page 396)*

2. A __?__ uses place value and a decimal point to show tenths, hundredths, and so on. *(page 380)*

3. In the decimal 5.41, the 4 is in the __?__ place. *(page 380)*

4. A decimal such as 3.7 can also be written as a __?__. *(page 382)*

5. An example of __?__ is 1.6 and 1.60. *(page 386)*

6. In the decimal 8.39, the 9 is in the __?__ place. *(page 380)*

7. You can __?__ the sum or difference of two decimals by rounding each to a whole number. *(page 396)*

Concept Check

Write the letter of the decimal that matches each model. *(page 380)*

8.

9.

10.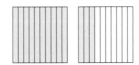

a. 0.3
b. 1.3
c. 0.03

Write a decimal and a fraction or a mixed number for each. *(page 382)*

11.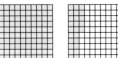

12.

13.

14.

Tell whether the decimals are equivalent.
Write *yes* or *no.* *(page 386)*

15.

16.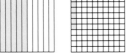

Compare. Use <, >, or = for ●.
(page 388)

17.

18.

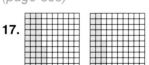

0.34 ● 0.25   1.4 ● 1.40

Estimate the sum or difference by using front-end digits. *(page 396)*

19. 5.30
$+2.14$

20. 8.04
-3.65

Estimate the sum or difference by rounding to the nearest whole number. *(page 396)*

21. 0.84
9.29
$+4.60$

22. 9.63
-2.86

Skill Check

Write each as a decimal. *(page 380)*

23. three tenths

24. $\dfrac{23}{100}$

25. $\dfrac{1}{10}$

26. $\dfrac{1}{100}$

27. $\dfrac{14}{100}$

Order the numbers from greatest to least. *(page 388)*

28. $0.59; 0.95; 5.9; 0.09$

29. $0.14; 4.1; 1.04; 1.40; 4.01$

Find the sum or difference. *(pages 396, 400, 402)*

30. 0.48
-0.11

31. 3.06
$+2.78$

32. 1.74
$+0.39$

33. 3.00
-2.41

34. 0.64
-0.45

35. $0.20 + 3.32 + 4 = n$

36. $7 - 3.6 = n$

37. $3.94 + 1 + 0.1 = n$

Problem-Solving Check

Solve by working backward. *(page 384)*

38. Fay took $3.00 of her savings to go shopping. When she came home, she put $0.85 back. She now has $5.75. How much money did she have before she went shopping?

39. Sean put posters on his bedroom walls. He put half the posters on one wall. He put 2 posters on each of the other 3 walls. How many posters did Sean put on all 4 walls?

Use estimation to solve. *(page 398)*

40. At the fair, Angela spent $6.25 for tickets, $3.79 for food, and $4.20 for a stuffed animal. About how much money did she spend at the fair?

41. Andrew ran 2.8 mi on Monday, 2.9 mi on Wednesday, and 3.1 mi on Friday. About how many miles did he run those 3 days?

Write a fraction or a mixed number and a decimal for each.

1.   2. 3.   4.

Write two equivalent decimals for the shaded part of each model.

5. 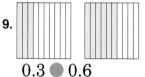 6. 7. 8.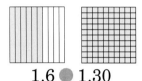

Compare. Use <, >, or = for ●.

9. 0.3 ● 0.6

10. 0.27 ● 0.72

11. 1.6 ● 1.30

Order the numbers from greatest to least.

12. 1.6; 0.16; 0.6; 0.06

13. 2.03; 3.02; 2.30; 3.2; 0.03

> I can estimate to see if the sum or difference is reasonable.

Round each decimal to the nearest whole number.

14. 0.52   15. 7.4   16. 3.09   17. 5.8

Find the sum or difference.

18. 5.42 + 3.13

19. 7.00 − 4.63

20. 0.73 − 0.54

21. 12.48 0.43 + 6.99

Solve.

22. Nancy spent $12.00 for a gift. Then she earned $5.00. She now has $16.00. How much money did she have before she bought the gift?

23. Lindsay put half her dolls on one shelf. She put 3 dolls on each of 3 other shelves and 1 doll on the last shelf. How many dolls does Lindsay have?

24. By using grocery coupons, Mrs. Sullivan saved $3.80 one week, $5.10 the following week, and $4.60 the third week. About how much money did she save with her coupons those 3 weeks?

25. Brad's bean plant grew 1.8 cm the first week. It grew 2.25 cm the second week and 1.75 cm the third week. About how tall was Brad's plant by the end of the third week?

School Olympics

Imagine that you are on a committee to develop individual sports activities for an athletic competition at your school. This athletic event for fourth, fifth, and sixth graders will be held in the fall. The winners will participate in School Olympics for all the schools in your county. Your task is to create one of these individual sports activities, provide training guidelines, and set achievement goals.

☭ Decide

Brainstorm about sports activities that would encourage participation by many students. Make a list.

Choose one of the activities.

List ways to get students interested in the competition.

Decide what sources you can investigate to gather information.

╬ Do

Research whether the activity you are planning already has performance records.

Conduct tryouts with committee members to get an idea about the timing, speed, and levels of skill and physical fitness required.

Outline the rules for the activity.

Share

Describe your sport to the class. Prepare a training chart and a table or graph of possible winning performance levels.

TALK ABOUT IT

Based on your tryouts, what should a student achieve to win the event?

Did your knowledge and investigation of Olympic events or other sports activities help in planning your event? Explain.

Because of the type of event, is it a good idea to have separate contests for girls and boys? Explain.

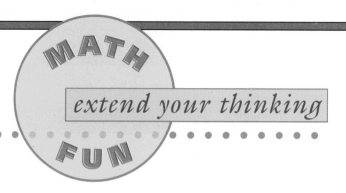

Activity

Model Decimals

Write the following decimals on separate cards: 0.4, 0.16, 0.05, 0.41, 1.06, 0.51, 0.15, 0.04, 0.60, 1.5, 1.44, 1.41, 1.05, 0.50. Spread the cards faceup.

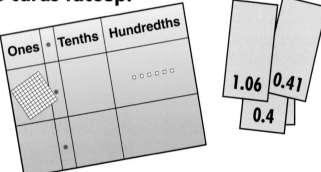

Play this game with a partner. Mentally select a decimal from one of the cards without telling your partner, and show it with place-value models. After you have finished, your partner has 5 seconds to choose the card with the decimal you modeled. If your partner is correct, he or she may keep the card. Take turns. The player with the most cards is the winner.

For an extra challenge, try this variation of the game.

Model a decimal that is not on one of the cards. Then give your partner 10 seconds to write the decimal you modeled.

Challenge
Extend Vocabulary

With a partner, use a dictionary to look up the following words. Notice that they all begin with *dec-*, like the word *decimal*. Tell how the meaning of each word is related to the meaning of the word *decimal*.

1. December
2. deciliter
3. decade
4. decapod
5. decagon
6. decathlon

Decimal Riddles

Use the clues in each riddle to find the decimal being described.

1. The digit in my hundredths place is 8. The digit in my ones place is 3. My tenths digit is the difference of those.

2. I have 6 ones and 8 hundredths. My tenths digit is 2 less than half of the hundredths digit.

Write the letter of the correct answer.

1. Which fraction shows $\frac{4}{20}$ in simplest form?

   A. $\frac{1}{5}$ B. $\frac{2}{10}$

   C. $\frac{1}{4}$ D. $\frac{2}{5}$

2. Which is the average of 41, 42, 46?

   A. 40 B. 42
   C. 43 D. 45

3. What is $\frac{2}{3}$ of 15?

   A. 5 B. 10
   C. 12 D. not here

4. What is the value of the digit 5 in 5,342,897?

   A. 50 B. 5,000
   C. 500,000 D. 5,000,000

5. $8\overline{)650}$

   A. 80 r1 B. 80 r2
   C. 81 r2 D. not here

6. Which decimal is equivalent to 0.3?

   A. 0.03 B. 0.30
   C. 0.33 D. 3.30

7. Which figure is *not* a polygon?

   A. ⌴ B. ☐

   C. ◇ D. ⇨

8. What is the name of this solid figure?

   A. cube B. cylinder
   C. cone D. pyramid

9. $6.4 - 2.17 = n$

   A. $n = 4.23$ B. $n = 4.33$
   C. $n = 4.37$ D. $n = 8.57$

10. $4,382$
    $\times \quad 4$

    A. 16,228 B. 16,288
    C. 17,436 D. 17,528

11. There are 24 students in Andrew's class. There are 4 more boys than girls. How many girls are there?

    A. 8 girls B. 10 girls
    C. 12 girls D. 14 girls

12. The play began at 8:15. It lasted 2 hours and 20 minutes. At what time did the play end?

    A. 9:35 B. 10:30
    C. 10:35 D. 10:45

DIVIDING
BY 2-DIGIT NUMBERS

Did you know ...

. . . that marine biologists study plants and animals in the world's oceans? The more we learn, the more wisely we can share the earth with these organisms.

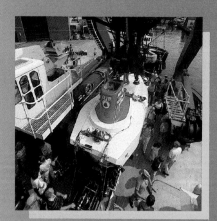

Timmy's Aunt Rita is a marine biologist. She is going to dive 13,000 feet in *Alvin*, a tiny submarine. Timmy knows that there are 5,280 feet in a mile. How can he use that information to find the depth in miles?

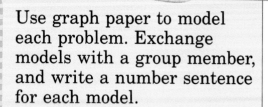

Carlos Mendez is an exercise specialist who works for the Bay Hill Health Club. From Monday through Friday he schedules 30-minute workouts. On Tuesday the workouts last 210 minutes. How many workouts does Carlos schedule on Tuesday?

Divide.

210	÷	30	=	n
↑		↑		↑
total minutes (dividend)		minutes in each workout (divisor)		number of workouts (quotient)

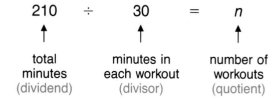

Building Understanding

Use centimeter graph paper, scissors, and a ruler to explore dividing by multiples of ten.

On your graph paper, draw a rectangle 21 squares by 10 squares. Cut out the rectangle. The rectangle has an area of 210 squares.

Talk About It

▶ How can you make groups of 30 squares from this rectangle?

▶ How many groups of 30 squares can you make?

▶ Write a division number sentence to show what you just did.

▶ What basic fact helps you find the quotient mentally?

▶ So, how many workouts does Carlos schedule?

Use graph paper to model each problem. Exchange models with a group member, and write a number sentence for each model.

a. $20\overline{)120}$

b. $30\overline{)90}$

c. $40\overline{)160}$

 Connection, pages 450–451

Making the Connection

You can see a pattern in the quotients when dividing by multiples of 10.

Example

$70\overline{)210}$ →

$70\overline{)2,100}$ →

$70\overline{)21,000}$ →

Place-Value Chart			
Thousands	**Hundreds**	**Tens**	**Ones**
			3
		3	0
	3	0	0

1. On the place-value chart, did the value of the digit 3 increase or decrease?

2. Make a pattern using the fact $12 \div 4 = 3$. Write a sentence to explain the pattern.

Record each quotient on a place-value chart.

3. $2\overline{)4}$
   $20\overline{)40}$
   $20\overline{)400}$

4. $9 \div 3$
   $90 \div 30$
   $900 \div 30$

5. $4\overline{)8}$
   $40\overline{)80}$
   $40\overline{)800}$

6. $15 \div 5$
   $150 \div 50$
   $1,500 \div 50$

Checking Understanding

On graph paper, make a model for each problem. Solve.

7. $540 \div 60 = n$

8. $140 \div 70 = n$

9. $180 \div 60 = n$

10. $360 \div 40 = n$

Write the basic fact that helps you find each quotient. Solve.

11. $30\overline{)150}$

12. $20\overline{)180}$

13. $30\overline{)270}$

14. $40\overline{)160}$

Record each quotient on a place-value chart.

15. $7\overline{)63}$
    $70\overline{)630}$
    $70\overline{)6,300}$

16. $4\overline{)28}$
    $40\overline{)280}$
    $40\overline{)2,800}$

17. $9\overline{)72}$
    $90\overline{)720}$
    $90\overline{)7,200}$

18. $8\overline{)64}$
    $80\overline{)640}$
    $80\overline{)6,400}$

Find the next number sentence in the pattern.

19. $40 \div 20 = \blacksquare$
        $400 \div 20 = \blacksquare$
        $4,000 \div 20 = \blacksquare$
        $\blacksquare \div \blacksquare = \blacksquare$

20. $3 \times \blacksquare = 15$
      $3 \times \blacksquare = 150$
      $3 \times \blacksquare = 1,500$
      $\blacksquare \times \blacksquare = \blacksquare$

21. $30 \div 6 = \blacksquare$
          $300 \div 60 = \blacksquare$
          $3,000 \div 600 = \blacksquare$
          $\blacksquare \div \blacksquare = \blacksquare$

ESTIMATING QUOTIENTS

Nancy Morrow works for the telephone company. Part of her job is to repair telephone lines. She repairs about the same number of lines each month. She repaired 68 phone lines last year. About how many telephone lines did she repair each month?

There are 12 months in a year.
So, you can estimate the quotient of $68 \div 12$.

Use compatible numbers. Since 12 is close to 10, change the divisor to 10. Change the dividend to the nearest number that can be easily divided by 10.

Compatible numbers are numbers that are easy to compute mentally.

$$68 \div 12$$
$$\downarrow \quad \downarrow$$
$$70 \div 10 = 7$$

So, Nancy repaired about 7 telephone lines each month.

More Examples

A. $83 \div 18 = n$
$\downarrow \quad \downarrow$
$80 \div 20 = 4$

B. $239 \div 11 = n$
$\downarrow \quad \downarrow$
$240 \div 10 = 24$

C. $613 \div 59 = n$
$\downarrow \quad \downarrow$
$600 \div 60 = 10$

Talk About It

▶ Why do you change the divisor to a multiple of 10?

▶ Name another estimation method you can use to estimate quotients.

Check for Understanding

Copy and complete. Use compatible numbers to estimate.

1. $223 \div 69 = n$
$\downarrow \quad \downarrow$
$210 \div \blacksquare = 3$

2. $302 \div 52 = n$
$\downarrow \quad \downarrow$
$\blacksquare \div 50 = 6$

3. $143 \div 19 = n$
$\downarrow \quad \downarrow$
$140 \div \blacksquare = \blacksquare$

Estimate the quotient.

4. $24\overline{)82}$ 5. $31\overline{)897}$ 6. $48\overline{)153}$ 7. $71\overline{)224}$ 8. $65\overline{)715}$

Idea Bank, page 455, Exercises 11–12

Practice

Copy and complete. Use compatible numbers to estimate.

9. $154 \div 32 = n$
↓ ↓
■ $\div 30 = 5$

10. $137 \div 21 = n$
↓ ↓
$140 \div$ ■ $= 7$

11. $249 \div 13 = n$
↓ ↓
$250 \div$ ■ $=$ ■

12. $410 \div 72 = n$
↓ ↓
$420 \div$ ■ $= 6$

13. $118 \div 64 = n$
↓ ↓
■ $\div 60 = 2$

14. $279 \div 73 = n$
↓ ↓
$280 \div$ ■ $=$ ■

Estimate the quotient.

15. $64\overline{)539}$ **16.** $92\overline{)715}$ **17.** $81\overline{)628}$ **18.** $45\overline{)288}$ **19.** $73\overline{)556}$

20. $22\overline{)168}$ **21.** $71\overline{)502}$ **22.** $54\overline{)354}$ **23.** $68\overline{)418}$ **24.** $43\overline{)172}$

Mixed Applications

25. Jill Nixon has 358 telephone directories to deliver to an apartment complex. If there are 12 buildings in the complex, about how many directories will each building receive?

26. Mr. Ring needs to order 132 telephone cords. The cords are packaged in boxes of 12. Will 10 boxes be enough? Why or why not?

27. The telephone company's customer-service office receives an average of 420 calls in a 2-week period. The office is open 5 days a week. About how many calls does it receive per day?

MIXED REVIEW

Estimate the product or quotient. You may use a calculator.

1. 29×42 **2.** 109×12 **3.** 63×98 **4.** 57×19 **5.** 288×18

6. $9\overline{)1,796}$ **7.** $5\overline{)3,056}$ **8.** $8\overline{)6,376}$ **9.** $5\overline{)108}$ **10.** $6\overline{)239}$

How would you estimate the quotient for $610 \div 90$?

WRAP UP...

Manny Donato works $7\frac{1}{2}$ hours per day in a radio factory. One of his jobs is to check the electrical systems of radios. He can check 30 radios each hour. Today he has 120 radios to check. How much time will Manny have to do other jobs?

Sometimes, you must identify and answer a question that is not given before you can solve the problem. This kind of problem requires more than one step to solve.

▶ **UNDERSTAND**

What are you asked to find?

What information is given?

▶ **PLAN**

What is the question that you must answer before you can solve the problem?

The hidden question is, "How long will it take Manny to check the radios?"

▶ **SOLVE**

How can you solve this problem?

Step 1 Find how long Manny will take to check the radios.	**Step 2** Find how many hours he has left for other jobs.

Step 1
Find how long Manny will take to check the radios.

$$120 \;\div\; 30 \;=\; \blacksquare$$

↑   ↑   ↑

| number of radios to check | number he can check each hour | number of hours needed to check the radios |

It will take Manny 4 hours to check the radios.

Step 2
Find how many hours he has left for other jobs.

$$7\frac{1}{2} \;-\; 4 \;=\; \blacksquare$$

↑   ↑   ↑

| number of hours he works | number of hours checking radios | number of hours left for other jobs |

Manny will have $3\frac{1}{2}$ hours left to do other jobs.

▶ **LOOK BACK**

How can you check your answer?

WHAT IF...   ... Manny has to check 150 radios? How long will it take him to check them?

Apply

Find the hidden question. Solve.

1. Ms. Hill uses a measuring cup to pour cocoa into a 2-gal jug. She pours 8 cups, and Jillie pours 4 cups. How many cups are left to pour?
HINT: 1 gal = 16 c

2. Stu Holden stopped at Mini-Mart on his way to the radio station. He bought 2 cans of juice for $0.89 each. How much change did he receive from $5.00?

3. On Monday the marketing department sold 19 ads. There were 34 ads sold on Tuesday. The department needs to sell 100 ads. How many more ads need to be sold?

Mixed Applications → **STRATEGIES** • Find the Hidden Question • Work Backward • Guess and Check • Act It Out • Draw a Picture

Choose a strategy and solve.

4. There are 45 people at a meeting. Twice as many women as men are at the meeting. How many women are there? how many men?

5. Joe Moore left the radio factory at 5:23 P.M. He spent 15 min waiting in traffic. Then it took him 42 min to drive home. At what time did he arrive home?

6. Demi had $50.00. He spent $12.95 on a birthday gift for his sister and $16.99 for a compact disc. How much did he have left?

7. Mr. Hahn took his two young sons to a radio museum and spent $17.50 for admission. A child's ticket cost $5.00. How much did Mr. Hahn's ticket cost?

8. Ted Woodland is a computer programmer at the radio station. On Monday he was at the station $8\frac{1}{2}$ hr. He spent 15 min talking with his boss, $\frac{1}{2}$ hr eating lunch, and 20 min talking on the telephone. How much time did he spend programming computers?

9. Kerry and Marsha live 18 mi apart. They plan to meet at Midway, which is halfway between their homes. Kerry has gone 7 mi toward Midway, and Marsha has gone 6 mi. How far apart are Kerry and Marsha?

Tara McCall is learning a new word processing system. She can type 80 words per minute. About how long will it take her to type a memo of 732 words?

Estimate. Use compatible numbers. $720 \div 80 = 9$

Divide. $732 \div 80 = n$

Step 1

Decide where to place the first digit in the quotient.

 no $\quad \overset{X}{80)\overline{732}}$ You *cannot* divide 7 by 80. Not enough hundreds.

no $\quad \overset{X}{80)\overline{732}}$ You *cannot* divide 73 by 80. Not enough tens.

yes $\quad \overset{\blacksquare}{80)\overline{732}}$ You *can* divide 732 by 80. There are enough ones.

So, place the first digit in the ones place.

Step 2

Divide. Use compatible numbers.
Think: $720 \div 80 = 9$
Write the 9 in the ones place of the quotient.

$$\begin{array}{r} 9 \\ 80)\overline{732} \\ -720 \\ \hline 12 \end{array}$$

← Multiply. 9×80
← Subtract. $732 - 720$
Compare. $12 < 80$

Step 3

Write the remainder in the quotient.

$$\begin{array}{r} 9\ r12 \\ 80)\overline{732} \\ -720 \\ \hline 12 \end{array}$$

The memo will take Tara a little more than 9 minutes. There will be 12 more words to type after 9 minutes.

Another Example

$$\begin{array}{r} 4\ r2 \\ 20)\overline{82} \\ -80 \\ \hline 2 \end{array}$$

← Think: $80 \div 20 = 4$
← Multiply. $4 \times 20 = 80$
← Subtract and compare.

Check by multiplying.

$$\begin{array}{r} 20 \\ \times\ 4 \\ \hline 80 \end{array}$$ Add the remainder.

$80 + 2 = 82$

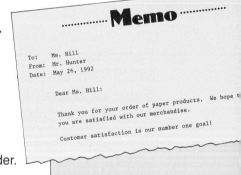

········· **Memo** ·········

To: Ms. Hill
From: Mr. Hunter
Date: May 26, 1992

Dear Ms. Hill:

Thank you for your order of paper products. We hope t you are satisfied with our merchandise.

Customer satisfaction is our number one goal!

Check for Understanding

Copy each problem. Draw ■ where the first digit in the quotient should be placed.

1. $40)\overline{45}$ 2. $30)\overline{196}$ 3. $60)\overline{125}$ 4. $20)\overline{67}$

Find the quotient. Check by multiplying.

5. $30)\overline{91}$ 6. $20)\overline{113}$ 7. $40)\overline{351}$ 8. $60)\overline{437}$

Practice

Copy each problem. Draw ▓ where the first digit in the quotient should be placed.

9. $40\overline{)144}$ **10.** $60\overline{)219}$ **11.** $50\overline{)256}$ **12.** $30\overline{)387}$ **13.** $70\overline{)633}$

Find the quotient. Check by multiplying.

14. $80\overline{)245}$ **15.** $40\overline{)286}$ **16.** $80\overline{)609}$ **17.** $60\overline{)565}$ **18.** $20\overline{)36}$

19. $40\overline{)159}$ **20.** $20\overline{)117}$ **21.** $70\overline{)136}$ **22.** $60\overline{)133}$ **23.** $40\overline{)225}$

24. $354 \div 40 = n$ **25.** $564 \div 70 = n$ **26.** $451 \div 50 = n$ **27.** $312 \div 70 = n$

28. $457 \div 30 = n$ **29.** $607 \div 20 = n$ **30.** $918 \div 70 = n$ **31.** $178 \div 40 = n$

Mixed Applications

32. The computer at the radio station shows that 216 T-shirts are in stock. The shirts are packaged in boxes of 36. How many boxes of shirts are there?

33. Tara typed an essay that was 62 lines long. If she typed an average of 18 words per line, about how many words did she use in the essay?

34. **Find Data** Can the students in your class form teams that have the same number on each team? Why or why not? If you can form teams, how many students will be on each team? How many teams will there be?

LOGICAL REASONING

Find the missing divisor and remainder for each.

HINT: The answers are multiples of 10.

35. $\overset{7\ \text{r}\ ▓▓}{▓▓\overline{)470}}$ **36.** $\overset{9\ \text{r}\ ▓▓}{▓▓\overline{)470}}$ **37.** $\overset{5\ \text{r}\ ▓▓}{▓▓\overline{)230}}$ **38.** $\overset{7\ \text{r}\ ▓▓}{▓▓\overline{)230}}$

How do you decide where to place the first digit?

WRAP
UP...

1. On Friday Mr. Ross shipped 35 packages. On Saturday he shipped twice as many packages. How many packages did he ship both days?

2. Grace is thinking of a three-digit number. The ones digit is one less than the hundreds digit. The hundreds digit is one less than the tens digit. The tens digit is half of ten. What is the number?

3. What is the probability of choosing a red marble from a bag of 15 marbles if there are 5 red marbles in the bag?

4. List the possible combinations of sandwiches you can make if you can use either turkey or roast beef and either wheat, rye, or white bread.

Write two equivalent decimals for the shaded part of each model.

5.

6.

Equivalent decimals are different names for the same amount.

Round each decimal to the nearest whole number.

7. 9.7   8. 0.63   9. 1.05   10. 33.5

Name each figure.

11.   12.   13.   14.

Write whether each angle is a *right,* an *acute,* or an *obtuse* angle.

15.   16.    17.   18.

Find the quotient. Check by multiplying.

19. 6)379   20. 4)304   21. 5)622   22. 8)345

Find the range and the average for each set of numbers.

23. 46, 58, 71, 25   24. 19, 14, 12   25. 34, 57, 16, 53

Spotlight ON
PROBLEM SOLVING

Understand
Plan
Solve
Look Back

Interpret the Answer

•Sometimes an answer can be interpreted in several ways. Always check to be sure that your solution answers the question.

Janice is a manager trainee for a sporting goods store. She is filling an order from the local school district for softballs. Janice is packing the softballs into boxes that hold 16 softballs each. There are 27 schools in the school district. Each school will receive 4 softballs. How many boxes will Janice have to send?

Talk About It

Work with a partner. Answer these questions.

a. Will 6 boxes of softballs be enough to fill the school district's order? Why or why not?

b. If Janice ships 7 boxes to the school district, how many extra softballs will the school district receive?

c. If Janice could ship only boxes that would be totally used, how many schools would not receive softballs? Explain.

Apply

Solve. Explain how to interpret the answer.

1. Each van of workers can hold 10 adults. If 68 workers signed up, how many vans are needed?

2. Heather and Stacey are studying to be physician's assistants. Together they have spent about $360 on books. Can you tell who spent more?

3. Scott ate 2 slices of pizza, and Lexie ate $\frac{1}{4}$ of the pizza. The pizza had 8 slices. Who ate more, Scott or Lexie? What fraction of the pizza was left over?

Tanaki Yoshira is the head chef at a Japanese restaurant. She serves rice with most of her dishes. She has 117 pounds of rice in her pantry. She uses 28 pounds of rice a week. How many weeks' supply does Tanaki have?

Divide. $117 \div 28 = n$

WORK TOGETHER

Building Understanding

Use place-value blocks to model the problem.

Step 1	**Step 2**	**Step 3**
To divide 117 by 28, start by showing 117 as 1 flat (hundred), 1 long (ten), and 7 units (ones).	Make as many groups of 28 blocks as you can. Regroup if needed.	Count how many groups you made. Count how many blocks are left.

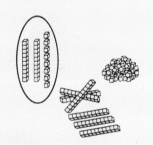

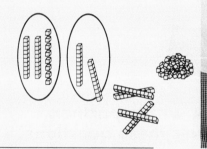

> **Talk About It**
>
> ▶ How did you regroup the flat and the longs?
>
> ▶ How many groups of 28 blocks did you make? Did you have any blocks left over?
>
> ▶ Complete: When 117 blocks are divided into groups of 28, there are ▮ groups with ▮ blocks left over.
>
> ▶ So, how many weeks' supply does Tanaki have? What do the remaining blocks represent?

422

Making the Connection

Use place-value blocks to model the problem. Record the
numbers as you complete each step.

Divide. $126 \div 31 = n$

Step 1	**Step 2**	**Step 3**
To divide 126 by 31, start by showing 126 as 1 flat, 2 longs, and 6 units.	Use compatible numbers to estimate. $120 \div 30 = 4$ So, try to make 4 groups of 31. 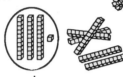	Make groups of 31. Count how many groups. Count how many units are left over. 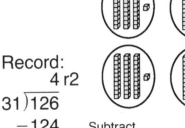
Record: $31\overline{)126}$	Record: 4 $31\overline{)126}$ -124 Multiply. 4×31	Record: $4\,r2$ $31\overline{)126}$ -124 Subtract. 2 Compare. $2 < 31$

Use place-value blocks to find the quotient. Record your work.

1. $11\overline{)48}$ 2. $23\overline{)136}$ 3. $14\overline{)87}$ 4. $23\overline{)121}$

Checking Understanding

Find the quotient. Use place-value blocks to help you.

5. $20\overline{)45}$ 6. $31\overline{)92}$ 7. $44\overline{)178}$ 8. $53\overline{)159}$ 9. $67\overline{)279}$

CALCULATOR

Find the quotient by using repeated subtraction. Subtract the
divisor until the display shows 0. The quotient is **the number of
times you subtract the divisor.**

Example $21\overline{)63}$

Press: 6 3 − 2 1 − 2 1 − 2 1 = [0.]

So, ■ = 3.

10. $36\overline{)180}$ 11. $16\overline{)128}$ 12. $55\overline{)385}$ 13. $99\overline{)693}$

Nina Nakano is an aeronautical engineer who works for NASA. She tracks space probes and communications satellites. The Tyco satellite orbits the earth at the same rate of speed 144 times in 24 days. How many orbits does it make each day?

Estimate. $140 \div 20 = 7$

Divide. $144 \div 24 = n$

Step 1
Decide where to place the first digit in the quotient.

no $\overset{\text{X}}{24\overline{)144}}$ You *cannot* divide 1 by 24. Not enough hundreds.

no $\overset{\text{X}}{24\overline{)144}}$ You *cannot* divide 14 by 24. Not enough tens.

yes $\overset{\blacksquare}{24\overline{)144}}$ You *can* divide 144 by 24. There are enough ones.

So, place the first digit in the ones place.

Step 2
Divide. Think: $2\overline{)14}$ or $20\overline{)140}$
Then multiply.

$$\overset{7}{24\overline{)144}}$$
$$\underline{-168}$$

Multiply. 7×24
You cannot subtract 168 from 144. So, the quotient is too large.

Step 3
Adjust the quotient. Since 7 is too large, try 6.

$$\overset{6}{24\overline{)144}}$$
$$\underline{-144}$$
$$0$$

Multiply. 6×24
Subtract. $144 - 144$
Compare. $0 < 24$

So, the Tyco satellite makes 6 orbits per day.

Talk About It

▶ How would you adjust the quotient if, after the subtraction step, the difference was larger than the divisor?

▶ Why was the estimate different from the answer?

Check for Understanding

Check whether the first digit in each quotient is correct. Adjust the quotient if necessary and solve.

1. $\overset{5}{16\overline{)72}}$ 2. $\overset{9}{42\overline{)379}}$ 3. $\overset{8}{34\overline{)272}}$ 4. $\overset{6}{56\overline{)394}}$ 5. $\overset{6}{27\overline{)175}}$

Practice

Find the quotient.

6. $23\overline{)115}$ **7.** $32\overline{)289}$ **8.** $56\overline{)448}$ **9.** $83\overline{)581}$ **10.** $47\overline{)152}$

11. $73\overline{)438}$ **12.** $45\overline{)225}$ **13.** $90\overline{)810}$ **14.** $75\overline{)255}$ **15.** $37\overline{)148}$

16. $234 \div 34 = n$ **17.** $112 \div 28 = n$ **18.** $306 \div 51 = n$ **19.** $176 \div 22 = n$

Mixed Applications

Use the table for Exercises 20–22.

Satellite	Length of Mission
Pamo	260 hr
Cernan	147 hr
Lukra	241 hr
Gibertti	192 hr
Motrax	302 hr

20. Which satellite had the longest mission? the shortest? Write the names of the satellites in order from longest to shortest mission.

21. Cernan and Lukra were launched at the same time. What was the combined length of time of their missions?

22. Find the length of each mission in days and hours. HINT: There are 24 hours in one day. Any remainders are the hours beyond whole days.

CHALLENGE • CALCULATOR

The letters *A, B, C,* and *D* stand for the numbers 637, 504, 494, and 399. Use a calculator and the clues below to find which letter stands for each number.

Clues:
A and *C* are divisible by 2.
B and *D* are divisible by 7.
B and *C* are divisible by 19.
A and *B* are divisible by 3.
C and *D* are divisible by 13.

23. $A = \blacksquare$ **24.** $B = \blacksquare$

25. $C = \blacksquare$ **26.** $D = \blacksquare$

How do you know that a digit in the quotient is too large?

WRAP UP...

Raul Diego works for Narcoosee Fire and Rescue Squad. He has worked during floods, fires, and earthquakes. The 75 workers are divided into rescue teams with at least 12 members on each team. How can the teams be made up so every worker is on a team?

You should consider both the quotient and the remainder when solving a problem.

▶ **UNDERSTAND**

What are you asked to find?

What information is given?

▶ **PLAN**

What operation can you use to solve the problem?

You can divide to find the number of groups. $75 \div 12 = n$

▶ **SOLVE**

How can you solve the problem?

$$
\begin{array}{r}
6\,r3 \\
12\overline{)75} \\
-72 \\
\hline
3
\end{array}
$$

So, there can be 6 teams with 12 workers on each team.

Since there are 3 extra workers, 3 of the teams will have 13 workers.

▶ **LOOK BACK**

How can you check your answer?

WHAT
IF...

...each of Narcoosee's rescue vehicles holds 8 people? How many vehicles will it take to transport the whole squad?

Apply

Solve. Interpret the quotient and the remainder.

(1) Whit wants to buy a bicycle for $129. He earns $6 a day by working as the rescue-center custodian. How many days will he have to work to earn enough money for the bicycle?

(2) Mr. Mills has 150 bottles of antiseptic to pack in boxes. Each box contains 12 bottles. Leftover bottles will be packed into emergency kits. How many bottles will Mr. Mills pack into emergency kits?

Mixed Applications → **STRATEGIES** • Use Estimation • Draw a Picture • Guess and Check • Write a Number Sentence

Choose a strategy and solve.

(3) Portia is making up first-aid kits. She puts 24 bandages in each kit. She has 293 bandages. In how many kits can she place the exact number of bandages?

(4) A human body has 68 bones in the face and hands. There are 138 bones in the rest of the body. What is the total number of bones in the body?

(5) Lucia drew a rectangle that was twice as long as it was wide. The rectangle had an area of 18 square units. What were the dimensions of Lucia's rectangle?

(6) From Raul Diego's home, it is 2.3 km to the hospital and 1.4 km to the rescue center. It is 3.2 km from the hospital to the rescue center. If he drives from his home to the hospital, back home, and then to the rescue center, how far does he drive?

WRITER'S CORNER

(7) Use the information from the table. Write two division problems that involve finding the average number of hours worked during the three-month period. Exchange with a partner and solve. Remember to interpret the quotient and remainder to determine your answer.

Rescue Center Volunteers			
	Hours Volunteered		
Name	April	May	June
Mr. King	126	134	127
Ms. Hall	100	120	90
Miss Lamb	47	56	60
Mr. Martin	15	22	36
Mrs. Miller	20	25	35

More Practice, Lesson 13.7, page H84

TWO-DIGIT QUOTIENTS

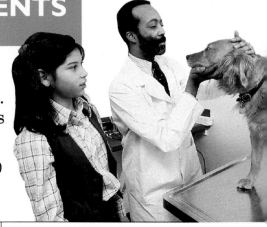

Otis Davis is training to become a veterinarian. There are 157 animals in the clinic where he works. Otis can examine 13 animals a day. How many days will it take him to examine all the animals?

Use compatible numbers to estimate. $150 \div 15 = 10$

Divide. $157 \div 13 = n$

Step 1	**Step 2**	**Step 3**
Decide where to place the first digit in the quotient.	Divide the tens. Think: $13\overline{)15}$ Write a 1 in the tens place in the quotient.	Divide the ones. Think: $13\overline{)27}$ Write a 2 in the ones place in the quotient.
no **X** $13\overline{)157}$ You *cannot* divide 1 by 13. Not enough hundreds.	$\begin{array}{r} 1 \\ 13\overline{)157} \\ -13\downarrow \\ \hline 27 \end{array}$ Multiply. 1×13 Subtract and bring down.	$\begin{array}{r} 12\ \text{r}1 \\ 13\overline{)157} \\ -13 \\ \hline 27 \\ -26 \\ \hline 1 \end{array}$ Multiply. 2×13 Subtract and compare. Think: $1 < 13$ So, write the remainder in the quotient.
yes ▪ $13\overline{)157}$ You *can* divide 15 by 13. There are enough tens.		
So, place the first digit in the tens place.		

It will take 12 days for Otis to examine 157 animals with 1 more animal to examine on the thirteenth day. So, it will take him 13 days to examine all the animals.

Use a calculator to find how many times you can subtract 12 from 204. Write a division number sentence to show this.

Check for Understanding

Copy each problem. Draw ▪ where the first digit in the quotient should be placed.

1. $32\overline{)65}$ 2. $41\overline{)168}$ 3. $54\overline{)579}$ 4. $79\overline{)266}$ 5. $18\overline{)198}$

Estimate. Then find the quotient. You may use a calculator.

6. $28\overline{)91}$ 7. $65\overline{)374}$ 8. $33\overline{)134}$ 9. $17\overline{)82}$ 10. $42\overline{)462}$

Practice

Copy each problem. Draw ▉ where the first digit in the quotient should be placed.

11. $27\overline{)335}$ **12.** $18\overline{)208}$ **13.** $16\overline{)64}$ **14.** $18\overline{)270}$ **15.** $43\overline{)320}$

Estimate. Find the quotient. Use a calculator.

16. $32\overline{)58}$ **17.** $79\overline{)188}$ **18.** $13\overline{)199}$ **19.** $47\overline{)251}$ **20.** $89\overline{)267}$

Find the quotient.

21. $14\overline{)588}$ **22.** $16\overline{)386}$ **23.** $30\overline{)690}$ **24.** $12\overline{)240}$ **25.** $25\overline{)556}$

Mixed Applications

Complete the table. Then use it for Exercises 26–28.

Hinds Veterinary Clinic		
Animal Food Purchased in 1991		
Animal Group	Amount per wk	Amount per yr
Dogs	▉	2,600 lb
Cats	25 lb	▉
Large Animals (horses, cows)	100 lb	▉

Remember: 1 year = 52 weeks

26. Was more food purchased for dogs or for cats?

27. How much food was purchased during the year for all animals?

28. How much more food was purchased per week for large animals than for cats?

CHALLENGE

29. Solve the problems in the pentagon. If the computations are done correctly, the sum of the remainders will be 57 and the sum of the quotients will be 67.

Decide where to place the first digit in the quotient.

29. ? 653
30. ? 499
31. ? 587
÷ 45
33. ? 729
32. ? 604

How do you find a quotient by using repeated subtraction?

DIVIDING MONEY

Lillian Cannon is the director of the Oak Land Day-Care Center. She plans to take the children to the circus. She paid $348 for the tickets. Each ticket cost $12. How many tickets did she buy?

Estimate by rounding. $350 ÷ $10 = 35

Divide. $348 ÷ $12 = n

Divide money like you divide whole numbers.

Step 1	**Step 2**	**Step 3**
Decide where to place the first digit in the quotient.	Divide the tens. Think: 12)34 Write 2 in the tens place in the quotient.	Divide the ones. Think: 12)108 Write 9 in the ones place in the quotient.
no X 12)348 You *cannot* divide 3 by 12. Not enough hundreds.	2 12)348 −24↓ 108 Multiply. 2 × 12 Subtract and bring down.	29 ← Remember: When $348 12)348 is separated into groups −24 of $12, the answer is 108 the number of tickets. −108 0 Multiply. 9 × 12 Subtract and compare.
yes ▪ 12)348 You *can* divide 34 by 12. There are enough tens.		
So, place the first digit in the tens place.		

So, Lillian bought 29 tickets to the circus.

Try these examples with a calculator.

A. $204 ÷ $34 = n   **Press:**

B. $0.96 ÷ 12 = n   **Press:**

• Why did you have to enter the zero in A but not in B?

Check for Understanding

Find the quotient.

1. 14)$336   2. 24)$312   3. 51)$408   4. $29)$203

5. $1,008 ÷ 16 = n   6. $576 ÷ 72 = n   7. $1,764 ÷ 18 = n

Idea Bank, page 455, Exercise 9

Practice

Find the quotient.

8. $16\overline{)\$368}$ 9. $\$22\overline{)\$44}$ 10. $\$10\overline{)\$290}$ 11. $33\overline{)\$990}$ 12. $\$42\overline{)\$882}$

13. $24\overline{)\$744}$ 14. $\$32\overline{)\$416}$ 15. $19\overline{)\$646}$ 16. $\$43\overline{)\$903}$ 17. $12\overline{)\$108}$

18. $\$798 \div \$21 = n$ 19. $\$567 \div \$63 = n$ 20. $\$1,440 \div \$18 = n$ 21. $\$2,392 \div \$52 = n$

Mixed Applications

22. Miss Cannon spends about $435 per year on school supplies. She spends the same amount for each of 29 children. How much does she spend on supplies for each child?

23. Danny Doerr works for a pool company and earns $375 per week. How much money does Danny earn in a month if he is usually paid 4 times a month?

24. Evan has 160 nickels. Each nickel wrapper holds 40 nickels. How many nickel wrappers can he fill?

25. Tandy placed 50 pennies in each of 16 wrappers. How many pennies did she put in wrappers? How much money does she have?

CHALLENGE • SOCIAL STUDIES CONNECTION

When you visit another country, your U.S. dollars may have to be changed. In Japan, for example, 1 U.S. dollar = 135 yen.

Use the data below for Exercises 26–28.

Foreign Money Exchanges (1991)
1 U.S. dollar = 5 francs (France)
1 U.S. dollar = 2 marks (Germany)
1 U.S. dollar = 1,100 lira (Italy)
Note: The value of the U.S. dollar changes almost daily in foreign countries.

26. How many U.S. cents are equivalent to 1 franc?

27. How many U.S. dollars would you exchange for 400 marks?

28. If you are going to Italy, how many lira will you get for 100 U.S. dollars?

On a calculator $\$2.63 + \$3.17 = \boxed{\qquad 5.8}$.
How do you write this as a money amount?

WRAP UP...

Vocabulary Check

Choose a word or words from the box to complete each sentence.

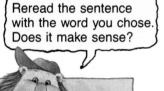

compatible
    numbers
digit
dividend
divisor
multiplication
quotient
regroup
remainder

Reread the sentence
with the word you chose.
Does it make sense?

1. In the division number sentence $156 \div 12 = 13$, the __?__ is 156. *(page 412)*

2. Numbers that are easy to compute mentally are __?__. *(page 414)*

3. You can use __?__ to check the solution of a division problem. *(page 418)*

4. In the division number sentence $350 \div 70 = 5$, the __?__ is 5. *(page 412)*

5. When you use place-value models to divide 143 by 21, you must __?__ the flat into 10 longs. *(page 422)*

6. In the division number sentence $150 \div 15 = 10$, the __?__ is 15. *(page 412)*

7. When there are not enough hundreds or tens to divide, place the first __?__ in the ones place. *(page 418)*

8. The __?__ must be less than the divisor. *(page 418)*

Concept Check

Write a division number sentence for each graph-paper model. *(page 412)*

9.

10.

Copy and complete. Use compatible numbers to estimate. *(page 414)*

11. $282 \div 69 = n$
    ↓   ↓
    ■ $\div 70 = 4$

12. $214 \div 17 = n$
    ↓   ↓
    $200 \div$ ■ $= 10$

13. $345 \div 44 = n$
    ↓   ↓
    $350 \div$ ■ $=$ ■

Copy each problem. Draw ■ where the first digit in the quotient should be placed. *(page 418)*

14. $20\overline{)165}$ 15. $40\overline{)239}$ 16. $33\overline{)297}$ 17. $56\overline{)575}$ 18. $77\overline{)800}$

    Idea Bank, page 455, Exercise 13

Write the division number sentence shown by each model. *(page 422)*

19. 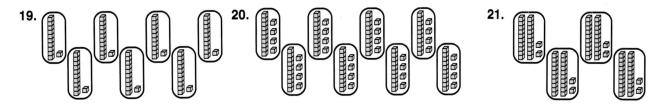 **20.** **21.**

Skill Check

Estimate the quotient. Use compatible numbers. *(page 414)*

22. $41\overline{)389}$ **23.** $62\overline{)372}$ **24.** $37\overline{)156}$ **25.** $44\overline{)211}$ **26.** $73\overline{)643}$

Find the quotient by using repeated subtraction. Use a calculator. *(page 428)*

27. $21\overline{)87}$ **28.** $30\overline{)120}$ **29.** $20\overline{)378}$ **30.** $57\overline{)265}$ **31.** $45\overline{)619}$

Find the quotient. *(pages 418, 422, 424, 428, 430)*

32. $80 \div 20 = n$ **33.** $240 \div 60 = n$ **34.** $270 \div 30 = n$ **35.** $480 \div 80 = n$

36. $14\overline{)94}$ **37.** $56\overline{)427}$ **38.** $23\overline{)255}$ **39.** $17\overline{)384}$ **40.** $\$29\overline{)\$348}$

41. $\$62\overline{)\$372}$ **42.** $\$44\overline{)528}$ **43.** $50\overline{)541}$ **44.** $73\overline{)365}$ **45.** $\$51\overline{)\$255}$

Problem-Solving Check *(pages 416, 426)*

46. Anson has 168 math books to pack in boxes. Each box can hold 18 books. How many boxes will Anson need to pack all the books?

47. Ava spent $16.79 for a curling iron and $5.19 for a set of headbands. How much change did she receive from $30.00?

48. Leo works stocking shelves at a supermarket. He has 300 cans of vegetables to place on the store shelves. He can fit 36 cans on a shelf. How many shelves can he fill with the cans?

49. Bo and Al packed apples into crates. Bo packed 87 crates, and Al packed 115 crates. Together they must pack 300 crates. How many more crates of apples do they need to pack?

CHAPTER TEST

Copy and complete. Use compatible numbers to estimate.

1. $163 \div 29 = n$
   ↓   ↓
    $\div 30 = 5$

2. $421 \div 56 = n$
   ↓   ↓
   $420 \div \blacksquare = 7$

3. $254 \div 41 = n$
   ↓   ↓
   $250 \div \blacksquare = \blacksquare$

Copy each problem. Draw ▥ where the first digit in the quotient should be placed.

4. $10\overline{)535}$

5. $43\overline{)517}$

6. $81\overline{)654}$

7. $29\overline{)487}$

Estimate the quotient. Use compatible numbers.

8. $44\overline{)378}$

9. $65\overline{)482}$

10. $39\overline{)258}$

11. $53\overline{)295}$

12. $21\overline{)307}$

Find the quotient.

13. $40 \div 20 = n$

14. $320 \div 40 = n$

15. $540 \div 60 = n$

16. $280 \div 70 = n$

17. $27\overline{)84}$

18. $30\overline{)571}$

19. $48\overline{)316}$

20. $59\overline{)634}$

21. $\$12\overline{)\$480}$

22. $40\overline{)83}$

23. $30\overline{)247}$

24. $56\overline{)575}$

25. $60\overline{)521}$

26. $37\overline{)\$4.44}$

Solve.

27. Ken had 1,000 folders to file. He filed 489 folders one week and 318 folders the next week. How many of the folders have not been filed?

28. Cathy the Caterer is making extra-long hero sandwiches. Each sandwich will serve 4 people. How many sandwiches should Cathy make to serve 67 people?

29. King Industries spent $1,948.12 on paper and $673.59 on supplies. The expense budget allows for $3,000.00. How much money is left in the budget for other expenses?

30. Rae wants to buy a video game that costs $79. She earns $5 a day working after school at a day-care center. How many days does she have to work at the day-care center to earn enough money to buy the video game?

Teamwork P-R-O-J-E-C-T

Who Do You Know?

You and your teammates will be on a new television show called *Who Do You Know?* You will be part of a team that has researched the life and career of a famous person. Your team can give no more than five clues to help the panel guess the famous person's identity.

  Decide

Discuss the type of career you would like to research.

Make a list of people that fit into this group. Choose one you would like to research.

Discuss possible sources of information about the person.

  Do

Prepare a short outline of the person's life and career. Include information about why the person is famous. List interesting facts or details about his or her early years, and about the education, training, or event that led to the career.

  Share

Work as a team to give no more than five clues to the other teams. The other teams are allowed to ask five questions. Take turns giving clues and answering questions.

CAREERS

Judge - Thurgood Marshall
Sandra Day O'Connor
William Rehnquist

Talk About It

- What interesting information did you find about this person?
- What makes this person's life outstanding?
- Does the person have outstanding accomplishments that are not related to the career?
- How does this person use math in his or her career?

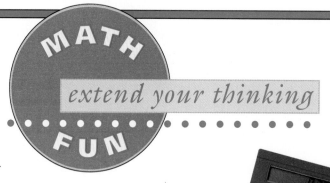

Number Match

In each of the following division problems, the quotient and the remainder are given. From each group of cards, select the dividend and the divisor that make the problem correct. Then complete the division.

1.  | 62 | 69 | 558 | 525 | ⟌ 8 r6

3.  | 41 | 240 | 38 | 364 | ⟌ 8 r36

2.  | 612 | 73 | 566 | 74 | ⟌ 7 r55

4.  | 33 | 210 | 184 | 39 | ⟌ 6 r12

Make up more problems like these. Exchange with a partner and solve.

Challenge

Calculator Trick

On a calculator, enter a six-digit number in which the last three digits are a repeat of the first three digits (Example: 289,289). Then follow these steps, using your calculator. (Do not clear between steps.)

Steps			Display
1.	÷	7 =	41327.
2.	÷	1 1 =	3757.
3.	÷	1 3 =	

What number do you see in the display? Try this with numbers you make up yourself. Does the trick always work?

Everyday Math

1. There are 648 muffins. There are 12 muffins in each box. There are 18 boxes in each crate. How many crates are there?

2. There are 480 offices in a building. There are 2 copy machines on each floor of the building. There are 32 offices on each floor. How many copy machines are in the building?

3. There are 6,256 books in the library. Each of 23 bookcases holds an equal number of books. How many books are in each bookcase?

Write the letter of the correct answer.

1. $131 \div 30 = n$

A. 3 r11   B. 3 r41
C. 4 r1   D. 4 r11

2.
$$\begin{array}{r} 496 \\ -228 \\ \hline \end{array}$$

A. 168   B. 262
C. 268   D. 278

3. $6\overline{)83}$

A. 13 r3   B. 13 r4
C. 14 r5   D. not here

4. $21\overline{)987}$

A. 46   B. 47
C. 47 r1   D. not here

5. Estimate the product by rounding the greater factor to the nearest hundred.
$894 \times 6 = \blacksquare$

A. 4,800   B. 5,400
C. 6,000   D. 6,400

6. Which is the area in square meters?

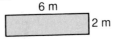

6 m
2 m

A. 8 sq m   B. 12 sq m
C. 16 sq m   D. 18 sq m

7. Which is in order from least to greatest?

A. 4.7; 4.07; 5.04
B. 4.7; 5.04; 4.07
C. 4.07; 4.7; 5.04
D. 4.07; 5.04; 4.7

8. Which decimal shows thirty and twenty-one hundredths in standard form?

A. 30.21   B. 31.20
C. 3,021   D. not here

9. Choose the correct unit. John's father is about six $\blacksquare$ tall.

A. inches   B. feet
C. yards   D. miles

10.
$$\begin{array}{r} \frac{1}{2} \\ +\frac{1}{4} \\ \hline \end{array}$$

A. $\frac{2}{6}$ B. $\frac{1}{6}$
C. $\frac{1}{8}$ D. $\frac{3}{4}$

11. What is the next figure in this pattern?

A. ◯   B. ▢
C. △   D. ⬡

12. Joel worked for $2\frac{1}{2}$ hours on Monday and $3\frac{1}{2}$ hours on Tuesday. If he was paid $5 per hour, how much did he earn?

A. $11   B. $20
C. $25   D. $30

COMPUTER Connection

Computers can do many kinds of work. They help writers, business people, artists, doctors, and lawyers. They can also do work for you in mathematics.

In this section you will explore LOGO, use a word processor, make a spreadsheet, and build a data base. You will be using the kinds of computer programs that many people use at their jobs and at home.

▶▶▶◁▷◁▷◁▷◁▷

Table of Contents

LOGO Graphics

LOGO is a computer language used to tell a computer how to draw pictures. You tell a triangle, called a turtle, to move forward, backward, to the right, or to the left. The center of the screen is its home. When you type the command DRAW, the turtle appears in the center of the screen. It is then ready to receive your commands. Below are some of the commands the turtle understands.

LOGO COMMANDS

FD 30	The turtle moves FORWARD 30 steps in the direction in which the turtle is pointing.
BK 50	The turtle moves BACKWARD 50 steps.
LT 90	The turtle turns to the LEFT a distance of 90.
RT 135	The turtle turns to the RIGHT a distance of 135.
PU	(PENUP) The turtle moves without leaving a trail.
PD	(PENDOWN) The turtle moves and leaves a trail.
DRAW	This clears the screen and brings the turtle HOME.

You can use different numbers and combinations of the commands to draw interesting pictures. The computer will remember and do a series of these commands if you put them in a **procedure**. Before you can write a procedure, you must give it a name. The name will tell the computer which set of instructions to follow.

For example, if you don't want to retype the commands to draw a square, you can put the instructions inside of a procedure called SQUARE. The procedure must begin with the word TO and finish with the word END. If you save the procedure on a formatted data disk, you can use the procedure again whenever you are using that disk.

At the Computer

1. After you learn how to use the LOGO commands on your computer, finish this procedure to draw a square. Each side is 40 steps long.

TO SQUARE
   FD ■
   RT 90
   FD ■
   RT 90
   FD ■
   RT ■
   FD ■
   RT ■
END

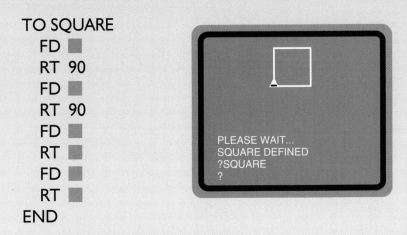

PLEASE WAIT...
SQUARE DEFINED
?SQUARE
?

2. Write procedures to teach the turtle to

   a. draw your initials.

   b. draw a large X on the screen.

   c. draw and name the geometric shapes below.

c.1   c.2   c.3

3. Add the same amount to or subtract the same amount from all the FD commands in the procedures to draw geometrically similar figures. Make sure you use the EDIT command to change your procedure.

Talk About It

▶ Are the figures still similar if you change the numbers of the turning commands?

▶ What is hard about turning the turtle?

▶ What is important about naming the procedure?

LOGO Graphics
The REPEAT Command

You can teach the turtle to repeat a procedure or a group of commands. The REPEAT command was used to make all of these polygons.

SQUARE   PENTAGON   OCTAGON

REPEAT 4 [FD 30 LT 90]   REPEAT 5 [FD 30 LT 72]   REPEAT 8 [FD 30 LT 45]

The number after the REPEAT tells the turtle how many times to do the other commands. What relationship do you see between the amount of the LEFT turn and the number of times the steps are repeated? Hint: The turtle must turn a total distance of 360 to close the figure.

Investigate

Type the commands for the square, pentagon, and octagon. For each figure, change the numbers after the REPEAT, FORWARD, and LEFT commands. Record the shapes you create. You can add other commands inside the brackets [ ] to create interesting patterns.

Talk About It

▶ What happens when you change only the number of the FORWARD command? the turning command?

▶ Did you ever move the turtle off the screen? If so, why?

▶ What kinds of figures did you draw?

▶ How can you use multiplication to pick the turning and REPEAT numbers for the polygon procedures?

▶ How can you make a triangle with the REPEAT command?

At the Computer

1. Use multiplication or division to find the missing number in each procedure. Then use the procedures to draw the polygons. Notice that a LT or RT command will draw the same polygon, but in a different place.

   a. TO HEXAGON
       REPEAT ■ [FD 30 RT 60]
       END

   b. TO DECAGON
       REPEAT 10 [FD 30 RT ■]
       END

HEXAGON DEFINED
?HEXAGON
?

DECAGON DEFINED
?DECAGON
?

2. How many times does the turtle have to make a RIGHT turn of 60 to travel a total distance of 360?

3. You can use the REPEAT command to make ovals. Edit the command

   REPEAT 36 [FD 10 RT 10]

   to draw large and small ovals like the ones below.

?DRAW
?
?

LOGO Graphics
Planning Your Drawings

As you learn more about the LOGO commands, you can make interesting drawings. These drawings must be planned before you begin to type the procedures. Use the following steps to help you plan and draw your designs.

PLANNING STEPS

a. Sketch the figure on dot paper. You can use dot paper to draw the figure the same way the turtle draws a figure.

b. Design a decision tree, or outline, to help you organize the steps you want the turtle to take.

c. Write a procedure the turtle will understand.

d. Test the procedure on your computer.

e. Change or debug your procedure if you find any errors.

Investigate

Use the programming steps to write procedures for these drawings.

1. quadrilateral whose perimeter equals 100 steps

2. pentagon whose sides are 30 steps

3. octagon whose perimeter equals 180

4. star pattern that uses a SQUARE procedure inside a REPEAT command

   Hint: TO STAR
                 REPEAT ■ [SQUARE RT 50]
                 END

5. your own creative design

Applying Math

If a figure can be folded so that its two parts are the same, the figure is symmetrical. The fold is the line of symmetry. A symmetrical drawing also needs careful planning.

a. Trace the figures.

b. Cut them out.

c. Fold each figure to find out whether it is symmetrical.

d. Write the numbers of the figures that have a line of symmetry.

6.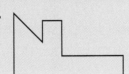

7.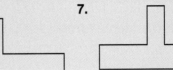

8.

9.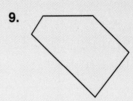

At the Computer

Create procedures for these figures, print the figures, and draw their lines of symmetry.

10.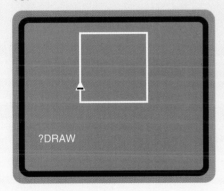

?DRAW

11.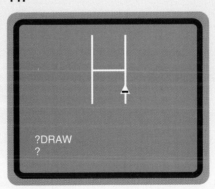

?DRAW
?

12.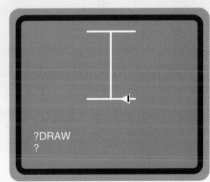

?DRAW
?

Talk About It

▶ Do all figures have a line of symmetry?

▶ Can a figure have more than one line of symmetry?

▶ How is symmetry used in architecture?

▶ Name objects at home, at school, or outdoors that are symmetrical.

Using Word Processing

You and your classmates can have fun writing math riddles. Think of a number. Then type clues on the computer so your classmates can guess the number. The riddles can be changed easily on the computer. One riddle can be turned into many riddles.

At the Computer

1. Type this riddle on your word processor. Save your work on a formatted data disk. Have one of your classmates guess the number.

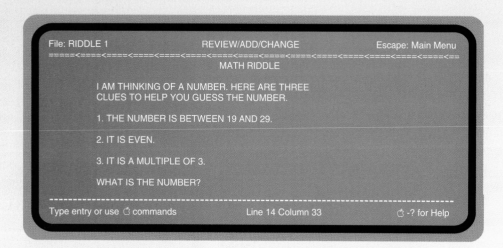

2. Use the problem above to make up new riddles. Retype only the words that will change the riddle.

Talk About It

▶ What can you do if your riddles have more than one answer?

▶ If your classmates can't guess the number, what can you do?

▶ Why can you type new riddles without typing all the words?

Investigate

It's a good idea to make two copies of your riddles. Make one copy with the answers and another copy without the answers. A **word processor** can store many math riddles in separate files. You can use file names that will help you remember what is in each file. Follow these steps to make a math riddle booklet.

WORD PROCESSING STEPS

a. Type a riddle in a word processing file. The last line should be "THE NUMBER IS _____."

b. Using a good file name, save the file on a formatted data disk. See how many characters a file name can be on *your* computer. A name like MULTRIDDLE can remind you that the riddle is about multiplication.

c. Learn how to copy a riddle from one file to another on *your* computer. Copy the file MULTRIDDLE into another file, called MULTANS. Type the answer for each riddle in the new file. Save your MULTANS file.

d. Repeat these steps with other riddles until you have enough riddles for a booklet.

e. Learn how to print the riddles on *your* printer.

At the Computer

3. Start your riddle booklet with this example.

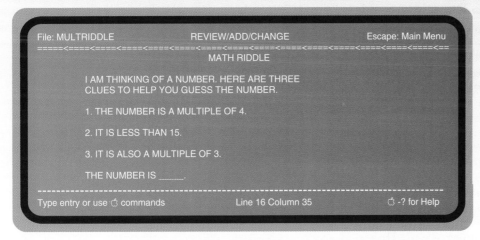

```
File: MULTRIDDLE          REVIEW/ADD/CHANGE              Escape: Main Menu
=====<====<====<====<====<====<====<====<====<====<====<====<====<====<==
                              MATH RIDDLE

     I AM THINKING OF A NUMBER. HERE ARE THREE
     CLUES TO HELP YOU GUESS THE NUMBER.

     1. THE NUMBER IS A MULTIPLE OF 4.

     2. IT IS LESS THAN 15.

     3. IT IS ALSO A MULTIPLE OF 3.

     THE NUMBER IS _____.

-------------------------------------------------------------------------
Type entry or use ⌂ commands        Line 16 Column 35        ⌂-? for Help
```

Spreadsheet Math
Organizing and Calculating Information

A **spreadsheet** is a computer program that helps you organize information. A spreadsheet can also add, subtract, multiply, and divide like a calculator. Carlita and Bryan Foster used a spreadsheet to plan the construction of a patio deck. They need to consider different measurements and costs to decide what size deck to build. Here is a spreadsheet of their choices.

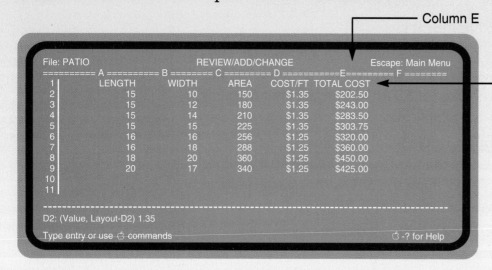

Column E

File: PATIO REVIEW/ADD/CHANGE Escape: Main Menu

	LENGTH	WIDTH	AREA	COST/FT	TOTAL COST
1	LENGTH	WIDTH	AREA	COST/FT	TOTAL COST
2	15	10	150	$1.35	$202.50
3	15	12	180	$1.35	$243.00
4	15	14	210	$1.35	$283.50
5	15	15	225	$1.35	$303.75
6	16	16	256	$1.25	$320.00
7	16	18	288	$1.25	$360.00
8	18	20	360	$1.25	$450.00
9	20	17	340	$1.25	$425.00
10					
11					

D2: (Value, Layout-D2) 1.35

Type entry or use ⌕ commands ⌕-? for Help

Row 1
The words TOTAL COST "live" in cell E1. The address is for column E and row 1.

The boxes in which you type the information are called **cells**. These cells are lined up in rows and columns. You can type a word, a number, or a formula in a cell. A **formula** tells the computer to perform a task.

Each cell has an address. The cell's address is like a home address. Your home address is made up of numbers and sometimes letters to show people where you live. The address of a cell also has a letter and a number. It tells you and the computer where the information "lives."

Talk About It

▶ What happens to the cost per foot as the area increases?

▶ Which row contains words?

▶ Which columns contain dollar values?

At the Computer

1. After you learn to use *your* spreadsheet program, type in Carlita and Bryan's spreadsheet.

2. What are the addresses of these words and numbers? For example, the address for the word LENGTH is A1.

   a. AREA   b. 15   c. $425.00
   d. $1.25   e. 340   f. $1.35

3. What lives in the cells that have these addresses? For example, cell E6 contains the number $320.00.

   a. A9   b. D5   c. E3
   d. B1   e. C11   f. D1

4. Work with three or four other students to find the cost of printing your names on T-shirts. Put all the information on a sheet of paper. Count the letters in each of your first and last names. Suppose each letter costs $.65. Find the cost of printing each student's full name.

5. Put your results in a spreadsheet like the one shown here. Use the same cells that the example uses. You can use the COPY or LAYOUT commands to arrange the information.

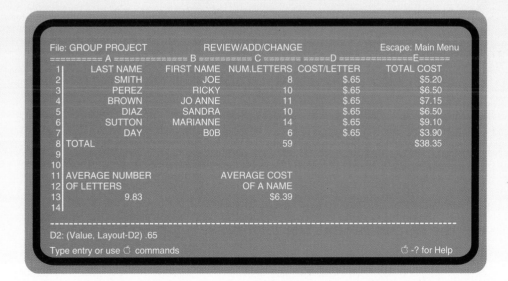

File: GROUP PROJECT   REVIEW/ADD/CHANGE   Escape: Main Menu

	A LAST NAME	B FIRST NAME	C NUM.LETTERS	D COST/LETTER	E TOTAL COST
1	LAST NAME	FIRST NAME	NUM.LETTERS	COST/LETTER	TOTAL COST
2	SMITH	JOE	8	$.65	$5.20
3	PEREZ	RICKY	10	$.65	$6.50
4	BROWN	JO ANNE	11	$.65	$7.15
5	DIAZ	SANDRA	10	$.65	$6.50
6	SUTTON	MARIANNE	14	$.65	$9.10
7	DAY	BOB	6	$.65	$3.90
8	TOTAL		59		$38.35
9					
10					
11	AVERAGE NUMBER		AVERAGE COST		
12	OF LETTERS		OF A NAME		
13	9.83		$6.39		
14					

D2: (Value, Layout-D2) .65

Type entry or use ⌂ commands   ⌂ -? for Help

Spreadsheet Math
Working with Formulas

A spreadsheet can be used as an organizer and a calculator. You can type a formula in any of the cells. The formula can tell the computer to add, subtract, multiply, or divide the numbers in any row or column of cells. Both the formula and the answer can live in the same cell, just as you can live at the same address as your family.

In the previous lesson, you calculated how much it cost to print names on T-shirts, and you organized the information on the spreadsheet. In this lesson, you will use spreadsheet formulas to answer these five questions.

a. If the cost per letter is $.65, how much will it cost to print each name?
b. What is the total number of letters?
c. How much will it cost to print everybody's name?
d. What is the average cost of printing a name?
e. What is the average number of letters in a name?

Here is the spreadsheet without the formulas.

File: GROUP PROJECT   REVIEW/ADD/CHANGE   Escape: Main Menu
========== A ========== ======== B ========== C ======== ====D ============== E======

	LAST NAME	FIRST NAME	NUM.LETTERS	COST/LETTER	TOTAL COST
1					
2	SMITH	JOE	8	$.65	?
3	PEREZ	RICKY	10	$.65	?
4	BROWN	JO ANNE	11	$.65	?
5	DIAZ	SANDRA	10	$.65	?
6	SUTTON	MARIANNE	14	$.65	?
7	DAY	BOB	6	$.65	?
8	TOTAL		?		?
9					
10					
11	AVERAGE NUMBER		AVERAGE COST		
12	OF LETTERS		OF A NAME		
13	?		?		
14					

(C2 * D2)
This formula tells the computer to see what numbers live in cells C2 and D2. The computer then multiplies the two numbers and puts the answer in cell E2.

C13

Type entry or use ○ commands   ○ -? for Help

Turn to page 449 to see the numbers that the formulas will calculate.

At the Computer

Using the example T-shirt spreadsheet or a spreadsheet with your own names, type in the formulas for the total cost. The ZOOM key on the AppleWorks program will let you see the spreadsheet in a format that shows the formulas. The same ZOOM key will bring back the values and the original format.

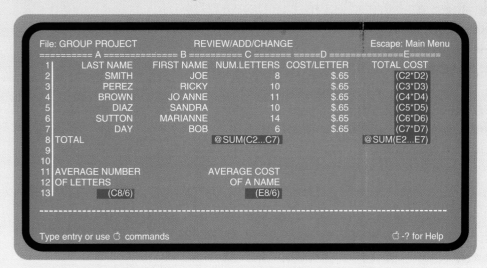

```
File: GROUP PROJECT              REVIEW/ADD/CHANGE              Escape: Main Menu
========== A ============== B ========== C ======= =====D =============E======
  1|      LAST NAME     FIRST NAME  NUM.LETTERS  COST/LETTER     TOTAL COST
  2|         SMITH         JOE           8          $.65         (C2*D2)
  3|         PEREZ         RICKY         10         $.65         (C3*D3)
  4|         BROWN         JO ANNE       11         $.65         (C4*D4)
  5|         DIAZ          SANDRA        10         $.65         (C5*D5)
  6|         SUTTON        MARIANNE      14         $.65         (C6*D6)
  7|         DAY           BOB           6          $.65         (C7*D7)
  8| TOTAL                         @SUM(C2...C7)          @SUM(E2...E7)
  9|
 10|
 11| AVERAGE NUMBER                  AVERAGE COST
 12| OF LETTERS                      OF A NAME
 13|         (C8/6)                          (E8/6)
--------------------------------------------------------------------
Type entry or use ⌂ commands                            ⌂-? for Help
```

1. Answer the five questions at the beginning of this lesson by looking at the example spreadsheet or your own spreadsheet.

2. Explain what the formula in cell E5 does.

3. What is the difference beween the formula in E5 and the formula in E2?

4. What is the address for the cell that has the formula @SUM (E2...E7)?

5. What are the addresses for the amount $.65?

6. Change some of the names so that they have more or fewer letters. What is the total cost of each new name?

Talk About It

▶ If the numbers of letters in the names change, what will happen to the totals?

▶ If the numbers change, do the formulas also change?

▶ Why is using a spreadsheet better than using a calculator?

Data Base

Searching and Ordering

A computer program called a **data base** will order a lot of information quickly. It can also find pieces of information hidden in long lists.

The fourth-grade class at Forest Town Elementary collected information from students in other grades about favorite things. Each fourth grader interviewed students to find out their favorite color, drink, food, and number. The fourth graders gave the other students lists of favorite things to choose from.

The fourth graders want separate lists of all the people who like blue, juice, chicken, and 9, but they don't want to search through a long list. They will let a data base computer program search the information for them. They will go through these steps.

DATA BASE STEPS

a. Enter the information into the data base program.

b. Fix, or edit, any typing mistakes.

c. Save the information on a formatted data disk.

d. Tell the computer to organize the information.

e. Tell the computer to first find all the students who like chicken in the food category.

f. Tell the computer to print a list of students for each category.

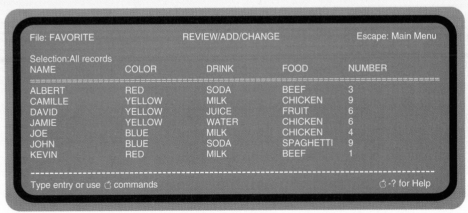

File: FAVORITE   REVIEW/ADD/CHANGE   Escape: Main Menu

Selection: All records

NAME	COLOR	DRINK	FOOD	NUMBER
ALBERT	RED	SODA	BEEF	3
CAMILLE	YELLOW	MILK	CHICKEN	9
DAVID	YELLOW	JUICE	FRUIT	6
JAMIE	YELLOW	WATER	CHICKEN	6
JOE	BLUE	MILK	CHICKEN	4
JOHN	BLUE	SODA	SPAGHETTI	9
KEVIN	RED	MILK	BEEF	1

Type entry or use ⌕ commands   ⌕-? for Help

The computer screen shows part of the fourth-grade information. The students used the data base program to order the information alphabetically by name.

The computer was directed to search all the data for the students who chose chicken as their favorite food. In a few seconds the screen displayed this data.

File: FAVORITE   FIND RECORDS   Escape: Review/Add/Change

Find records containing CHICKEN
Press a =F to change Find.

NAME	COLOR	DRINK	FOOD	NUMBER
CAMILLE	YELLOW	MILK	CHICKEN	9
JAMIE	YELLOW	WATER	CHICKEN	6
JOE	BLUE	MILK	CHICKEN	4

Type entry or use ⌂ commands   ⌂-? for Help

At the Computer

1. Order this data base or one like it alphabetically.

2. Use the data base to find students who like your favorite color, drink, food, or number.

- A data base organizes, sorts, and finds information normally kept in a list or on file cards.
- A record contains several types of information about a person or item. This is a record.

  JAMIE   YELLOW   WATER   CHICKEN   6
- A category (field) is the type of information in a data base. **NAME, COLOR, DRINK, FOOD,** and **NUMBER** are the names of the categories in the student records.
- Sorting is the computer's way of organizing or ordering the information.

Talk About It

▶ In what other ways can you organize the records?

▶ How would you change the student data base to order the students by favorite number?

▶ What step of setting up a data base takes the longest time?

▶ What are other uses for a data base?

IDEA BANK

LOGO IDEAS

1. Write a procedure to make a circle. Then change it to make a bigger circle with the same center.

2. Use the circle procedure in Exercise 1 to make a happy face.

3. Draw polygons with five, six, and eight equal sides. Change the sizes of the figures.

4. See if the turtle understands decimals. Can it move 9.5 steps? Will it turn 40.5?

WORD PROCESSING IDEAS

5. Write directions on how to use a calculator to add a column of numbers.

6. Write directions to a classmate explaining how to add two fractions. Also explain how a spreadsheet can add fractions with the same denominator.

7. Explain to an alien visitor how to draw a hexagon with LOGO. Teach him or her how to write a procedure to draw the figure.

8. Write a mystery story about your favorite number. The reader will need to guess the number from your clues. Make sure that your clues are specific. Only one number should fit the description.

SPREADSHEET IDEAS

9. Get a sales ad from your Sunday newspaper. Use your spreadsheet to find fifteen items that you can buy for less than $500.00.

10. Make a calendar that shows how much television you watched last week.

11. Make a table of numbers that shows multiplication facts.

12. Make a table of numbers that shows division facts.

DATA BASE IDEAS

13. Use the data base to type 30 vocabulary words. Tell your data base program to put the words in alphabetical order.

14. Make a phone-number list of your relatives or friends. Tell the computer to put the names in alphabetical order.

15. Ask a group of 4 or 5 classmates these questions.

    a. What is your full name?

    b. What is your favorite number?

    c. Which is your birthday month? (pick 1 through 12)

    d. On what day were you born? (pick 1 through 31)?

    Put the information in a data base. Compare the information. Did any of your classmates pick their birthday month or day as their favorite number?

16. Find another way to compare the information in a – d above. Did the computer compare the numbers for you?

Student **H**andbook

Bridge Lessons

CHAPTER 1

Place Value • Developing Number Sense

Number Patterns

Evan's class is going to the space center, so the students are lining up in pairs. Today there are 18 students in class. Does each student have a partner?

All even numbers make pairs.

Use your counters. Show 18 in pairs.

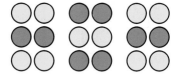

18 is even.

All odd numbers have 1 left over.

Show 19 in pairs.

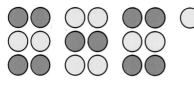

19 is odd.

Even numbers end in 0, 2, 4, 6, or 8.
Odd numbers end in 1, 3, 5, 7, or 9.

Since 18 ends in 8, it is an even number.
So, each student in Evan's class has a partner.

Begin at zero and count by twos to name even numbers.

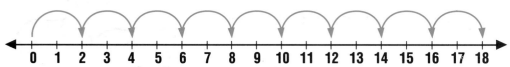

Talk About It

▶ Can each person in your classroom have a partner? How can you find out?

▶ Suppose you want to count by twos and name odd numbers. With what number should you begin?

Another Method

You can skip-count to complete number patterns.

a. 2, 4, 6, 8, ▨, ▨, ▨

HINT: Count by twos.

b. 10, 15, 20, ▨, ▨, ▨

HINT: Count by fives.

Practice

Write the number. Tell whether it is odd or even.

1. 17   2. 11   3. 22   4. 33   5. 48   6. 27   7. 72

8. 92   9. 104   10. 155   11. 203   12. 444   13. 739   14. 947

15. 1,210   16. 5,555   17. 342   18. 475   19. 7,039   20. 947   21. 1,300

Use the number line. Write the missing numbers in the pattern.

22.

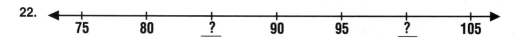

75   80   ?   90   95   ?   105

Write the missing numbers in the pattern.

23. 70, 60, 50, ■, 30, ■, 10, 0

24. 88, 90, 92, 94, ■, 98, ■

25. 35, 37, 39, ■, ■, 45, 47, ■

26. 300, 400, ■, ■, 700, ■, 900, ■

You can find odd or even number patterns in sums. Use the examples to help you.

Even numbers end in 0, 2, 4, 6, or 8.

$6 + 6 = 12$
$2 + 6 = 8$

27. Is the sum of two even numbers an even number or an odd number?

$2 + 7 = 9$
$6 + 1 = 7$

28. Is the sum of an even number and an odd number even or odd?

$3 + 5 = 8$
$5 + 9 = 14$

29. Is the sum of two odd numbers even or odd?

Solve.

30. There are 7 numbers. The numbers start at 48 and end at 60. They are all even numbers. Write them.

31. Steve is counting backward by tens: 80, 70, 50, 40, 30. Write a sentence to tell the mistake he made.

32. The house numbers of the first three houses on Mindy's street are 915, 917, and 919. Mindy lives in the fourth house. What is her house number?

33. Jacob is 8 years old. His brother is 3 years older. Is the age of Jacob's brother an even or an odd number?

Adding and Subtracting Whole Numbers

Fact Families

Two addition sentences can be written with the numbers 3, 6, and 9.

$$3 + 6 = 9 \qquad 6 + 3 = 9$$

Two subtraction sentences can be written with the numbers 3, 6, and 9.

$$9 - 6 = 3 \qquad 9 - 3 = 6$$

These four number sentences make up a fact family.

> A **fact family** is a set of related addition and subtraction number sentences using the same numbers.

More Examples

A. 4, 5, 9
$4 + 5 = 9$
$5 + 4 = 9$
$9 - 5 = 4$
$9 - 4 = 5$

B. 7, 8, 15
$7 + 8 = 15$
$8 + 7 = 15$
$15 - 7 = 8$
$15 - 8 = 7$

C. 4, 4, 8
$4 + 4 = 8$
$8 - 4 = 4$

D. 5, 6, 11
$5 + 6 = 11$
$6 + 5 = 11$
$11 - 6 = 5$
$11 - 5 = 6$

Talk About It

Use your counters.

▶ What is the fact family for 2, 3, and 5?

▶ What is the fact family for 1, 7, and 8?

▶ How many facts are in the fact family for 5, 5, and 10? What are they?

▶ How many facts are in the fact family for 3, 3, and 6? What are they?

Name a related subtraction fact.

a. $4 + 5 = 9$ **b.** $7 + 9 = 16$ **c.** $6 + 4 = 10$ **d.** $3 + 4 = 7$

Practice

Write the set of numbers for each fact family.

1. $3 + 7 = 10, 7 + 3 = 10, 10 - 3 = 7, 10 - 7 = 3$

2. $8 + 9 = 17, 9 + 8 = 17, 17 - 8 = 9, 17 - 9 = 8$

3. $9 + 5 = 14, 5 + 9 = 14, 14 - 5 = 9, 14 - 9 = 5$

4. $6 + 9 = 15, 9 + 6 = 15, 15 - 9 = 6, 15 - 6 = 9$

Write the fact family for each set of numbers.

5. $5, 7, 12$ 6. $4, 6, 10$ 7. $9, 7, 16$ 8. $8, 4, 12$

Find the missing number to complete each fact.

9. $3 + \blacksquare = 12, 9 + \blacksquare = 12, 12 - \blacksquare = 9, 12 - \blacksquare = 3$

10. $8 + \blacksquare = 14, 6 + \blacksquare = 14, 14 - \blacksquare = 6, 14 - \blacksquare = 8$

Write a related subtraction fact.

11. $5 + 7 = 12$, so $\blacksquare - \blacksquare = \blacksquare$.   12. $8 + 5 = 13$, so $\blacksquare - \blacksquare = \blacksquare$.

Write a related addition fact.

13. $15 - 8 = 7$, so $\blacksquare + \blacksquare = \blacksquare$.   14. $12 - 7 = 5$, so $\blacksquare + \blacksquare = \blacksquare$.

15. Choose an addition fact. Write the fact family for it.

16. Choose a subtraction fact. Write the fact family for it.

Solve.

Maria collects pictures of horses. She started with 14 pictures. She lost 5.

17. How many pictures does she have now? Write the number fact to solve the problem.

18. Write the three other facts in the same fact family.

Adding and Subtracting Whole Numbers

Counting Money

Debbie has one $5 bill, one $1 bill, 2 quarters, 2 dimes, 1 nickel, and 3 pennies. How much money does she have?

Count: $5.00 $6.00 $6.50 $6.70 $6.75 $6.78

So, Debbie has $6.78 in all.

Count by nickels to $1.00.
- How many nickels are in $1.00?

Count by dimes to $1.00.
- How many dimes are in $1.00?

Count by quarters to $1.00.
- How many quarters are in $1.00?

Count by $1 bills to $5.00.
- How many $1 bills are in $5.00?

> Remember, a dollar sign and a decimal point show money amounts.
> Examples $3.98 $5.08 $7.14
> In $0.98 the zero means no dollars.

> To count coins and bills, I start with the bill of greatest value and count to the coin of least value.

Count: $5.00 $8.00 $8.50 $8.60 $8.70 $8.71

Read: eight dollars and seventy-one cents

More Examples

A.

Read: three dollars and fifty-four cents

B.

Read: seven dollars and sixty-two cents

Practice

Use your play money. Count the money and write the amount.

1.

2.

3.

4.

Write the letter for the set of money that shows the same amount.

5.    a.    b.

6.    a.    b.

7.    a.   b.

8.    a.    b.

Solve.

9. Linc has three $1 bills, 10 dimes, 6 nickels, and 48 pennies. Does he have enough money to buy a plant for $4.19?

10. Casey has one $5 bill, 8 quarters, and 4 dimes. How much money does Casey have?

11. Larry wants to buy a calendar for $0.75, a notebook for $0.80, and an eraser for $0.35. How much do the three items cost in all?

12. Bethany earned $2.50 helping her grandmother clean the house. Bethany wants to buy a hair clip for $3.07. How much more money must she earn?

Multiplication and Division • Using Facts

Exploring Arrays

WORK TOGETHER

An **array** shows objects in rows and columns.

Use square tiles or square pieces of paper.
Make an array with 3 rows and 3 columns.

Now, make an array with 4 rows and 4 columns.
Next, make an array with 5 rows and 5 columns.

Talk About It

▶ What multiplication fact is shown by each array?

▶ What shape is formed by each array?

Now Try This

Make an array with 3 rows and 4 columns.

Now, make an array with 4 rows and 5 columns.
Next, make an array with 5 rows and 6 columns.

Talk About It

▶ What multiplication fact is shown by each array?

▶ What shape is formed by each array?

Practice

Write the multiplication sentence for each array.

1.

2.

3.

4.

5.

6.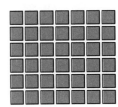

7.

8.

9.

10. Which arrays in Exercises 1–9 form squares?

11. What do you notice about the factors when the array forms a square?

Use graph paper to draw an array. Find the product.

| 12. | 7
×7 | 13. | 6
×9 | 14. | 7
×9 | 15. | 8
×8 | 16. | 3
×6 | 17. | 9
×9 | 18. | 4
×7 |

19. Ken made a bulletin board from squares of cork. He used 3 rows of 6 squares. How many squares did Ken use?

20. Susan made a quilt by sewing squares of fabric together. Her quilt was 7 squares long and 5 squares wide. How many squares did Susan use to make her quilt?

21. Work with a classmate. Use 24 square tiles. Make as many different arrays as you can. Show your arrays on graph paper. Write the multiplication fact for each array.

Multiplication and Division • Using Facts

Exploring Division

WORK TOGETHER

Draw 3 circles on a sheet of paper. Use 18 counters.

Put 1 counter in each circle. Then put another counter in each circle. Do this until all the counters are placed equally in the 3 circles.

Talk About It

▶ Do you have the same number of counters in each circle? If not, start with the 18 counters again, and place them equally in the circles.

▶ How many counters are there in all? How many circles? How many counters are in each circle?

Use your 18 counters.
Put them in 6 equal groups.

Talk About It

▶ How many counters are there in all? How many groups? How many counters are in each group?

Fill in the missing numbers.

When _?_ counters are divided equally into _?_ groups, there are _?_ counters in each group. _?_ divided by _?_ equals _?_ .

Practice

You can divide to find how many red marbles are in each group.

1. How many marbles are there in all?

2. How many groups are there?

3. How many marbles are in each group?

Read: Twenty divided by four equals five.
Write: $20 \div 4 = 5$

4. What does the 20 stand for?

5. What does *divided by* mean?

6. What does *equals 5* mean?

7. What does the division sign stand for?

Answer the questions for each picture.

  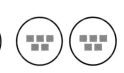

8. How many in all?
   How many groups?
   How many in each group?
   $15 \div 3 = $ ▓

9. How many in all?
   How many groups?
   How many in each group?
   $12 \div 4 = $ ▓

10. How many in all?
   How many groups?
   How many in each group?
   $10 \div 2 = $ ▓

Divide. Use counters and circles.

11. $16 \div 4 = $ ▓

12. $8 \div 2 = $ ▓

13. $27 \div 3 = $ ▓

14. $21 \div 7 = $ ▓

15. $14 \div 2 = $ ▓

16. $20 \div 5 = $ ▓

17. $18 \div 3 = $ ▓

18. $18 \div 6 = $ ▓

CHAPTER 4

Time, Graphing, and Data

Time After the Hour

Peter is going to a movie at the mall. The clocks show the time that the movie begins. What time do the clocks show?

Read: three-thirty
or thirty minutes after three
Write: 3:30

Rhea and Jean are going swimming. What times does the clock show?

Read: two-fifteen,
fifteen minutes after two,
or quarter after two
Write: 2:15

If the girls swim for 30 minutes, at what time will they finish?

Read: two forty-five,
forty-five minutes after two,
or quarter to three
Write: 2:45

Show 8:15 on your clock. Show 8:30. Now, show 8:45.

- What number does the minute hand point to at 15 minutes after the hour? 30 minutes? 45 minutes?

- How many minutes pass from 15 minutes after the hour to 45 minutes after the hour?

More Examples

A.

4:30

B.

6:45

C.

10:15

D.

9:00

Practice

Use your clockface to help you answer Exercises 1–4.

a.    b.    c.    d.

1. Write the time shown on each clock.

2. Write the time 1 hour later than shown.

3. Write the time 30 minutes later than shown.

4. Write the time 15 minutes later than shown.

Count by fives to show the minutes that have passed from the first time to the second time.

5.

6.

5, ■, ■, ■, ■

5, ■, ■, ■

Use your clockface. Solve.

7. Nancy was 30 minutes late for the baseball game. The game started at 6:00. At what time did she get to the game?

8. Betty's soccer team began its warm-up at 7:30. The game began 15 minutes later. At what time did the game begin?

9. Sam watched television for 30 minutes. He started watching television at 1:15. At what time did he stop watching?

10. Ginger's lunch period starts at 11:45 and ends at 12:30. How long is the lunch period?

CHAPTER 5

Multiplying by 1-Digit Numbers

Regrouping Ones and Tens

To save on gasoline, Mr. Perez bought a car that gets 34 miles to a gallon. How many miles can he drive on 5 gallons of gasoline?

$$5 \times 34 = \blacksquare$$

Use your place-value materials.

Step 1

Multiply the ones.
$5 \times 4 = 20$ ones
Regroup 20 ones as 2 tens 0 ones.

tens	ones
2	
3	4
×	5
	0

Step 2

Multiply the tens.
$5 \times 3 = 15$ tens
Add the 2 tens.
$15 + 2 = 17$ tens
Regroup 17 tens as 1 hundred 7 tens.

hundreds	tens	ones
	2	
	3	4
×		5
1	7	0

So, Mr. Perez can drive 170 miles on 5 gallons of gasoline.

Talk About It

▶ Why were the ones regrouped? How were they regrouped?

▶ Why were the tens regrouped? How were they regrouped?

More Examples

A.
$$\begin{array}{r} 21 \\ \times\ 4 \\ \hline 84 \end{array}$$
No Regrouping

B.
$$\begin{array}{r} {}^{2}\ \\ 13 \\ \times\ 7 \\ \hline 91 \end{array}$$
Regrouping Ones

C.
$$\begin{array}{r} 51 \\ \times\ 5 \\ \hline 255 \end{array}$$
Regrouping Tens

D.
$$\begin{array}{r} {}^{1}\ \\ 86 \\ \times\ 3 \\ \hline 258 \end{array}$$
Regrouping Ones and Tens

Practice

Copy and complete.

1.
T	O
	4	5
×		3
---	---	---
		5

2.
H	T	O
	1	2	6
×			4
---	---	---	---
			4

3.
H	T	O
	5	7	9
×			6

4.
H	T	O
	3	2	4
×			3
---	---	---	---
		7	

5.
H	T	O
	5	4	6
×			2

6.
H	T	O
	7	4	3
×			8

Find the product. Use place-value materials to help you.

7. $\begin{array}{r} 62 \\ \times\ 4 \\ \hline \end{array}$
8. $\begin{array}{r} 62 \\ \times\ 6 \\ \hline \end{array}$
9. $\begin{array}{r} 26 \\ \times\ 2 \\ \hline \end{array}$
10. $\begin{array}{r} 33 \\ \times\ 2 \\ \hline \end{array}$
11. $\begin{array}{r} 51 \\ \times\ 4 \\ \hline \end{array}$
12. $\begin{array}{r} 54 \\ \times\ 6 \\ \hline \end{array}$

13. $\begin{array}{r} 12 \\ \times\ 7 \\ \hline \end{array}$
14. $\begin{array}{r} 13 \\ \times\ 3 \\ \hline \end{array}$
15. $\begin{array}{r} 23 \\ \times\ 2 \\ \hline \end{array}$
16. $\begin{array}{r} 91 \\ \times\ 9 \\ \hline \end{array}$
17. $\begin{array}{r} 29 \\ \times\ 4 \\ \hline \end{array}$
18. $\begin{array}{r} 14 \\ \times\ 6 \\ \hline \end{array}$

19. $\begin{array}{r} 43 \\ \times\ 2 \\ \hline \end{array}$
20. $\begin{array}{r} 82 \\ \times\ 4 \\ \hline \end{array}$
21. $\begin{array}{r} 31 \\ \times\ 5 \\ \hline \end{array}$
22. $\begin{array}{r} 92 \\ \times\ 8 \\ \hline \end{array}$
23. $\begin{array}{r} 23 \\ \times\ 5 \\ \hline \end{array}$
24. $\begin{array}{r} 17 \\ \times\ 4 \\ \hline \end{array}$

25. $8 \times 12 = $ ▓
26. $7 \times 11 = $ ▓
27. $5 \times 75 = $ ▓
28. $4 \times 42 = $ ▓

Solve.

29. Danny and his family went to visit his grandfather, who lives 78 miles away. How many miles did they drive going there and coming back?

30. In Jan's class, each student had to bring in 3 empty milk cartons for an art project. There are 25 students in the class. How many milk cartons will be brought in?

31. Mr. Fields spent $15 on gasoline for each of the 8 rental cars he uses for his business. How much did he spend on gasoline for all 8 cars?

32. Ellen goes to ballet class 2 times a week. The class is 12 miles away. How far does Ellen travel to class and back home in one week?

CHAPTER 7

Measurement

Temperature • Degrees Fahrenheit

Temperature can be measured in degrees Fahrenheit (°F).

WORK TOGETHER

Use a thermometer.

- Find the temperature in your classroom.
  Is the temperature lower or higher than 68°F?

- Find the temperature in a sunny window.
  Is the temperature lower or higher than 80°F?

- Find the temperature of a glass of water.
  Is the temperature lower or higher than 50°F?

- Put ice cubes in a glass of water.
  Find the temperature of the water.
  Is the temperature lower or higher than 40°F?

Write: 68°F
Read: sixty-eight degrees Fahrenheit

Practice

Choose the more reasonable temperature in °F.

1.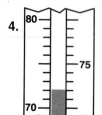
25°F or 65°F

2.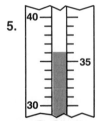
40°F or 99°F

3.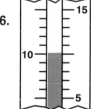
60°F or 120°F

Write each temperature in °F.

4.

5.

6.

7.

8. The temperature on July 4 was 100°F. That was 10 times the temperature on January 1. What was the temperature on January 1?

9. Mrs. Garcia likes the classroom temperature to be 72°F. Is the room too hot or too cold?

Temperature • Degrees Celsius

Temperature can be measured in degrees Celsius (°C).

WORK TOGETHER

Use a thermometer.

- Find the temperature in your classroom. Is the temperature lower or higher than 20°C?

- Find the temperature in a sunny window. Is the temperature lower or higher than 30°C?

- Find the temperature of a glass of water. Is the temperature lower or higher than 10°C?

- Put ice cubes in a glass of water. Find the temperature of the water. Is the temperature lower or higher than 0°C?

Write: ⁻20°C (For temperatures below 0°C, write a minus sign [−].)

Read: 20 degrees below 0

100°C	Water will boil
58°C	Highest weather temperature ever recorded
37°C	Normal body temperature
32°C	Warm day
20°C	Room temperature
10°C	Cool day
0°C	Water will freeze
-25°C	Cold day

Practice

Choose the more reasonable temperature in °C.

1.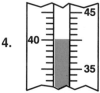
⁻5°C or 20°C

2.
25°C or 5°C

3.
80°C or 100°C

Write each temperature in °C.

4.  5. 6. 7.

8. The temperature was 32°C in the afternoon. It was 18°C at night. How much colder was the temperature at night?

9. Marlo placed a Celsius thermometer in a dish of ice cubes. About what temperature did the thermometer read after a few minutes?

CHAPTER 8

Dividing by 1-Digit Numbers

Quotients with Remainders

When you divide, you show groups with an equal number in each group. Use counters to help you understand division.

WORK TOGETHER

Building Understanding

Use 28 counters. Put them in groups of 7.

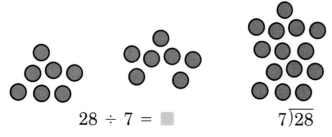

$$28 \div 7 = \blacksquare \qquad\qquad 7\overline{)28}$$

Talk About It

▶ How many groups of 7 did you make?

▶ Are any counters left over?

Use 33 counters.
Put them in 4 equal groups.

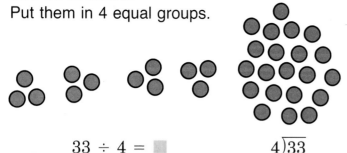

$$33 \div 4 = \blacksquare \qquad\qquad 4\overline{)33}$$

Talk About It

▶ How many counters are in each of the 4 groups?

▶ How many counters are left over?

In division, the amount left over is called the **remainder.**

Practice

Write the division number sentence for each picture.

1.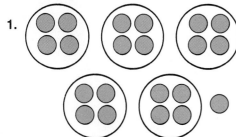

2.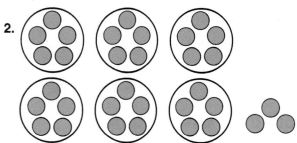

Use your counters to find each quotient.

3. Use 18 counters.
   Put them in groups of 6.
   $18 \div 6 = \blacksquare$

4. Use 29 counters.
   Put them in 3 equal groups.
   $29 \div 3 = \blacksquare$

Solve.

5. For $18 \div 6$, how many groups of 6 counters did you make?

6. For $29 \div 3$, how many counters were in each of the 3 groups?

7. How can you check your division when there is a remainder?

8. How can you divide without using counters?

9. How are multiplication and division different?

Use your counters to find the quotients.

10. $4\overline{)24}$ 11. $8\overline{)13}$ 12. $3\overline{)20}$ 13. $7\overline{)29}$

14. $2\overline{)19}$ 15. $5\overline{)22}$ 16. $9\overline{)36}$ 17. $8\overline{)48}$

Write a number sentence. Solve.

18. Sally had 34 pencils to share with her group. Including Sally there are 8 members in Sally's group. How many pencils will each member receive? How many pencils will be left over?

19. Barry brought 22 cans of juice to the party. There were 9 children including Barry at the party. How many cans of juice could each child have? How many cans were left?

CHAPTER 9

Geometry

Exploring Perimeter

WORK TOGETHER

Building Understanding

The distance around a figure is called the **perimeter.**
Find the distance around a book by using paper clips.

Talk About It

▶ Will you need about 5 or about 50 paper clips?

▶ To the nearest paper clip, how many paper clips equal the distance around your book?

Now use connecting cubes.

▶ Will you need more than or fewer than 10 connecting cubes?

▶ To the nearest connecting cube, how many cubes equal the distance around your book?

Use the width of your hand. Find the distance around your desk top.

▶ To the nearest hand, what is the distance around your desk top?

Use your foot as a unit of measure. Find the distance around your classroom with your footsteps. Have a partner count the steps. Then count your partner's footsteps. Compare the numbers.

Talk About It

▶ Why might the numbers of each partner's footsteps be different?

▶ Would the distance around the classroom equal *more* or *fewer* footsteps for someone with the largest feet in the class?

Choose an object in your classroom.
Find its perimeter with three different units of measure.
Copy this table. Record your answers.

Object: ?			
Unit of Measure	1. ?	2. ?	3. ?
Perimeter	?	?	?

4. How does the size of the unit of measure affect the numbers you get?

Find the perimeter of each figure by using the width of a pencil.

5.

6.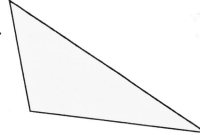

Find the perimeter.

7.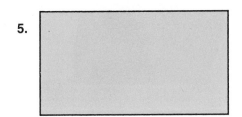

8.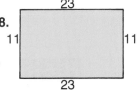

9.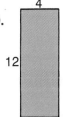

10.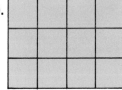

11.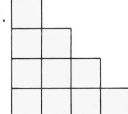

12.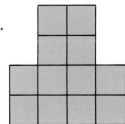

CHAPTER 10

Understanding Fractions and Mixed Numbers

Explore Comparing Fractions

You can use fraction pieces to compare fractions.

WORK TOGETHER

Shelly ate $\frac{1}{4}$ of her pizza. Kevin ate $\frac{3}{4}$ of his pizza. Who ate more pizza?

Use fraction pieces to compare the fractions.

Show $\frac{1}{4}$ and $\frac{3}{4}$ with the fraction pieces.

Compare the fractions. Which is greater?

$\frac{3}{4}$ is greater than $\frac{1}{4}$.

So, Kevin ate more pizza.

Show $\frac{1}{3}$ and $\frac{2}{3}$ with fraction pieces.

Compare the fractions.
Which is greater? Use <, >, or =.

$$\frac{\blacksquare}{3} > \frac{\blacksquare}{3}$$

Show $\frac{2}{6}$ and $\frac{2}{8}$ with fraction pieces.

Compare the fractions. Which is greater?

$$\frac{2}{\blacksquare} > \frac{2}{\blacksquare}$$

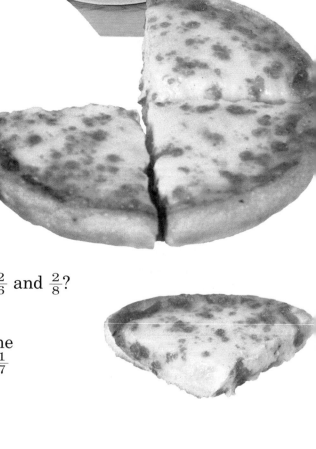

Talk About It

▶ Is it easier for you to compare $\frac{1}{4}$ and $\frac{3}{4}$ or $\frac{2}{6}$ and $\frac{2}{8}$? Why?

▶ What happens to the size of the pieces as the denominator gets larger? $\frac{1}{2}, \frac{1}{3}, \frac{1}{4}, \frac{1}{5}, \frac{1}{6}, \frac{1}{7}$

Practice

Study the example.

Example

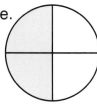

$\frac{2}{4}$ of the circle is shaded.

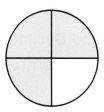

$\frac{3}{4}$ of the circle is shaded.

Compare. Write $<$, $>$, or $=$ for ●.

1.

$\frac{1}{3}$ ● $\frac{2}{3}$

2.

$\frac{3}{4}$ ● $\frac{2}{4}$

3.

$\frac{2}{6}$ ● $\frac{3}{6}$

4.

$\frac{1}{2}$ ● $\frac{3}{4}$

5.

$\frac{5}{8}$ ● $\frac{3}{8}$

6.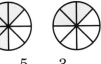

$\frac{3}{5}$ ● $\frac{4}{5}$

7.

$\frac{1}{3}$ ● $\frac{1}{2}$

8.

$\frac{1}{4}$ ● $\frac{3}{4}$

9.

$\frac{4}{6}$ ● $\frac{1}{3}$

10.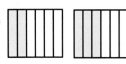

$\frac{1}{4}$ ● $\frac{1}{2}$

11.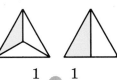

$\frac{2}{3}$ ● $\frac{1}{2}$

12.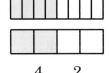

$\frac{4}{8}$ ● $\frac{2}{4}$

Solve.

13. On Monday $\frac{1}{3}$ of the class saw a film about soccer. On Tuesday $\frac{1}{4}$ of the class saw the film. On which day did more students see the film?

14. Matt ate $\frac{3}{4}$ of his oatmeal bar. Yoko ate $\frac{7}{8}$ of her oatmeal bar. Who ate more?

15. Fran had $6. She spent $\frac{1}{3}$ of her money for a snack. She spent $\frac{1}{6}$ of her money on a notebook. Did she spend more on the snack or on the notebook?

16. Maggie baked some muffins. She gave away $\frac{2}{5}$ of them. She kept $\frac{6}{10}$ of them for herself. Did she give away or keep more of the muffins?

CHAPTER 12

Understanding Decimals

Fractions and Decimals

Sandy and Mack play a game called "Rainbow." The gameboard is divided into 10 equal parts. What fraction of the gameboard is green?

Green takes up 1 of 10 equal parts, or $\frac{1}{10}$, of the gameboard.

One tenth can be written as a fraction, $\frac{1}{10}$, or as a decimal, 0.1.

Write: $\frac{1}{10}$ **Write:** 0.1   **Read:** one tenth

A decimal is a number that uses place value and a decimal point to show tenths, hundredths, and so on.

Place-Value Chart	
Ones	Tenths
0	1

A zero is used to show that there are no ones.   decimal point

WORK TOGETHER

Use graph paper. Cut a figure 10 squares wide and 10 squares long. Color 2 strips red.

- What fraction names the part that is colored red?

- What decimal names the part that is colored red?

Color the rest of the strips red.

- Why is $\frac{10}{10}$ the fraction name for the whole number?

- Why is 1.0 the decimal name for the whole figure?

More Examples

A.

$\frac{3}{10}$ or 0.3

B.

$\frac{5}{10}$ or 0.5

C.

$\frac{1}{10}$ or 0.1

Practice

Write the decimal that names the shaded part in each figure.

1.

2.

3.

4.

5.

6.

Write each fraction as a decimal.

7. $\dfrac{5}{10}$ **8.** $\dfrac{1}{10}$ **9.** $\dfrac{9}{10}$ **10.** $\dfrac{7}{10}$ **11.** $\dfrac{8}{10}$ **12.** $\dfrac{2}{10}$

Write each decimal as a fraction.

13. 0.2   **14.** 0.6   **15.** 0.5   **16.** 0.3   **17.** 0.7   **18.** 0.4

Which number matches the picture? Write **a, b,** or **c.**

19.

   a. 0.3

   b. $\dfrac{3}{5}$

   c. 0.6

20.

   a. 0.4

   b. 0.2

   c. $\dfrac{2}{5}$

21.

   a. 0.8

   b. $\dfrac{1}{10}$

   c. $\dfrac{4}{5}$

Solve. Answer Exercises 22–24 with a fraction and with a decimal.

22. Lola was at bat 10 times. She had 6 hits. In what fraction of her times at bat did she have a hit?

23. Of the team's 10 base hits, Peter made 4 of them. What fraction of the base hits did Peter make?

24. There were 10 players on Sam's team. If 2 of them made a home run, what fraction of the team made a home run?

25. After 3 innings the baseball game was called off because of rain. What fraction of the game was not played? HINT: There are 9 innings in a baseball game.

School-Home Connection

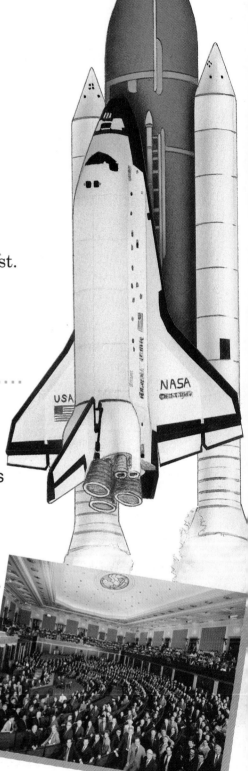

CHAPTER I

Place Value • Developing Number Sense

Application: Exploring Space

Some spacecraft have taken material into space. This material is called the craft's payload. The weight of various payloads is shown in this table.

Spacecraft	Payload (in pounds)
Titan 3C	25,000
Saturn V	280,000
Saturn I	32,000

Order the weights of the payloads from greatest to least.

Now Try This

Research the weights of the payloads of Russian spacecraft. Order the weights from greatest to least.

· ·

CHAPTER 2

Adding and Subtracting Whole Numbers

Application: Population and the House of Representatives

There are a total of 435 members in the House of Representatives. The number of members from each state depends on the population of that state.

If there is one representative for every 500,000 people, how many representatives would a state with a population of 4,700,000 have? You can use repeated subtraction to find the answer.

4,700,000 – 500,000 = 4,200,000 ← 1 representative
4,200,000 – 500,000 = 3,700,000 ← 1 representative, and so on.

There would be 9 representatives.

Now Try This

Determine the number of representatives from your state.

CHAPTER 3

Multiplication and Division: Using Facts

Application: Racetracks

Racetracks can be of different lengths. Some may be 2 miles around and others may be 3 miles around.

If a car races around a 3-mile track 5 times, how far does it go?

$$5 \times 3 = 15$$

The car travels 15 miles.

Now Try This

Find the length in miles of the Indianapolis 500 racetrack. About how many times do the drivers have to travel around the track to go a total of 500 miles? Use a calculator.

CHAPTER 4

Time, Graphing, and Data

Project: Taking Inventory

Stores take inventory to find how many of each item has been sold. This helps them know when to reorder items.

Now Try This

Keep track of how many slices of bread are eaten by your family each day for a week. Record the data in a table like this.

Day	Tally	Number of Slices Eaten
Sunday		
Monday		

Use the data in your table to make a bar graph. Predict how many slices of bread your family will eat next week.

CHAPTER 5

Multiplying by 1-Digit Numbers

Application: Purchasing Clothes

When you go shopping and buy more than one of an item, you can use multiplication to find the total cost.

Find the total cost of 3 shirts that cost $38 each, and 2 pairs of shoes that cost $24 a pair. Then find how much change you would receive from $200.

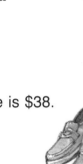

$3 \times 38 = 114$

$2 \times 24 = \underline{48}$

162 The total cost is $162.

200

-162

38 The change is $38.

Now Try This

When you go shopping with your family, pay for a purchase. Check the change to make sure it is correct.

. . . .

CHAPTER 6

Multiplying by 2-Digit Numbers

Application: Using Expanded Form to Multiply

An easy way to multiply two-digit numbers is to write the numbers in expanded form and then find the sum of the partial products.

$12 \times 46 = \blacksquare$

a. Write each factor in expanded form, and make a chart for multiplying.

b. Fill in the chart.

c. Add each row across to find the partial products.

d. Add the partial products.

46   12

$40 + 6$ $10 + 2$

expanded form

×	40	6
10	400	60	→ 460
2	80	12	→ + 92

552

Now Try This

Use this method to find the product.

1. $15 \times 32 = \blacksquare$ 2. $21 \times 35 = \blacksquare$ 3. $18 \times 48 = \blacksquare$

CHAPTER 7

Measurement

Project: Making a Möbius Strip

A Möbius strip is a twisted surface in space that has some unusual properties. For example, a Möbius strip is a one-sided surface.

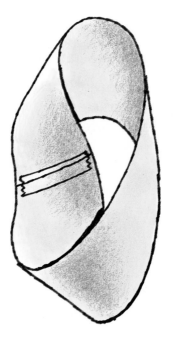

Now Try This

Cut a strip of paper about 2 inches wide and 12 inches long. Make a half twist in the strip, and tape the ends together.

To show that the strip has only one side, try this. Using a marker, draw a wide line along the center of the strip without lifting the marker. What happens?

Cut the strip in half along the line you drew. Describe what happens.

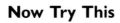

CHAPTER 8

Dividing by 1-Digit Numbers

Application: Measuring in Picas

Publishers often measure the length of a page in picas. One inch is 6 picas.

How many inches are 570 picas?

570 ÷ 6 = 95

95 inches

How many picas are 11 inches?

11 × 6 = 66

66 picas

Now Try This

Measure the length of a page in your math book in inches. Then determine how long the page is in picas.

How many inches and how many picas long is your local newspaper?

CHAPTER 9

Geometry

Application: Tessellating

Shapes that can fill a plane without producing holes or overlaps are said to tessellate the plane. A square tessellates a plane.

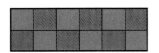

Now Try This

From a piece of cardboard, cut out a triangle having sides of equal length. Trace the triangle on a sheet of paper to make a tessellation. What other regular polygon tessellates a plane?

CHAPTER 10

Understanding Fractions and Mixed Numbers

Application: Fractions and the International Flag Code

Sailors use flags from the international flag code to give signals to other ships. They can clip flags together to form messages.

Here are two of the flags in the international code.

 This flag represents the letter *C*. It is $\frac{2}{5}$ blue, $\frac{2}{5}$ white, and $\frac{1}{5}$ red.

 This flag represents the letter *L*. It is $\frac{2}{4}$ black and $\frac{2}{4}$ yellow. What other fraction could you use to express the part that is black and the part that is yellow?

Now Try This

Research the international flag code.

1. Which flag is $\frac{1}{2}$ red and $\frac{1}{2}$ blue?

2. What fraction represents the part of the *Q* flag that is yellow?

3. Draw three other letter flags that are divided into equal parts. Express the colors of each flag as fractions.

CHAPTER 11

Using Fractions and Exploring Probability

Application: Using Recipes

Suppose you want to serve twice as many people as the number stated in a recipe. You will need to double the amount of each ingredient in the recipe.

If a recipe calls for $\frac{1}{2}$ cup of flour and you are doubling the recipe, you will need $\frac{1}{2} + \frac{1}{2} = \frac{2}{2}$, or 1 cup of flour.

Now Try This

Find a recipe. Rewrite it for twice as many people.

CHAPTER 12

Understanding Decimals

Application: Making a Number Palindrome

A palindrome is a word or a number that reads the same backward as it does forward. These are word palindromes.

wow   madam   peep   mom

Follow these steps to make a number palindrome with decimals.

1. Write any decimal with three digits.

2. Reverse the digits, keeping the decimal point between the same two digits. Add the two numbers.

$$
\begin{array}{r}
4.61 \\
+16.4 \\
\hline
21.01 \\
+10.12 \\
\hline
31.13
\end{array}
$$

3. Repeat Step 2 until you get a palindrome.

Now Try This

Find the palindrome for each number.

1. 1.27   2. 36.3   3. 32.9   4. 5.83

CHAPTER 13

Dividing by 2-Digit Numbers

Application: Unit Pricing

Smart shoppers use unit prices to compare brands of foods or different sizes of the same brand. Then the shoppers can see which is the best buy.

A unit price is the price per unit of an item. You can use division to find unit prices. Suppose one 28-ounce box of cereal costs $3.36, and a 36-ounce box of the same cereal cost $3.96. To find the better buy, calculate the unit price, which is the price per ounce, of each box. Divide the total cost by the number of ounces.

$$\overset{0.12 \text{ per ounce}}{28\overline{)\$3.36}} \qquad \overset{0.11 \text{ per ounce}}{36\overline{)\$3.96}}$$

The 36-ounce box costs less per ounce, so it is the better buy.

Now Try This

Find the unit prices of foods such as cereal, rice, or pasta at a grocery store. Calculate the unit price for different sizes of the same brand, or for the same sizes of different brands. Compare the unit prices and determine the better values. Record what you find in a chart.

PHOTO CREDITS KEY: (t) top, (b) bottom, (l) left, (r) right, (c) center **TABLE OF CONTENTS:** iv(t), HBJ/Jerry White; iv(b) NASA; v, DiMaggio/Kalish/The Stock Market; vi(t), Cary Wolinsky/Stock, Boston; vi(b), HBJ/Earl Kogler; vii(t), HBJ/Rob Downey; vii(b), E.R.Degginger; viii(t), Frank Martin/TSW; viii(b), ix(b), HBJ/MariaParaskevas; ix(b), HBJ/J. White; x, HBJ/Debi Harbin; xi, Richard Hutchings/InfoEdit; xii, Rick Stewart/Allsport USA; xiii(t), HBJ/Maria Paraskevas; xiii(b), HBJ Photo; xiv(t), Bob Daemmrich/Stock, Boston; xiv(bl), NASA; xiv(br), HBJ/Terry Sinclair. **INTRODUCTION:** xvi–xvii, HBJ/Richard Haynes; xviii–xxii, HBJ/Terry Sinclair; xxiii(t) HBJ/J. White; xxiii(b) HBJ/Victoria Bowen. **CHAPTER 1:** xxiv, NASA; xxiv–1(background), NASA; 1, HBJ/J. White; 2, HBJ/Maria Paraskevas; 4(t), Chris Bjornberg/ PhotoResearchers; 4(b), HBJ/J. White; 5, HBJ/Earl Kogler; 6, 8, 9(all), HBJ/J. White; 10(t), Courtesy Celestron International; 10(b), HBJ/John Lei; 11(all), NASA; 12, R.B. Sanchez/The Stock Market; 13, Imtek Imagineering/Masterfile; 15, HBJ/J. White; 16, HBJ; 17,National Optical Astronomy Observatories; 18, JPL/NASA; 19,Julian Baum/SPL/Photo Researchers; 20, HBJ/J. White; 21, John Bova/Photo Researchers; 22(t), NASA; 22(b), HBJ/J. White; 24(t), Julian Baum/SPL/Photo Researchers; 24(b), HBJ/ J. White; 29, HBJ/Maria Paraskevas; 30, HBJ/Britt Runion. **CHAPTER 2:** 32, HBJ/Charlie Burton; 32–33(background), Dagmar Fabricius/Stock, Boston; 33, Robin Smith/ TSW; 36, Bob Higbee/Berg & Assoc.; 39, HBJ/J. White; 40, DiMaggio/Kalish/The Stock Market; 41, Bob Daemmrich/Stock, Boston; 42, David Young-Wolf/PhotoEdit; 44, E.R. Degginger; 45, Ray Shaw/The StockMarket; 48(t), Hugh Rogers/Monkmeyer Press; 48(b), HBJ/J. White; 50, Viesti Associates, Inc.; 51, HBJ/Earl Kogler; 52, William Johnson/ Stock, Boston; 53, Pat & Tom Leeson/Photo Researchers; 54, Luis Villota/The Stock Market; 55(t)(b), HBJ/J. White; 56, HBJ/Earl Kogler; 58(t), Paul Conklin/Monkmeyer Press; 58(c), HBJ/ Maria Paraskevas; 58(b), HBJ/Victoria Bowen; 59, HBJ/Maria Paraskevas; 60, E.R. Degginger; 65, Luis Castaneda/The Image Bank. **CHAPTER 3:** 68, HBJ/J. White; 68–69(background), Kirk Schlea/Berg & Assoc.; 68–69, Robert Beck; 70, HBJ/Victoria Bowen; 71, HBJ/Rob Downey; 72, Bob Daemmrich/Stock, Boston; 73, Peter Vadnai/The Stock Market; 74, Bob Daemmrich/TSW; 75, Paul Sutton/duomo; 76, David Young-Wolf/PhotoEdit; 78, HBJ/Earl Kogler; 79, Cary Wolinsky/Stock, Boston; 80(t), Edith G. Haun/Stock, Boston; 80(c), Ellis Herwig/Stock, Boston; 80(b), E.R. Degginger; 82, HBJ/J. White; 84, Kirk Schlea/Berg & Assoc.; 85, HBJ/David Krueger; 88, Guido Alberto Rossi/The Image Bank; 92, Ken Levine/Allsport; 93, Al Tielemans/duomo; 94, Alvis Upitis/The Image Bank; 95, Mitchell Layton/duomo; 96, Alan & Sandy Cary; 97, HBJ Photo; 98(l), Grafton Marshall Smith/The Image Bank; 98(r), 99, Tony Freeman/PhotoEdit; 100, Nancy Dudley/Stock, Boston; 105(l), David Young-Wolf/PhotoEdit; 105(l), Tony Freeman/PhotoEdit; 105(r), Kaz Morr/The Image Bank. **CHAPTER 4:** 108, HBJ/John Petrey; 108–109(background), 109, HBJ/J. White; 110, HBJ/Rob Downey; 111, E.R. Degginger; 112(t), HBJ/J. White; 112(b), Miro Vintoniv/The Picture Cube; 113, Tony Freeman/PhotoEdit; 114, HBJ/Terry Sinclair; 116(t), HBJ/Rob Downey; 116(b), HBJ/ J. White; 118, HBJ Photo; 120, HBJ/Maria Paraskevas; 121, Artsteet; 122, Sybil Shackman/Monkmeyer Press; 124, HBJ/Earl Kogler; 128, Paul Conklin/Monkmeyer Press; 130(t), HBJ/Maria Parashevas; 130(b), 131, HBJ/Downey; 132, HBJ/J. White; 134, Myrleen Ferguson/PhotoEdit; 135, E.R. Degginger; 136, 137, HBJ/Rob Downey; 138, HBJ/ Charlie Burton; 138(action figures), HBJ/Terry Sinclair; 139(t), Tony Freeman/PhotoEdit; 139(b), Peter Glass/Monkmeyer Press; 143, HBJ/Earl Kogler. **CHAPTER 5:** 146–147, 146–147(background), Jim Bush Photography; 148(t)(b), HBJ/Debi Harbin; 150, Sybil Shackman/Monkmeyer Press; 152(t)(c)(b), HBJ/Maria Paraskevas; 153, HBJ/ Debi Harbin; 154(t), HBJ/Maria Paraskevas; 154(b), 156, HBJ/J. White; 158, HBJ/Richard Haynes; 159, Jim Bush Photography, Inc.; 162(t), Julie Marcotte/Stock, Boston; 162(c), John Kelly/The Image Bank; 162(b), Grant V.Faint/The Image Bank; 163(l), Julie Marcotte/Stock, Boston; 163(r), Cary Wolinsky/Stock, Boston; 164, HBJ/Earl Kogler; 166, Bob Daemmrich/Stock, Boston; 168, 169, HBJ/J. White; 173, HBJ/Earl Kogler; 174, HBJ/J. White. **CHAPTER 6:** 176, Steve Niedorf/The Image Bank, 176–177(background), Neena M. Wilmot/Stock/Art Images; 177, HBJ/J. White; 178, Tony Freeman/ PhotoEdit; 180, D. Morrison/The Picture Cube; 181, Jose Carrillo/Stock, Boston; 182, Arnold J. Kaplan/The Picture Cube; 183, HBJ/J. White; 184, HBJ/Rob Downey; 186, HBJ/Maria Paraskevas; 187, Gabe Palmer/Mugshots; 188(t), Doug Plummer/ Photo Researchers; 188(b), Tom Myers; 189, Robert Marien/Ro-Ma Stock; 192(t), Frank Martin/TSW; 192(b), Steve Maines/Stock, Boston; 196, Bob Daemmrich/Stock, Boston; 198, HBJ/J. White; 203,HBJ/Maria Paraskevas. **CHAPTER 7:** 206, The George Yarrall Spectrum Quilt, The Kentucky Museum, Western Kentucky University, Bowling Green, Kentucky; 206–207(background), Alfred Hochrein/Berg & Assoc.; 207, Tom McCarthy/The Stock Solution; 208, 209, HBJ/Maria Paraskevas; 210(t), L.H. Mantell/The Stock Market; 210(c), Elizabeth Zuckerman/PhotoEdit; 210(b), James P. Rowan/TSW; 214, 216, HBJ/ J. White; 218, HBJ/Maria Paraskevas; 219, HBJ/Annette Stahl; 222, HBJ/Britt Runion; 224, HBJ/J. White; 226. HBJ/Earl Kogler; 227, Nancy Sheehan/The Picture Cube; 228(t), David Young-Wolff/PhotoEdit; 228(b), HBJ/Annette Stahl; 230(all), HBJ/Charlie Burton; 231, NASA; 232(t), Roy Morsch/The Stock Market; 232(b), William Johnson/Stock, Boston; 233(t)(b), HBJ/J. White; 237, HBJ/Maria Paraskevas. **CHAPTER 8:** 240, Don Johnson/The Stock Market; 240–241(background), Tom Tracy/The Stock Market; 240–241, HBJ/Richard Haynes; 242, HBJ/Britt Runion; 244, HBJ/ Richard Haynes; 246, HBJ/Debi Harbin; 247, HBJ/Maria Paraskevas; 248, Lawrence Migdale/Stock, Boston; 250, HBJ/Earl Kogler; 252(t)(b)(all), HBJ/J. White; 255(t), Romilly Lockyer/The Image Bank; 255(l), Ken Straiton/The Image Bank; 255(r), Marcel ISY-Schwart/The Image Bank; 256, Dick George/Tom Stack & Assoc.; 258, HBJ/J. White; 260(t), Susan Krutzler; 260(b), HBJ/Rodney Jones; 262, Bill Binzen/The Stock Market; 264, HBJ/Debi Harbin; 265, HBJ/Rob Downey; 266, 271(l), HBJ/J. White; 271(r), HBJ/Earl Kogler. **CHAPTER 9:** 274, Cy Furlan/Berg & Assoc.; 274–275(background), Alan J. Bedding/TSW; 275(t), E.R.Degginger; 275(b), Murray & Assoc./TSW; 276, HBJ/Debi Harbin; 278, 280, 281, HBJ/Maria Paraskevas; 285, HBJ/J. White; 288(t), HBJ/Debi Harbin; 288(b), HBJ/Debi Harbin; 292, Artstreet; 294(t)(b), HBJ/Rob Downey; 296, HBJ/Britt Runion; 298, 300, HBJ/J. White; 301, Aripi Duyck/The Image Bank; 302, HBJ/Debi Harbin; 304, HBJ/J. White; 306, 308, HBJ/Maria Paraskevas. **CHAPTER 10:** 316, HBJ/J. White; 316–317(background), Brian Parker/Tom Stack & Assoc.; 317, Jose Carrillo/Stock, Boston; 318, HBJ/Debi Harbin; 320, HBJ/J. White; 322, HBJ/Richard Haynes; 324, 325, HBJ/Rob Downey; 326(t), HBJ/Greg Leary; 326(b), HBJ/Maria Paraskevas; 328, HBJ/Rob Downey; 331, Eric Wheater/The Image Bank; 334(l), HBJ/Maria Paraskevas; 334(r), HBJ/Greg Leary; 336, Richard Hutchings/InfoEdit; 338(t)(b), HBJ/Britt Runion. **CHAPTER 11:** 346, HBJ/J. White; 346–347(background), Barton Stabler/The Image Bank; 347, UPI/Bettmann Newsphotos; 348,HBJ/Britt Runion; 350, HBJ/Debi Harbin; 352, HBJ/Rob Downey; 354(t), HBJ/ Britt Runion; 354(b), HBJ/Earl Kogler; 356, HBJ/Charlie Burton; 358(t), Tony Freeman/PhotoEdit; 358(b), Tony Freeman/PhotoEdit; 361, HBJ/Linda & David Phillips; 362, HBJ/J. White; 364, 366, HBJ/Richard Haynes; 368(t)(b), HBJ/Maria Paraskevas; 369(t) (b), HBJ/Britt Runion; 370, HBJ/Richard Haynes. **CHAPTER 12:** 378, Steven E. Sutton/duomo; 378–379(background), Paul J. Sutton/duomo; 379, Adam J. Stoltman/duomo; 380(t)(b)(all), HBJ/Victoria Bowen; 381(l)(r), HBJ/Maria Paraskevas; 382, Mike Powell/Allsport USA; 384, 385, HBJ/Richard Haynes; 386(r), HBJ/Maria Paraskevas; 386(r), VGV/duomo; 388, Steven E. Sutton/duomo; 389, HBJ/Annette Stahl; 390(t), Heinz Kluetmeier/Sports Illustrated; 390(b), HBJ/Rodney Jones; 391, HBJ/Maria Paraskevas; 394(t), Rick Stewart/Allsport USA; 394(b), David Young-Wolff/PhotoEdit; 395, Allsport USA; 396, 397, HBJ/Victoria Bowen; 398, Robert Tringali/Sportschrome, Inc.; 400, David Madison/duomo; 402, Steven E. Sutton/duomo. **CHAPTER 13:** 410, Hank Morgan/Photo Researchers; 410–411 (background), Ralph Oberlander/Stock, Boston; 411, TomStack/Tom Stack & Assoc.; 412(t) (b), HBJ/Maria Paraskevas; 412, HBJ/Victoria Bowen; 414, Richard Pasley/Stock, Boston; 416, Michael Salas/The Image Bank; 418, Steve Dunwell/The Image Bank; 422(t) (b), HBJ/Maria Paraskevas; 424(t), NASA; 424(b), E.R. Degginger; 425, Peter Menzel/Stock, Boston; 426, HBJ/J. White; 428(t), Mike Malyszko/Stock, Boston; 428(b Alan &Sandy Carey; 430, Bob Daemmrich/Stock, Boston; 435, HBJ/Britt Runion; 436, HBJ/J. White. **COMPUTER CONNECTION:** 438, Tim Bieber/The Image Bank; 438–439, HBJ/J. White; 439, Jon Feingersh/Tom Stack & Assoc.; 456(t), HBJ/J. White; 456(b)–H1, HBJ/Debi Harbin. **STUDENT HANDBOOK:** H1, HBJ/John Lei; H2, NASA; H3, HBJ/Annette Stahl; H4, HBJ/J. White; H5(t), Alan & Sandy Carey; H5(b), Alix Coleman/Grant Heilman; H6, HBJ/Burnell Caldwell; H7(all), HBJ/Chris Lawrey; H8, HBJ/Rob Downey; H10, HBJ/Victoria Bowen; H11, HBJ/Beverly Brosius; H12, HBJ/Richard Haynes; H14, John Michael/International Stock Photo; H18, U.S. Capitol Historical Society; H20, HBJ/Maria Paraskevas; H22, HBJ, Maria Paraskevas; H24, HBJ/Terry Sinclair; H26, U.S. Capitol Historical Society; H27(t), Pascal Rondeau/Allsport USA; H27(b), HBJ/Charlie Burton; H29, HBJ/Richard Haynes; H31, HBJ/Terry Sinclair.

ILLUSTRATOR CREDITS

Ernie Albanese: 355, 373; **Dave Blanchette:** 115, 120, 121, 122, 123, 124, 226, 227, 257, 266, 399; **Tim Bowers:** xv, 14, 26, 28, 46, 62, 64, 86, 102, 104, 140, 142, 160, 170, 172, 190, 200, 202, 220, 234, 236, 254, 268, 270, 290, 310, 312, 330, 340, 342, 360, 372, 374, 392, 404, 406, 420, 432, 434, M1; **Shirley Breuel:** 13, 18, 20, 35; **Sheila Braun:** 93, 101, 262; **Jane Chambless:** 228, 229, 235; **Suzanne Clee:** 320, 327; **William Colrus:** 61, 183, 245, 249, 251, 301, 323, 364–367; **Nancy Didion:** 57, 214, 217, 222, 223; **Eldon Doty:** xi, 34, 37, 43, 51; **Len Ebert:** 289, 292, 308, 319, 431; **Ruth Flanigan:** 48, 229, 254, 307; **Kathy Hendrickson:** 196, 224, 225, 297, 298; **Anne Kennedy:** 17, 49, 51, 76; **John Kilgrew:** 77, 211; **Loretta Krupinski:** 383, 390, 415, 419; **Polly Lewis:** 197, 210, 211, 212, 280; **Heather Meikenhous:** 82, 83, 94, 118, 119; **Susan Miller:** 12, 23; **Bill Ogden:** 3, 8, 9, 38, 56, 84, 93, 136, 137, 138, 159, 180, 185, 209; **Michael O'Reilly:** 299; **PC & F:** x, 276, 283–286, 300, 302, 306, 309; **Tom Powers:** 7; **Den Schofield:** 167, 194, 230, 231, 370; **Jean & Mov-sien Tseng:** 90; **George Ulrich:** 90, 168; **Lane Yerkes:** 199, 215, 263, 267, 293.

More Practice

CHAPTER 1

Lesson 1.1 *(pages 2–3)*

Use graph-paper models to help you answer each question.

1. How many more than 1,000 is 1,500?
2. What is 300 more than 700?

Here are some statements about 1,000. Write *true* or *false.*

3. There are more than 1,000 chairs in the classroom.

4. You can run fast for 1,000 seconds.

5. 1,000 dimes is greater than ten dollars.

Lesson 1.2 *(pages 4–5)*

Copy and complete.

1. $30 = \blacksquare$ tens
2. $700 = \blacksquare$ hundreds
3. $1,240 = \blacksquare$ tens
4. $21 = \blacksquare$ ones
5. $4,000 = \blacksquare$ hundreds
6. $70 = \blacksquare$ ones

Match each number with its value. Write the correct letter.

a. 9 tens   b. 76 hundreds   c. 19 hundreds

d. 467 tens   e. 500 ones   f. 42 tens

7. 1,900   8. 500   9. 7,600   10. 90   11. 420   12. 4,670

Lesson 1.3 *(pages 6–7)*

Express each number in two other ways.

1. three hundred forty
2. six thousand, three hundred eleven
3. 2,934
4. 832
5. 7,390
6. $8,000 + 500 + 20 + 3$

Lesson 1.4 *(pages 8–9)*

Each week the students in Mr. Sampson's English class must choose from four kinds of books to read. Use the table to solve Exercises 1–4.

1. How many students chose adventure books?

2. How many students chose poetry?

3. How many more students chose a biography than a mystery?

4. Which category was chosen the least number of times?

Categories of Books	
Biography	ЖЖ //
History	///
Poetry	ЖЖ
Mystery	//
Adventure	ЖЖ ЖЖ ////

Lesson 1.5 *(pages 10–11)*

Write the value of the digit 6 in each number.

1. 49,632　　2. 684,913　　3. 83,276　　4. 362,931　　5. 807,650

Express each number in two other ways.

6. thirty-three thousand, eight hundred one

7. two hundred thirty thousand, one hundred twenty

8. nine thousand, seven hundred sixty-four

Lesson 1.6 *(pages 12–13)*

Write the number that is 1,000,000 more.

1. 9,432,111　　2. 80,296,400　　3. 63,290,000　　4. 29,024,913

Write the number that is 1,000,000 less.

5. 1,293,180　　6. 40,864,971　　7. 27,288,640　　8. 51,335,702

Name the period shown by the blue digits.

9. 2,379,812　　10. 90,286,313　　11. 47,810,677　　12. 9,280,732

13. 4,691　　14. 513,678　　15. 705,811,542　　16. 7,895,061

Lesson 1.7 (pages 16–17)

Compare. Write $<$, $>$, or $=$ for ●.

1. 3,120 ● 1,854
2. 2,612 ● 3,512
3. 798 ● 789
4. 7,894 ● 7,893
5. 9,002 ● 9,007
6. 482 ● 482
7. 6,438,298 ● 6,483,293
8. 3,982,463 ● 3,982,436

Write the numbers, using the symbol that means *is less than.*

9. 92; 29
10. 423; 432
11. 32; 23
12. 4,289; 4,928
13. 321; 362
14. 8,240; 8,204
15. 612; 621
16. 1,293; 1,393

Write the numbers, using the symbol that means *is greater than.*

17. 411; 401
18. 783; 703
19. 265; 256
20. 5,250; 5,550
21. 4,301; 4,300
22. 9,100; 9,010
23. 429; 492
24. 6,023; 6,320

Using the number 12,949, write the number that is

25. 1 more.
26. 10 more.
27. 100 more.
28. 10 less.
29. 1,000 more.
30. 1,000 less.
31. 1 less.
32. 100 less.

Lesson 1.8 (pages 18–19)

Write each group of numbers in order from least to greatest.

1. 635; 630; 640
2. 3,706; 3,760; 3,710; 3,701
3. 289; 265; 286; 270
4. 8,418; 9,460; 1,664
5. 12,210; 12,201; 13,100; 13,101
6. 1,062; 1,026; 1,260
7. 13,420; 13,204; 14,420
8. 80,912; 81,209; 82,921
9. 42,856; 43,012; 42,658

Choose the letter that describes how each group of numbers is ordered.

a. from least to greatest
b. from greatest to least

10. 8,920; 8,290; 7,920
11. 492; 534; 643; 652
12. 51,281; 51,218; 51,208; 50,999
13. 82; 89; 101; 153
14. 673; 669; 658; 649
15. 17,060; 17,600; 17,606

Lesson 1.9 *(pages 20–21)*

Complete the pattern.

1. □ □ △ △ ○ ○ □ □ △ △ ○ ○ ___?___

2. □ □ □ □ □ □ □ □ ___?___

3. ⊂ ∪ ⊃ ∩ ⊂ ∪ ⊃ ∩ ⊂ ___?___

4. □ ∇ □ △ □ ∇ □ △ ___?___

Linda has created a code using numbers. When she says 4, the answer is 15. When she says 10, the answer is 21. When she says 35, the answer is 46.

5. What is the pattern?

6. What is the answer when she says 9?

7. What is the answer when she says 15?

8. If the answer is 44, what did she say?

Lesson 1.10 *(pages 22–23)*

Write the missing ordinal numbers.

1. 41st, 42nd, ▪, ▪, 45th

2. 201st, ▪, ▪, 204th, 205th

Use the calendar to answer each question.

3. What is the date of the third Wednesday?

4. What is the date of the day before the second Tuesday?

5. What is the date of the day after the first Saturday?

November						
Sun	Mon	Tue	Wed	Thu	Fri	Sat
						1
2	3	4	5	6	7	8
9	10	11	12	13	14	15
16	17	18	19	20	21	22
23	24	25	26	27	28	29
30						

Lesson 1.11 *(pages 24–25)*

Estimate by rounding to the nearest ten cents and to the nearest dollar.

1. $10.19
2. $0.73
3. $62.91
4. $0.84
5. $29.63

Estimate by rounding to the nearest thousand or to the nearest ten dollars.

6. 2,500
7. $15.91
8. 48,291
9. $769.34
10. $219.38

CHAPTER 2

Lesson 2.1 *(pages 34–35)*

Find the sum. Name the addition-fact strategy.

1. $3 + 4 = \blacksquare$ **2.** $7 + 0 = \blacksquare$ **3.** $6 + 7 = \blacksquare$ **4.** $8 + 8 = \blacksquare$

5. $7 + 3 = \blacksquare$ **6.** $8 + 0 = \blacksquare$ **7.** $5 + 5 = \blacksquare$ **8.** $11 + 3 = \blacksquare$

Find the sum.

9. $6 + 3 = \blacksquare$ **10.** $12 + 0 = \blacksquare$ **11.** $6 + 6 = \blacksquare$ **12.** $5 + 6 = \blacksquare$

13.	**14.**	**15.**	**16.**	**17.**	**18.**
8	4	9	6	8	9
+9	+0	+1	+2	+4	+3

19.	**20.**	**21.**	**22.**	**23.**	**24.**
6	9	3	5	1	4
+0	+9	+6	+3	+6	+5

Lesson 2.2 *(pages 36–37)*

Find the sum. Check by grouping the addends differently.

1. $(8 + 1) + 7 = \blacksquare$ **2.** $2 + (3 + 6) = \blacksquare$ **3.** $8 + 3 + (7 + 2) = \blacksquare$

4. $(4 + 7) + 8 = \blacksquare$ **5.** $5 + (6 + 4) = \blacksquare$ **6.** $(7 + 2) + (3 + 6) = \blacksquare$

Look for tens. Find the sum.

7.	**8.**	**9.**	**10.**	**11.**	**12.**
1	3	5	6	2	8
8	4	9	8	7	4
+9	+7	+5	+4	+8	+6

Lesson 2.3 *(pages 38–39)*

Estimate the sum by using front-end and rounding methods.
Then use a calculator to find which estimate is closer to the
exact answer.

1.	**2.**	**3.**	**4.**	**5.**
114	$9.86	$10.42	803	$4.19
+537	+ 3.12	+ 3.04	+591	+ 6.83

6. $598 + 402 + 187 = \blacksquare$ **7.** $\$3.98 + \$7.04 + \$2.18 = \blacksquare$

Lesson 2.4 *(pages 40–41)*

Solve by drawing a picture.

1. Anna, Pablo, Dirk, and Heather sit in the same row. Anna sits in the second seat. Anna sits between Pablo and Heather. Dirk sits next to Pablo. In what seat does Dirk sit?

2. Four students have birthdays in October. Jason's birthday comes before Rodney's. Kristin's birthday comes between Rodney's and Jason's. Melinda's birthday comes after Rodney's. Whose birthday comes first?

3. Henry, Eric, Mary Jo, and Sue Ellen are standing in line for lunch. Henry is just behind Eric. Mary Jo is between Henry and Sue Ellen. Who is first in line?

4. Four students live on the same street near Piney Elementary. Pedro's house is farther from school than Tiffany's. Jim's house is between Pedro's and Tiffany's. Tiffany's house is farther from school than Ny's. Whose house is farthest from school?

Lesson 2.5 *(pages 42–43)*

Find the sum. Circle the columns in which you needed to regroup.

| 1. 34 +63 | 2. 84 +15 | 3. 56 +24 | 4. 34 +49 | 5. 74 +19 | 6. 29 +39 |

Lesson 2.6 *(pages 44–45)*

Find the sum. Circle the columns in which you needed to regroup.

| 1. 241 +753 | 2. 375 +506 | 3. 520 +369 | 4. $4.73 + 2.85 | 5. 425 +182 | 6. $3.65 + 1.23 |

Lesson 2.7 *(pages 48–49)*

Find the sum.

| 1. 24 51 +13 | 2. 836 979 + 13 | 3. 670 580 + 66 | 4. 94 374 +667 | 5. $ 1.98 42.06 + 9.62 | 6. 8,291 1,041 + 312 |

7. $909 + 117 + 283 + 2,104 = \blacksquare$

8. $269 + 348 + 711 + 98 = \blacksquare$

Lesson 2.8 *(pages 50–51)*

Estimate the difference by rounding.

1. 529
    −347

2. 652
    −275

3. $3.19
    − 1.83

4. $17.86
    − 8.15

5. 863
    −491

6. 7,685
    −2,594

7. 634
    −295

8. $7.36
    − 4.88

9. $16.34
    − 7.92

10. $8.12
    − 1.51

11. 3,493
    −1,507

12. 2,838
    −1,217

13. $12,107 - 6,212 = $ ■

14. $\$2,913 - \$151.04 = $ ■

15. $38,420 - 999 = $ ■

Lesson 2.9 *(pages 52–53)*

Find the difference.

1. 93
    −21

2. 64
    −59

3. 66
    −34

4. 70
    −65

5. 76
    −47

6. 95
    −69

7. 85
    −38

8. 68
    −61

9. 84
    −54

10. 56
    −37

11. 99
    −78

12. 92
    −58

13. $59 - 21 = $ ■

14. $38 - 17 = $ ■

15. $68 - 49 = $ ■

16. $84 - 15 = $ ■

17. $78 - 40 = $ ■

18. $91 - 32 = $ ■

Lesson 2.10 *(pages 54–55)*

Find the difference.

1. 582
    −350

2. $6.39
    − 3.52

3. 498
    −259

4. 661
    −490

5. 319
    −224

6. $7.04
    − 3.02

7. $9.26
    − 1.73

8. $6.53
    − 5.16

9. 875
    −389

10. 712
    −114

11. 545
    −253

12. $7.46
    − 6.97

13. $395 - 162 = $ ■

14. $757 - 429 = $ ■

15. $882 - 491 = $ ■

16. $452 - 189 = $ ■

17. $905 - 611 = $ ■

18. $614 - 427 = $ ■

19. $520 - 276 = $ ■

20. $213 - 99 = $ ■

21. $333 - 299 = $ ■

Lesson 2.11 *(pages 56–57)*

Use the table to answer the questions.

1. Susan has $5.00 to spend for lunch. List the different combinations of lunches that can be made by selecting one item from each category.

Lunch Menu		
Entrées	Turkey Sandwich	$3.19
	Stuffed Potato	$2.75
Side Orders	Tossed Salad	$1.43
	Fruit	$0.85
Beverages	Milk	$0.75
	Juice	$1.00

2. How much more money would she need to buy the sandwich, salad, and juice?

3. How much change would Susan receive if she ordered the least expensive item from each category?

Lesson 2.12 *(pages 58–59)*

Find the difference.

1. $3.00
   − 0.59

2. $10.00
   − 5.67

3. 600
   −415

4. 4,000
   − 298

5. $80.00
   − 62.81

6. 2,500
   − 759

7. $5.90
   − 3.09

8. 607
   −169

9. $23.00
   − 7.59

10. 900
    −892

11. 717 − 409 = ■

12. 307 − 108 = ■

13. 8,000 − 1,908 = ■

Lesson 2.13 *(pages 60–61)*

First, estimate the sum or difference. Then, use a calculator or pencil and paper to find the exact answer.

1. 3,805
   +4,778

2. 5,697
   −5,286

3. 17,804
   − 5,921

4. 28,358
   + 4,629

5. 4,070
   −3,648

6. 9,832
   +7,045

7. 78,906
   +43,697

8. 27,025
   −14,892

9. 5,093
   − 785

10. 41,005
    − 1,426

11. 96,421 + 3,592 = ■

12. 13,572 − 4,905 = ■

13. 63,000 − 14,521 = ■

CHAPTER 3

Lesson 3.1 (pages 70–71)

Write three other facts for each fact family.

1. $12 \div 6 = 2$
2. $3 \times 8 = 24$
3. $35 \div 5 = 7$
4. $6 \times 3 = 18$

Lesson 3.2 (pages 72–73)

Find the product.

1. $\begin{array}{r} 8 \\ \times 3 \\ \hline \end{array}$
2. $\begin{array}{r} 2 \\ \times 4 \\ \hline \end{array}$
3. $\begin{array}{r} 3 \\ \times 2 \\ \hline \end{array}$
4. $\begin{array}{r} 5 \\ \times 2 \\ \hline \end{array}$
5. $\begin{array}{r} 3 \\ \times 7 \\ \hline \end{array}$
6. $\begin{array}{r} 2 \\ \times 2 \\ \hline \end{array}$
7. $\begin{array}{r} 9 \\ \times 2 \\ \hline \end{array}$

8. $\begin{array}{r} 6 \\ \times 3 \\ \hline \end{array}$
9. $\begin{array}{r} 2 \\ \times 6 \\ \hline \end{array}$
10. $\begin{array}{r} 7 \\ \times 2 \\ \hline \end{array}$
11. $\begin{array}{r} 3 \\ \times 8 \\ \hline \end{array}$
12. $\begin{array}{r} 3 \\ \times 4 \\ \hline \end{array}$
13. $\begin{array}{r} 2 \\ \times 8 \\ \hline \end{array}$
14. $\begin{array}{r} 3 \\ \times 3 \\ \hline \end{array}$

Lesson 3.3 (pages 74–75)

Find the product.

1. $\begin{array}{r} 4 \\ \times 4 \\ \hline \end{array}$
2. $\begin{array}{r} 5 \\ \times 2 \\ \hline \end{array}$
3. $\begin{array}{r} 7 \\ \times 4 \\ \hline \end{array}$
4. $\begin{array}{r} 6 \\ \times 5 \\ \hline \end{array}$
5. $\begin{array}{r} 3 \\ \times 4 \\ \hline \end{array}$
6. $\begin{array}{r} 5 \\ \times 7 \\ \hline \end{array}$
7. $\begin{array}{r} 4 \\ \times 8 \\ \hline \end{array}$

8. $\begin{array}{r} 6 \\ \times 4 \\ \hline \end{array}$
9. $\begin{array}{r} 5 \\ \times 8 \\ \hline \end{array}$
10. $\begin{array}{r} 9 \\ \times 4 \\ \hline \end{array}$
11. $\begin{array}{r} 4 \\ \times 5 \\ \hline \end{array}$
12. $\begin{array}{r} 5 \\ \times 3 \\ \hline \end{array}$
13. $\begin{array}{r} 5 \\ \times 5 \\ \hline \end{array}$
14. $\begin{array}{r} 5 \\ \times 9 \\ \hline \end{array}$

Lesson 3.4 (pages 76–77)

Write **a, b, c,** or **d** to tell which property is shown.

a. Order Property   **b.** Property of One   **c.** Zero Property   **d.** Grouping Property

1. $1 \times 7 = 7$
2. $5 \times (7 \times 2) = (5 \times 7) \times 2$
3. $8 \times 0 = 0$

4. $6 \times 3 = 3 \times 6$
5. $(8 \times 2) \times 4 = 8 \times (2 \times 4)$
6. $5 \times 0 = 0$

Use the multiplication properties to solve.

7. $4 \times 5 = 20$
$5 \times 4 = \blacksquare$
8. $2 \times 9 = 18$
$9 \times 2 = \blacksquare$
9. $(6 \times 1) \times 2 = 12$
$6 \times (1 \times 2) = \blacksquare$
10. $9 \times 0 = 0$
$5 \times 0 = \blacksquare$

11. $(2 \times 3) \times (3 \times 2) = \blacksquare$
12. $1 \times (693 \times 1) = \blacksquare$
13. $(586 \times 0) \times 887 = \blacksquare$

Lesson 3.5 *(pages 78–79)*

If the problem has too little information, write what fact is missing. If the problem has too much information, tell what fact is not needed. Solve the problem if you can.

1. John wins 4 bags of marbles with 9 marbles in each bag. He also wins 3 boxes of pencils. How many marbles does he win?

2. Wednesday is Scout Day at the fair. There are 8 Brownie troops from Northridge Elementary and 6 Brownie troops from Concord Elementary. How many Brownie Scouts go to the fair?

3. The owner of a concession stand ordered 600 hot dog buns and 800 hamburger buns. How many cases of each did he order?

4. There are 8 cars on the space shuttle ride. Each car holds 6 people. José rides the space shuttle 4 times. How many people can the ride carry?

Lesson 3.6 *(pages 80–81)*

Find the product.

1. 7 $\times 3$	2. 4 $\times 6$	3. 6 $\times 7$	4. 7 $\times 7$	5. 5 $\times 6$	6. 7 $\times 2$	7. 6 $\times 8$

8. $7 \times 5 = \blacksquare$ 9. $3 \times 6 = \blacksquare$ 10. $7 \times 8 = \blacksquare$ 11. $9 \times 6 = \blacksquare$

Lesson 3.7 *(pages 82–83)*

Find the product.

1. 8 $\times 7$	2. 9 $\times 3$	3. 8 $\times 9$	4. 9 $\times 9$	5. 5 $\times 8$	6. 4 $\times 9$	7. 8 $\times 3$

8. $6 \times 9 = \blacksquare$ 9. $8 \times 8 = \blacksquare$ 10. $8 \times 2 = \blacksquare$ 11. $9 \times 5 = \blacksquare$

Lesson 3.8 *(pages 84–85)*

Find the product.

1. 6 $\times 3$	2. 9 $\times 7$	3. 8 $\times 4$	4. 5 $\times 6$	5. 7 $\times 7$	6. 4 $\times 6$	7. 2 $\times 9$

8. $7 \times 3 = \blacksquare$ 9. $2 \times 9 = \blacksquare$ 10. $8 \times 8 = \blacksquare$ 11. $6 \times 9 = \blacksquare$

Lesson 3.9 *(pages 88–89)*

Complete. Write another number sentence to show the inverse operation.

1. $28 \div 7 = \blacksquare$
2. $8 \times 6 = \blacksquare$
3. $54 \div 6 = \blacksquare$
4. $20 \div 5 = \blacksquare$

Find the missing factor.

5. $4 \times \blacksquare = 36$
6. $\blacksquare \times 3 = 27$
7. $\blacksquare \times 8 = 64$
8. $5 \times \blacksquare = 30$

9. $7 \times \blacksquare = 21$
10. $\blacksquare \times 4 = 24$
11. $\blacksquare \times 9 = 63$
12. $\blacksquare \times 4 = 16$

Lesson 3.10 *(pages 90–91)*

Complete the number sentence.

1. $4 \times \blacksquare = 28$
2. $6 \times \blacksquare = 36$
3. $\blacksquare \times 8 = 56$
4. $4 \times \blacksquare = 32$

Find the quotient.

5. $2\overline{)16}$
6. $3\overline{)24}$
7. $2\overline{)8}$
8. $3\overline{)12}$
9. $2\overline{)14}$
10. $3\overline{)27}$

11. $2\overline{)10}$
12. $3\overline{)15}$
13. $3\overline{)21}$
14. $2\overline{)6}$
15. $2\overline{)18}$
16. $3\overline{)6}$

Lesson 3.11 *(pages 92–93)*

Find the missing factor.

1. $4 \times \blacksquare = 20$
2. $\blacksquare \times 7 = 28$
3. $9 \times \blacksquare = 45$
4. $\blacksquare \times 8 = 32$

Find the quotient.

5. $40 \div 5 = \blacksquare$
6. $12 \div 4 = \blacksquare$
7. $30 \div 5 = \blacksquare$
8. $36 \div 4 = \blacksquare$

Complete the table.

9.

Divide by 4	
12	3
16	$\blacksquare$
8	$\blacksquare$
32	$\blacksquare$
4	$\blacksquare$

10.

Divide by 4	
24	6
0	$\blacksquare$
36	$\blacksquare$
20	$\blacksquare$
28	$\blacksquare$

11.

Divide by 5	
25	5
15	$\blacksquare$
40	$\blacksquare$
35	$\blacksquare$
0	$\blacksquare$

12.

Divide by 5	
45	9
30	$\blacksquare$
5	$\blacksquare$
20	$\blacksquare$
10	$\blacksquare$

Lesson 3.12 (pages 94–95)

Write a number sentence and solve.

1. Liza reads an average of 4 biographies a month. How many biographies does Liza read in 6 months?

2. José collects baseball cards. He collected 58 cards the first week, 37 the second week, and 64 the third week. How many cards did he collect?

3. Shelly has 1 dozen oatmeal muffins to share with her chess club. There are 5 other members. How many will she give to each member?

4. Joey bought supplies for his lawn service. He paid $3.19 for a gas can, $8.69 for hedge clippers, and $2.99 for work gloves. How much did he spend in all?

Lesson 3.13 (pages 96–97)

Find the quotient.

1. $5 \div 5 = $ ▨

2. $28 \div 1 = $ ▨

3. $0 \div 6 = $ ▨

4. $12 \div 1 = $ ▨

5. $37 \div 1 = $ ▨

6. $0 \div 16 = $ ▨

7. $7 \div 7 = $ ▨

8. $49 \div 1 = $ ▨

9. $9\overline{)0}$

10. $6\overline{)6}$

11. $4\overline{)0}$

12. $1\overline{)4}$

13. $7\overline{)7}$

14. $1\overline{)27}$

Lesson 3.14 (pages 98–99)

Complete the number sentence.

1. ▨ $\times 7 = 42$

2. ▨ $\times 6 = 36$

3. $6 \times$ ▨ $= 54$

4. $7 \times$ ▨ $= 21$

Find the quotient.

5. $7\overline{)49}$

6. $3\overline{)18}$

7. $7\overline{)35}$

8. $6\overline{)24}$

9. $4\overline{)32}$

10. $7\overline{)14}$

11. $54 \div 9 = $ ▨

12. $28 \div 7 = $ ▨

13. $56 \div 7 = $ ▨

14. $30 \div 5 = $ ▨

Lesson 3.15 (pages 100–101)

Find the quotient.

1. $9\overline{)9}$

2. $9\overline{)36}$

3. $8\overline{)16}$

4. $9\overline{)36}$

5. $9\overline{)45}$

6. $8\overline{)64}$

7. $9\overline{)18}$

8. $8\overline{)56}$

9. $8\overline{)40}$

10. $8\overline{)72}$

11. $8\overline{)8}$

12. $9\overline{)81}$

13. $8\overline{)24}$

14. $9\overline{)63}$

15. $7\overline{)42}$

16. $8\overline{)48}$

17. $6\overline{)54}$

18. $7\overline{)56}$

CHAPTER 4

Lesson 4.1 *(pages 110–111)*

Write the time in two different ways.

1.    2.    3.    4.

5. a quarter past six   6. ten thirty-five   7. four forty   8. one twenty-eight

Lesson 4.2 *(pages 112–113)*

Write the time by using numbers and A.M. or P.M.

1. The restaurant starts serving breakfast.   2. There is heavy traffic after work.   3. The newspaper is delivered.   4. The movie matinee starts.

      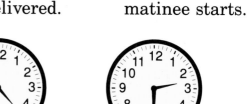

Write A.M. or P.M. to complete each sentence.

5. Go to gym class at 1:45 ■.

6. Eat lunch at 12:14 ■.

7. Practice baseball at 4:30 ■.

8. Wake up at 7:45 ■.

Lesson 4.3 *(pages 114–115)*

Choose the most reasonable unit of time for each
(sec, min, hr, d, wk, mo, yr).

1. School lasts about 8 ■.

2. It takes 4 ■ to earn a college degree.

3. It takes about 10 ■ to walk across the street.

4. To make a sandwich takes about 5 ■.

5. There are about 4 ■ in one month.

6. The school year lasts about 10 ■.

Lesson 4.4 *(pages 116–117)*

Complete the table. Remember to use A.M. and P.M. correctly.

Activity	Starting Time	Ending Time	Elapsed Time
1. Eating lunch	12:12 P.M.	12:47 P.M.	■
2. Soccer game	11:30 A.M.	■	2 hr 15 min
3. Art class	■	12:56 P.M.	1 hr 11 min

Lesson 4.5 *(pages 118–119)*

Use the calendars to answer Exercises 1–4.

1. How many days have passed between January 19 and February 10?

2. How many weeks have passed between March 4 and March 25?

3. What is the date of the third Friday in April?

4. How many Sundays are there in January?

JANUARY						
S	M	T	W	T	F	S
					1	2
3	4	5	6	7	8	9
10	11	12	13	14	15	16
17	18	19	20	21	22	23
24	25	26	27	28	29	30
31						

FEBRUARY						
S	M	T	W	T	F	S
	1	2	3	4	5	6
7	8	9	10	11	12	13
14	15	16	17	18	19	20
21	22	23	24	25	26	27
28	29					

MARCH						
S	M	T	W	T	F	S
		1	2	3	4	5
6	7	8	9	10	11	12
13	14	15	16	17	18	19
20	21	22	23	24	25	26
27	28	29	30	31		

APRIL						
S	M	T	W	T	F	S
					1	2
3	4	5	6	7	8	9
10	11	12	13	14	15	16
17	18	19	20	21	22	23
24	25	26	27	28	29	30

Lesson 4.6 *(pages 120–121)*

Use the schedule to answer Exercises 1–3.

1. Sara wants to take the tour on Friday. What time must she start if she wants to return by 11:00 A.M.?

2. How many tours are available on Saturday?

3. The 8:10 A.M. tour is 11 minutes late. What time will it now end?

Factory Tour Schedule		
Starting Time	Ending Time	Days
6:22 A.M.	10:00 A.M.	Sunday only
7:20 A.M.	10:56 A.M.	Daily except Saturday and Sunday
7:50 A.M.	11:30 A.M.	Saturday and Sunday only
8:10 A.M.	11:48 A.M.	Daily
8:40 A.M.	12:20 P.M.	Daily except Sunday

Lesson 4.7 (pages 122–123)

Use the frequency table to answer Exercises 1–3.

1. How many cans were collected in all?

2. On which day were the fewest cans collected? the most?

3. How many more cans were collected on Wednesday than on Friday?

Recycling Project	
Day	**Number of Cans Collected**
Monday	98
Tuesday	140
Wednesday	219
Thursday	154
Friday	87
Saturday	256

Lesson 4.8 (pages 124–125)

Use the pictograph to answer Exercises 1–2.

1. Who read the fewest books?

2. How many books did Sara read? Joe? Karl?

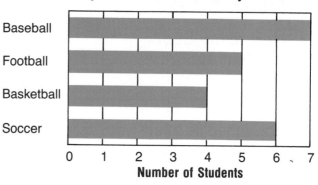

Lesson 4.9 (pages 128–129)

Use the bar graph to answer Exercises 1–3.

1. Which sport was chosen by the most students? the fewest?

2. How many students chose football? baseball?

3. Did more students choose soccer or basketball?

Sports Activities Chosen by Students

Lesson 4.10 (pages 130–131)

Use the frequency table. Make a bar graph.

Name	Heartbeats per Minute
Hector	76
Frank	72
Dawn	74
Steve	75
Julie	82

Lesson 4.11 *(pages 132–133)*

Use the map of the state fair to write the ordered pair for each attraction.

1. Food Booths

2. First-aid station

3. Rides and Games

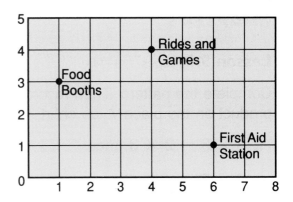

Lesson 4.12 *(pages 134–135)*

Use the line graph to answer Exercises 1–2.

1. Which day had the highest average temperature? the lowest?

2. What was the average temperature on Monday? on Tuesday?

AVERAGE TEMPERATURE FOR ONE WEEK IN JANUARY

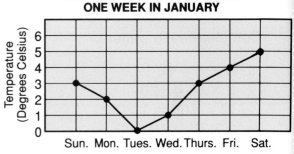

Lesson 4.13 *(pages 136–137)*

This table shows the number of sandwiches that were sold in a week. Use the data to make a line graph.

Day	Number of Sandwiches Sold
Monday	45
Tuesday	20
Wednesday	15
Thursday	50
Friday	35

Lesson 4.14 *(pages 138–139)*

Use the graph to answer Exercises 1–2.

1. What kind of graph is shown?

2. How many more students are on the baseball team than on the football team?

School Teams	Each 🚶 stands for 10 students.	
Baseball	🚶 🚶 🚶 🚶 🚶 🚶	
Football	🚶 🚶	
Basketball	🚶 🚶 🚶 🚶 🚶	

CHAPTER 5

Lesson 5.1 *(pages 148–149)*

Complete the pattern. Then record the product on the place-value chart.

1. $2 \times 3 = 2 \times 3$ ones

2. $2 \times \blacksquare = 2 \times 3$ tens

3. $2 \times 300 = 2 \times \blacksquare$

4. $2 \times \blacksquare = 2 \times \blacksquare$

Place-Value Chart			
Thousands	Hundreds	Tens	Ones
			$\blacksquare$
		$\blacksquare$	$\blacksquare$
	6	0	0
6 ,	0	0	0

Complete each pattern.

5. $3 \times 4 = \blacksquare$
   $3 \times \blacksquare = 120$
   $\blacksquare \times 400 = 1{,}200$
   $3 \times \blacksquare = 12{,}000$

6. $5 \times 4 = \blacksquare$
   $5 \times \blacksquare = 200$
   $\blacksquare \times 400 = 2{,}000$
   $5 \times \blacksquare = 20{,}000$

7. $6 \times 8 = \blacksquare$
   $6 \times \blacksquare = 480$
   $\blacksquare \times 800 = 4{,}800$
   $6 \times \blacksquare = 48{,}000$

Lesson 5.2 *(pages 150–151)*

Estimate the product. Name the strategy that you used.

1. $8 \times 413 = \blacksquare$

2. $4 \times 5{,}124 = \blacksquare$

3. $6 \times 39 = \blacksquare$

4. $8 \times 294 = \blacksquare$

Estimate the product.

5. 87
   $\times\ 3$

6. 621
   $\times\ \ 4$

7. 49
   $\times\ 7$

8. 647
   $\times\ \ 6$

9. $1{,}789$
   $\times\ \ \ \ 5$

10. $8{,}019$
    $\times\ \ \ \ 2$

11. 964
    $\times\ \ 8$

12. $2{,}829$
    $\times\ \ \ \ 4$

13. 646
    $\times\ \ 2$

14. $3{,}912$
    $\times\ \ \ \ 5$

Lesson 5.3 *(pages 152–153)*

Find each product using place-value blocks on a mat and the partial-product method.

1.

H	T	O
5	6	5
$\times$		3

2.
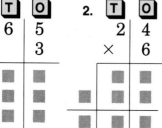

T	O
2	4
$\times$	6

3.

H	T	O
1	8	4
$\times$		2

4.

T	O
3	9
$\times$	4

5.

H	T	O
6	1	2
$\times$		6

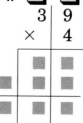
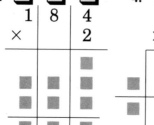
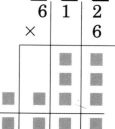

Lesson 5.4 *(pages 154–155)*

Estimate the product.

1. 37
× 4

2. 55
× 3

3. 44
× 6

4. 79
× 3

5. 86
× 2

Find the product.

6. 85
× 5

7. 43
× 7

8. 61
× 3

9. 76
× 5

10. 23
× 4

11. 32
× 6

12. 18
× 9

13. 54
× 8

14. 95
× 4

15. 49
× 7

16. 67
× 3

17. 87
× 2

18. 28
× 8

19. 16
× 5

20. 94
× 6

21. $5 \times 64 =$ ■

22. $7 \times 17 =$ ■

23. $8 \times 49 =$ ■

24. $3 \times 78 =$ ■

Lesson 5.5 *(pages 156–157)*

Find the product.

1. 413
× 2

2. 243
× 4

3. 326
× 3

4. 146
× 5

5. 182
× 4

6. 170
× 5

7. 192
× 3

8. 405
× 2

9. 315
× 3

10. 248
× 4

11. 481
× 2

12. 119
× 7

13. 109
× 8

14. 265
× 3

15. 188
× 5

16. $(2 \times 1) \times 416 =$ ■

17. $3 \times (111 \times 3) =$ ■

18. $(2 \times 3) \times 110 =$ ■

19. $4 \times (322 \times 5) =$ ■

20. $1 \times (4 \times 524) =$ ■

21. $(313 \times 2) \times 2 =$ ■

22. The carousel can carry 115 people. How many people will ride if it is filled 5 times?

23. The roller coaster can carry 132 people. How many people will ride if it is filled 6 times?

Lesson 5.6 *(pages 158–159)*

Solve. Make a flowchart and *work backward*.

1. Tyrel collects baseball cards for a hobby. If you take the number of baseball cards he collected last week, add 25, and divide by 3, the result is 23. How many baseball cards did Tyrel collect?

2. Darcy and her sister, Sue, went shopping. Darcy bought a game for $8.98 and a notebook for $1.29. Then Sue gave her $3.00. Darcy had $4.83 left. How much did Darcy have before she went shopping?

3. The Edgewood Elementary School put on 5 performances of their school play. If you take the number of people who attended all 5 performances, add 497, and subtract 21, the result is 1,372. How many people attended the play?

4. Miko baked apple muffins to serve as refreshments for the monthly meeting of the science club. If you take the number of muffins she baked, add 46, and divide by 11, the result is 8. How many muffins did Miko bake?

Lesson 5.7 *(pages 162–163)*

Estimate the product.

1. $7 \times 685 = $ ■

2. $4 \times 309 = $ ■

3. $8 \times 47 = $ ■

4. $5 \times 353 = $ ■

Find the product.

5. 513
   × 7

6. 209
   × 8

7. 820
   × 4

8. 83
   × 5

9. 88
   × 8

10. 47
    × 8

11. 783
    × 6

12. 341
    × 4

13. 64
    × 7

14. 657
    × 9

Lesson 5.8 *(pages 164–165)*

Estimate. Then use a calculator to find the product.

1. 2,318
   × 5

2. 1,703
   × 2

3. 6,129
   × 4

4. 3,199
   × 3

5. 8,256
   × 2

6. 7,429
   × 3

7. 1,925
   × 6

8. 2,489
   × 7

9. 4,964
   × 5

10. 5,721
    × 2

Lesson 5.9 (pages 166–167)

Tell which method of computation you would use to solve the
problem. Write *mental math, paper and pencil,* or *calculator.*
Then, solve.

1. There were 5 buses that could
   hold 20 students each. How many
   students could go on the field
   trip if all 5 buses were used?

2. What if the buses could hold
   23 students each? How many
   students could go on the field
   trip now?

3. The cost of the field trip is
   $12.97 for each student. What is
   the total cost if 137 students
   attend the outing?

4. Each student was to contribute
   $5.00 toward the cost of the trip.
   If 100 students were going on the
   trip, how much money would
   they contribute in all?

Lesson 5.10 (pages 168–169)

Estimate by rounding to the next higher dime or dollar. Then
find the product.

1. $4 \times \$3.15 = $ ■

2. $8 \times \$1.62 = $ ■

3. $5 \times \$0.37 = $ ■

4. $2 \times \$0.41 = $ ■

5. $9 \times \$1.69 = $ ■

6. $6 \times \$8.14 = $ ■

7. $7 \times \$2.55 = $ ■

8. $3 \times \$4.15 = $ ■

9. $9 \times \$7.32 = $ ■

Find the product.

10. $1.82
    × 2

11. $0.56
    × 8

12. $3.19
    × 5

13. $6.09
    × 4

14. $0.94
    × 3

15. $12.43
    × 2

16. $5.19
    × 6

17. $14.52
    × 3

18. $0.76
    × 9

19. $6.55
    × 5

20. $10.22
    × 4

21. $17.23
    × 2

22. $7.58
    × 5

23. $0.66
    × 8

24. $15.93
    × 4

25. $18.39
    × 4

26. $0.73
    × 7

27. $4.76
    × 9

28. $1.59
    × 2

29. $13.24
    × 5

CHAPTER 6

Lesson 6.1 (pages 178–179)

Copy and complete. Use a basic fact to help you.

1. $3 \times 30 = \blacksquare$
   $30 \times 30 = \blacksquare$
   $30 \times 300 = \blacksquare$

2. $10 \times 8 = \blacksquare$
   $100 \times 8 = \blacksquare$
   $100 \times 80 = \blacksquare$

3. $5 \times 60 = \blacksquare$
   $50 \times 60 = \blacksquare$
   $500 \times 600 = \blacksquare$

Find the product.

4. $40 \times 40 = \blacksquare$

5. $10 \times 8,000 = \blacksquare$

6. $5,000 \times 30 = \blacksquare$

7. $1,000 \times 90 = \blacksquare$

8. $\begin{array}{r} 50 \\ \times 10 \\ \hline \end{array}$

9. $\begin{array}{r} 6,000 \\ \times \quad 200 \\ \hline \end{array}$

10. $\begin{array}{r} 9,000 \\ \times \quad 70 \\ \hline \end{array}$

11. $\begin{array}{r} 200 \\ \times 600 \\ \hline \end{array}$

12. $\begin{array}{r} 20,000 \\ \times \quad 500 \\ \hline \end{array}$

13. $\begin{array}{r} 200 \\ \times \quad 90 \\ \hline \end{array}$

14. $\begin{array}{r} 7,000 \\ \times \quad 400 \\ \hline \end{array}$

15. $\begin{array}{r} 30 \\ \times 80 \\ \hline \end{array}$

16. $\begin{array}{r} 300 \\ \times 900 \\ \hline \end{array}$

17. $\begin{array}{r} 80,000 \\ \times \quad 80 \\ \hline \end{array}$

Lesson 6.2 (pages 180–181)

Estimate.

1. $14 \times 84 = \blacksquare$

2. $39 \times 45 = \blacksquare$

3. $335 \times 62 = \blacksquare$

4. $108 \times 26 = \blacksquare$

5. $\begin{array}{r} \$4.92 \\ \times \quad 18 \\ \hline \end{array}$

6. $\begin{array}{r} \$9.23 \\ \times \quad 34 \\ \hline \end{array}$

7. $\begin{array}{r} \$1.27 \\ \times \quad 99 \\ \hline \end{array}$

8. $\begin{array}{r} \$6.95 \\ \times \quad 82 \\ \hline \end{array}$

9. $\begin{array}{r} \$1.13 \\ \times \quad 45 \\ \hline \end{array}$

Lesson 6.3 (pages 182–183)

Multiply.

1. $\begin{array}{r} 33 \\ \times 70 \\ \hline \end{array}$

2. $\begin{array}{r} 29 \\ \times 40 \\ \hline \end{array}$

3. $\begin{array}{r} 16 \\ \times 80 \\ \hline \end{array}$

4. $\begin{array}{r} 95 \\ \times 10 \\ \hline \end{array}$

5. $\begin{array}{r} 17 \\ \times 40 \\ \hline \end{array}$

6. $\begin{array}{r} 12 \\ \times 50 \\ \hline \end{array}$

7. $\begin{array}{r} 65 \\ \times 70 \\ \hline \end{array}$

8. $\begin{array}{r} 32 \\ \times 30 \\ \hline \end{array}$

9. $\begin{array}{r} 27 \\ \times 80 \\ \hline \end{array}$

10. $\begin{array}{r} 68 \\ \times 20 \\ \hline \end{array}$

Find n.

11. $n \times 20 = 60 \times 30$

12. $30 \times n = 20 \times 60$

13. $80 \times 90 = 90 \times n$

Lesson 6.4 *(pages 184–185)*

The table below shows the number of students taking part in after-school activities. Use the information in the table to copy and complete the bar graph.

Activity	Number of Students
Arts & Crafts	5
Cooking	9
Dancing	2
Gymnastics	6

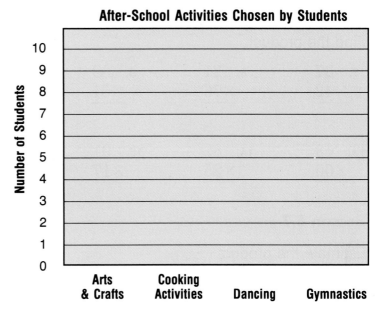

Lesson 6.5 *(pages 186–187)*

Solve using partial products. Then solve using the shorter way.

1.
```
   42
 × 13
-----
    6
  120
   20
 +400
```

2.
```
   63
 × 18
-----
   24
  480
   30
 +600
```

3.
```
   17
 × 52
-----
   14
   20
  350
 +500
```

Write a number sentence. Solve.

4. Jackie can make 3 woven bracelets in one hour. If she works 4 hours a day for 8 days, how many bracelets can she make?

5. Mrs. Ramos arranged 10 rows with 7 computers in each row and 6 more rows with 8 computers in each row. How many computers did she arrange in all?

6. Alan read 4 books a month for 4 months. For the next 4 months, he read 5 books a month. How many did he read in those 8 months?

7. Pat packed a dozen oranges into each of 23 boxes. How many oranges did she pack?

Lesson 6.6 (pages 188–189)

Estimate first. Then find the product.

1. 73
   ×48

2. 29
   ×18

3. 58
   ×47

4. 86
   ×54

5. 78
   ×42

6. 67
   ×33

Find the product.

7. 37
   ×42

8. 21
   ×76

9. 89
   ×61

10. 39
    ×19

11. 94
    ×37

12. 49
    ×43

13. 63
    ×60

14. 82
    ×25

15. 91
    ×17

16. 47
    ×34

17. 54
    ×49

18. 71
    ×42

Lesson 6.7 (pages 192–193)

Estimate the product.

1. 531
   × 69

2. 298
   × 52

3. 716
   × 19

4. 475
   × 34

5. 882
   × 28

Find the product.

6. 304
   × 94

7. 247
   × 67

8. 329
   × 53

9. 728
   × 64

10. 209
    × 35

11. 536
    × 60

12. 428
    × 56

13. 892
    × 38

14. 639
    × 28

15. 375
    × 46

Lesson 6.8 (pages 194–195)

Estimate first. Then find the product.

1. 307
   × 14

2. 178
   × 23

3. 2,891
   × 79

4. 40,799
   × 63

5. 898
   × 22

6. 414
   × 66

7. 1,982
   × 12

8. 25,293
   × 14

Lesson 6.9 *(pages 196–197)*

Solve by using *guess and check.*

1. Mr. Davis planted rows of bushes in front of his house. The number of rows times the number of bushes in each row is 24. The difference between the number of rows and the number of bushes in each row is 5. How many rows of bushes and how many bushes in each row did Mr. Davis plant?

2. Angel is putting 45 tomato plants on shelves in the nursery. The difference between the number of shelves and the number of plants on each shelf is 4. How many shelves did Angel use, and how many plants did he put on each shelf?

3. There are 25 workers at the Watertown Garden Club Fair. There are 4 times as many men working as women. How many men and women are working at the fair?

4. Jackson bought two plants at the fair for $20.00. One of the plants cost $10.00 more than the other plant. How much did each plant cost?

Lesson 6.10 *(pages 198–199)*

Find the product. You may use a calculator.

1. $0.79
   × 14

2. $0.99
   × 12

3. $38.16
   × 30

4. $50.73
   × 15

5. $69.23
   × 11

6. $13.79
   × 26

7. $1.49
   × 78

8. $45.74
   × 60

9. $16.05
   × 53

10. $0.68
    × 70

Use the table to solve Exercises 11–13.

11. Mr. Jimenez sells 27 tulips on Friday. How much money is collected for tulips?

12. On Saturday, 64 marigolds are sold. How much money is collected for marigolds?

13. Mrs. Jimenez sells one customer 14 geraniums and 18 daffodils. How much money does she collect?

Jimenez Nursery Price List	
Flower	Cost
Geranium	$2.49
Daffodil	$1.63
Marigold	$1.87
Tulip	$2.65

CHAPTER 7

Lesson 7.1 *(pages 208–209)*

Find the length of each in centimeters, inches, blips, and your
units. Use rulers and string.

1. the length of your
   hand

2. an eraser

3. a paintbrush

4. the distance from
   your elbow to your
   fingertips

5. a paper clip

6. a shoelace

Lesson 7.2 *(pages 210–212)*

Choose the more reasonable measurement.

1.

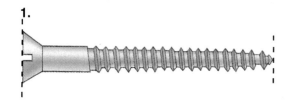

   5 cm or 50 cm

2.

   4 cm or 4 dm

3.

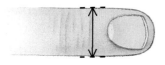

   1 cm or 1 dm

4.

   6 cm or 600 cm

Lesson 7.3 *(pages 214–215)*

Choose the appropriate unit for each. Write *in., ft, yd,* or *mi.*

1. The width of a stamp
   is about 1 __?__ .

2. The distance across
   the United States is
   about 2,800 __?__ .

3. The length of a car is
   about 10 __?__ .

Which is longer?

4. 3 yd or 3 ft

5. 200 mi or 200 ft

6. 4 yd or 4 mi

7. 43 in. or 43 ft

8. 64 yd or 64 ft

9. 14 in. or 14 ft

Lesson 7.4 *(pages 216–217)*

Draw a picture to solve.

1. Three of Keisha's friends live in the same apartment building. Sam lives 2 floors above Keisha. Keisha lives on the 3rd floor, which is 1 floor above Peter. Julie lives 5 floors above Peter. On which floor does Julie live?

2. A fence encloses the apartment building. The fence is 44 feet long and 28 feet wide. It comes in 4-foot-long pieces. How many pieces of fencing were used to build this fence?

3. Paul arranged five pieces of fruit in a row. The plum was next to the orange. The orange was beside the apple. The strawberry was between the apple and the pear. Which piece of fruit was in the middle?

4. Cindy made an array with 42 tiles. Every other row consisted of red tiles. The rows between the red-tiled rows consisted of blue tiles. The center tile of each red-tiled row was black. She put 7 tiles in each row. How are the tiles arranged?

Lesson 7.5 *(pages 218–219)*

Using an inch ruler and a string, find the perimeter of each.

1. the top of a table
2. a lunch tray
3. a square that you draw

4. your backpack
5. a chalkboard eraser
6. the seat of your chair

Write a number sentence to find the perimeter of each figure.

7.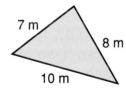

8.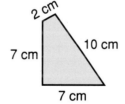

9.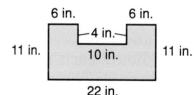

Solve. You may use a calculator.

10. A rectangular swimming pool is 7 ft wide and 22 ft long. Find the perimeter.

11. A square has sides that measure 19 cm each. Find the perimeter of the square.

Lesson 7.6 *(pages 222–223)*

Choose the appropriate unit of measure.

1.

1 c or 1 qt

2.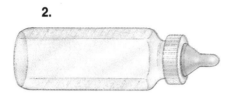

1 c or 1 qt

3.

2 c or 2 gal

Solve.

4. Mr. Turner prepares 12 cups of soup for his family's lunch. How many pints are in 12 cups?

5. Marshall wants to double a recipe that calls for 8 oz of milk and 3 tsp of cocoa. What are the new measurements?

Lesson 7.7 *(pages 224–225)*

Use more than one step to solve.

1. Jeff is using a cup to pour some lemonade into a gallon jug. It will take 16 cups to fill the jug. He pours 8 cups and his sister pours 4 cups. How many cups are left to pour?

2. The Stone family buys fruits and vegetables from a roadside stand. Sean buys 4 tomatoes, each weighing about 6 ounces, and an apple weighing 8 ounces. How many ounces of fruits and vegetables did he buy in all?

3. Janet works at her job for 3 hours each night from Monday through Thursday. She works 4 hours on Saturday. She earns $5 an hour. How much does she earn in one week?

4. Brittany spent $11.00 on four books at the book fair. Two of the books cost $2.79 each. Another book cost $1.85. How much did the fourth book cost?

Lesson 7.8 *(pages 226–227)*

Choose the appropriate unit for each. Write *mL* or *L.*

1. a glass of apple juice

2. soup in a spoon

3. gasoline in a car

4. a bathtub of water

5. a jug of milk

6. a cup of cream

Lesson 7.8 *(pages 226–227)* *(continued)*

Complete.

7. 3 L = ▓ mL   8. ▓ mL = 5 L   9. 8 L = ▓ mL

10. ▓ mL = 2 L   11. ▓ mL = 1 L   12. 9 L = ▓ mL

Lesson 7.9 *(pages 228–229)*

Choose the more reasonable measurement.

1. a car tire
   10 g or 10 kg

2. a bicycle
   20 g or 20 kg

3. a flashlight battery
   100 g or 100 kg

4. a pencil
   5 g or 5 kg

5. a bar of soap
   200 g or 200 kg

6. a refrigerator
   150 g or 150 kg

Lesson 7.10 *(pages 230–231)*

Choose the appropriate unit to measure each.
Write *oz*, *lb*, or *T*.

1.    2.   3.

Complete. You may use a calculator.

4. 2 lb = ▓ oz   5. 5 lb = ▓ oz   6. 9 T = ▓ lb

7. 3 lb = ▓ oz   8. 5 T = ▓ lb   9. 4 lb = ▓ oz

Lesson 7.11 *(pages 232–233)*

Write *multiply* or *divide* to tell how to change the units.

1. tons to pounds   2. miles to yards   3. ounces to pounds

4. inches to feet   5. pints to cups   6. feet to yards

Complete. Use a calculator.

7. 60 ft = ▓ yd   8. ▓ oz = 7 lb   9. 24 gal = ▓ qt

10. 6,000 lb = ▓ T   11. 16 c = ▓ pt   12. 7 ft = ▓ in.

CHAPTER 8

Lesson 8.1 *(pages 242–243)*

Tell how many digits will be in each quotient.

1. $5\overline{)500}$
2. $3\overline{)9,000}$
3. $7\overline{)14}$
4. $5\overline{)3,000}$

Complete the pattern.

5. $\overset{7}{6\overline{)42}}$ $\overset{70}{6\overline{)420}}$ $\overset{\blacksquare\blacksquare\blacksquare}{6\overline{)4,200}}$

6. $\overset{6}{4\overline{)24}}$ $\overset{60}{4\overline{)240}}$ $\overset{\blacksquare\blacksquare\blacksquare}{4\overline{)2,400}}$

Lesson 8.2 *(pages 244–245)*

Use multiplication to find the quotient.

1. $3\overline{)25}$
2. $6\overline{)47}$
3. $8\overline{)15}$
4. $9\overline{)47}$
5. $8\overline{)43}$

6. $4\overline{)34}$
7. $3\overline{)11}$
8. $7\overline{)51}$
9. $7\overline{)17}$
10. $9\overline{)30}$

Solve.

11. My quotient is 5, and my divisor is 8. My dividend is 47. I am the remainder. What number am I?

12. If you divide me by 4, my remainder is 2. I am a multiple of 10. What two-digit number am I?

Lesson 8.3 *(pages 246–247)*

Tell what money amount is represented by the place-value materials.

1.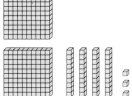

2.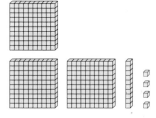

3.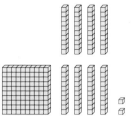

Solve.

4. In one episode of the television show *Dandy Lions,* Dandy and 3 friends are building a clubhouse. The materials will cost $54.00. If they share the cost equally, how much will each person pay?

5. In another episode, Dandy has to pack 68 books into boxes. Each box will hold 8 books. How many boxes will Dandy need to pack all the books?

Lesson 8.4 (pages 248–249)

Choose the letter of the best estimate. Write the method you used.

1. $6\overline{)249}$ **a.** 20   **b.** 30   **c.** 40

2. $4\overline{)337}$ **a.** 60   **b.** 70   **c.** 80

3. $7\overline{)209}$ **a.** 30   **b.** 40   **c.** 50

Estimate the quotient by looking for pairs of compatible numbers.

4. $4\overline{)179}$ **5.** $5\overline{)249}$ **6.** $9\overline{)631}$ **7.** $8\overline{)317}$ **8.** $3\overline{)236}$

9. $315 \div 6 = n$ **10.** $426 \div 5 = n$ **11.** $432 \div 6 = n$ **12.** $651 \div 8 = n$

Lesson 8.5 (pages 250–251)

Choose a strategy and solve.

1. The state fair had 137 exhibits last year. This year there were 176 exhibits. How many more exhibits were there this year?

2. Roberto buys a book and a pen. The book costs two times as much as the pen. Together they cost $9.00. How much does Roberto pay for each item?

3. Four students are growing plants for a science project. Miranda's plant is shorter than Tina's. Karl's plant is taller than Tina's and shorter than Anthony's. Whose plant is shortest?

4. Kim sells plants to 16 customers. Each customer buys 7 plants. How many plants does Kim sell altogether?

Lesson 8.6 (pages 252–253)

Find the quotient. Check by multiplying.

1. $3\overline{)95}$ **2.** $6\overline{)88}$ **3.** $5\overline{)46}$ **4.** $8\overline{)93}$ **5.** $3\overline{)98}$

6. $2\overline{)47}$ **7.** $7\overline{)79}$ **8.** $2\overline{)42}$ **9.** $2\overline{)67}$ **10.** $5\overline{)56}$

11. $47 \div 3 = n$ **12.** $82 \div 5 = n$ **13.** $33 \div 2 = n$ **14.** $84 \div 4 = n$

15. $91 \div 4 = n$ **16.** $75 \div 2 = n$ **17.** $59 \div 3 = n$ **18.** $62 \div 7 = n$

Lesson 8.7 *(pages 256–257)*

Find the quotient. Check by multiplying.

1. $4\overline{)299}$ 2. $6\overline{)443}$ 3. $2\overline{)133}$ 4. $4\overline{)889}$

5. $6\overline{)752}$ 6. $5\overline{)459}$ 7. $5\overline{)238}$ 8. $7\overline{)848}$

9. $747 \div 8 = $ ▨   10. $605 \div 9 = $ ▨   11. $193 \div 2 = $ ▨

Lesson 8.8 *(pages 258–259)*

Estimate. Then find the quotient.

1. $7\overline{)775}$ 2. $4\overline{)835}$ 3. $9\overline{)969}$ 4. $7\overline{)514}$

5. $4\overline{)671}$ 6. $6\overline{)185}$ 7. $4\overline{)920}$ 8. $3\overline{)120}$

9. $645 \div 6 = n$ 10. $959 \div 8 = n$ 11. $811 \div 2 = n$

Lesson 8.9 *(pages 260–261)*

Find the quotient. Check by multiplying.

1. $7\overline{)\$9.38}$ 2. $6\overline{)\$8.52}$ 3. $4\overline{)\$9.72}$ 4. $7\overline{)\$6.65}$

5. $5\overline{)\$4.80}$ 6. $8\overline{)\$8.56}$ 7. $2\overline{)\$1.58}$ 8. $5\overline{)\$5.95}$

9. $\$6.23 \div 7 = n$ 10. $\$7.11 \div 3 = n$ 11. $\$7.66 \div 2 = n$

Lesson 8.10 *(pages 262–263)*

Write which method you would use to solve the problem. Write
mental math, *paper and pencil*, or *calculator*. Then, solve.

1. Jane bought a calculator for
   $17.95 and a battery for $1.75.
   She gave the clerk $20.00. How
   much change did she receive?

2. On Monday, Betty sold
   6 calculators. She sold
   14 calculators on Tuesday
   and 9 calculators on Wednesday.
   How many calculators did she
   sell in all?

Lesson 8.10 (pages 262–263) (continued)

3. Mr. Alexander earns $1,600 a month at his job. If there were 20 working days last month, how much did he earn per day?

4. Mrs. Taylor spent $12.97 at the art supply store, $48.93 at the grocery store, and $11.15 at the dry cleaners. How much money did she spend?

Lesson 8.11 (pages 264–265)

Use the table to find the averages.

1. What is Pam's average test score?

2. What is Joe's average test score?

3. What is Carlos's average test score?

4. What is Rosa's average test score?

5. Who has the highest average test score?

	Week 1	Week 2	Week 3
Joe	98	83	95
Pam	95	89	98
Carlos	87	92	94
Rosa	90	85	95

Lesson 8.12 (pages 266–267)

Find the median, range, and average for each set of numbers.

1. 45, 30, 15

2. 65, 41, 14

3. 24, 15, 27, 34, 10

4. 10, 22, 32, 44, 60, 28, 14

5. 15, 17, 28

6. 15, 151, 79, 85, 20

Use the table for Exercises 7–9.

7. Find the median and range for
   a. the number of books Darcy read.
   b. the number of books José read.
   c. the number of books Mary read.

8. Find and list the average number of books read monthly by each student.

9. Which student had the highest average?

Number of Books Read Each Month					
	Jan.	Feb.	Mar.	Apr.	May
Desmond	10	4	8	6	12
José	3	8	13	11	10
Darcy	6	11	4	9	10
Jacob	9	8	3	10	5
Mary	12	4	6	11	7
Sara	3	12	8	7	5

CHAPTER 9

Lesson 9.1 *(pages 276–277)*

Write whether each is a picture of a *plane* figure or a *solid* figure.

1.  **2.**   **3.**   **4.**

Name the solid figure represented by each.

5.   **6.**  **7.**   **8.**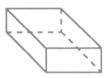

Lesson 9.2 *(pages 278–279)*

Write *yes* or *no* to tell whether the figure is a polygon. Give a reason for your answer.

1.   **2.**   **3.**   **4.**

Lesson 9.3 *(pages 280–282)*

Find the area in square units.

1.   **2.**   **3.**

4.  **5.** 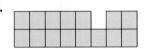 **6.**

Lesson 9.4 *(pages 284–285)*

1. Matt has $1,500 in play money. He has $500 in $20 bills, and $800 in $50 bills. The rest of the money is in $10 bills. How much money are the $10 bills worth?

2. Diane takes pictures along the Mississippi River. One roll of film is enough for 36 pictures. Diane took 18 pictures on Monday and 8 pictures on Tuesday. How many pictures are left on the roll?

3. Mrs. Stoddard earns $9.00 an hour as a secretary. She works 8 hours a day, 5 days a week. How much does she earn in 4 weeks?

4. On Tuesday, Jan's Boutique received a delivery of dresses and coats. There were 3 cartons of dresses with 12 dresses in each, and 4 cartons of coats with 8 coats in each. How many coats and dresses were delivered?

Lesson 9.5 *(pages 286–287)*

Identify each figure. Write *line segment, line,* or *ray.*

1.
2.
3.
4.

Lesson 9.6 *(pages 288–289)*

Write whether each example is a *right,* an *acute,* or an *obtuse* angle.

1.
2.
3.
4.

Lesson 9.7 *(pages 292–293)*

Write whether each picture suggests *intersecting lines, parallel lines, perpendicular lines,* or *rays.*

1.
2.
3.
4.

Lesson 9.8 (pages 294–295)

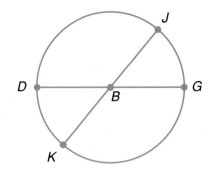

1. Name the center of this circle.

2. Name a radius

3. Name a diameter.

Lesson 9.9 (pages 296–297)

Write whether each pair of figures is *congruent*, *similar*, or *both*.

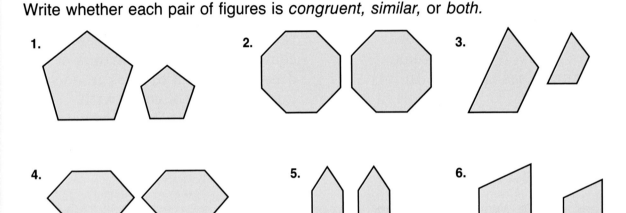

1.

2.

3.

4.

5.

6.

Lesson 9.10 (pages 298–299)

Mr. Jameson's art students are designing jewelry. They are making necklaces using small round beads. The beads are red, blue, green, and purple.

1. Josie wants to make a necklace using 24 green beads and 6 purple beads. Make a model to show what her necklace might look like.

2. Tony is making a 16-inch necklace with all the different colors of beads. A 16-inch necklace can hold 40 beads. Show some designs Tony could make.

3. Bess wants to make a necklace with a pattern of 2 red beads, 3 blue beads, 1 green bead, 2 red, 3 blue, 1 green, and so on. Make a model to show what her necklace will look like if she uses 42 beads.

4. Jake plans to use red and green beads to make a bracelet. He will use a pattern of 5 red, then 5 green, then 5 red, and so on. Show what the bracelet will look like if he uses 20 beads.

Lesson 9.11 *(pages 300–301)*

How many lines of symmetry does each figure have?

1.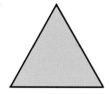

2.

3.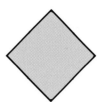

4.

Lesson 9.12 *(pages 302–303)*

Tell how each polygon was moved. Write *flip*, *slide*, or *turn*.

1.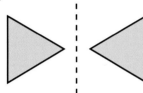

2.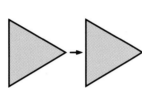

3.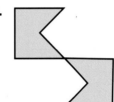

4.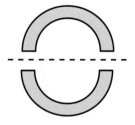

Lesson 9.13 *(pages 304–305)*

Tell how many faces, edges, and corners each figure has.

1.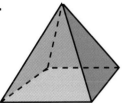

2.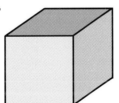

3.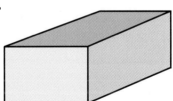

Lesson 9.14 *(pages 306–308)*

Find the volume of each in cubic units.

1.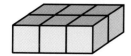

2.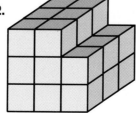

3.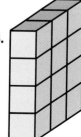

CHAPTER 10

Lesson 10.1 *(pages 318–319)*

Write *part of a whole* or *part of a group* to describe each example.

1.

$\dfrac{1}{5}$

2.

$\dfrac{5}{6}$

3.

$\dfrac{1}{4}$

4.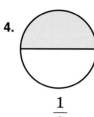

$\dfrac{1}{2}$

5. Write the letters of the figures that show thirds.

a. 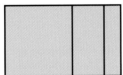   b. 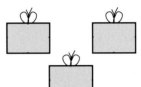   c. 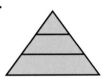   d.

6. What are three other ways that you could read or write $\frac{1}{7}$?

Lesson 10.2 *(pages 320–321)*

Write a fraction for the shaded part.

1. 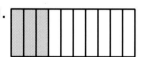   2.   3. 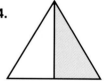   4.

Draw a figure, and shade part of it to show the fraction.

5. $\dfrac{7}{8}$ 6. $\dfrac{5}{9}$ 7. $\dfrac{3}{4}$ 8. $\dfrac{2}{6}$ 9. $\dfrac{4}{12}$

Write the letter of the fraction for each picture.

10.   11. 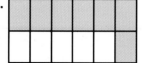   12. 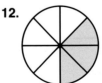   13.

a. $\dfrac{7}{12}$ b. $\dfrac{1}{5}$ c. $\dfrac{2}{3}$ d. $\dfrac{3}{8}$

Lesson 10.3 *(pages 322–323)*

Write a fraction for the shaded part.

1.
2. △ △ △ △
   △ △ △ △
   △ △
3.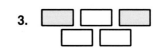
4. ///////
   //////

Draw a picture of a group, and shade part of it to show the fraction.

5. $\dfrac{4}{5}$ 6. $\dfrac{8}{8}$ 7. $\dfrac{5}{9}$ 8. $\dfrac{11}{12}$ 9. $\dfrac{1}{6}$ 10. $\dfrac{6}{10}$

Lesson 10.4 *(pages 324–325)*

Use the pictures to help you complete Exercises 1–3.

1.
2. △ △   △ △
   △ △   △ △   △ △
3.

$\dfrac{1}{4}$ of 12 = ▨ $\dfrac{2}{5}$ of 10 = ▨ $\dfrac{1}{2}$ of 6 = ▨

Copy and complete. Use multiplication and division to help you.

4. $\dfrac{2}{3}$ of 18 = ▨   5. $\dfrac{6}{9}$ of 36 = ▨   6. $\dfrac{1}{5}$ of 20 = ▨   7. $\dfrac{2}{4}$ of 24 = ▨

Lesson 10.5 *(pages 326–327)*

Solve each problem by *acting it out*.

1. Of the 36 students in Leslie's class, $\dfrac{5}{6}$ attended the assembly on nutrition. How many students attended the assembly?

2. The computer class was divided into 7 groups. If there were 28 students in the class, how many students were in each group?

3. Allen counted the money in his pocket. He had 2 $1 bills, 5 quarters, 4 dimes, and 2 nickels. How much money was in Allen's pocket?

4. Calvin cut a sheet of notebook paper into strips. He made 7 cuts. How many strips of paper did he have?

Lesson 10.6 (pages 328–329)

Look at the first figure in each exercise. Then choose the figure that shows a fraction equivalent to the first figure. Write **a, b,** or **c.**

1.    a. 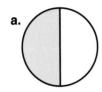   b. 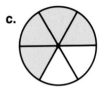   c.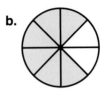

2.    a.    b.   c.

3.   a.   b.   c.

Write two equivalent fractions for each.

4. $\dfrac{1}{3}$ 5. $\dfrac{1}{2}$ 6. $\dfrac{5}{12}$ 7. $\dfrac{3}{5}$ 8. $\dfrac{2}{7}$

Lesson 10.7 (pages 332–333)

Complete.

1. 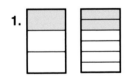   2. 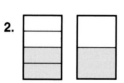   3. 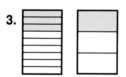   4.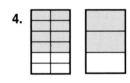

$\dfrac{1}{3} = \dfrac{\blacksquare}{6}$ $\dfrac{2}{4} = \dfrac{\blacksquare}{2}$ $\dfrac{3}{9} = \dfrac{\blacksquare}{3}$ $\dfrac{8}{\blacksquare} = \dfrac{\blacksquare}{3}$

5. $\dfrac{8}{10} = \dfrac{8 \div 2}{10 \div 2} = \dfrac{\blacksquare}{\blacksquare}$ 6. $\dfrac{9}{12} = \dfrac{9 \div 3}{12 \div 3} = \dfrac{\blacksquare}{\blacksquare}$

7. Look at the fractions. Write the letter of the fractions that are in simplest form.

a. $\dfrac{5}{9}$ b. $\dfrac{8}{12}$ c. $\dfrac{11}{12}$ d. $\dfrac{1}{3}$ e. $\dfrac{9}{12}$ f. $\dfrac{6}{8}$

Write each fraction in simplest form.

8. $\dfrac{8}{12}$ 9. $\dfrac{5}{15}$ 10. $\dfrac{8}{10}$ 11. $\dfrac{4}{6}$ 12. $\dfrac{8}{16}$

13. $\dfrac{6}{18}$ 14. $\dfrac{7}{14}$ 15. $\dfrac{6}{8}$ 16. $\dfrac{3}{9}$ 17. $\dfrac{8}{24}$

Lesson 10.8 *(pages 334–335)*

Choose a strategy and solve.

1. Julia bought two trees at the nursery for $20.00. One of the trees cost $8.00 more than the other. How much did each tree cost?

2. In the high jump, Allen won the event. If you take the number of centimeters Allen jumped, subtract 55, and divide by 2, the result is 51. How many centimeters did Allen jump in the high jump?

3. Dean was unloading 18 boxes of apples and bananas. Each box weighed 28 pounds. How many pounds of fruit did he unload? Write the number sentence and then solve.

4. Chris spent $0.69 for shoelaces for his running shoes. He gave the clerk $1.00. He received 1 penny and some nickels in change. How many nickels did he receive?

Lesson 10.9 *(pages 336–337)*

Write the fraction for each figure. Then compare using <, >, or =.

1. 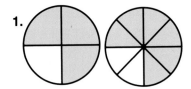   2.   3.

Draw a picture for each fraction. Then compare using <, >, or = for 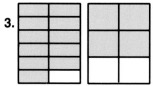.

4. $\dfrac{5}{8}$ ⬤ $\dfrac{7}{8}$

5. $\dfrac{1}{3}$ ⬤ $\dfrac{2}{6}$

6. $\dfrac{3}{4}$ ⬤ $\dfrac{2}{3}$

7. $\dfrac{1}{2}$ ⬤ $\dfrac{3}{8}$

Lesson 10.10 *(pages 338–339)*

Draw a picture to show each mixed number or fraction.

1. $\dfrac{7}{6}$

2. $4\dfrac{2}{5}$

3. $\dfrac{16}{5}$

4. $2\dfrac{1}{3}$

5. $\dfrac{7}{3}$

Write a mixed number for each picture.

6.   7.   8.

CHAPTER 11

Lesson 11.1 *(pages 348–349)*

Estimate the shaded part of each. Write *about* 0, *about* $\frac{1}{2}$, or *about* 1.

1. 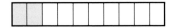 **2.** **3.**

4. **5.** **6.**

Estimate each. Draw pictures to show your estimate.
Write *about* 0, *about* $\frac{1}{2}$, *about* 1, or *about* $1\frac{1}{2}$.

7. $\frac{2}{8} + \frac{3}{4} = $ ▩

8. $\frac{2}{3} + \frac{1}{6} = $ ▩

9. $\frac{3}{7} + \frac{1}{8} = $ ▩

10. $\frac{2}{3} + \frac{10}{12} = $ ▩

Lesson 11.2 *(pages 350–351)*

Find the sum. Use fraction pieces.

1. $\begin{array}{r} \frac{1}{5} \\ + \frac{3}{5} \\ \hline \end{array}$

2. $\begin{array}{r} \frac{2}{7} \\ + \frac{4}{7} \\ \hline \end{array}$

3. $\begin{array}{r} \frac{1}{4} \\ + \frac{2}{4} \\ \hline \end{array}$

4. $\begin{array}{r} \frac{5}{12} \\ + \frac{2}{12} \\ \hline \end{array}$

5. $\begin{array}{r} \frac{3}{11} \\ + \frac{5}{11} \\ \hline \end{array}$

Use fraction pieces to find the sum. You may write the sum in simplest form.

6. $\frac{1}{4} + \frac{1}{4} = \frac{▩}{▩}$

7. $\frac{2}{6} + \frac{1}{6} = \frac{▩}{▩}$

8. $\frac{3}{10} + \frac{5}{10} = \frac{▩}{▩}$

9. $\frac{2}{8} + \frac{4}{8} = \frac{▩}{▩}$

10. $\frac{11}{24} + \frac{1}{24} = \frac{▩}{▩}$

11. $\frac{3}{15} + \frac{7}{15} = \frac{▩}{▩}$

Write the letter of the number sentence that helps you add the fraction pieces in each pair of pictures.

12. **13.**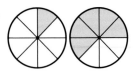

14. **15.**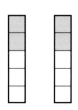

a. $\frac{1}{3} + \frac{2}{3} = \frac{3}{3}$

b. $\frac{9}{15} + \frac{5}{15} = \frac{14}{15}$

c. $\frac{2}{5} + \frac{2}{5} = \frac{4}{5}$

d. $\frac{1}{8} + \frac{5}{8} = \frac{6}{8}$

Lesson 11.3 *(pages 352–353)*

Use fraction pieces to find the difference.

1. $\dfrac{9}{10}$
   $-\dfrac{6}{10}$

2. $\dfrac{7}{8}$
   $-\dfrac{2}{8}$

3. $\dfrac{6}{7}$
   $-\dfrac{3}{7}$

4. $\dfrac{8}{9}$
   $-\dfrac{3}{9}$

5. $\dfrac{10}{10}$
   $-\dfrac{3}{10}$

6. $\dfrac{6}{8} - \dfrac{2}{8} = \dfrac{\blacksquare}{8}$

7. $\dfrac{5}{6} - \dfrac{1}{6} = \dfrac{\blacksquare}{6}$

8. $\dfrac{9}{12} - \dfrac{6}{12} = \dfrac{\blacksquare}{12}$

9. $\dfrac{7}{8} - \dfrac{6}{8}$

10. $\dfrac{5}{7} - \dfrac{2}{7}$

11. $\dfrac{7}{8} - \dfrac{3}{8}$

12. $\dfrac{3}{4} - \dfrac{1}{4}$

Lesson 11.4 *(pages 354–355)*

Make a model to solve.

1. Frank is making a seating chart for the sports banquet. He needs to seat the coach, assistant coach, and team manager at the head table. What arrangements can he make with the head coach in the middle seat?

2. Elise wants to make a rectangular arrangement out of 24 squares. If one side must be 8 squares, what will be the dimensions of the rectangle?

3. Brad painted $\frac{3}{10}$ of a board green and $\frac{3}{5}$ of it yellow. Did he paint the whole board?

4. Amy mixed $\frac{1}{2}$ cup of red paint and $\frac{2}{3}$ cup of white paint together. Was this more than or less than 1 cup?

Lesson 11.5 *(pages 356–357)*

Use fraction pieces to find the common denominator.

1. $\dfrac{3}{4}$ and $\dfrac{2}{8}$

2. $\dfrac{1}{2}$ and $\dfrac{1}{4}$

3. $\dfrac{2}{3}$ and $\dfrac{1}{6}$

4. $\dfrac{3}{5}$ and $\dfrac{4}{10}$

Use fraction pieces to change unlike fractions into like fractions.

5. $\dfrac{1}{3}$ and $\dfrac{1}{6}$

6. $\dfrac{1}{4}$ and $\dfrac{3}{8}$

7. $\dfrac{1}{9}$ and $\dfrac{2}{3}$

8. $\dfrac{5}{12}$ and $\dfrac{1}{2}$

Use fraction pieces to find the sum or difference.

9. $\dfrac{3}{5} + \dfrac{1}{10} = n$

10. $\dfrac{2}{3} + \dfrac{2}{9} = n$

11. $\dfrac{3}{4} - \dfrac{1}{8} = n$

12. $\dfrac{5}{6} - \dfrac{3}{12} = n$

Lesson 11.6 *(pages 358–359)*

Copy and complete. Use fraction pieces to help you.

1. $\dfrac{2}{3} \rightarrow \dfrac{\blacksquare}{\blacksquare}$
    $+\dfrac{1}{12} \rightarrow \dfrac{\blacksquare}{\blacksquare}$
    $\dfrac{\blacksquare}{\blacksquare}$

2. $\dfrac{11}{12} \rightarrow \dfrac{\blacksquare}{\blacksquare}$
    $-\dfrac{3}{6} \rightarrow \dfrac{\blacksquare}{\blacksquare}$
    $\dfrac{\blacksquare}{\blacksquare}$

3. $\dfrac{2}{7} \rightarrow \dfrac{\blacksquare}{\blacksquare}$
    $+\dfrac{14}{21} \rightarrow \dfrac{\blacksquare}{\blacksquare}$
    $\dfrac{\blacksquare}{\blacksquare}$

4. $\dfrac{9}{10} \rightarrow \dfrac{\blacksquare}{\blacksquare}$
    $-\dfrac{4}{5} \rightarrow \dfrac{\blacksquare}{\blacksquare}$
    $\dfrac{\blacksquare}{\blacksquare}$

Find the sum or difference. Use fraction pieces to help you.

5. $\dfrac{2}{3} + \dfrac{2}{6}$

6. $\dfrac{4}{9} - \dfrac{1}{3}$

7. $\dfrac{1}{2} + \dfrac{2}{10}$

8. $\dfrac{3}{4} - \dfrac{1}{2}$

9. $\dfrac{1}{8} + \dfrac{1}{16}$

10. $\dfrac{1}{4} + \dfrac{5}{12}$

11. $\dfrac{7}{10} - \dfrac{1}{5}$

12. $\dfrac{2}{5} - \dfrac{4}{15}$

Lesson 11.7 *(pages 362–363)*

Find the sum or difference. You may write your answer in simplest form.

1. $2\dfrac{1}{8}$
    $+3\dfrac{4}{8}$

2. $4\dfrac{4}{10}$
    $-4\dfrac{3}{10}$

3. $3\dfrac{2}{8}$
    $+4\dfrac{5}{8}$

4. $8\dfrac{5}{6}$
    $-5\dfrac{3}{6}$

5. $6\dfrac{1}{3}$
    $+2\dfrac{2}{3}$

6. $7\dfrac{3}{6}$
    $-5\dfrac{1}{6}$

7. $6\dfrac{1}{7}$
    $+3\dfrac{3}{7}$

8. $8\dfrac{5}{8}$
    $-5\dfrac{1}{8}$

Lesson 11.8 *(pages 364–365)*

Use a customary ruler to measure each to the nearest unit.
Use $\frac{1}{2}$ inch, $\frac{1}{4}$ inch, or $\frac{1}{8}$ inch.

1.

2.

3. [pencil image]

4. Measure the length of your index finger.

5. Measure the distance between your desk and the desk that is next to yours.

6. Draw a line segment that measures $2\frac{3}{8}$ inches long.

Lesson 11.9 *(pages 366–367)*

Make an organized list to solve.

1. Rosa has a silver necklace and a gold necklace. She can wear a red, black, or striped blouse. List the different combinations of blouses and necklaces she can wear.

2. Using the digits 2, 3, 5, and 9, list all the four-digit numbers you can with 9 in the ones place.

3. Mrs. Reys is planting rows of flowers. She is planting 1 row each of marigolds, zinnias, and pansies. List the different ways she can plant the rows of flowers.

4. A clown is selling red, yellow, and orange balloons at the fair. The balloons are either round or oblong. What are the different choices of balloons he is selling?

Lesson 11.10 *(pages 368–369)*

Look at the spinner. Find the probability of landing on each color.

1. red

2. blue

3. green

4. yellow

Lesson 11.11 *(pages 370–371)*

1. Copy and complete the tree diagram. List the possibilities.

   If you order the lunch special, you may choose from a hot or cold entrée with a salad, vegetable, or fruit.

   Tree Diagram   *Possibilities*

   hot entrée — salad   hot entrée; salad

   cold entrée

2. How many possible combinations are there in all?

3. Write a multiplication sentence to find all the possible combinations.

CHAPTER 12

Lesson 12.1 (pages 380–381)

On graph paper, draw a model for each decimal. Then write each decimal in words.

1. 0.35
2. 0.79
3. 1.25
4. 2.42
5. 5.06

Write each decimal.

6. four tenths

7. eighty-four hundredths

8. one and five tenths

9. six and two hundredths

10. three and twenty-one hundredths

11. nine and one hundredth

Lesson 12.2 (pages 382–383)

Write the decimal.

1. $\dfrac{8}{10}$

2. $\dfrac{42}{100}$

3. $\dfrac{18}{100}$

4. $\dfrac{3}{10}$

5. $\dfrac{4}{100}$

6. $35\dfrac{9}{10}$

7. $1\dfrac{4}{10}$

8. $6\dfrac{1}{100}$

9. nine and six tenths

10. thirteen hundredths

11. eight and nine hundredths

12. seven and three hundredths

13. two and ninety-four hundredths

14. four hundredths

Lesson 12.3 (pages 384–385)

1. Sandi gave half of her bracelets to her sister. Then she gave 4 bracelets to a friend. She had 6 bracelets left. How many bracelets did Sandi have to start with?

2. Sanchez spent half of his money for a movie ticket and $5 for snacks. He spent $1 at a coffee shop after the movie, and had no money left. How much money did Sanchez have at the start?

3. Of the 30 students in Mona's class, half are boys. Five of the boys have blond hair and 7 have brown hair. The rest of the boys have red hair. How many boys have red hair?

4. Kara used half of the mushrooms in a package for making a salad. Then she used half of the mushrooms that were left to make an omelet. There were 8 mushrooms left. How many mushrooms had been in the package?

Lesson 12.4 *(pages 386–387)*

Write two equivalent decimals for the shaded part of each model.

1.   **2.**   **3.** 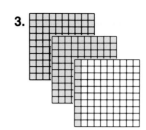 **4.**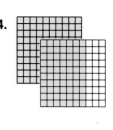

Tell whether the decimals are equivalent. Write *yes* or *no.*

5. 12.20 and 12.02   **6.** 4.3 and 4.30   **7.** 8.14 and 8.41   **8.** 1.1 and 1.10

Write an equivalent decimal for each.

9. 0.2   **10.** 5.30   **11.** 4.7   **12.** 0.90

Lesson 12.5 *(pages 388–389)*

Compare. Use <, >, or = for ●.

1.

0.39 ● 0.24

2.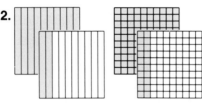

1.2 ● 1.20

3.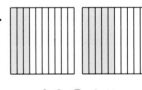

0.3 ● 0.5

4. 0.31 ● 0.2   **5.** 1.12 ● 1.21   **6.** 4.3 ● 4.30   **7.** 0.8 ● 0.28

8. 3.70 ● 3.7   **9.** 0.54 ● 0.45   **10.** 0.26 ● 0.6   **11.** 5.35 ● 5.53

Order the decimals from least to greatest.

12. 4.06; 6.40; 0.46; 0.64   **13.** 1.34; 1.43; 1.32; 1.47

Lesson 12.6 *(pages 390–391)*

Round each decimal to the nearest whole number.

1. 6.29   **2.** 0.96   **3.** 1.7   **4.** 6.8   **5.** 21.39

6. 4.3   **7.** 2.09   **8.** 14.92   **9.** 9.78   **10.** 21.08

Lesson 12.7 *(pages 394–395)*

Find the sum and difference for each pair of pictures.

1. 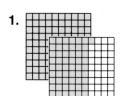 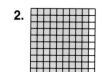   **2.** 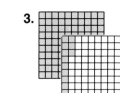   **3.**

Use graph paper to draw models for each problem. Solve.

4. $0.73 + 0.19 = n$ **5.** $1.17 + 0.54 = n$ **6.** $1.67 - 1.09 = n$

Show each problem on a place-value chart. Solve.

7. $7.6 - 4.7 = n$ **8.** $2.0 - 1.31 = n$ **9.** $3.79 + 1.83 = n$

Lesson 12.8 *(pages 396–397)*

Estimate by using front-end digits.

| **1.** 7.32 $+4.21$ | **2.** 8.35 -6.87 | **3.** 95.72 -12.36 | **4.** 10.78 $+20.10$ | **5.** 76.43 -14.23 |

Estimate by rounding to the nearest whole number.

6. $6.18 - 3.6 = n$ **7.** $2.3 + 8.9 + 1.6 = n$ **8.** $42.05 + 7.88 + 4.5 = n$

Estimate the sum or difference by using either method.

| **9.** 11.90 $- 8.71$ | **10.** 3.29 16.43 $+ 4.95$ | **11.** 0.79 3.21 $+4.69$ | **12.** 7.10 2.93 $+10.07$ | **13.** 13.78 $- 3.21$ |

Lesson 12.9 *(pages 398–399)*

Use estimation to solve.

1. Jarvis spent $3.98 for a breakfast sandwich, $0.98 for juice, and $1.29 for a piece of melon. About how much did he spend on breakfast?

2. Maria rides the bus 2.1 km to get to school. Then she walks 1.5 km to go to piano lessons. From there she must ride the bus 4.2 km to get back home. About how far does Maria travel?

Lesson 12.9 *(pages 398–399)* (continued)

3. Andrew bought a baseball glove for $11.49 and a baseball for $5.99. About how much change did he receive from $20.00?

4. Angie has saved $30.00 for some new clothes. Can she buy two blouses she wants that each cost $14.75?

Lesson 12.10 *(pages 400–401)*

Find the sum.

1. $\begin{array}{r} 4.8 \\ +7.6 \\ \hline \end{array}$

2. $\begin{array}{r} 2.3 \\ +9.7 \\ \hline \end{array}$

3. $\begin{array}{r} 0.05 \\ +0.39 \\ \hline \end{array}$

4. $\begin{array}{r} 34.98 \\ +43.06 \\ \hline \end{array}$

5. $\begin{array}{r} 12.06 \\ +27.14 \\ \hline \end{array}$

6. $\begin{array}{r} 45.00 \\ +34.28 \\ \hline \end{array}$

7. $\begin{array}{r} 9.48 \\ +20.10 \\ \hline \end{array}$

8. $\begin{array}{r} 10.29 \\ +16.90 \\ \hline \end{array}$

9. $\begin{array}{r} 5.36 \\ 4.51 \\ +7.87 \\ \hline \end{array}$

10. $\begin{array}{r} 1.76 \\ 8.06 \\ 5.60 \\ +7.15 \\ \hline \end{array}$

11. $7.00 + 1.39 + 0.94 = n$

12. $17.85 + 2 + 3.9 = n$

13. $4.36 + 8.20 + 0.7 = n$

14. $14.7 + 5 + 11.0 = n$

15. $25.67 + 5.1 + 3.2 = n$

16. $9 + 21.8 + 13.04 = n$

17. $4.2 + 22.4 + 44.2 = n$

18. $16.99 + 2.4 + 8 = n$

Lesson 12.11 *(pages 402–403)*

Find the difference.

1. $\begin{array}{r} 8.9 \\ -3.6 \\ \hline \end{array}$

2. $\begin{array}{r} 7.5 \\ -4.1 \\ \hline \end{array}$

3. $\begin{array}{r} 6.3 \\ -2.5 \\ \hline \end{array}$

4. $\begin{array}{r} 6.22 \\ -4.38 \\ \hline \end{array}$

5. $\begin{array}{r} 81.42 \\ -43.75 \\ \hline \end{array}$

6. $\begin{array}{r} 19.38 \\ -17.54 \\ \hline \end{array}$

7. $\begin{array}{r} 67.24 \\ -15.96 \\ \hline \end{array}$

8. $\begin{array}{r} 77.3 \\ -47.5 \\ \hline \end{array}$

9. $\begin{array}{r} 9.5 \\ -8.7 \\ \hline \end{array}$

10. $\begin{array}{r} 5.23 \\ -0.64 \\ \hline \end{array}$

11. $13.17 - 1.48 = n$

12. $52.64 - 13.83 = n$

13. $69.48 - 43.98 = n$

14. $6.18 - 0.39 = n$

15. $92.36 - 4.72 = n$

16. $91.46 - 15.07 = n$

17. $56.01 - 3.98 = n$

18. $20.5 - 12.09 = n$

19. $44.60 - 3.3 = n$

CHAPTER 13

Lesson 13.1 *(pages 412–413)*

Write the basic division fact that helps you find each quotient. Solve.

1. $40\overline{)320}$ 2. $70\overline{)280}$ 3. $80\overline{)640}$ 4. $90\overline{)540}$

On graph paper, draw a model for each problem. Solve.

5. $810 \div 90 = n$ 6. $180 \div 30 = n$ 7. $240 \div 80 = n$ 8. $490 \div 70 = n$

Record each quotient on a place-value chart.

9. $6\overline{)42}$

   $60\overline{)420}$

   $60\overline{)4,200}$

10. $7\overline{)35}$

    $70\overline{)350}$

    $70\overline{)3,500}$

11. $3\overline{)21}$

    $30\overline{)210}$

    $30\overline{)2,100}$

12. $8\overline{)72}$

    $80\overline{)720}$

    $80\overline{)7,200}$

Lesson 13.2 *(pages 414–415)*

Copy and complete. Use compatible numbers to estimate.

1. $162 \div 41 = n$
   $\downarrow \quad \downarrow$
   $\blacksquare \div 40 = 4$

2. $223 \div 74 = n$
   $\downarrow \quad \downarrow$
   $210 \div \blacksquare = 3$

3. $369 \div 58 = n$
   $\downarrow \quad \downarrow \quad \downarrow$
   $360 \div \blacksquare = \blacksquare$

Choose the best estimate. Write **a, b, c,** or **d.**

4. $21\overline{)63}$ a. 2   b. 3   c. 4   d. 5

5. $58\overline{)239}$ a. 2   b. 3   c. 4   d. 5

6. $75\overline{)731}$ a. 6   b. 7   c. 8   d. 9

7. $42\overline{)339}$ a. 6   b. 7   c. 8   d. 9

Estimate the quotient. Use compatible numbers.

8. $72\overline{)506}$ 9. $58\overline{)379}$ 10. $53\overline{)359}$ 11. $24\overline{)131}$

12. $32\overline{)161}$ 13. $11\overline{)451}$ 14. $46\overline{)490}$ 15. $83\overline{)573}$

16. $29\overline{)218}$ 17. $61\overline{)475}$ 18. $94\overline{)551}$ 19. $38\overline{)130}$

Lesson 13.3 (pages 416–417)

Find the hidden question. Solve.

1. The Turners are traveling 800 miles to Memphis by car. The first day they drive 480 miles. They drive 240 miles before noon the second day. How many miles are left?

2. The Turner family is camping along the Mississippi River. Mary is reading a 250-page book by Mark Twain. She read 50 pages on Monday and 38 pages on Tuesday. How many pages does she have left to read?

3. On Monday, the nursery had 73 ferns. Mrs. Tucker sold 40 ferns on Tuesday. She sold 31 ferns on Wednesday. How many ferns does she have left?

4. Mr. Jacob needs some new gardening tools. He buys a spade for $2.69 and a hoe for $5.19. He gives the store owner $20.00. How much change does he receive?

Lesson 13.4 (pages 418–419)

Copy each problem. Draw ■ where the first digit in the quotient should be placed.

1. $30\overline{)126}$ 2. $50\overline{)169}$ 3. $60\overline{)371}$ 4. $80\overline{)329}$ 5. $40\overline{)293}$

Find the quotient. Check by multiplying.

6. $70\overline{)371}$ 7. $20\overline{)191}$ 8. $60\overline{)315}$ 9. $30\overline{)283}$ 10. $70\overline{)224}$

11. $40\overline{)132}$ 12. $50\overline{)471}$ 13. $80\overline{)409}$ 14. $90\overline{)461}$ 15. $30\overline{)294}$

Lesson 13.5 (pages 422–423)

Use place-value blocks to find the quotient. Record your work.

1. $16\overline{)52}$ 2. $19\overline{)109}$ 3. $23\overline{)191}$ 4. $32\overline{)168}$ 5. $41\overline{)252}$

Find the quotient. Use place-value blocks to help you.

6. $30\overline{)62}$ 7. $29\overline{)92}$ 8. $22\overline{)189}$ 9. $53\overline{)491}$ 10. $41\overline{)615}$

11. $49\overline{)314}$ 12. $85\overline{)618}$ 13. $73\overline{)412}$ 14. $13\overline{)127}$ 15. $27\overline{)264}$

16. $294 \div 37 = n$ 17. $151 \div 25 = n$ 18. $529 \div 53 = n$

Lesson 13.6 *(pages 424–425)*

Find the quotient.

1. $34\overline{)78}$ 2. $23\overline{)97}$ 3. $41\overline{)96}$ 4. $22\overline{)56}$ 5. $32\overline{)64}$

6. $42\overline{)281}$ 7. $61\overline{)211}$ 8. $82\overline{)495}$ 9. $31\overline{)265}$ 10. $83\overline{)352}$

11. $60\overline{)445}$ 12. $50\overline{)323}$ 13. $73\overline{)596}$ 14. $83\overline{)593}$ 15. $62\overline{)350}$

16. $52\overline{)421}$ 17. $31\overline{)174}$ 18. $43\overline{)225}$ 19. $61\overline{)537}$ 20. $54\overline{)334}$

21. $365 \div 72 = n$ 22. $694 \div 81 = n$ 23. $417 \div 63 = n$

24. $257 \div 61 = n$ 25. $394 \div 40 = n$ 26. $747 \div 92 = n$

Solve.

27. Robert unpacks 200 screwdrivers. He puts 24 screwdrivers in each compartment. How many compartments does he fill? How many screwdrivers are left over?

28. Gayle is setting up a display of 258 tape measures. She puts 32 tape measures in each stack. How many stacks does she make? How many tape measures are left over?

Lesson 13.7 *(pages 426–427)*

Solve. Interpret the quotient and the remainder.

1. Sharon bought enough paint to paint 286 square feet of fence. Each can of paint will cover about 45 square feet. How many full cans will she use?

2. Mr. Crane needs to replace 13 light bulbs that have burned out. The light bulbs are sold in packages of 4. How many packages does he need to buy?

3. Wesley has 178 nails to put in packages. Each full package will have 24 nails. How many full packages will he have?

4. The warehouse has 342 shovels. Each of the 43 stores in this area is to get the same number of shovels. How many shovels will be left in the warehouse?

Lesson 13.8 *(pages 428–429)*

Copy each problem. Draw ■ where the first digit in the quotient should be placed.

1. $33\overline{)419}$ 2. $29\overline{)617}$ 3. $17\overline{)143}$ 4. $82\overline{)941}$ 5. $41\overline{)516}$

Estimate. Find the quotient. Use a calculator.

6. $41\overline{)83}$ 7. $63\overline{)197}$ 8. $14\overline{)298}$ 9. $25\overline{)507}$ 10. $72\overline{)394}$

Find the quotient.

11. $43\overline{)994}$ 12. $29\overline{)795}$ 13. $38\overline{)808}$ 14. $20\overline{)516}$ 15. $23\overline{)498}$

16. $40\overline{)872}$ 17. $24\overline{)504}$ 18. $78\overline{)943}$ 19. $57\overline{)768}$ 20. $34\overline{)889}$

21. $13\overline{)568}$ 22. $17\overline{)483}$ 23. $50\overline{)270}$ 24. $32\overline{)217}$ 25. $65\overline{)386}$

26. $253 \div 52 = n$ 27. $499 \div 28 = n$ 28. $365 \div 77 = n$

29. $614 \div 46 = n$ 30. $870 \div 26 = n$ 31. $716 \div 67 = n$

Lesson 13.9 *(pages 430–431)*

Find the quotient.

1. $\$21\overline{)\$315}$ 2. $33\overline{)\$66}$ 3. $\$16\overline{)\$144}$ 4. $\$34\overline{)\$782}$

5. $41\overline{)\$369}$ 6. $\$24\overline{)\$384}$ 7. $\$12\overline{)228}$ 8. $\$45\overline{)\$810}$

9. $\$891 \div \$33 = n$ 10. $\$1,232 \div 56 = n$ 11. $\$2,205 \div \$63 = n$

12. $\$3,182 \div 74 = n$ 13. $\$108 \div 36 = n$ 14. $\$1,449 \div \$21 = n$

Solve.

15. Ling spends $8.28 for tubes of caulking. She buys 12 tubes. How much does each tube of caulking cost?

16. Mrs. Lawrence bought 11 cans of spray paint. Her total was $9.79. How much did each can of paint cost?

The Learning Resources can be traced, colored, and cut out. These resources can be used as tools to help you understand math concepts and solve problems.

Multiplication Table

×	0	1	2	3	4	5	6	7	8	9
0	0	0	0	0	0	0	0	0	0	0
1	0	1	2	3	4	5	6	7	8	9
2	0	2	4	6	8	10	12	14	16	18
3	0	3	6	9	12	15	18	21	24	27
4	0	4	8	12	16	20	24	28	32	36
5	0	5	10	15	20	25	30	35	40	45
6	0	6	12	18	24	30	36	42	48	54
7	0	7	14	21	28	35	42	49	56	63
8	0	8	16	24	32	40	48	56	64	72
9	0	9	18	27	36	45	54	63	72	81

Number Lines

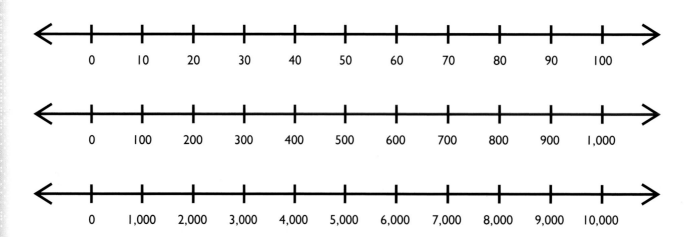

Plane Geometric Shapes

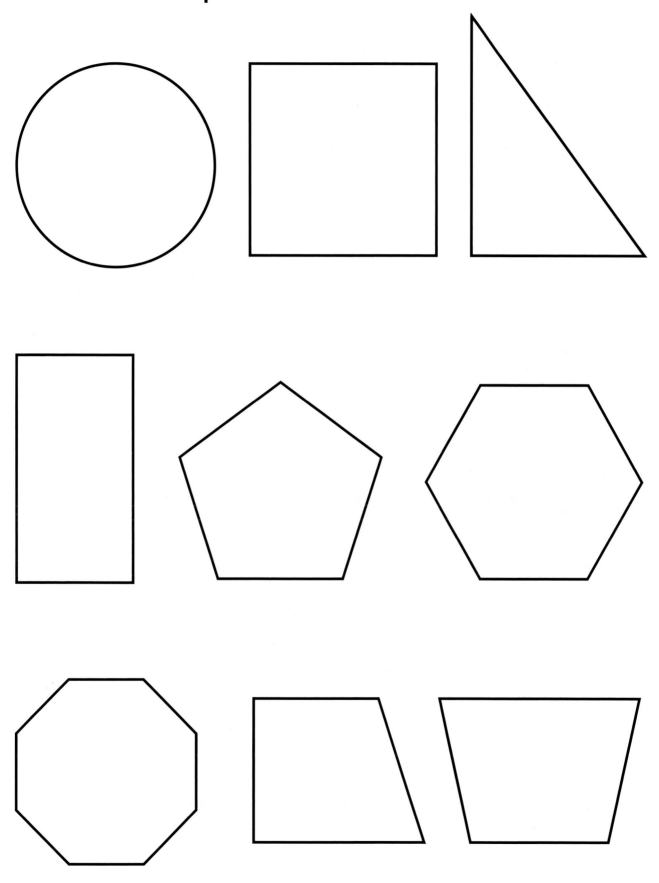

Fraction Circles

Fraction Bars

| $\frac{1}{10}$ | | | | | | | | | |

| $\frac{1}{9}$ | | | | | | | | |

| $\frac{1}{8}$ | | | | | | | |

| $\frac{1}{7}$ | | | | | | |

| $\frac{1}{6}$ | | | | | |

| $\frac{1}{5}$ | | | | |

| $\frac{1}{4}$ | | | |

| $\frac{1}{3}$ | | |

| $\frac{1}{2}$ | |

| 1 |

Solid Geometric Pattern

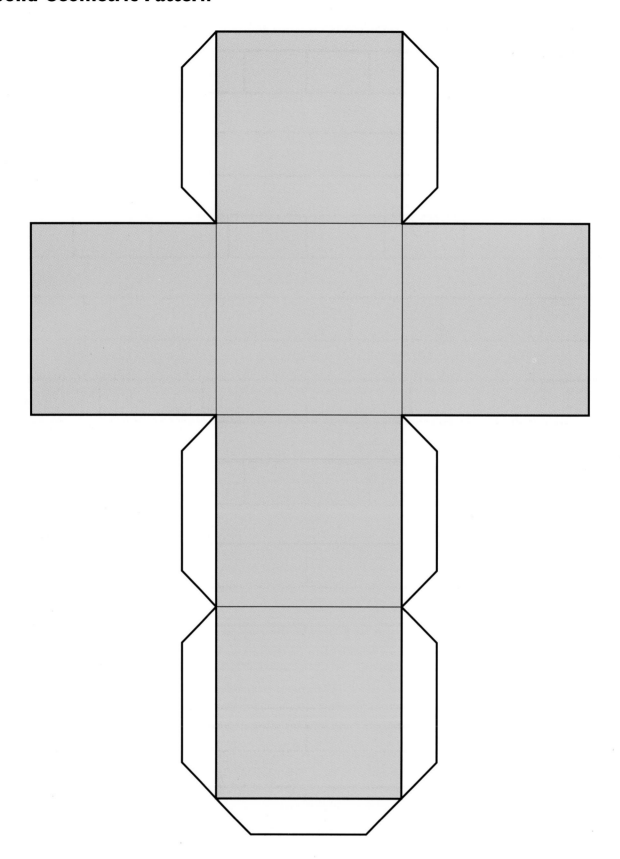

Solid Geometric Pattern

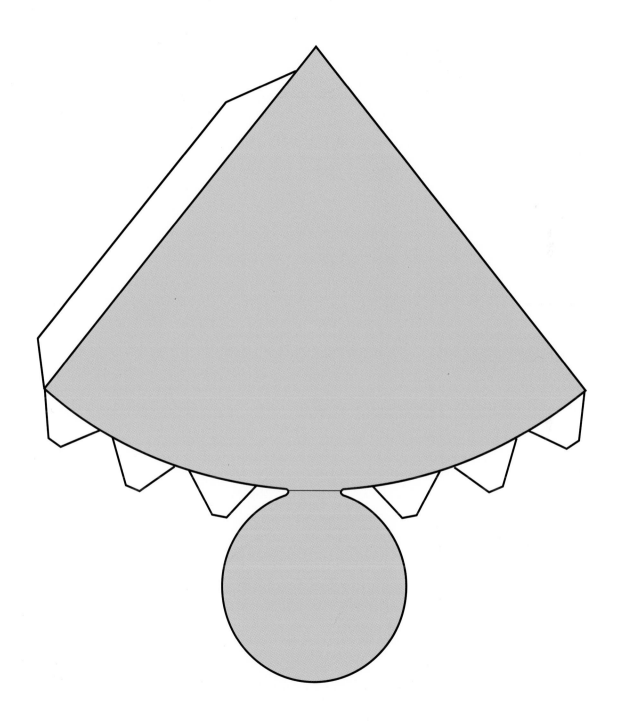

Solid Geometric Pattern

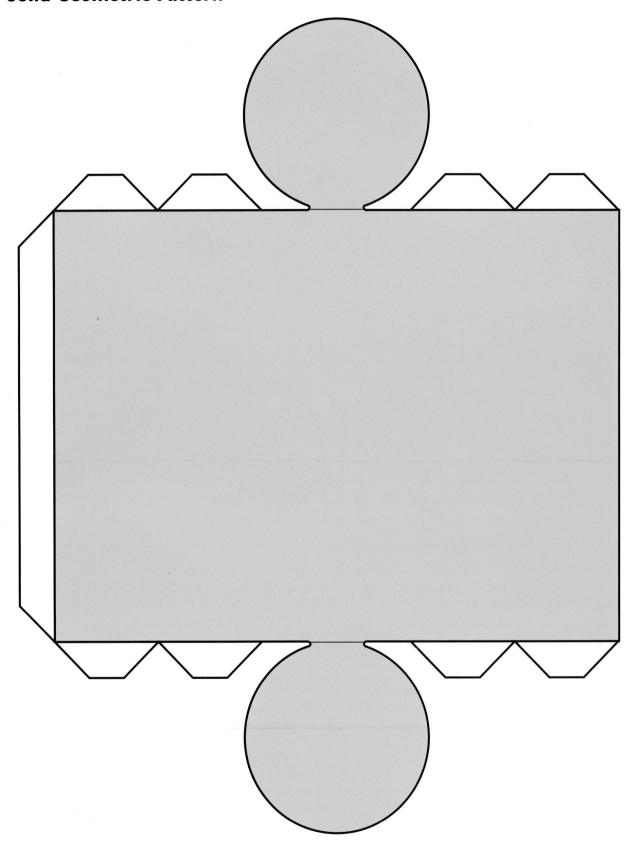

Solid Geometric Pattern

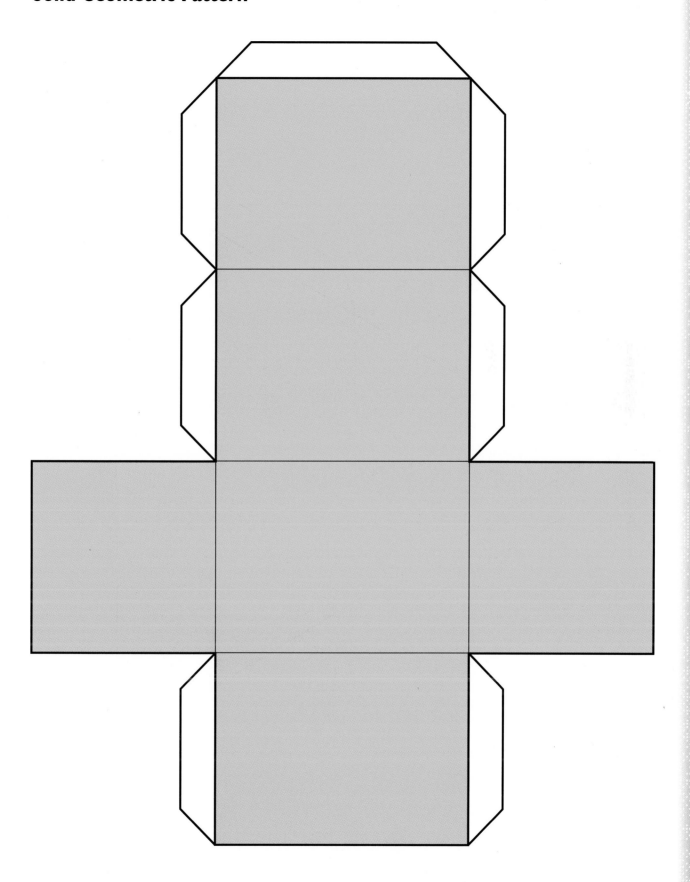

Solid Geometric Pattern

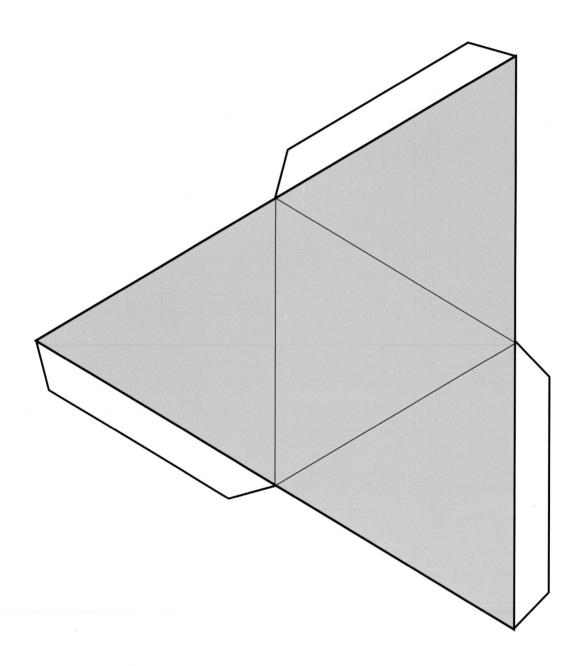

Tangram

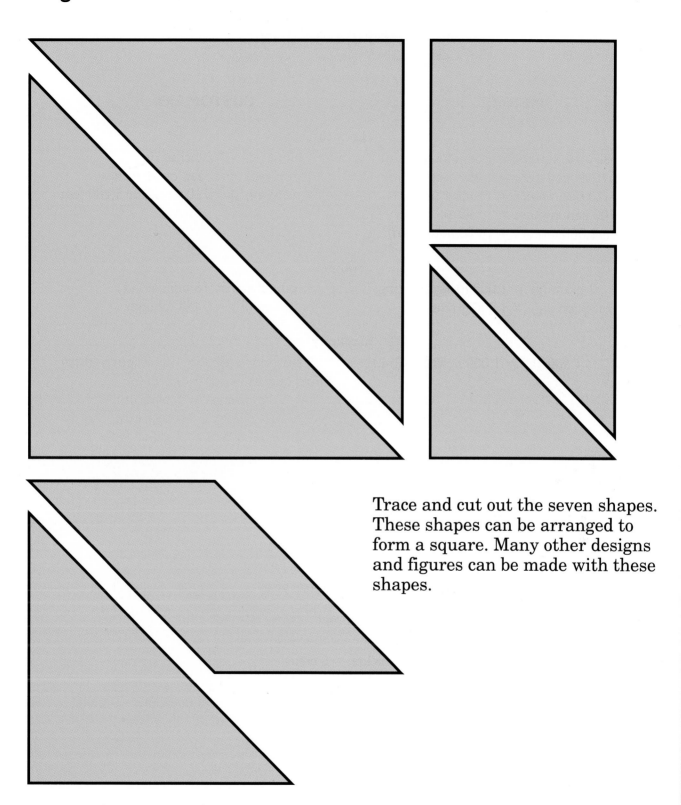

Trace and cut out the seven shapes. These shapes can be arranged to form a square. Many other designs and figures can be made with these shapes.

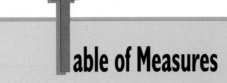

Table of Measures

METRIC	CUSTOMARY

Length

METRIC	CUSTOMARY
10 millimeters (mm) = 1 centimeter (cm)	1 foot (ft) = 12 inches (in.)
10 centimeters = 1 decimeter (dm)	1 yard (yd) = 3 feet, or 36 inches
10 decimeters = 1 meter (m)	1 mile (mi) = 1,760 yards, or 5,280 feet
100 centimeters = 1 meter	
1,000 meters = 1 kilometer (km)	

Weight

METRIC	CUSTOMARY
1 gram (g) = 1,000 milligrams (mg)	1 pound (lb) = 16 ounces (oz)
1 kilogram (kg) = 1,000 grams	1 ton (T) = 2,000 pounds

Capacity

METRIC	CUSTOMARY
1 liter (L) = 1,000 milliliters (mL)	3 teaspoons (tsp) = 1 tablespoon (tbsp)
	8 fluid ounces (fl oz) = 1 cup (c)
	2 cups = 1 pint (pt)
	2 pints = 1 quart (qt)
	4 quarts = 1 gallon (gal)

Time

60 seconds (sec) = 1 minute (min)
60 minutes = 1 hour (hr)
24 hours = 1 day (d)
7 days = 1 week (wk)
12 months (mo), or 52 weeks, or 365 days = 1 year (yr)
366 days = 1 leap year

Money

1 penny = 1 cent (¢)
1 nickel = 5 cents
1 dime = 10 cents
1 quarter = 25 cents
1 half dollar = 50 cents
1 dollar ($) = 100 cents

Symbols

< is less than
> is greater than
= is equal to
°F degrees Fahrenheit
°C degrees Celsius

Glossary

A

acute angle An angle that has a measure less than a right angle (90°) *(page 288)*

addend Any of the numbers that are added *(page 34)*
   Example: 2 + 3 = 5
      The addends are 2 and 3.

A.M. The time between midnight and noon *(page 112)*

analog A kind of clock that displays the digits 1–12 and uses minute and hour hands to tell the current time *(page 110)*

angle A figure formed by two rays that meet at a common endpoint *(page 288)*
   Example:

area The number of square units needed to cover a flat surface *(page 280)*

array An arrangement of objects in rows and columns *(page 70)*

average The number found by dividing the sum of a set of numbers by the number of addends *(page 264)*

B

bar graph A graph that uses bars of different heights or lengths to show and compare information *(page 128)*

C

capacity The amount a container can hold when filled *(page 222)*

cardinal number A number that tells how many items are in a group *(page 22)*
   Example:

   The cardinal number of the group is 3.

cell In a spreadsheet, a block area in which data or formulas can be entered. The cell is located by an address consisting of a letter and a number. *(page 454)*

centimeter (cm) A unit of length in the metric system *(page 208)*
      100 centimeters = 1 meter
      Example:
      |— 1 cm —|

circle A flat, round shape with all points on the circle the same distance from the center point *(page 294)*
   Example:

closed figure An outline of a shape that begins and ends at the same point *(page 278)*
   Examples:

common denominator   A common multiple of two or more denominators *(page 356)*

compatible numbers   Pairs of numbers that are easy to compute mentally *(page 248)*

cone   A three-dimensional, or solid, figure with one vertex and a circular base *(page 276)*
Example:

congruent figures   Figures that have the same size and shape *(page 296)*
Example:

counting on   A method used to find the sum when one addend is 1, 2, or 3 *(page 34)*
Example: 6 + 2 = 8
Think: 6, . . . 7, 8.

cube   A three-dimensional, or solid, figure with six congruent square faces *(page 276)*
Example:

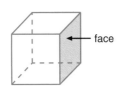
← face

cup (c)   A customary unit for measuring capacity *(page 222)*
8 ounces = 1 cup

cylinder   A three-dimensional, or solid, figure with two faces that are parallel, congruent circles *(page 276)*
Example:

data   Information, such as text, formulas, or numbers, that can be organized, sorted, found, or used *(page 122)*

data base   A computer program used to organize, sort, and find the kind of information that is normally kept in a list or on file cards *(page 465)*

decimal   A number that uses place value and a decimal point to show values less than one, such as tenths, hundredths, and so on *(page 380)*

decimal point   A period used in decimal numbers to separate the whole number part from the decimal part *(page 394)*

decimeter (dm)   A unit of length in the metric system *(page 210)*
10 decimeters = 1 meter

degree Celsius (°C)   A standard unit for measuring temperature in the metric system *(page H16)*

degree Fahrenheit (°F)   A standard unit for measuring temperature in the customary system *(page H17)*

denominator   The number below the bar in a fraction. It tells the total number of equal parts or groups into which the whole or group has been divided. *(page 320)*

Example: $\dfrac{3}{4}$ ← denominator

diameter   A line segment that passes through the center of a circle and has its endpoints on the circle *(page 295)*

difference   The answer to a subtraction problem *(page 50)*
Example: 7 − 3 = 4
The difference is 4.

---

dividend   The number that is to be divided in a division problem *(page 244)*
Example: 2)̅3̅5̅ or 35 ÷ 5
The dividend is 35.

divisor   The number that divides the dividend *(page 244)*
Example: 3)̅1̅8̅ or 18 ÷ 3
The divisor is 3.

doubles   Two addends that are the same *(page 34)*

doubles plus one   A method used to find the sum when one addend is one more than the other *(page 34)*
Example: 3 + 4 = 7
Think: 1 more than 3 + 3.

edge   The line segment where two faces of a three-dimensional, or solid, figure meet *(page 304)*
Example:

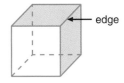

elapsed time   The time that passes from the start of an activity to the end of that activity *(page 116)*

equals (=)   The symbol used to compare two numbers that are the same value *(page 16)*

equivalent decimals   Two or more decimals that name the same amount *(page 386)*

equivalent fractions   Two or more fractions that name the same amount *(page 328)*
Example: $\frac{3}{4} = \frac{6}{8}$

estimate   To find an answer that is close to the exact answer *(page 150)*

expanded form   A way to write numbers by showing the value of each digit *(page 6)*
Example: 253 = 200 + 50 + 3

face   A flat surface of a three-dimensional, or solid, figure *(page 304)*
Example:

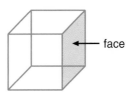

fact family   A set of related addition and subtraction or multiplication and division number sentences *(page 70)*

factor   A number that is multiplied by another number to find a product *(page 148)*
Example: 4 × 7 = 28
The factors are 4 and 7.

field   The type of information in a data base, such as names or phone numbers *(page 465)*

foot (ft)   A unit of length in the customary system *(page 214)*
12 inches = 1 foot

formula   In a spreadsheet, a set of instructions that tells the computer to do a calculation or to perform a task *(page 458)*

fraction   A number that names part of a whole or part of a group *(page 318)*
Examples:

$\frac{1}{3}$ of the region is shaded. $\frac{1}{3}$ of the group of pencils is circled.

frequency table   A table that uses numbers to show how often an item occurs *(page 122)*

front-end estimation   The method using only the front-end digits to estimate a sum, difference, product, or quotient *(page 38)*

gallon (gal)   A customary unit for measuring capacity *(page 222)*
   4 quarts = 1 gallon

gram (g)   A metric unit used to measure weight *(page 228)*
   1,000 grams = 1 kilogram

graph   A drawing used to show and compare information *(page 184)*

graphic   Art or design made using a grid *(page 440)*

greater than (>)   A symbol used to compare two numbers with the greater number given first *(page 16)*
   Example: 8 > 6

Grouping Property of Addition   The property which states that the way addends are grouped does not change the sum *(page 36)*

Grouping Property of Multiplication   The property which states that the way factors are grouped does not change the product *(page 76)*
   Example:
      $(2 \times 3) \times 4 = 2 \times (3 \times 4)$
      $6 \quad \times 4 = 2 \times \quad 12$
      $24 = 24$

hexagon   A polygon with six sides and six vertices *(page 278)*

inch (in.)   A unit of length in the customary system *(page 208)*
   Example:

1 inch

intersecting lines   Two lines that cross at exactly one point *(page 292)*
   Example:

$\overleftrightarrow{AB}$ and $\overleftrightarrow{CD}$ intersect at point E.

interval   The space between two points on the scale of a graph *(page 128)*

inverse operations   Opposite operations, such as multiplication and division, that undo each other *(page 88)*
   Example: $3 \times 4 = 12$ and
      $12 \div 4 = 3$

kilogram (kg)   A metric unit used to measure weight *(page 228)*
   1,000 grams = 1 kilogram

kilometer (km)   A unit of length in the metric system *(page 210)*
   1,000 meters = 1 kilometer

label   Text in a spreadsheet read as a character, not as a number value *(page 454)*

less than (<)   A symbol used to compare two numbers with the lesser number given first *(page 16)*
   Example: 6 < 8

like fractions Fractions with the same denominator *(page 336)*

    Example: $\frac{2}{5}$ and $\frac{3}{5}$

line A straight path extending in both directions with no endpoints *(page 286)*

line graph A graph that uses a line to show how something changes over a period of time *(page 134)*

line of symmetry A line that divides a shape into two congruent parts *(page 300)*

    Example:

line segment Part of a line with two endpoints *(page 286)*

liter (L) A metric unit of capacity *(page 226)*

    1,000 milliliters = 1 liter

LOGO A computer language used primarily to draw graphic designs. It can also perform calculations. *(page 440)*

mass The amount of matter of an object *(page 228)*

median The middle number in an ordered series of numbers *(page 264)*
    Example: 4 is the median of
    1, 3, 4, 6, 7.

meter (m) A unit of length in the metric system *(page 210)*
    100 centimeters = 1 meter

mile (mi) A unit of length in the customary system *(page 214)*
    5,280 feet = 1 mile

milliliter (mL) A metric unit of capacity *(page 226)*
    1,000 milliliters = 1 liter

mixed number A number that is made up of a whole number and a fraction or a whole number and a decimal *(page 338)*
    Example: $2\frac{1}{2}$; 2.5

multiple A number that is the product of a given number and another whole number *(page 148)*

number line A line with equally spaced points named by numbers *(page 16)*
    Example:

numerator The number above the bar in a fraction. It tells how many of the equal parts of the whole are being considered. *(page 320)*

    Example: $\frac{2}{3}$ ← numerator

obtuse angle An angle that has a measure greater than a right angle (90°) *(page 288)*

octagon A polygon with eight sides and eight vertices *(page 278)*

open figure A set of points that does not completely enclose a region in the same plane *(page 276)*
    Examples:

Glossary

ordered pair   A pair of numbers used to locate a point on a grid. The first number tells the left-right position and the second number tells the up-down position. *(page 132)*

Order Property of Multiplication
The property which states that when the order of two factors is changed, the product is the same *(page 76)*
   Example: $5 \times 7 = 7 \times 5$
   $35 = 35$

ordinal numbers   A number telling order or position *(page 22)*
   Examples: first; second

ounce (oz)   A customary unit used to measure weight *(page 230)*
   16 ounces = 1 pound

outcome   A possible result in a probability experiment *(page 368)*

··········**P**········

parallel lines   Lines in a plane that stay exactly the same distance apart *(page 292)*
   Example:

partial product   A method of multiplying where the ones, tens, hundreds, and so on are multiplied separately and then the products added together *(page 153)*

pentagon   A polygon with five sides and five vertices *(page 278)*

perimeter   The distance around a figure *(page 218)*

period   Each group of three digits in a number *(page 10)*
   Example:

Periods	
thousands	ones
2 6 7	5 3 1

A comma separates periods.

perpendicular lines   Two lines that intersect to form right angles *(page 292)*
   Example:

pictograph   A graph that uses pictures to show and compare information *(page 124)*

pint (pt)   A customary unit for measuring capacity *(page 222)*
   2 cups = 1 pint

plane   A flat surface that extends without end in all directions *(page 276)*

plane figure   A closed figure that lies on a flat surface *(page 276)*
   Examples:

P.M.   The time between noon and midnight *(page 112)*

polygon   A closed plane figure formed by three or more line segments joined at their endpoints *(page 279)*

pound (lb)   A customary unit used to measure weight *(page 230)*
   16 ounces = 1 pound

probability   The chance that a given event will occur *(page 368)*

procedure   A set of commands that tells the computer what to do *(page 440)*

product   The answer to a multiplication problem *(page 148)*
   Example: $6 \times 2 = 12$
   The product is 12.

Property of One for Multiplication
The property which states that the
product of any number and 1 is the
number *(page 76)*
    Examples: $5 \times 1 = 5$
                  $16 \times 1 = 16$

pyramid   A three-dimensional, or solid,
figure whose base is a polygon and
whose faces are triangles with a
common vertex *(page 276)*

quadrilateral   A polygon with four
sides and four vertices *(page 278)*

quart (qt)   A customary unit for
measuring capacity *(page 222)*
    2 pints = 1 quart

quotient   The answer in a division
problem *(page 244)*
    Example: $27 \div 3 = 9$
       The quotient is 9.

radius   A line segment with one
endpoint at the center of a circle and
the other endpoint on the circle
(page 295)

range   The difference between the
greatest and least numbers in a set of
data *(page 264)*

ray   A part of a line that begins at one
endpoint and extends forever in only
one direction *(page 286)*

record   In a data base, information
for one particular person or item
(page 452)

rectangle   A polygon with four sides
and four right angles *(page 278)*

rectangular prism   A three-dimensional, or solid, figure in which
the parallel bases are rectangles
(page 276)
    Example:

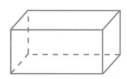

regroup   To exchange equal amounts
(page 42)

relative copy   A copy of a cell or group
of cells. The computer makes changes
in the new cells to reflect their position
in the spreadsheet. *(page 448)*

remainder   The amount left over when
you find the quotient *(page 244)*
    Example: 3 r4 The remainder is 4.
         5)19

right angle   An angle that forms a
square corner and measures 90°
(page 288)
    Example:

round   To express a number to the
nearest thousandth, hundredth, tenth,
one, ten, hundred, thousand, and so on
(page 24)
    Examples: 473 rounded to the
       nearest hundred is 500.
       37.85 rounded to the nearest tenth
       is 37.9.

similar figures   Figures that have the
same shape but may not have the
same size *(page 296)*

simplest form   A fraction whose
numerator and denominator have no
common factor greater than 1 *(page 332)*

sphere Any round object whose curved surface is the same distance from the center at all points *(page 304)*
   Example:

spreadsheet A computer program that organizes information in rows and columns and makes calculations with numbers and formulas *(page 448)*

square A polygon with four equal sides and four right angles *(page 278)*

square centimeter (sq cm) A metric unit for measuring area *(page 281)*

square inch (sq in.) A customary unit for measuring area *(page 281)*

standard form A way to write numbers using the digits 0–9, with each digit having a place value *(page 6)*

sum The answer in an addition problem *(page 34)*
   Example: $2 + 3 = 5$ The sum is 5.

survey A collection of data that lists choices *(page 122)*

symmetric figure A figure that can be folded in half so that its two parts match exactly *(page 300)*

tablespoon (tbsp) A customary unit for measuring capacity *(page 222)*
   3 teaspoons = 1 tablespoon

tally table A table that uses tally marks to show how often something occurs *(page 122)*
   Example: ||||\ = 5

ton (T) A customary unit used to measure weight *(page 230)*
   2,000 pounds = 1 ton

triangle A polygon with three sides *(page 278)*

turtle The triangle in the computer language LOGO that is directed to draw graphic designs *(page 440)*

unlike fractions Fractions that have different denominators *(page 336)*
   Example: $\frac{3}{4}$ and $\frac{2}{3}$

vertex The point at which two rays of an angle or two or more line segments meet *(page 278)*

volume The measure of the space inside a solid figure *(page 306)*

word processor A computer program used to write text, such as letters, reports, word problems, or memos *(page 446)*

yard (yd) A unit of length in the customary system *(page 214)*
   3 feet = 1 yard

Zero Property for Multiplication The property which states that the product of zero and any number is zero *(page 76)*
   Examples: $13 \times 0 = 0$
   $0 \times 7 = 0$

Index

Mental math, 43, 45, 83, 166,
262, 369
multiplication, 178–179
Metersticks, 239
Metric system
capacity, 226–227
centimeters, 208–212,
218–219, 295
cubic centimeters, 308
decimeters, 210–212
grams, 228–229
kilograms, 228–229
kilometers, 210–212
length, 210–212
liters, 226–227
mass, 228–229
meters, 210–212
milliliters, 226–227, 308
square centimeters, 281–282
Millions, 12–13
Missing factors, 88–89, 92–94,
98, 100, 244
Mixed numbers, 338–339
adding, 362–363
and decimals, 382–383
subtracting, 362–363
Mixed Reviews, 7, 25, 39, 43,
81, 91, 99, 125, 131, 151, 163,
189, 193, 223, 233, 249, 259,
287, 295, 329, 353, 357, 383,
401, 415
Möbius strips, H29
Money
best buys, 238
change, H28
cost analysis, 105
counting, H6–H7
dimes, 2–3, 58–59, 168–169,
247, 326, 381, H6–H7
dividing, 247, 260–261,
430–431, H32
dollars, 2–3, 58–59, 152,
168–169, 247, 326, 381,
431, H6–H7
francs, 431
liras, 431
marks, 431
multiplying, 168–169,
196–199
nickels, H6–H7
pennies, 2, 58–59, 228, 247,
326, 381, H6–H7
quarters, 326–327, H6–H7
regrouping, 58–59
rounding, 24–25, 38, 168, 430
shillings, 431
subtracting, 54–55, 58–59
telephone bills, 271
unit prices, H32
More Practice, H34–H85
Multiples
common, 356

of hundred, 148–150
of ten, 148–150, 182–183,
412–414
of thousand, 148–150
Multiplication
and addition, 70, 74
arrays, H8–H9
with calculators, 164–165,
174, 180, 204, 230,
232–233, 413
for changing units, 232–233
and division, 70–71, 88–89,
244–245
by eight, 82–83
estimating products,
150–151, 154–156,
162–165, 168–172,
180–181, 188–189,
192–195, 198
expanded form of, H28
factors, 72, 85, 88, 178
by five, 74–75
by four, 74–75
Grouping Property of, 76–77
mental math, 178–179
of money amounts, 168–169,
196–199
by multiples of ten, 182–183
by nine, 82–83
by one, 76–77
Order Property of, 76–77, 80
partial products, 153,
186–187, H28
patterns in, 148–149
products, 72, 85, 88, 178–179
Properties of, 76–77
Property of One, 76–77
regrouping, 152–157,
162–172
by seven, 80–81
by six, 80–81
tables, 72, 74, 80, 82, 84–85
by three, 72–73
by two, 72–73
by two-digit numbers,
186–189, 192–202
of whole numbers, 70–85,
88–89, 148–157, 162–172,
174, 178–183, 186–202,
204, H8–H9, H14–H15,
H27–H29
by zero, 76–77
Zero Property, 76–77, 84

Number lines, H3
in multiplying, 72
in rounding, 24, 390–391

Numbers
adding, 34–39, 42–49, 60–64,
349–351, 357–359,
362–363, 396–401, H4–H5,
H31
cardinal, 22–23
comparing, 16–19, 336–337,
388–389, H22–H23
decimals, 380–408, H24–H25,
H31
dividing, 70–71, 88–104,
242–249, 252–253,
256–262, 265–270,
412–434, 436, H10–H11,
H18–H19, H27, H29, H32
even, H2–H3
expanded form of, 6–7, 10–11
factors of, 106
fractions, 318–325, 327–329,
332–342, 348–365,
H22–H25, H30–H31
mixed, 338–339, 362–363
multiplying, 70–85, 88–89,
148–157, 162–172, 174,
178–183, 186–202, 204,
H8–H9, H14–H15,
H27–H29
odd, H2–H3
ordered pairs, 132–133, 144
ordering, 18–19, 388, H26
ordinal, 22–23
palindromes, 66, H31
place value, 2–7, 10–13, 16,
18, 24
prime, 106
rounding, 24–25, 30, 38,
50–51, 154, 162, 168, 180,
188, 192, 348–349,
390–391, 394–395, 400, 430
square, 85
standard form of, 6–7, 10–13
subtracting, 50–55, 58–64,
349, 352–353, 357–359,
362–363, 396–397,
402–403, H4–H5, H26
in words, 6–7, 10–13
Number sense, 5, 7, 11, 25, 30,
35, 37, 45, 53, 55, 61, 77, 81,
85, 115, 193, 215, 229, 249,
359, 365, 387, 401
developing, H2–H3
estimating, 51, 59, 181
expressing numbers, 6–7
logical reasoning, 403
Numerators, 320, 322, 325,
338–339, 351, 353, 358

Octagons, 279, 286, 293, 442
Open figures, 278

use a table, 8–9
use estimation, 398–399
work backward, 158–159, 384–385
write a number sentence, 94–95
Products, 72, 85, 88
estimating, 150–151, 154–156, 162–165, 168–172, 180–181, 188–189, 192–195, 198
partial, 153, 186–187, H28
zeros in, 178–180, 182–183
Project. *See* Teamwork Projects
Properties
of Addition, 37
Grouping, 36, 76–77
of Multiplication, 76–77
of One, 76–77
Order, 76–77, 80
Zero, 76–77, 84
Puzzles, 66, 106, 174, 204, 272, 376
tangrams, 313
Pyramids, 277
triangular, 304–305

Quadrilaterals, 279
rectangles, 218–219, 279–282, 286, 297, 309
squares, 218–219, 279–282, 293, 298–299, 440–442, H30
Quotients, 88, 94, 96–101, 242–245, 248–249, 252–253, 256–261, 412–415, 418–419, 423–434, 436
checking, 252–253, 256–257, 261–262
estimating, 248–249, 252, 256, 258–260, 414–415, 418, 423–424, 428–430
of one, 96–97
zeros in, 258–259

R

Radius, 295
Ranges, 264, 266–268
Rays, 286–288
Reading Connection, 129
Rectangles, 279–282, 286, 297
area of, 280–282, 284, 309
perimeter of, 218–219
squares, 218–219, 279–282, 293, 298–299, 440–442, H30

Rectangular prisms, 277, 304–309
cubes, 276–277, 304–307
volume of, 306–309
Regrouping
in addition, 42–45, 48–49, 60–61, 400
in division, 246
money, 58–59
in multiplication, 152–157, 162–172, 182, 188, 192, 194, H14–H15
in subtraction, 52–55, 58–61, 402
Remainders, 244–246, 252, 256, 261, 339, 418–419, 422–429, 436, H18–H19
interpreting, 426–427
Repeated subtraction, 423, 428–429
Reviews
Chapter, 26–27, 62–63, 102–103, 140–141, 170–171, 200–201, 234–235, 268–269, 310–311, 340–341, 372–373, 404–405, 432–433
Cumulative, 31, 67, 107, 145, 175, 205, 239, 273, 315, 345, 377, 409, 437
and Maintenance, 14, 46, 86, 126, 160, 190, 220, 254, 290, 330, 360, 392, 420
Mixed, 7, 25, 39, 43, 81, 91, 99, 125, 131, 151, 163, 189, 193, 223, 233, 249, 259, 287, 295, 329, 353, 357, 383, 401, 415
Riddles, 408, 446–447
Rounding
decimals, 390–391, 394–395, 400
fractions, 348–349
money amounts, 24–25, 38, 168, 430
whole numbers, 24–25, 30, 50–51, 154, 162, 180, 188, 192
Rulers, 208–209, 218–219, 239, 295, 364–365

S

Schedules, 120–121, 133
School-Home Connections, H26–H32
Science Connections, 231, 257
Similar figures, 296–297
Simplest form, 332–333

Slides, 302–303
Social Studies Connections, 19, 75, 263, 431
Solid figures, 276–277, 304–309
cones, 277, 304–305
cubes, 276–277, 304–307
cylinders, 277, 304–305
edges of, 304–305
faces of, 276, 304–305
prisms, 277, 304
pyramids, 277, 304–305
spheres, 304–305
vertices of, 304–305
Spheres, 304–305
Spotlight on Problem Solving
analyze and compare data, 127
analyze data, 291
analyze relationships, 47
check the solution, 255
check the solution for reasonableness, 191, 331
draw conclusions, 221
interpret the answer, 421
make predictions, 15, 393
solve the problem in another way, 361
write questions, 87, 161
Spreadsheets, 448–451, 455
Square numbers, 85
Squares, 279–282, 293, 298–299, 440–442, H30
magic, 43
perimeters of, 218–219
Standard form, 6–7, 10–13
Statistics, 122–142
analyzing data, 115, 127, 135, 137–139, 179, 209, 253, 291, 301, 401
averages, 264–268
bar graphs, 128–131, 138, 143, 184–185, 335, H27
collecting data, 122–123
comparing data, 127
finding data, 9, 131, 165, 229, 419
line graphs, 134–139
medians, 264, 266–268
organizing data, 9, 121, 123, 143
pictographs, 124–125, 138–139, 155
predictions, 15, 393
ranges, 264, 266–268
surveys, 143
Subtraction
and addition, H4–H5
with calculators, 55, 60–61, 423
of decimals, 396–397, 402–403

MATH FUN MAGAZINE

These brainteasers don't stump me!

Have fun solving these brain teasers!

▸ As you learn
▸ new things this year,
▸ you will be able
▸ to solve problems
▸ that might have
▸ stumped you at first.
▸ So, keep trying!

Seeing is not Believing

Sometimes your eyes can play tricks on you.
You may not see what is really there.
See if you can solve each puzzle without being fooled.

1. Which line on the left extends to the right?

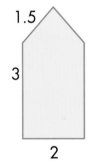

2. Which figure has the greater perimeter? Do not add the lengths of the sides.

Figure A   Figure B

3. Which center circle is larger?

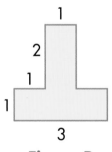

4. Is the hat taller than it is wide or wider than it is tall?

Don't Get BOXED IN

These problems are all about boxes. Don't jump to a quick conclusion and get boxed in without checking all the facts!

1. Ten full crates of peanuts weigh 410 pounds. An empty crate weighs 10 pounds. How much do the peanuts alone weigh?

2. There are 3 separate boxes that are the same size. Inside each box there are 2 separate small boxes. Inside each of the small boxes there are 4 smaller boxes. How many boxes are there altogether?

3. Three empty cereal boxes weigh 9 ounces. Each box holds 11 ounces of cereal. How much do 2 full boxes of cereal weigh together?

4. There are 4 boxes stacked on a shelf. The boxes are stacked from the heaviest on the bottom to the lightest on the top. Box A is heavier than Box D but lighter than Box C. Box C is heavier than Box A but lighter than Box B. In what order are the boxes stacked?

5. This box is made up of small boxes. How many small boxes are used to make the large box?

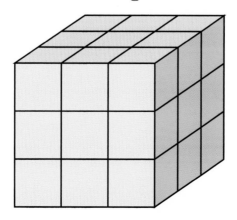

MAgic SumS

1. Copy the wheel onto your paper. Write numbers 1 through 13, one in each circle, so that the sum of any three numbers in a line is 21.

   HINT: Think about the numbers 1 through 6 on a clockface.

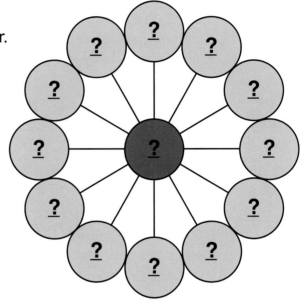

2. Copy the pentagon onto your paper. Write a number in each circle so that the sum of each side is the same.

   HINT: There may be more than one correct answer.

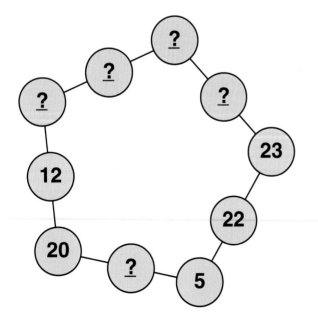

M4

H·O·W · IS · Y·O·U·R
MEMORY?

Nested shapes are figures within figures. This drawing is an example of nested shapes. Study the drawing carefully. Then cover the drawing so that you cannot see it. Now, answer the questions from your memory of the drawing.

1. What is the largest shape in the drawing?

2. What is the smallest shape in the drawing?

3. Is the circle inside or outside the pentagon?

4. In which corner is the fish?

5. How many squares are in the drawing?

DISAPPEARING
DIGITS

**Tim did his math homework correctly,
but he made one big mistake.
He wrote some problems and answers
in disappearing ink.**

**Copy the problems on a sheet of paper.
Replace the digits that have disappeared.**

1.
```
      8
  +  36
  ------
   6,965
```

2.
```
    ,73
  +5,1 6
  ------
   9,9 8
```

3.
```
     5
  -2 7
  ----
   553
```

4.
```
     6
  -358
  ----
    12
```

5.
```
     4
  x  3
  ----
     4
  ------
   1,104
```

6.
```
     3
  x  5
  ----
    18
     7
  ----
     9
```

7.
```
          3
      _____
  4 | 546
      4
  --------
          0
```

8.
```
          7
      _____
  2 | 408
     -2
  --------
          8
  --------
          0
```

ONE BLOCK

Solve this math word puzzle and be Number 1!
Use the letters O, N, and E
in the word ONE to complete the word
in each row of the stack of blocks.

● Each of the letters O, N, and E
  must be used in each of the rows.

● The letters may be used in any order
  and may be repeated as needed.

● Write each completed word on your own paper.

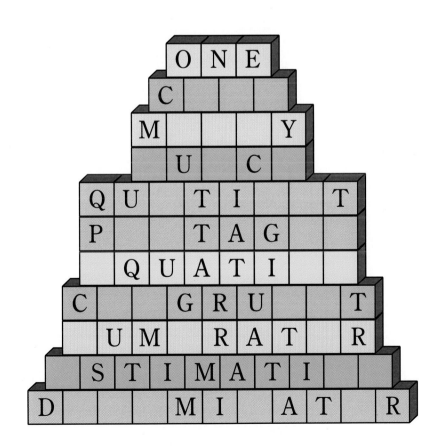

VENDING MACHINE
Arithmetic

The vending machine contains the four items shown. The machine takes only quarters, dimes, and nickels.

What combination of three coins could you use to purchase

1. a bag of peanuts?
2. a granola bar?
3. dried fruit?
4. cheese crackers?

What combination of five coins could you use to purchase

5. a bag of peanuts?
6. a granola bar?
7. dried fruit?
8. cheese crackers?

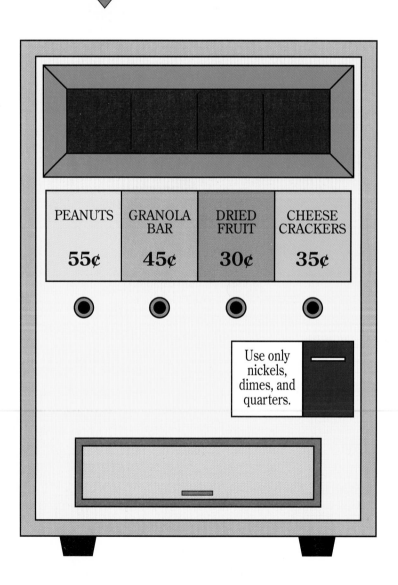

PEANUTS	GRANOLA BAR	DRIED FRUIT	CHEESE CRACKERS
55¢	45¢	30¢	35¢

Use only nickels, dimes, and quarters.

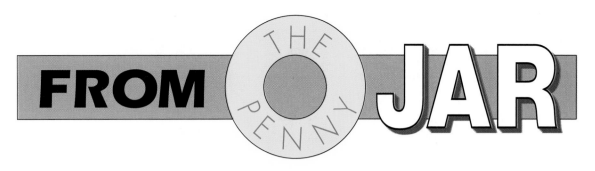
**You may find it helpful to use pennies to solve these puzzles.
For each puzzle, draw a picture of your solution.**

1. How could you arrange 12 pennies into 4 rows with
4 pennies in each row?

2. How could you arrange 9 pennies into 2 rows with
5 pennies in each row?

3. How could you arrange 4 pennies in such a way that
all of them are the same distance apart?

4. How could you change 10 pennies into four and
one-half dozen?

triangles
triangles Everywhere

You don't have to be a square to solve triangular puzzles!

How many triangles can you find in this quilt pattern?

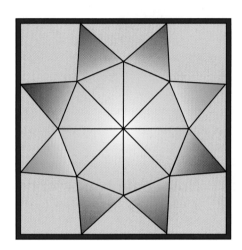

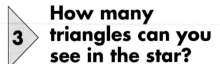

2 **How many different kinds of geometric shapes can you see in the six-pointed star? Name them.**

3 **How many triangles can you see in the star?**

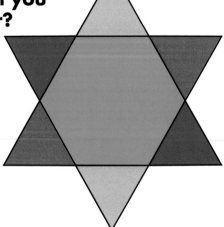

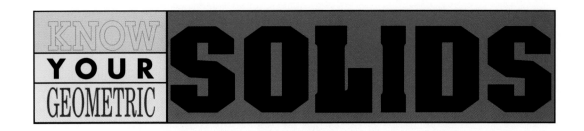

Part of each geometric solid is hidden from view.
Match each solid with its name.

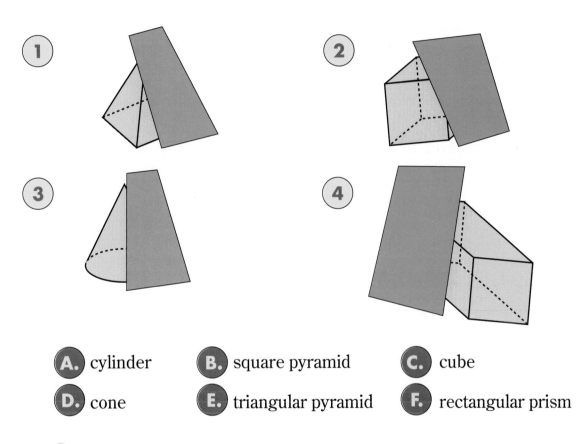

1

2

3

4

A. cylinder   B. square pyramid   C. cube

D. cone   E. triangular pyramid   F. rectangular prism

5 Which face is not part of this geometric solid?

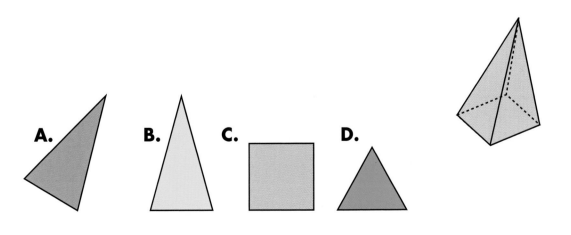

A.   B.   C.   D.

On AND On

**Many patterns go on and on without stopping.
By carefully studying the patterns,
you can predict how they will continue.**

1. What three numbers come next?

. . ., **237, 316, 395, 474, ? , ? , ? , . . .**

2. What six numbers come next?

1, 7, 2, 8, 3, 9, 4, ? , ? , ? , ? , ? , ? , . . .

3. What three figures come next?

★⊕★↑★△★⊖★↓ ? ? ? . . .

4. Draw the design that would come next.

?

5. It may not be apparent, but this pattern
takes number know-how. Draw the next three shapes.

∞ ‖ ♡ 8 ⋈ ? ? ? . . .

DO YOU HAVE Good Connections

**Finding likenesses can help you to compare things.
Examine the first comparison to help you
complete the second comparison.**

1. Celsius is to **0°** as Fahrenheit is to

A. 0°   **B.** 32°   **C.** 100°   **D.** 212°

2. **6** is to **36** as **10** is to

A. 20   **B.** 50   **C.** 60   **D.** 100

3. The numbers **1** through **12** are to a clock
as the numbers **1** through **100** are to

A. eggs   **B.** a parking meter   **C.** a thermometer
D. coins

4. Stop is to  as yield is to

5. 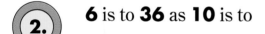 is to

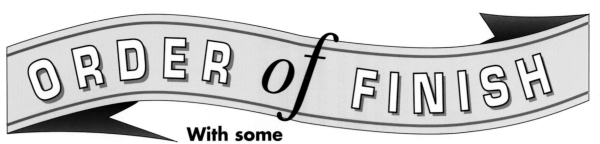

ORDER of FINISH

With some logical reasoning and modeling, you can solve each of these "order of finish" puzzles.

1. The Sailing Club members raced in the Lazer Regatta. *Wet Rabbit* finished in second place. *Sea Wind* came in last. *Lightning* finished two places before *Sea Wind*. *Star* finished before *Wet Rabbit,* and *Long Shot* finished after *Lightning*. What was the order of finish of the sailboats?

2. At a track meet, the javelin throw comes after the pole vault event. The 100-yard dash comes before the pole vault. The relay race comes between the 100-yard dash and the pole vault. Which event is first?

3. There were five contestants in the soapbox derby. Pam came in first. Bill finished last. Mark finished ahead of Jane. Sue finished after Jane. Who came in second? third? fourth?

4. Georgio won second prize in a dance contest. Gigi came in next to last. Shep placed just ahead of Gigi. Tina came in right after Georgio. Jose did not place sixth. Where did Mark place? List the entire order of finish.

Pentominos

Trace and cut out the pentomino pieces below.

A.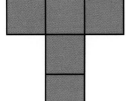

B.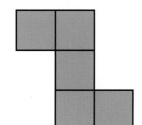

C.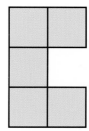

D.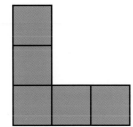

E.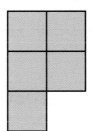

F.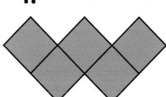

1. **Which pentomino is different from the others? Explain.**

2. **Which pentomino will form a rectangle with itself?**

3. **Which three pentominos can be put together to make a rectangle with a perimeter of 16 units?**

TRAFFIC SIGN Arithmetic

**Traffic signs tell motorists how to proceed.
These traffic signs will help you solve number sentences.**

Count the number of sides on each traffic sign.

 ? sides

YIELD **? sides**

SPEED LIMIT 35 **? sides**

SCHOOL CROSSING **? sides**

200 E 300 GRANT ST. **? sides**

ONE WAY **? sides**

STOP **? sides**

**Use what you know about the number of sides on the
figures to solve each number sentence.**

1. **SPEED LIMIT 35** × **YIELD** × **SCHOOL CROSSING** = **?**

2. **SPEED LIMIT 35** + **STOP** − **YIELD** = **?**

3. **YIELD** + **SCHOOL CROSSING** + (**200 E 300 GRANT ST.** × **YIELD**) = **?**

4. (**ONE WAY** + **SPEED LIMIT 35**) ×  = **?**

5. **Use the traffic signs and mathematical operations to
draw number sentences for 6, 19, and 25.**

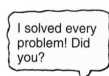
I solved every problem! Did you?

M16